THE PLAY OF POWER

MARGARET RICH GREER

The Play of Power

MYTHOLOGICAL

COURT DRAMAS

OF

Calderón de la Barca

PRINCETON UNIVERSITY PRESS

PRINCETON, NEW JERSEY

Library of Congress Cataloging-in-Publication Data

Greer, Margaret Rich.
The play of power : mythological court dramas of Calderón
de la Barca / Margaret Rich Greer.
p.   cm.
Includes bibliographical references and index.
ISBN 0-691-06857-7
1. Calderón de la Barca, Pedro, 1600–1681—Criticism and
interpretation.   2. Mythology in literature.   3. Spain—Court and
courtiers—History—17th century.   4. Politics and literature—
Spain—History—17th century.   5. Spain—Politics and
government—17th century.   I. Title.
PQ6312.G74   1991
862'.3—dc20   90-44110

Publication of ths book has been aided by a grant from
The Program for Cultural Cooperation Between Spain's
Ministry of Culture and United States Universities

This book has been composed in Monotype Bembo

Printed in the United States of America by
Princeton University Press,
Princeton, New Jersey

1   3   5   7   9   10   8   6   4   2

To Jim and Emily

CONTENTS

ILLUSTRATIONS

ACKNOWLEDGMENTS

THE STUDY that follows—my attempt to understand and explain the mythological court-spectacle plays of Pedro Calderón de la Barca—is a result of my fascination with three rather divergent subjects: politics, the music and spectacle of opera, and the theatrical world of Golden Age Spain. The last I owe to graduate classes with Alec Parker; it was he who first suggested Calderón's mythological plays as a topic worthy of more thoughtful attention than they had hitherto received. I am also indebted to him for the model of intellectual rigor and clarity that he set for his students. Although this study has taken a different route from the one he had envisioned, it would not have been possible without the grounding he provided.

I have also enjoyed and learned from long conversations with Alban Forcione, who supported this project throughout and commented on the manuscript with great care and insight, for which I am very grateful. Louise Stein's help has been invaluable with regard to the development of music and spectacle in Spain and other European nations. She generously supplied me with a copy of her dissertation and read my manuscript with critical attention, correcting my ignorance in many areas. Thomas Walker provided a new perspective on early Italian opera, and with an equal mastery of modern electronic media, supplied early librettos with amazing speed. Fred DeArmas also read the entire manuscript and made a number of valuable suggestions. Other friends and colleagues who have strengthened the study through their comments and assistance include, but are not limited to: Don Cruickshank, John Varey, Henry Sullivan, Susana Hernández-Araico, Shirley Whitaker, Lee Fontanella, John Logan, Ron Surtz, Stan Zimic, Douglass Parker, George Mariscal, Mark Franko, François Rigolot, and Pietro Frassica.

Invaluable also has been the assistance of a number of colleagues in Spain, including the staff of the Sección de Raros y Manuscritos of the Biblioteca Nacional, and in particular its director, Manuel Sánchez Mariana; the staff of the Archivo del Palacio; Jaime Moll and Mercedes Dexeus, Vicenta Cortés and Gerardo Kurtz. For financial support, I thank the Fulbright Commission and the Comité Conjunto Hispano Norteamericano for grants for research in Spain in 1980–1981 and again in 1985; the Spanish Embassy, which provided summer research money through the Américo Castro fellowship; the Mellon Foundation for the preceptorship that allowed an extra semester of sabbatical to write the bulk of the manuscript; and the Humanities Council at Princeton University for assistance with the cost of illustrations.

ACKNOWLEDGMENTS

Portions of Chapters 2, 3, 5, 6, and 7 have appeared in "Bodies of Power in Calderón: *El nuevo palacio del Retiro* and *El mayor encanto, amor*" in *Conflicts of Discourse: Spanish Literature of the Golden Age*, ed. Peter Evans (Manchester University Press, 1990); in "Art and Power in the Spectacle Plays of Calderón de la Barca," *PMLA* 104 (1989); in "The Play of Power: Calderón's *Fieras afemina Amor* and *La estatua de Prometeo*," *Hispanic Review* 55 (1988); and in my edition of Pedro Calderón de la Barca, *La estatua de Prometeo* (Edition Reichenberger, 1986). I am grateful to Edition Reichenberger, the Manchester University Press, *PMLA* and *Hispanic Review* for permission to reprint this material.

And last, my thanks to my husband, Bob, who did not type this manuscript, did not read proofs for me, did not sit at my feet while I read him each chapter, or otherwise play the classic academic spouse—but who supports my research wholeheartedly, as long as I don't ask him to read it. He keeps me in touch with sanity and life outside the academic walls.

THE PLAY OF POWER

ONE

Introduction

What is the relationship between art and power? What should it be? Plato, as is well known, would have had all poets excluded from his ideal republic because their imitative fictions stimulate undesirable passions and undermine obedience to law and the authority of reason and truth. In contrast, Günther Grass maintains that only writers who critically engage the established powers can legitimately be included in the community of responsible intellectuals. Edward Said extends the question to include critical practice, maintaining that literary critics cannot escape implication in political discourse by avoiding the subject or denying its importance because such silence functions as an acquiescence in the prevailing political system.

Whether or not a critic subscribes to Said's position, an understanding of the complex symbiosis between art and power is essential to any critical evaluation of the court plays that Pedro Calderón de la Barca wrote for the Spanish Hapsburg courts of Felipe IV and Carlos II between 1635 and 1680. These dramas were part of—and in important senses a culmination of—the great vogue of spectacular court entertainments that spread throughout Europe in the sixteenth and seventeenth centuries, accompanying the advance of absolutism on the European political stage. Their expulsion from the canon of viable dramatic works in the course of the eighteenth century resulted from the combined effects of the change in aesthetic taste—the advent of neoclassicism—and the dynastic change in Spain that brought in Bourbon kings and their Italian wives, who preferred Italian-style opera for their court spectaculars.[1] Furthermore, their continued exclusion from critical attention until recent years has been the result of aesthetic judgments strongly influenced by political considerations.

Menéndez y Pelayo represented the majority opinion of past critics when he called the mythological drama an "inferior genre" and said of the plays:

> En estas comedias mitológicas, como en toda especie de drama de espectáculo, el poeta queda siempre en grado y en categoría inferior al maquinista y al pintor escenógrafo. Eran obras que se destinaban al solaz de los Reyes y de la corte, . . . y en las cuales más se atendía al prestigio de los ojos que a la lucha de los afectos y los caracteres, ni a la verdad de la expresión (*Calderón* 365–366).

Hoy no tienen más interés que el histórico y el de algunos buenos versos
acá y allá esparcidos y casi ahogados en un mar de enfática y culterana
palabrería. Juzgar a Calderón por tales dramas sería evidente injusticia. Bus-
car en ellos pasión, interés, caracteres y color de las respectivas épocas, fuera
necedad y desvarío (*Teatro* lxiii–lxiv).

For Menéndez y Pelayo, then, the mythological court play is a "play of
power" in the sense of a frivolous pastime of the powerful—a game having
neither artistic merit nor meaningful relationship to society—either in the days
of Calderón or in succeeding ages.[2] A contemporary critic (Maraniss 87) echoes
Menéndez y Pelayo's condemnation of Calderón's court mythological plays in
even harsher terms: "Lacking any serious mimetic or intellectual substance, they
have no religious, moral, political, social or metaphysical content; they have
only a style."

Even as attentive a reader of Calderón as Cascardi comes to essentially the
same conclusion, praising plays such as *Eco y Narciso* as brilliant crystallizations of
Calderón's theatrical showmanship but then continuing: "For all their outward
energy and exuberance, they are static. Because there are no deep motives for
the action of these plays, it would be a mistake to consider them as truly dramatic. Their only dynamism is that of the self-contained, motionless lyric"
(130). Cascardi's evaluation, he makes clear, is based on the judgment that art
has in these plays become totally subservient to the interests of power. He finds
in them Calderón's technical mastery "turned to wholly uncritical ends," because from the date of his "appointment as court dramatist" he dedicated himself
not only to shoring up collective social values felt to be threatened but also to
expressing those values "filtered through the royal optic" in order to congratu-
late the ineffective kings Felipe IV and Carlos II (xi–xii). In sum, the plays have
been condemned as at best, extravagant baubles to entertain the court, and at
worst, servile and mendacious flattery of a decadent monarchy.

Contrary to this traditional current, an increasing number of critics in recent
years are reconsidering Calderón's court plays and finding them dramatic works
of continuing vitality, containing profound explorations of human life and social
organization.[3] However, the majority of the favorable critics read the plays as
allegories of general human experience, divorced from the spectacular form in
which they were presented and the political setting in which they took shape.
In so doing, they overlook Calderón's greatest achievements in these spectacles:
(1) the coherent use of the newest dramatic techniques, combining music,
dance, perspective scenery, and complex stage machinery to enhance rather
than overpower his poetic text, exploiting to the full the inherent polyphony of
the theatrical idiom to produce masterpieces of dramatic illusion; (2) the
achievement of a complex discourse of power that combined celebration of the
monarch with a tactful critique of his policy.

The discomfort of succeeding generations with the apparent subservience of the creative mind to the uses and pleasures of absolute monarchs has been a primary factor in the neglect of the mythological plays. It is in the reconsideration of this relationship of art and power that we can fully appreciate Calderón's achievement. To achieve such an understanding of the myth plays requires, I believe, a prior reflection on what Gadamer (xxii) calls our "effective-historical consciousness." We must become aware of certain prejudices that mediate our reading of Calderón and distance our interpretation of his works from the conditions of their reception in his day, as best we can reconstruct them.[4] To that end, we should first recognize that discomfort with the close relationship between art and power is a modern phenomenon, arising with the ideal of the self-supporting writer and the advent of political liberalism, which considers individual (and artistic) integrity to depend on a position of critical independence from the established order and all totalizing systems of thought. Lope de Vega could claim to be the first writer who lived by the fruits of his pen, but the prevailing pattern was still the dependence of artists on the patronage of the wealthy and powerful.[5] As terHorst points out, Golden Age Spanish drama began and ended at court, in the *églogas* of Juan del Encina and the court plays of Calderón. Although there were contemporary critics of the court spectaculars, their criticisms were directed against the extravagance of the events in times of war and popular privation or their distraction of rulers from more important tasks, not against the dedication of artistic creativity to political ends.[6]

Secondly, it should be noted that the persistence of this prejudice in the case of Calderón's work has been encouraged by the predominant conservativism of Golden Age drama criticism. As Goodman and Elgin observe, "That a text has a single right interpretation that is determined by and entirely in accord with the author's intentions has been, and perhaps still is, like absolute realism, the most popular view" (568). With notable exceptions, this has been the prevailing critical practice among students of Golden Age drama, probably reinforced in Calderón's case by what Boris Tomashevskii describes as the weight of an author's "ideal biography," or the legend of his life, in shaping the subsequent reception of his works.[7] Calderón was not only Catholic but also became a priest at fifty-one years of age, after which he stopped writing works for the public theatres and wrote only *autos sacramentales* (allegorical religious pieces staged open-air as part of the Corpus Christi celebrations) and court dramas. Although he was never appointed "court dramatist," as Cascardi states, he did enjoy immense stature at court and was even granted a modest royal pension in his later years. These facts, combined with the weight of his "ideal biography" and the fact that many, if not most, readers of the court plays bring to their first reading a previous familiarity with Calderón's autos sacramentales, have encouraged the reading of the myth plays as similarly orthodox allegories, either philosophical or specifically religious in content. For example, Aubrun says, "Calderón fit de cette classe d'opéras à grand spectacle le support de quelques thèmes théologiques" (ix), while Wilson and Moir describe the plays as "a kind of secular *autos*, which hint at philosophical or religious truths" (113–114), and Paul Mooney (175) goes to the extreme of saying that Calderón's principal concern in *La estatua de Prometeo* is the presentation of religious dogma.

To go beyond this mediated reading of the myth plays will require the examination of (1) the basic codes of the court spectacular; (2) the feasibility of critical discourse in the Hapsburg court; and (3) the hermeneutical practices traditionally applied to classical myth. Without calling into question Calderón's orthodox Catholicism—nor his fundamental support of the Hapsburg monarchy—attention to these elements should permit an appreciation of the complex discourse of power operant in these works.

If we are to rescue these plays from undeserved neglect, however, the first problem is delimiting the corpus of Calderonian court spectaculars. The classic form was a three-act drama whose plot derived from classical mythology, performed with elaborate perspective scenery and stage machinery, rich costuming, music and dance, in celebration of an occasion of state such as a royal birthday, wedding, or the birth of a prince. We have eleven extant Calderonian plays that clearly fit this description: *El mayor encanto, amor* (1635); *Los tres mayores prodigios* (1636); *La fiera, el rayo y la piedra* (1652); *Fortunas de Andrómeda y Perseo* (1653); *Celos aun del aire matan* (1660);[8] *Apolo y Climene* (1661); *El hijo del sol, Faetón* (1661); *Eco y Narciso* (1661); *Ni Amor se libra de amor* (1662); *Fieras afemina Amor* (1672);[9] and *La estatua de Prometeo* (1670–1674).[10] Three other works clearly belong in the same category, differing only in their shorter length: *El golfo de las sirenas* (1657), which Calderón christened an "égloga piscatoria"; *El laurel de Apolo* (1657–1658); and *La púrpura de la rosa* (1660), his first experiment with a work sung in its entirety.

But a neat line cannot be drawn around the corpus at this point. Calderón wrote other plays not based on classical myths for court performance. He drew the plots of *El jardín de Falerina* (1648–1649?)[11] and *Hado y divisa de Leonido y Marfisa* (1680) from chivalric materials, that of *El monstruo de los jardines* (1661) from legends of Achilles' childhood and adolescence. In others, such as *Amado y aborrecido* (1650–1656) and *Fineza contra fineza* (1671), mythic gods and goddesses (Venus and Diana, Venus and Cupid, respectively) intervene only at the end to assure a happy resolution of the plot.

Only in the case of *Hado y divisa de Leonido y Marfisa*, for which detailed records of the performance survive, can we be certain these plays began as full-fledged court spectacles. Although *Fineza contra fineza* was performed for the birthday of the Queen Mother, Mariana of Austria, normally the occasion for a spectacular play, that text contains no stage directions that would seem to indicate an elaborate court production. However, the absence of such stage directions is not proof of a simple original design, for it was common practice, after the first spectacular production at court, to repeat the play in a simpler form in the public theatres or for private performances before the royalty, and the surviving texts may derive from those simplified performances. Such was clearly the case with *La estatua de Prometeo* (see Greer introduction 208–214).

As the dates above indicate, Calderón composed the great majority of his court plays after his entry to the priesthood in 1650. Although he then gave up writing for the public theatres, this involved less of a change in the overall nature of his production than has generally been supposed (Cruickshank and Page xiii).[12] The mythological court plays did become a much more substantial part of his total output, but he also continued to write cape-and-sword plays and plays of royal intrigue akin to *La vida es sueño*, albeit for the court rather than the public theatres. Therefore, a chronological boundary does exist within Calderón's production, as do demarcations between mythic and nonmythic, spectacular and nonspectacular, and courtly and noncourtly plays, but these boundaries are impossible to mark with consistency and precision.

Rather than attempting a precise definition of this Calderonian genre, I will focus on its prototypical form, the mythological court-spectacle play; I will, however, conclude with a study of one nonmythological court spectacle, *Hado y divisa de Leonido y Marfisa*, because its use of chivalric figures rather than gods is illustrative, by indirection, of the purpose of the mythic material and the subtlety with which Calderón suited the subject to the royal occasion.

DEVELOPMENT OF THE COURT SPECTACLE

Calderón's mythological court plays, while a genre unique to Spain, were also part of an explosion of spectacular court entertainment throughout Europe in the sixteenth and seventeenth centuries. Such spectacles were, in a general sense, both a tool and an expression of absolutist rule. They focused attention, within the state and in rival courts, on the importance of the prince, serving the Machiavellian end of dazzling potential internal and external opponents with their displays of wealth and power, and, at least in their earlier formulations, the Platonic end of providing an image of an ideal state that was to serve as a model for ruler and subjects. The monarch was central to this image, as Strong points out, because

> in a Europe dominated by the problem of rival religious creeds and the breakdown of the Universal Church, the monarch not only established himself as the arbiter in religious matters but gradually became adulated as the sole guarantor of peace and order within the State. Before the invention of the mechanical mass media of today, the creation of monarchs as an "image" to draw people's allegiance was the task of humanists, poets, writers and artists. During the sixteenth and seventeenth centuries the most profound alliance therefore occurred between the new art forms of the Renaissance and the concept of the prince (*Splendour* 19).

7

At the same time, the spectacles often expressed specific political goals of the rulers, whether it be the full political union of England and Scotland under James, the desire to achieve peace between warring religious factions in the Valois court festivals, or the affirmation of absolute personal rule in the Caroline masques.[13]

Rulers saw in these brilliant shows of wealth not only a tool for forging internal unity but also a useful instrument in foreign policy that could impress rival monarchs with a show of power. Two years after the 1635 renewal of war between Spain and France, some 300,000 ducats were spent on public festivities in Madrid to celebrate the election of Felipe IV's cousin Ferdinand III as emperor of the Holy Roman Empire, and some voices were raised in protest at the expense, but the contemporary chronicle *Noticias de Madrid* commented: "Dicen los discursistas que tan grande acción ha tenido otro fin que el de recreación y pasatiempo, y que fue también ostentación para que el Cardenal Richelieu, nuestro amigo, sepa que aún hay dinero en el mundo que gastar y con que castigar a su Rey . . ." (qtd in Deleito y Piñuela 215). Since a lasting peace with France was not secured until 1659, Cardinal Richelieu, himself a master in the political value of theatre, appears not to have been unduly intimidated by the display.[14]

Precisely the ostentation of the display, the dominant role played by the visual spectacle, has, however, repelled two centuries of readers, both in Spain and other European traditions. The same condemnation of the spectacles as empty show long predominated with respect to the English masque, but as Ewbank points out, such criticism comes primarily from eighteenth- to twentieth-century literary scholars, who have an inherent bias in favor of language over visual codes. For the literate Renaissance and baroque theatregoer, well versed in reading emblems and heraldic devices, however, meaning might be conveyed with equal if not greater effect by visual images. As Strong says: "Fêtes speak to the visual sense in a lost vocabulary of strange attributes which we can no longer easily read but which, by the close of the sixteenth century, was a perfectly valid silent language within the make-up of the educated Roman mind" (*Splendour* 56).[15] From royal entries to court ballets and masques, meaning was conveyed less by reasoned discourse than a succession of allegorical images, generally kings or gods bearing the attire or devices associated with ideal princely virtues. We can still find guides to the vocabulary of these devices in the emblems of Alciati; the *imprese,* or personal devices, symbolizing the royal houses, and the mythological manuals that codified and interpreted classical myths for the Renaissance reader (Strong, *Splendour* 56–58).

Gombrich even maintains that for such a man, visual images carried not a lesser but a greater weight of meaning For the inheritor of the hermetic tradition and one who sees the universe as a unified, hierarchical whole, "the image not only *represents,* but captures something of, or participates in the nature of, what is represented" (Gordon 17). In Gombrich's words, "For them a truth condensed into a visual image was somehow nearer the realm of absolute truth than one explained in words. It was not what these images said that made them important, but the fact that what was said was also 'represented' " (qtd in Gordon 17).

The spectacles served the interests not only of the Renaissance prince but also of humanists interested in reviving the lost dramatic forms of classical antiquity. Inspired by reading the *De architectura* of the Roman architect-engineer Vitruvius on Greek theatre construction, stage scenery, and machinery, they developed the proscenium arch, perspective stage scenery, and machinery for increasingly elaborate stage effects.[16] A similar humanistic preoccupation with the nature and use of music and dance in ancient Greece resulted in new modes of performance for theatrical music and stage dancing that are the forebears of modern opera and ballet.[17]

The overwhelming choice for the subject matter of the spectacles, the figures and stories of classical mythology, satisfied the humanists' desire to revive a classical world and the rulers' interest in the legitimizing power of association with divine forebears. The terrain for such association had long been prepared, particularly by the Sicilian writer Euhemerus of the third century B.C., whose theory of mythological interpretation was essentially that the gods were originally kings who had been idealized to the status of gods by their societies.[18] Euhemerism reappeared in Renaissance mythographies, along with a variety of allegorical and analogical forms of mythological interpretation.

While the creators of court entertainment may have used mythology allegorically, their purpose was not that of Christianizing or spiritualizing myths, either in Hapsburg Spain or other European courts. As Orgel rightly points out: "Modern historians of the subject regularly claim that Renaissance mythographers spiritualized and internalized their fables. In fact, the truth more often seems to me just the opposite. The pressure is not toward spiritualizing the physical, but toward embodying and sensualizing the moral and abstract. The increasing tendency in the Renaissance to illustrate mythographies, and to treat them as iconologies—systems of images—is clear evidence of this" ("Royal Theatre" 264).

The roots of the dramatic techniques used in the court spectacles can be traced back to the late fifteenth century when a group of short dramatic pieces, usually called *favole pastorali*, were presented in the courts of northern Italy, in Mantua, Ferrara, and Milan.[19] The plays have in common pastoral elements, mythological themes, classical inspiration, and music. Of the six favole pastorali extant today, the most famous are *Favola d'Orfeo* by Angelo Poliziano, *Cefalo* by Niccolò da Correggio, *Pasithea* by Gaspare Visconti, and *Danae*, composed by Baldassare Taccone, with sets designed by Leonardo da Vinci. These short pieces, written as distractions by scholars and men of politics, were presented at gala occasions to members of the court, or sometimes to the residents of the city. Poliziano's *Orfeo* was a kind of *intermedio*, or "entre-mets," apparently staged at a banquet given by Cardinal Gonzaga in Mantua during Carnival of 1480 (Pyle 1–3, 53, 198).

The mythological and allegorical *intermedi* that evolved from these first pieces were presented not between the courses at a banquet but between the acts of comedies, those of Plautus and Terence in the vernacular and their Renaissance descendants. A great variety of intermedi existed, suited to the means available and the occasion celebrated, from simple instrumental interludes peformed by hidden musicians to extremely elaborate and spectacular productions such as those for the 1589 celebration of the marriage of Christina of Lorraine and Ferdinand de'Medici.[20] Their greatest development took place in Florence, where the infant Medici dynasty employed art in general, and court spectaculars in particular, to legitimize its rule and discourage any lingering republican instincts in its domain. The complex of artistic codes displayed in the courtly intermedi—elaborate scenery, stage machinery, music, dance, and mythological subject matter—spread from Italy throughout the courts of Europe, evolving into different forms in response to local traditions and preferences of the monarchs. While in Italy and Vienna this complex gave birth to opera, in France the *ballet de cour* became the form of choice, as had the court masque in England. In Spain, which possessed a vigorous dramatic tradition, permanent theatres in several cities, and a number of professional troupes by the last two decades of the sixteenth century, the spectacle play became the predominant form after the theatre-loving Felipe IV ascended the throne in 1621.[21]

Of this complex of artistic elements, however, it was the visually spectacular ingredients—illusionistic perspective scenery and stage machinery—that aroused most admiration from the majority of contemporary viewers and gave such great importance to the role of stage architects that in Italy, France, and England, and in non-Calderonian Spanish court plays, they often overshadowed the creative role played by authors of their poetic texts. Although the ancient authors Vitruvius and Pollux mentioned the use of scenery and machinery only briefly, this classical "authorization" set off an immense activity in Renaissance and baroque theatre development (Lawrenson 20–21).

If the inspiration came from classical sources, the details for these theatrical "reconstructions" and innovations had to be worked out by Renaissance scholar-artists. With respect to scenery, the crucial developments were Filippo Brunelleschi's discovery of the mathematical laws of perspective in the early fifteenth century, the codification of techniques for giving painting the illusion of spatial depth by Leon Battista Alberti in his *Della pittura* (1436), and explanation of techniques for constructing perspective scenery and the use of the angled stage in *De Archittetura* (1545) of Sebastiano Serlio. On this technical foundation, theatre design moved from an architectural background to a painted illusionistic backdrop, and finally to the sort of perspective scenery used by Bernardo Buontalenti for the 1589 intermedi: a stage framed by a proscenium arch with ranks of side wings receding behind it to the back of the stage where a back shutter closed off the view.[22]

In the one set of Spanish drawings we have that clearly shows these slanted side wings, or *bastidores* (those from the 1690 production in Valencia of Calderón's *La fiera, el rayo y la piedra*) four sets of wings were used. This was not the premiere of the work, however, and although Valencia was an important theatre center, it probably lacked the resources to stage a production comparable to those in the Buen Retiro in Madrid. The larger the number of bastidores, the more precision could be achieved in the perfection of the illusion, and by the early eighteenth century, a plan of the royal theatre in the Buen Retiro Palace shows eleven pairs of slots for bastidores.

Not all the impetus for theatrical innovation came from secular humanists, however; stage architects could also draw on the tradition of mechanical devices and stage effects employed in medieval mystery plays, which by the fifteenth century could include lightning, thunder, rain, conflagrations, and such miracles as the resurrections of saints. Perhaps their most impressive contribution was the "glory," the clouds on which the gods descended from heaven, a technique transferred from religious painting to sacred theatre and thence to the court stages (Lawrenson 44). Again, Brunelleschi's name occupies a primary position. The mechanical principles he used to build vast structures he also applied to enrich the visual splendour of the Florentine *sacre rappresentazioni*, with machinery such as that which brought down the Angel of Annunciation, escorted by a circle of boys dressed as angels, as he delivered his message to the Virgin. Leonardo da Vinci clearly understood Brunelleschi's devices, which he applied in his designs for a number of court spectaculars, including those for Taccone's *Danae*. One of his drawings for this favola pastorale depicts the cloud-borne appearance of a deity, and the text calls for numerous other ascents and descents.

The other effect much loved by spectators was frequent and rapid changes of scenery. Vitruvius mentioned the use of revolving scenery, known as *periaktoi*, and Vasari introduced this in a 1569 Medici spectacle. But the real advances in this field depended on great sixteenth-century progress by hydraulic engineers, some of whom doubled as scenographers. This advance derived from the rediscovery of the mechanical principles of Hero of Alexander (first century A.D.), disseminated and elaborated by Giovanni Battista Aleotti. Still there were complaints that the scene changes were done awkwardly and often constituted more of a distraction than an enchancement. With the 1638 publication of Nicolà Sabbattini's *Practica di fabricar scene e machine ne'teatri*, stage designers in all European courts had available an illustrated textbook explaining the methods for rapid scene changes.

Another factor important in the dissemination of new developments in stage scenery and machinery was the Accademia del disegno founded in Florence by the noted scenographer Giuglio Parigi. Here both scientists and artists learned civil and military architecture, mathematics, Euclidean geometry, as well as the design of stage machinery and the application of the new science of perspective to stage scenery. It was a graduate of Parigi's academy, Cosimo Lotti, who brought the latest techniques to Spain (Amadei de Pulice 38).[23]

COURT SPECTACLES IN HAPSBURG SPAIN

Although a variety of court entertainments had been staged under previous Spanish kings, Carlos I and Felipe II were not interested in theatre; royal patronage of the theatre began under Felipe III and quickly intensified on his son's accession to the throne. Even as a child, Felipe IV had demonstrated a great predilection for the theatre. In the restricted sphere of palace life, one of the few pleasures permitted the young prince was the performance of *comedias*, "a lo que se aplicaba el joven príncipe con el mayor gozo, recitando o representando él mismo, incluso en fiestas preparadas *ad hoc* ante la real familia, con otros jóvenes de las más nobles casas" (Deleito y Piñuela 12). As a young adult, he added to this natural inclination a taste for the attractive actresses of the *corrales*, the public theatres. In order to ingratiate himself with the Felipe and secure his position as favorite, the count-duke of Olivares encouraged his appetite in both these areas.

Furthermore, once Felipe was on the throne, Olivares employed theatrical events (in a strict sense and in more general terms) to enhance the power of the king's image for domestic and foreign consumption. As Brown and Elliott's apt metaphor puts it, the entire Spanish Hapsburg court, with its exceptionally elaborate and formal etiquette and protocol, was a sort of theatre production in itself:

> The court of the King of Spain resembled a magnificent theater in which the principal actor was permanently on stage. The stage instructions were meticulously detailed; the scenery was imposing, if a little antiquated; and the supporting cast was impressively large. All that was needed was a director of genius to orchestrate the action and make the necessary dispositions to secure the most brilliant scenic effects. In the Count-Duke of Olivares, who had learned his craft in Seville, that most theatrical of cities, the perfect direction was ready to hand (31).

> In Olivares's scheme of things, the king was to be the focal point of Spain's cultural and artistic life. Shining in the reflected splendor of his patronage, the leading poets, playwrights and artists of the age would all revolve around him, magnifying his glory and giving luster to his reign (40).

12

To that end, this "director" quickly sent to Italy to get the best stage manager available, one who could make that "antiquated scenery" the rival of any in Europe. Olivares sent orders to the Spanish ambassador to the papal court to bring back a *fontanero*—an engineer specializing in the construction of fountains and garden waterworks. The ambassador returned in 1626 with Cosimo Lotti, who made an immediate impression as Shergold reports: "Lope de Vega compares him to Hero of Alexandria in his skill in constructing mechanical figures, and on his arrival in Spain he is reported to have made a satyr's head which moved its eyes, ears, and hair, and opened its mouth to make such ferocious cries that it terrified all those who were not forewarned against it" (275–276). With the arrival of Lotti, a new era began in court theatre in Spain. Lotti worked in Spain for a number of years, and after his death in 1643 (Whitaker 44 n.2), he was succeeded by another Italian engineer, Baccio del Bianco, who designed court plays until his death in 1657.[24]

Neither the use of illusionist stage scenery nor machine-produced stage effects were new to Spain in the seventeenth century. It was the sophistication and scale of their use that was novel. Spanish painters had long been fully cognizant of scientific perspective and had applied it to the creation of scenery for a court play as early as 1570 when an Amadís representation in Burgos was said to have scenery "puesta en muy buen perspectiua" (Shergold, *History* 296). This was probably a correct use of perspective on a two-dimensional sheet of canvas used as a backdrop, however. Lotti created a three-dimensional perspective scene in 1627 for Lope de Vega's "opera" *La selva sin amor,* with cutout figures to heighten the effect (Shergold, *History* 296). He also greatly extended the use of machinery to change scenes rapidly, so that the stage could be quickly and repeatedly transformed from a sumptuous palace to a humble village or fearsome cavern. All the machinery necessary for this *trompe-l'oeil* theatre was incorporated in the Coliseo of the Buen Retiro Palace, the new royal theatre inaugurated in 1640.

Mechanical devices were also being used to produce striking stage effects before the arrival of Lotti, both in court entertainments and, to a more limited extent, in the public theatres, but again, he multiplied their use in a variety of ways. A system of pulleys and winches could make actors ascend or descend rapidly, pull chariots through the "heavens" above the stage, and even transport whole temples. For the climactic final scene of Calderón's *Fortunas de Andrómeda y Perseo* (stage designs by Baccio del Bianco), a temple appears in the air and descends to the stage; twenty-six actors emerge from it, play out the final scene, and then return to the temple, which is wafted into the heavens again. Clouds or other celestial apparitions could be made to appear to grow or diminish, thanks to a series of mechanical arms that folded in and out. Trapdoors made mountains or palaces rise into view or sink suddenly from sight as if destroyed.

A mechanism called a *bofetón* either rotated or sprang open to make characters seem to appear or disappear as if by magic. Sea scenes were often created, with sea monsters or ships appearing or disappearing and fish moving up and down with the illusionistic water, creating effects so realistic that on one occasion they were reported to have caused seasickness among the ladies of the court (Shergold, *History* 222–223, 276).

Such effects were attainable only because of the staggering development of mechanics in the sixteenth century. The pleasure they afforded was therefore double, residing not only in wonder and delight in the effects achieved but also in the triumph of apparent total human control of the physical world. Serlio, commenting on the theoretical value of spectacle in his influential book *De Architettura*, highlights both the pleasures to man's eyes and the wonder of their manufacture by "mens hands":

> Among all the things that may bee made by mens hands, thereby to yeeld admiration, pleasure to sight, and to content the fantasies of men; I think it is placing of a Scene, as it is shewed to your sight, where a man in a small place may see built by Carpinters or Masons, skilful in Perspective work, great Palaces, large Temples, and diverse Houses, both neere and farre off. . . . In some other Scenes you may see the rising of the Sunne with his course about the world: and at the ending of the Comedie, you may see it goe downe most artificially, where at many beholders have been abasht. And when occasion serveth, you shall by Arte see a God descending downe from Heaven; you also see some Comets and Stars shoot in the skyes . . . which things, as occasion serveth, are so pleasant to mens eyes, that a man could not see fairer with mens hands (qtd in Srong, *Splendour* 192).

Another observer bypassed amazement at the effects to marvel at the machines. Federigo Zuccaro, a Roman mannerist painter, described his delight at these mechanical triumphs of human organization and engineering on seeing the backstage machinery in Mantua in 1608:

> It was delightful to see the windlasses mounted over the machines, the cables of optimum strength, the ropes and lines by which the machines were moved and guided, and the many stagehands who were needed to keep the apparatus in operation. Every man was at his station, and at a signal the machinery could be raised, lowered, moved, or held in a particular position. More than 300 workers were engaged and had to be directed, which required no less experience and skill than it did foresight and reason (qtd in Strong, *Splendour* 193).

Whether a number of workers as large as three hundred were ever needed in Spain we do not know, but production records for Calderón's last court play,

Hado y divisa de Leonido y Marfisa, list the names of sixty-nine men needed to handle the machinery for scene changes and another thirty-six who worked in the wings (Shergold and Varey, *Representaciones* 34).

The wonder of many of the stage effects was heightened by the introduction of artificial lighting, which made it possible to stage the spectacles at night. The flickering light of candles or wax torches, suggests Varey, may also have softened the artificiality of the painted bastidores and thus heightened the illusion of reality (Varey, "Scenes" 61). The amount of wax required to light the stage and theatre for such productions was astounding. For the premiere of Calderón's *Fortunas de Andrómeda y Perseo,* the royal waxworks had to supply 695 pounds of wax (Shergold and Varey, *Representaciones* 18, 58).

The enthusiasm of sixteenth- and seventeenth-century princes and less exalted spectators for these spectacular effects usually worked to the detriment of the play as a dramatic text, for the power and glory afforded to the architect exceeded the control of the playwright. Ben Jonson's prolonged and ultimately losing battle with the English stage architect Inigo Jones for control of the court masque is well known, and of the French ballet de cour, Christout says: "Il n'y a pas lieu de s'étonner . . . de la minceur des 'livrets' que n'étaient que le support du spectacle, fussent-ils signés de Molière ou de Corneille" (3). In describing his court spectacle, *La selva sin amor,* Lope de Vega pointed out the subordination of his dramatic verse (which he calls an "eclogue") to Lotti's effects: "lo menos que en ella hubo fueron mis versos. . . . El bajar de los dioses, y las demás transformaciones requería más discurso que la égloga, que, aunque era el alma, la hermosura de aquel cuerpo hacía que los oídos se rindiesen a los ojos (300)."[25]

A primary reason for Calderón's success in achieving a unique level of dramatic integrity in his mythological court plays was precisely his refusal to surrender control of the production to the engineers, whether Cosimo Lotti, Baccio del Bianco, or their Spanish successors. The history of Calderón's first complete spectacle play, *El mayor encanto, amor,* gives us evidence of his insistence on the priority of dramatic coherence over spectacle.[26] The original idea for the play was that of Cosimo Lotti, who in a memorandum to Calderón described a long list of devices to be included in the event. Calderón replied with a firm statement of rejection: "Avnque está trazada con mucho ynjenio, la traza de ella no es representable por mirar más a la ynbención de las tramoyas que al gusto de la representación" (qtd in Rouanet). He continued that if he were to write the play, he could not follow Lotti's list but that he was willing to select a number of the devices suggested. He did use a substantial number and even introduced one or two new effects. In effect, Calderón used Lotti's memorandum much as he often used works of other playwrights—as an idea to be reworked for maximum dramatic effectiveness.

15

Music

The effectiveness of the court spectacular relied not only on dazzling the eyes of its audience but on serving a feast for all the senses with music, dance, and even olfactory delights. Descriptions of Spanish court festivals often include accounts of sweet fragrances released during the performance, such as that of *Fieras afemina Amor*. In this play, a volcano that occupied the whole stage suddenly threw off clouds of thick smoke that darkened the whole theater, but with the additional surprise that it was "sin molestia del auditorio, porque estaban compuestos de olorosas gomas; de suerte que lo que pudiera ser fastidio de la vista se convirtió en lisonja del olfato" (Calderón, *Fieras* 154). For a 1655 performance, forty *arrobas* (about a thousand pounds) of oil of jasmin were ordered from Genoa, along with other fragrant ingredients, because "se dice ha de ser aquel día toda una gloria, sin que tengan los sentidos más que desear" (Barrionuevo 1:147). Unfortunately, at a distance of three or four centuries, these elements of the spectacle are harder to recreate because less documentation of them has survived than have descriptions of visual effects and dramatic texts. In the case of music, this is particularly true for Spain since two of the largest collections of Spanish music were destroyed in the eighteenth century—that in the royal library and music archive of the Alcázar palace, by fire, and that of King Joam IV of Portugal, by earthquake (Stein, "Music" 2). However, the recent work of Louise Stein in particular has gone far toward reconstructing the nature and development of seventeenth-century Spanish theatre music on the basis of the surviving evidence.[27]

Use of music in Spanish theatre was not an invention of the court plays. Music was closely associated with Spanish drama, both religious and secular, from its earliest roots in medieval liturgy and court pageantry; the association continued as the theatre developed a more extended and coherent shape in the Renaissance. Many of Juan del Encina's dramatic works conclude with a sung *villancico*,[28] as do several of the plays of Torres Naharro. Gil Vicente goes far beyond this, using music extensively and often to great expressive effect in a number of his dramatic works (Cotarelo y Mori, *Entremeses* cclxxvi–cclxxvii; Livermore 92–95).

Lope de Vega, in his ironic but ultimately serious *Arte nuevo de hacer comedias en este tiempo* (1609), made a general declaration of independence from the precepts of classical drama yet retained a roughly Aristotelian place for music in his formula for poetic imitation in popular theatre.[29] In practice as well as theory, he set the pattern for the use of music that was to prevail in the corrales throughout the seventeenth century. In these theatres, music and dance entertained the audiences before, after, and between the acts. Within the play, music was used "realistically," as it was in Italian comedies (Pirrotta and Povoledo 78), in situations that involve music in daily life. For example, trumpets would announce important entrances and drums a summons to battle; a maidservant would sing a love lament to entertain her lovelorn mistress; and weddings would be celebrated with onstage singing and dancing, and offstage choruses would intone refrains that expressed some mysterious divine or supernatural truth. In plays with some addition of stage machinery, music would be used strategically to mask the noise made by descending and ascending *tramoyas*. Most of the songs were either drawn from or modeled after traditional songs of the *cancionero popular*, and their musical structure was conservative (Stein, "Music" 18–29, 81).

Instruments specifically called for in stage directions of such plays include trumpets and drums for military scenes, shawms in religious scenes, and rustic instruments such as rough flutes, shepherd's pipes, bagpipes, and tambourines for peasant scenes. A guitar, harp, or *vihuela* might be used onstage to accompany a courtly song, and there are a few mentions of the use of bowed stringed instruments for accompaniment. In many cases, the stage directions mention only "música," leaving its specific nature up to the discretion—and the possibilities—of the *autor de comedias* (theatre-company owner-director) (Stein, "Music" 18–29). Knowledge of this pattern of music in the popular theatre is important to understanding the spectacle plays, for very few departed entirely from this standard national model.

In the decades around the turn of the seventeenth century, while the popular comedia form was being consolidated in Spain,[30] in Italy revolutionary changes in court theatre music were taking place that would lead to the establishment of opera. As in the case of theatre design and stage machinery, the impetus came from humanists interested in ancient Greek music, which they believed to have had great psychological power, a capacity to arouse or to still a variety of emotions in the human soul, which "modern music" did not possess. They were particularly interested in finding a means of communicating the words of the text, obscured by the prevailing polyphonic style of music, and in enhancing the affective power of the human voice.[31] Lacking samples of actual Greek music, their understanding of it derived from study of Plato and other theoretical commentaries on music, from which they deduced that "the secret of Greek music lay in the perfect union of words and melody, a union to be achieved by making the former dominate and control the latter" (Grout 36).

In the interest of a clear and natural declamation of the text, therefore, contrapuntal writing was replaced by solo voices with a simple continuo accompaniment, preferably played by the singer himself, and composers strove to find a middle way between speech and song, tending either toward what we now know as recitative and aria as the balance moved between dramatic declamation and lyricism, between "recitar cantando" and "cantar recitando" (Pirrotta 241–257). The development of an effective declamatory style was essential if Renaissance poets and composers were to create dramas sung in their entirety, which they presumed to have existed in Greece. Musicologists debate about which

17

work should be considered the first opera, but Jacopo Peri's setting of *Euridice* (libretto by Ottavio Rinuccini), performed in Florence in 1600 for the marriage of Henri IV of France and Maria de'Medici, is certainly crucial in its establishment.

While the Florentine innovation of wholly sung drama with the new *stile recitativo* spread to other Italian cities—Mantua, Rome, and Venice—opera found only a tardy and limited reception in Spain. In the first two decades of the seventeenth century, there was little specifically court theatre, perhaps because Felipe III preferred dancing, at which he apparently excelled, and Queen Margarita is reported to have disapproved of theatrical entertainments (Stein, "Music" 102–108).[32] The preferred form of court festivity was the *sarao*, a "large-scale, organized ball built around traditional figured dances" (Stein, "Music" 110–111). They can be considered theatrical in their elaborate "staging" and protocol, but they did not involve even minimal dramatic texts. Significantly, a large dancing hall rather than a theatre was built in the palace at Valladolid in 1605 (Stein, "Music" 111, 117).

Masques or pageants were staged to celebrate the marriage of Felipe III and Margarita in 1598 in Denia and Valencia; others were organized in Madrid in 1601, 1602, and 1603, and an elaborate masque capped the celebration of Felipe IV's birth in Valladolid in 1605. Their features were characteristic of other European royal celebrations in the Renaissance *fêtes* tradition—

> the use of triumphal carriages and floats, the staging of non-dramatic spectacles arranged in *tableaux vivants,* the use of music as a background or nonparticipative force (the musicians are not in costume and do not take part in the staged activity), the use of dancing in conjunction with the tableaux, and the participation of members of the royal family in the masque and the dancing. . . . The musical part of each spectacle was essential, but the characters in the scenes did not sing or play instruments as part of a story (Stein, "Plática" 19).

While such events were eminently theatrical, they did not have plots, dialogues, or any other written dramatic text.

A few events founded on written texts were staged during royal sojourns at country houses, particularly at the estate of the king's *valido* (the royal favorite, roughly equivalent to a prime minister), the duke of Lerma. Two simple spectacle plays were performed there, Lope's *El premio de la hermosura* in 1614 and *El caballero del sol* by Luis Vélez de Guevara in 1617, as was a loosely linked series of masques by Mira de Amescua, also in 1617. Under the circumstances, the machinery employed seems to have been relatively limited, consisting of such standard effects as the discovery of a ship or the descent and ascent on a cloud of the young prince, the future Felipe IV, who played the role of Cupid.[33] Like the earlier masques, these were amateur productions, acted by members of the royal family and their attendants, with the exception of the Mira de Amescua masques, in which professional actors participated along with courtiers. Although the music in these events continued to serve some of the nondramatic functions for which it was employed in earlier court entertainments, such as hiding machine noise and accompanying danced interludes, these plays and masques also included more dramatic use of music. Actors in costume sang solos and duets and small ensemble songs onstage, within the roles of their assigned characters. They did not, however, reflect any influence of the new Italian operatic theories, which seem not to have penetrated the court of Felipe III. Unfortunately, none of the scores for these performances have survived, but based on other evidence, Stein believes that they reflected a dual tradition: that of the courtly Renaissance fêtes and that of the Spanish comedia, with its more dramatic use of popular musical forms. As in the public theatres, solo singing was often accompanied only by a guitar, the characteristic accompaniment for singing of ballads, both on and off the public stage. While the popular traditions thus penetrated the court theatre, Stein points out that a properly majestic tone was set by more lavish instrumentation and by "use of courtly figured dance that rarely if ever graced the stages of the public *corrales*" ("Music" 135). These early spectacle plays thus displayed a pattern that would continue in Calderón's more ambitious works: the blending of elements from the European court tradition with others from the comedia ("Music" 123–136).

As we have seen, court theatre came to life with the ascent of Felipe IV to the throne in 1621. During the royal sojourn in Aranjuez the following year, three "splendid amateur productions" (Shergold 268) were staged on specially constructed outdoor stages: *La gloria de Niquea* by Juan de Tassis y Peralta, the count of Villamediana; *Querer por sólo querer* by Antonio Hurtado de Mendoza; and Lope de Vega's *El vellocino de oro*.[34] They altered the previous pattern more by their number than by stylistic innovations, however, for the latter two in particular were in subject matter and use of music closely akin to *El premio de la hermosura* and *El caballero del sol*, although their production seems to have been more spectacular.

La gloria de Niquea, on the other hand, did bring somewhat more of an Italian flavor to the Spanish court. Its author, the ill-fated aristocratic poet Villamediana, had come in contact with Marino and other Italian poets while in Italy from 1611 to 1615 (Villamediana 12–13) and had probably attended court entertainments there (Stein, "Music" 138). Villamediana employs a good deal of Italianate (seven- and eleven-syllable) verse in this loosely plotted two-act piece in which Amadís frees the enchanted Princess Niquea.[35] Although later editions called his work a comedia, he called it an *invención*, which, by Hurtado de Mendoza's description of it, was not required to abide by rules of unity of plot but aimed at amusing the court by its variety and its visual splendour: "esto que estrañara el pueblo por comedia, y se llama en Palacio invención, no se mide a los precetos comunes de las farsas que es una fábula unida, ésta se fabrica de variedad desatada, en que la vista lleva mejor parte que el oído, y la ostentación consiste más en lo que se ve, que en lo que se oye" (qtd in Stein, "Music" 140).

The visual splendour was entrusted to an Italian engineer, Giulio Cesare Fontana, superintendent of the fortifications of Naples (Stein, "Music" 139), who built a large stage reminiscent of the Olympic in Vicenza with an ornate architectural facade behind it. On the stage were two huge statues of Mercury and Mars, with scenery representing woods and a mountain fifty feet wide and eighty feet in circumference that divided into two parts to reveal gardens with flowers and fountains but was so constructed that one man could manipulate it. It also had steps leading up to a niche filled with wild beasts that was later used to discover other special effects such as an "Infierno de amor" with flames. Other effects included cloud-borne ascents and descents, triumphal cars, trees that opened to reveal nymphs, a flying dragon, and a throne on which sat the Goddess of Beauty, a nonspeaking part played by the Queen (Shergold, *History* 269–270).[36]

Italian influence seems not to have extended to the music, however. Although the score is lost, Stein's evaluation ("Music" 142–151) based on textual evidence indicates that the sections set to music were not those of Italianate verse but those in the traditional Spanish octosyllable, and music seems to have been used much as it was in the comedia. She speculates that the traditional use of music may have been due to the general control and perhaps partial composition of the music by the Flemish royal chapelmaster Matthieu Rosmarin, or Mateo Romero as he was called in Spain, who had taught the king both French and music, and had achieved an unusually powerful position in court for a musician. The only real musical novelty of the piece, she finds, was the reiterative use of music as a supernatural force. Throughout the piece, hidden choruses sang enigmatic warnings and encouragement to Amadís, and La Noche (Night), played by a black Portuguese maidservant, controlled the powerful hero with her song of "dark confusion." Comparison of this song with another song of Night in the 1579 open-air Florentine celebration of Francesco dei Medici and Bianca Capello, however, illustrates very different performance conditions in the two courts: "The song, a madrigal setting by Piero Strozzi for the "Chariot of the Night," was sung by the noble and expert singer Giulio Caccini to the accompaniment of a viol consort. In the Spanish play, Night sings to the accompaniment of a simple guitar, her text is in the traditional octosyllabic romance meter, and she is played by a lowly servant" ("Music" 145 n.23). The musical scheme for *La gloria de Niquea* did avail itself fully of the musical resources of the court, employing several choirs of singers and a variety of instruments, including "trumpets, drums, shawms, cornettos, sackbuts, flutes, viols, violins, lutes, guitars and theorbos" ("Music" 142).

In 1627, the year after Cosimo Lotti's arrival in Spain, an attempt was made to introduce the new Italian musical style and Italianate staging to the Madrid court, and to secure a royal appointment for Lotti in the bargain, with the performance of the first Spanish opera, *La selva sin amor*, whose text was written by Lope de Vega.[37] The impetus for the production apparently came not from the king but from Lotti himself, with the support of the Florentine embassy, which wished to secure both its own and Lotti's position in the young king's favor. The time seemed ideal, for the young king was known not only for his fascination with the theatre but also for his love of music. First planned for performance in the Casa de Campo, then a royal park, for the August birthday of the Infanta María, future queen of Hungary, the production had to be postponed because of a series of crises for the royal family: the death of Felipe and Isabel's only daughter at less than two years of age, a severe illness of the king, and the death of another daughter born in October, who lived only one day. It was ultimately staged in the Salon of the Palace in December to cheer up the queen, despondent after the death of yet another royal infant (Whitaker 49, 52–58).

Lope's text for *La selva* was as thin as those that Christout described for the ballet de cour; less than seven hundred lines of text (the average comedia has three thousand or more), it had only one act, divided into seven scenes. With one short exception, the entire text is in Italianate seven- and eleven-syllable verse (Stein, "Music" 169). He described his work accurately as a "pastoral eclogue," for it transforms Madrid and the river Manzanares into an Arcadia in which "dramatic conflict" revolves around Cupid's challenge of transforming shepherds and shepherdesses dedicated to the worship of the cold-hearted Daphne into loyal followers of Venus and Cupid (Amor). As we have seen, Lope himself said that his text was the least important element in a festival in which eyes prevailed over ears.

Judging from his own account, Lope was much more impressed by Lotti's staging than by the new music. He reported in some detail the changeable perspective scenery and stage effects, which included a maritime scene with ships that fired their cannons and answering salvos from castles; fish dancing in moving waves that appeared perfectly lifelike under the artificial light; Venus in a chariot drawn by two swans conversing with her son Cupid, who fluttered about overhead; and a smooth transformation of the maritime scene into one of a wood much like that near the bridge across the Manzanares, including views of the Casa del Campo and Palace. Of the music he has much less to say, except that it was completely sung, "cosa nueva en España," that instrumentalists were hidden from view, and that the music underscored the emotions of the text, its wonder, complaints, sorrows, and loves (Whitaker 46–47).

Composition of that music was entrusted to Filippo Piccinini, a noted lute and theorbo player of Bolognese origin who had been employed in the Spanish court since 1613 and met regularly to play with the king, his brothers, and the chapelmaster, Romero (Whitaker, 53–54). The score for *La selva* has been lost, but diplomatic correspondence indicates that the music was primarily in *stile recitativo*, a completely new musical genre for both the king and his chapelmaster. Piccinini himself, an instrumentalist rather than a vocalist or composer who had left Italy years before when recitative and accompanied monody were just becoming known, found himself unable to complete the task. An amateur musician, Bernardo Monanni, who had come to Madrid with Lotti in 1626 and served there as secretary of the Tuscan embassy until 1642, came to his assistance and in fact composed the two longest scenes of the play (Whitaker, 53–54; Stein, "Music" 161–167).

On hearing his text set to this music, according to Tuscan embassy correspondence, Lope was enraptured. The king was reported to be equally taken with the music, which he played through himself, and with the production as a whole, for he attended almost all the rehearsals. If this is not a biased exaggeration by the parties promoting the production, the puzzle is the "studied indifference" (Stein, "Music" 176) with which the new music was generally received. Perhaps, says Stein, this was due to the "lackluster quality of Piccinini's setting" or the Spanish preference for their established style of solo song. Yet another explanation might be that Olivares, who fully appreciated the power of theatre as an image-making force, was decidedly unmusical and not inclined to import musicians capable of implanting the new music. Whatever the explanation, there were no further experiments with opera until 1660 when Calderón and the Spanish composer Juan Hidalgo turned their hands to the task (Stein, "Music" 174).

DANCE

If the work of a musicologist attempting to recreate seventeenth-century Spanish theatre music requires a work of creative reconstruction from fragmentary documentation, that of the dance historian presents an almost impossible challenge. Twentieth-century musicians may have to translate the seventeenth-century scores into the modern notation system, but dancers have no score and only the scantiest of written descriptions. Dance steps and choreography were taught and transmitted orally. Even the lengthy descriptions of court fiestas are little help, for they concentrated on visual effects, which they described at length; some provide considerable detail regarding accompanying music, but danced passages rarely merit more than a brief comment: "They sing and dance." Or "The performance ended with a handsome dance."

In France, where dance took pride of place in the court spectacular, we find most explanation of the dance, particularly in philosophical terms. Ballet was said to be the mirror of man, of nature, and of morality. According to Claude

François Menestrier, it rivaled the theatre, for whereas comedy could only imitate actions of the people and tragedy those of the great, dance could combine the serious and the ridiculous, the natural and fantastic, fiction and history, and could thereby imitate and explain at the same time "la nature des choses" (qtd in McGowan 14). Horace's dictum "Ut pictura poesis" was transferred to dance, which, like painting, was considered "silent poetry." Like painting, poetry, and music, it at once expressed and spoke to the soul. Colletet said of dance in 1632: "Comme la Poësie est un vray tableau de nos passions et la Peinture un discours muet véritablement, mais capable néantmoins de réveiller tout ce qui tombe dans notre imagination: ainsi la Danse est une image vivante de nos actions, et une expression artificielle de nos secrètes pensées" (qtd in McGowan 12).

One Spanish theoretician of theatre, José Antonio Gonçalez de Salas, describes this representative quality of dance as almost pictorially specific.[38] Citing Lucian, he says that the fable that Proteus could transform himself into different forms derived from his dancing ability:

> El haber sido insigne Maestro de Bailar, i Dançar, i tener grande excelencia en la imitación varia de las cosas, que representaba dançando. i las Mudanças que de una forma hacia a otra, ia imitando al árbol, ia a las aguas, ia a las fieras, después se las fingieron Transformaciones . . . i no hai cosa más parecida a las Mudanças, que hoi se usan en los Bailes nuestros, pues ia en ellos se imita al que nada, ia al que siega, ia al que texe, i assí a otras infinitas differencias (f.120).

The central and much-repeated conception of the dance drawn from Pythagorean cosmology was that dance reflected the harmonious movement of the spheres. In the Pythagorean-Platonic tradition, perfect correspondence binds together all parts of the divinely ordered cosmos, at once stable and in constant movement. The mathematically perfect revolutions of the heavenly spheres witnesses this order as the bodies move in concord, producing a celestial harmony not materially audible to human ears (Heninger 178–179). A seventeenth-century Spanish dancing master, Esquivel Navarro, expresses this idea succinctly: "En quanto al origen de la Dança, es cosa indubitable . . . que es vna imitación dela numerosa armonía que las Esferas celestes, Luzeros, y Estrellas fixas y errantes traen en concertado mouimiento entre sí" (f.1r).[39] After citing various contradictory opinions on who invented dancing (including Theseus, Pyrrhus, and an anonymous man in Zaragoza), he explains his belief that it was Tubal Cain:

> Mas mi sentir es, que Tubal Cain inuentor del instrumento Músico, lo fue del Dançado, o alguno de los primeros que le oyessen tañer y no se haze duro de creer, pues auiendo sido hombre muy jouial, quién duda que al passo que tañía el instrumento, se mouería dançando? Pues vemos produzir

a cada causa su semejante, y conforme son las causas, produzen sus efectos: así como el estruendo bélico de la caxa de guerra, inquieta y altera los ánimos, incitando a la pelea: y si se oye vna biguela [vihuela], parece que combida a Dançar lo sonoro de sus acentos; y assí el que Dança, ajuste los compasses de los mouimientos con los instrumentos (f.2r).[40]

Esquivel's history of dance reflects the common belief that music and dance were analogous in their purpose, that of expressing human feelings and passions, and also in the effect on the soul of the spectator. This power, it was believed, derived from the correspondence among all parts of the universe; as human beings shared the qualities of all inferior beings, so they also experienced the desire to communicate with the superior Being, of which they are a pale reflection. Says McGowan: "Par l'emploi d'une musique qui imitant exactement les proportions de l'harmonie des sphères on croyait au XVIe siècle pouvoir, comme les anciens, attirer les influences planétaires sur l'ame humaine, impressionnable parce que son harmonie était proportionée à celle des cieux" (19).

Both music and dance, then, not only reflected the harmony of the spheres but were also capable of drawing that heavenly accord down to govern the affairs of terrestial beings. Two choruses in the 1594 ballet de cour of Jean Dorat, *L'Epithalame*, celebrate dance as the transformer of primitive chaos, the conserver of harmony (and hierarchy) on earth:

JOUVENCEAUX: Le monde est faict par discorde accordance:
Le Roy craint Dieu, et les Princes le Roy,
Qui vont donnans au peuple bas la Loy.
Dansons ainsi pour n'avoir discordance.

PUCELLES: L'un doit porter à l'autre obeissance
Du plus petit jusques au grant des grans,
Sans rompre l'ordre et sans troubles les rangs,
Pour danser tous en bonne convenance.

Dancers following the king's lead in the ball are like orderly stars that follow the sun that brings abundance in its wake:

PUCELLES: Nous ne scaurions aller en decadence,
Puisque le Roy Charles mene le bal;
Comm'un Soleil que va d'à mont à val,
En conduisant d'astres grand'abondance
(qtd in McGowan 21).

The union of the arts that humanists in other countries cultivated in opera and drama was in France promoted in the ballet de cour. In his preface to one of the first major ballets, *Le Balet Comique de la Royne* (1581), its author, Beaujoyeulx, said that in this union of music, poetry, and the dance, "J'ay toutesfois donné le premier tiltre & honneur à la danse, & le second à la substance" (p. eiij). He also makes explicit the political goal of his work, that of curing wounds and re-establishing harmony after recent religious strife. Both in its organization and in its political goals, this ballet presents interesting parallels and contrasts with Calderón's first surviving court spectacle play, *El mayor encanto, amor*, and it will be considered at greater length in a subsequent chapter.

The power of dance was never cultivated with such philosophical or political fervor in Spain, but neither was its contribution to the constitution of the public figure of the king ignored. Felipe II's chaplain, Antonio de Obregón y Cerceda, in a book he dedicated to the future Felipe III, said that dancing was necessary for kings and monarchs because "el arte del dançado muestra a traer bien el cuerpo, serenidad en el rostro, graciosos mouimientos, fuerça en las piernas, y ligereza" (Esquivel Navarro f.4v). Felipe III obviously took this advice to heart, for as we have seen, he preferred saraos and máscaras over other forms of court entertainment, and one author said that theatre did not flourish at his court "por ser su majestad el más airoso danzarín de su tiempo y gustar mucho de mostrar esta galantería a los saraos que se hacían en fiestas de años" (Bances Candamo 29).[41] Futhermore, although such organized balls generally lacked the poetic allegorical base of the French ballet de cour, they also published a similar message of order and hierarchy.

> Each moment of the sarao—the entrances and seating of the monarchs, the sequence of dancers, the choreography—was carefully planned in advance, in accordance with the *etiquetas de palacio* or court protocol. The dancing master of the royal household was usually responsible for the choreography and the pairing of the dance partners. The saraos were pre-arranged to allow King Philip to display his prowess as a dancer and to exhibit the unity of the royal couple as they danced together before the court (Stein, "Music" 111).

Such events did not end with the advent to the throne of Felipe IV, who Esquivel (f.4v–5) said was also a skilled dancer. However, given his love for the theatre, dramatic productions took center stage among court entertainments.

Dance, like music, had traditionally been associated with theatre in Spain, although not with the approval of all observers: in 1616, the complaints against the scandalous nature of theatrical dancing brought the Council of Castile to forbid all dancing in the theatre. Predictably, the order was not long enforced (Ivanova 77). In the corrales, dances often began and concluded the theatrical event, filled in between acts, and as in the case of music, complemented such scenes within the plays as weddings and other rustic celebrations. They were sometimes danced only to instrumental accompaniment, sometimes partly spoken, and sometimes sung by the dancers themselves, which Gonçalez de Salas, writing in 1633, considered a difficult novelty: "I lo que más es, los mismos que

Dançan i Bailan cantan juntamente, primor i elegancia en estos últimos años introducida, i summamente difficultosa, siendo fuerça que estorba, para la concentuosa harmonía de la voz, el spíritu alterado i defectuoso con los agitados movimientos" (f.121). He says, however, that in this feat, Spanish dancers are only following the model set by the "Ancients." Throughout his discussion of dance, in fact, Gonçalez de Salas is concerned with defending the legitimacy of this often-excoriated art form by demonstrations of its antiquity.

A distinction was made between two kinds of dance, "baile" and "danza," and it was surely the former that called forth the protests of the pious. González de Salas described the difference as follows: "Las *danzas* son de movimientos más mesurados y graves, y en donde no se usa de los brazos sino de los pies solos: los *bailes* admiten gestos más libres de los brazos y de los pies juntamente" (f.119). While using *baile* in one sense as a generic term for "dance," the *Diccionario de Autoridades* published in 1726 drew the same general distinction, defining *bailar* as "hacer mudanzas con el cuerpo, y con los pies y brazos, con orden, y a compás, siguiendo la consonancia del instrumento que se tañe," and quoted the earlier dictionary of Covarrubias, who believes the word derives from a Greek word *ballo*, "que significa arrojar, porque los que bailan se arrojan con los saltos y mudanzas." The *danza* is a much more stately affair: "baile serio en que a compás de instrumentos se mueve el cuerpo, formando con las mudanzas de sitio vistosas y agradables plantas." Cotarelo includes among the bailes such dances as the *contrapás, chacona, fandango, guineo, jácara, pasacalle, seguidillas, tarantela*, and *villano*, while he terms danzas the *alemana, branle, españoleta, furioso, gallarda, gitano, hacha, morisca, pavana, saltarelo, serranía, turdión*, and *zapateado*. In general, these refer to popular versus courtly dances, but bailes of a popular origin were often adopted by court circles in a refined form while a parallel popular version continued to be danced elsewhere (Brooks 35–37; Cotarelo, "Entremeses" clxiv–clxx, ccxxxiii–cclxvii). The inclusion of dances with such names as *gitano*, *morisca*, and *serranía* among "courtly" danzas obviously attests to this process.

In the 1605 sarao for the birth of the future Felipe IV, dances included the pavana, gallarda, turdión, madama de Orleans, and the danza de la hacha. The pavana allegedly earned its name because its stateliness was reminiscent of the movements of the peacock. It was usually danced with the gallarda, a gayer and more sprightly partnered court dance. The turdión, or tordion, was a similar dance that required less virtuosity in its execution. By at least one account, the danza de la hacha, or "torch dance," served as the finishing touch to all saraos.[42] The torneo, a figured dance that evolved from earlier mock tournaments and equestrian ballets (Brooks 393), was danced during the second act of Lope's 1617 court play *El premio de la hermosura* and also in Hurtado de Mendoza's *Querer por sólo querer* (Stein, "Music" 152). Many of these dances are also named as having been performed at court masques in the reigns of Felipe IV and Carlos II. For one máscara, violin music accompanied the entrance of the princess and her eighteen ladies-in-waiting, all wearing masks and the same color and cut of dress. The princess then sat by the king until her turn to dance. A lady-in-waiting danced a gallarda, and four others danced the españoleta, followed by solo and group performances of gallardas, the madama de Orleans, torneo, la galeria de amor, la alemana, and the *pie de gibao*.[43] At a masque given by the duke of Cadiz in 1673, music of several instruments heralded the entry of six pages dressed as Mars, Alcides, Adonis, Love, Mercury, and Science. Singing as they danced, they recited allegorical verses, then performed court dances, including the torneo, españoleta and la hacha, ending with a lively jácara (Brooks 32).[44]

None of this proves that these are the sort of dances that were performed as part of Calderón's court spectaculars. We have no descriptions of the dance employed, nor can we even be sure of the extent of its use. Calderón characteristically included only brief stage directions with his texts, leaving the specifics up to the director or writing a separate memorandum spelling out the effects to be employed. Absence of stage directions indicating that certain portions were sung and/or danced does not therefore constitute proof that they were merely spoken. When Juan de Vera Tassis published *La estatua de Prometeo* after Calderón's death, he added a stage direction, "Cantando y baylando," where none had existed in the first editions of the work. Vera Tassis, a friend of Calderón, would probably have seen the play performed, and his memory that the section was danced can be presumed accurate. Furthermore, on the somewhat more complete manuscript version of this play, the prompter wrote in at the same point a more specific indication of the type of dance: "Quatro cruzados en alas." A different hand also wrote "Builtas" ("vueltas") by a scene in the first act, which was surely a dance indication;[45] in the case of another court play, *Los celos hacen estrellas* by Juan Vélez de Guevara, the stage direction for a scene danced by "labradores y ninfas" read in one version: "Vaylen y canten, y Glauco y Licio," while another version says: "Baylan, y cantan, y Glauco, Y Licio. Bueltas afuera."[46] This is only fragmentary evidence, but it does indicate that the use of dance extended beyond the limited number of scenes for which it is specifically indicated in our texts.

While the court-spectacle plays may not have incorporated the well-known dances in the clearly recognizable form of a pavana or a gallarda, it seems logical that the choreography would not have differed much from a court sarao or máscara. Who could have been responsible for the design of the dances? Barring the most unlikely possibility that a dancing master was specially hired for the job but never mentioned in any *relación* or payment, the only two possibilities would have been the royal dance master or the director or another member of one of the professional troupes who ordinarily handled dancing in the corrales. Either would probably have used the steps and patterns with which he was familiar and that pleased his audience, perhaps altering them somewhat to suit the occasion. This conclusion is supported by the fact that the description of the performance of *Las fortunas de Andrómeda y Perseo* that accompanies the manuscript of the play refers to the dance of the signs of the zodiac that ended the opening *loa* first as a sarao and then as a máscara.

Since Brooks (154, 157) points out that the same aristocratic dances were known throughout Europe, we might again have recourse to French sources for a more precise description. The 1581 *Ballet comique* of Beaujoyeulx ended with the sort of grand *danse horizontale* that became the rule in court ballets:

Les violons changèrent de son & se prindrent à sonner l'entrée du grant Balet, composé de quinze passages, disposez de telle façon qu'à la fin du passage toutes tournoyent tousjours la face vers le Roy: devant la majesté duquel estans arrivées, dansèrent le grand Balet à quarante passages en figures Géométriques, & icelles toutes justes & considérées en leur diamètre, tantost en quarré, & ores en rond, & de plusieurs & diverses façons, & aussi tost en triangle, accompagné de quelque autre petit quarré, & autres petites figures. Lesquelles figures n'estoyent si tost marquées par les douze Naiades, vestues de blanc . . . que les quatre Dryades habillées de verd ne les veinssent rompre: de sorte que l'une finissant, l'autre soudain prenoit son commencement. A la moitié de ce Balet se feit une chaîne, composée de quatre entrelacemens différens l'un de l'autre, tellement qu'à les voir on eust dit que c'estoit une bataille rangée, si bien l'ordre y estoit gardé, & si dextrement chacun s'estudioit à observer son rang & cadence; de manière que chacun creut qu'Archimède n'eust peu mieux entendre les proportions Géométriques, que ces princesses & dames les pratiquoyent en ce Balet (56).

Drawing from a manuscript by a Spanish dancing master, Juan Antonio Jaque, describing the construction of a number of dances apparently from the latter half of the seventeenth century, Ivanova draws a pictures similar to that of the *Ballet comique*: "From this manuscript it will be seen that the Spaniards seemed to be very fond of figures that formed and reformed endlessly in various ways, half and full circles, danced clockwise or anticlockwise, with quarter turns giving the impression of charmingly original shapes of a petal or scallop design in the ground patterns" (86). Furthermore, one survival to the present of Spanish Renaissance dance attests to the validity of this description. Since the sixteenth century, if not earlier, a select group of choirboys has been trained to dance in the Cathedral of Seville. Brooks, who has studied this tradition in depth, says: "The dance steps, which date from the Renaissance period, are still recognizable despite a flattening of style over the centuries" (122). Presumably, the geometric patterns she observes in modern dances also derive from the Renaissance: "The ten dancers perform the steps in a series of interweaving geometric patterns, moving forward, sideways, and backwards to complete curves, circles, crosses, stars, and lines" (122–123). The similarity of these dances, in sacred and secular contexts and across national boundaries, is understandable, given their philosophical ground in the belief that such dance brought down to earth the ordered harmony of the heavens.

Nevertheless, similarity should not be presumed to mean identity, for there were national variations in the performance of steps and in dance forms. Brooks quotes a fascinating study by Marco Fabrito Caroso, *Della nobilità di dame* (1600) that compares the double step as executed in Italy, France, and Spain. In Italy, it consisted of "three steps moving forward, with the left, the right, and the left foot again, and then the right foot was brought up to the left on the fourth beat, with a subtle *plie-relevé* before settling gracefully to the neutral position." The French version "began with two quick springing steps called *trabuchetti*, but the first was done in a backwards direction, and the second to the side, followed by the same step pattern as in the Italian double. . . ." The Spanish double, however, "commenced with the performance of two *trabuchetti*, followed by six, rather than three steps forward. This step, thus, provided a sprightly and virtuosic variation to the double" (157). In fact, Brook believes that complex footwork, hip movements, and the use of shell castanets characterized Spanish dance even in the pre-Christian era, and that its rhythmic complexity and sensuality were reinforced first by Moorish contributions and then by the arrival of Gypsy bands. This, she says, maintained an eastern influence in popular dance that wove itself into the "fabric of Spanish culture" (30).

Whether or not Spanish court dance differed from that in other European courts in this same manner can be only a matter of speculation. What does seem to be true, however, is that forms of dance from the popular theatre persisted in the developing court theatre, coexisting with aristocractic forms. *Fieras afemina Amor* seems to offer a typical mix, for its loa ends with a máscara of the months of the year and signs of the zodiac that must have been a stately, geometric dance.[47] The concluding touch of this performance was not the courtly danza de la hacha, however; rather, eight actresses came on stage, out of costume (i.e., as themselves) to sing and dance a lively "fin de fiesta" that must have taken the form of a popular dance. Manuela de Escamilla's part in it proved such a crowd-pleaser that she was often asked for repeat performances and was even awarded a modest royal subsidy.[48]

As we shall see in Chapter 6, the opening dance of "divine harmony" on earth was appropriate for the idealized image with which Calderón opened the event, a courtly vision of an entire universe centered around the Spanish Hapsburg court. With certain adjustments to suit the particular royal referents, their aesthetic preferences, and current political program, it could have found a home on any European court stage. The loa combined all the classic elements of the court spectacle: it was set against a splendid set, a perspective scene of the heavens, with artificial light producing the effect of twinkling stars; the performers were attired in costumes of rich blue (see Plate 2 and Chapter 6); the twelve signs of the zodiac made their airborne appearance, thanks to the stage machinery; and instrumental and vocal music framed a poetic text that exalted the monarchs by linking them with classical heroes and mythic deities. All these ingredients blended to produce a spectacular visual image of the extension of heavenly harmony to earth, as machines lowered the twelve signs to the stage where in a geometric dance they wove their "eternal" beauty through the temporal realm of the twelve months.

The concluding dance, however, was uniquely Spanish, as the actors and actresses shed their mythic personages and appeared as common subjects, singing praises of their boy-king with a lively dance and a little drum, a *tamborilillo* "como los que tienen los muchachos para sus juegos" (DicAut). Taking up the symbolic images of the loa and the play, the *fin de fiesta* transformed them into a popular celebration that brought the symbolic language of the court spectacle "down to earth" in a stylistic movement parallel to the machine-borne descent of the zodiacal signs of the loa.[49]

In a sense, this movement is characteristic of Calderón's appropriation of the multiple codes of the court spectacle. While he in no way made of such spectacle a popular form, he did bring it into a fertile contact with popular traditions and with the political realities of court life. Mastering the ingredients of the court spectacle in the broader European movement, Calderón combined them with elements from the Spanish theatrical heritage to generate a machine play that added to the visual splendor of the form a new capacity for thematic complexity. This unique blend will be the focus of the chapters that follow.

Calderón, Master of Polyphony:
Las fortunas de
Andrómeda y Perseo

BY THE DEFINITION of Roland Barthes (259), "le théâtre constitue un objet sémiologique privilégié puisque son système est apparemment original (poly-phonique) par rapport à celui de la langue (qui est linéaire)." Calderón achieved in his court-spectacular plays a true mastery of the polyphony of the theatrical idiom and produced works that combined this dramatic coherence with a the-matic complexity that was perhaps unique in the history of the European court spectacular. He first displays his full command of the form in the 1653 play *Las fortunas de Andrómeda y Perseo*, which he prefaces with a superb prologue that constitutes, in effect, his dramatized poetics of the court spectacle.[1]

In order to appreciate Calderón's achievement in the context of the pan-European tradition from which it grew, I would first like to follow the story of Andromeda and Perseus through a number of incarnations on European court stages prior to its dramatization by Calderón. I make no attempt at an exhaustive survey but present samples that illustrate the differing ways the common ele-ments of poetry, music, dance, and scenic effect could be combined as the vogue of the court spectacle spread throughout Europe and adapted to aesthetic prefer-ences in the courts that took it up.[2] The Perseus-Andromeda story is a good vehicle for such a comparative view because it was worked and reworked from the beginnings of the court spectacular in the late fifteenth-century favole pas-torali to opera two centuries later, by artists of such calibre as Leonardo da Vinci, Lope de Vega, and Corneille as well as Calderón.

PERSEUS'S GENESIS AT COURT:
THE ALLIANCE OF ART AND POWER

Leonardo contributed his artistic and engineering talents to the favola entitled *Danae,* a splendid illustration of the birth of the court spectacular in the alliance of art and power. The play was conceived and performed by a group of artists and humanists at the palace of Gian Francesco Sanseverino, count of Caiazzo, for the duke of Milan, Lodovico Sforza. Sforza, also known as Lodovico il Moro, was renowned for his usurpation of power from the rightful ruler, Gian

Galeazzo, and was accused of having opened the door to foreign domination of Italy to secure his own power; on the other hand, with his lavish patronage of Leonardo and other artists, he made of Milan one of the most splendid courts of all Europe. Baldassare Taccone, who wrote the play, stated proudly in his prologue that the audience included many other princes and illustrious spectators as well as Sforza at its performance on the last day of January 1496. It was reputedly considered a great event among the high society of Milan (Steinitz 35).

The creators and performers of the piece also involved the cream of Milan's community of artists. Leonardo served as set designer and stage architect, and left a sketch, today in the Metropolitan Museum of Art, that lists the actors of the piece. King Acrisius was played by the sculptor Gian Christoforo Romano, one of the favorite artists of Béatrice d'Este, Lodovico's wife.[3] He was, according to Steinitz, a humanist and courtier to suit the model drawn by Castiglione in *Il Cortegiano,* a man versed in a number of arts and possessed of a magnificent voice that may have served him well in *Danae.* Jupiter was played by Gian Francesco Tantio, a writer and well-known personality in Milan; Franco Romano played Danae (it was the custom for men to play women's parts), and Mercury was played by Gian Battista da Ossma, or Ussmate. Taccone himself played the faithful servant Siro, a most appropriate role since his high rank in the court derived from his service as chancellor to Lodovico (Steinitz 36).

Taccone's addition of the character of Siro to the traditional story is doubly significant: first, it foregrounds and legitimizes the role of those who dedicate their lives to serving powerful lords, as do the artists who create the work; second, Siro is a familiar character type in classical comedy (Pyle 184), and his addition is therefore characteristic of modifications to mythic plots in the court spectacular, for the manner of presentation in each court was influenced by local theatrical traditions and the preferences of the ruler feted. Poets repeatedly reworked the plots of the mythological tales to suit the circumstances. Taccone introduces a number of other variants to the tale, probably to provide material for more spectacular effects. The most fertile source for poets of court spectaculars is Ovid's *Metamorphoses,* but that account mentions Danae only in passing; Pyle identifies Boccaccio's compendium, the *Genealogiae deorum gentilium libri,* as Taccone's most probable source.

Two elements in the Danae-Perseus-Andromeda story made it particularly appropriate for court spectacles: first, Perseus's aerial rescue of Andromeda from the sea monster provided an opportunity for impressive visual effects and a convenient image for the king's heroic preservation of the nation from its enemies; second, the tale contains the motif of a monarch whose offspring appear to jeapordize the security of the ruler and/or the realm, a theme whose relevance was all too apparent in many courts. After a prologue that previews the action, Taccone's drama opens with the latter motif, as King Acrisius tells his councillors of the prophecy that he would die at the hand of a son of his beautiful daughter Danae. To prevent this, he has his faithful servant Siro lock her up in a tower that no man can penetrate. Acrisius may have locked out men, but not Jupiter, who falls madly in love with Danae, and the heavens light up magnificently to display him seated among the gods. Dispatched by Jupiter, Mercury repeatedly descends and ascends to plead his case, with a sonnet for Danae and a bribe for the incorruptible Siro. When these methods fail, Jupiter transforms himself into gold, which rains down from heaven as the god dissolves, and hidden instruments close the third act with a crescendo: "e qui sonorono tanti instrumenti che è cosa inumerabile e incredibile" (35).[4]

Surprised by Danae's tolerance of her solitude, Acrisius sends Siro to visit her. He discovers that she is pregnant and after agonizing in fear of what the king will do, finally tells him the truth. Acrisius puts Siro in chains and orders that Danae be drowned at sea. At this point, Taccone takes leave of the traditional story in which Danae is put to sea in a box or a little boat with her infant son, Perseus, and is later miraculously rescued by a kind fisherman who cares for the abandoned pair as his own. In Taccone's version, Jupiter takes pity on Danae; as she is being led off to her death, he transforms her into a star that ascends slowly toward the heavens to the accompaniment of thunderous music: "e lì si vide di terra nascere una stella e a poco a poco andare in cielo con tanti soni che'l pareva ch'i palazzo cascasse" (41). Although the volume of this music may have been used primarily for dramatic effect, knowing that music often served to mask machine noise, we might speculate that Leonardo's engineering skill did not extend to creating a star that could rise in silence.

The last act, also unique to Taccone, is again characteristic of future court spectacles, which almost invariably dispel the tragic notes in the story in order to end the event with the celebratory note appropriate to the royal festivity. The act opens with nymphs singing in praise of the new star and dancing as they approach Jupiter to ask for an explanation of the miracle. He sends Hebe, goddess of immortality, toward earth, and she speaks to Acrisius from midair, calming his fury. Learning that the newborn Perseus is the son of a god, he pardons Danae, whereupon Hebe restores his youth and his beard falls off. At the same time, Siro's chains burst open, and Apollo descends to earth, praising loyal service:

> E quest advien chi serve con gran fede
> E con sincerità Dei e signori,
>   chè chi ben serve tutti gli altri excede (44).

The play ends with wishes for a long life and prosperity for Lodovico, a most fitting climax for this work in which art so clearly serves power and power in turn supports artistic innovation.

Although the "book" for the play is short and transitions between scenes abrupt, the performance was reported to have lasted three hours, perhaps because of the time occupied by the operation of the machines or musical interludes, as well as the performance of intermedi between the acts. Pirrotta (37) classifies this *Danae* as a "hybrid drama" that draws from classical traditions both its basic subject matter and five-act form yet retains elements of the tradition of popular sacred theatre in the disregard for unity of time and action, the verse form (predominantely octaves, except for two passages in *terza rima*[5] and the two sonnets exchanged by Jupiter and Danae), and the machinery Leonardo designed, which drew on Brunelleschi's accomplishments in the Florentine religious drama.[6]

Despite the treasure of Leonardo's sketch, many questions remain about the staging, for his drawings are but planning sketches accompanied by a number of mathematical calculations and do not represent any of the effects exactly as we read them in the text. The clearest drawing shows a divinity in a *mandorla* surrounded by flames in a large niche flanked by two smaller niches;[7] the divinity thus transported might be Danae transformed into a star, but given the shape of the figure and the appearance of the word *herald* to the left of it, more probably represents Apollo (Pirrotta and Povoledo 295–296). The more ambiguous sketch may represent the openings in the "heavens" through which the airborne figures (Mercury, Danae, Hebe, and Apollo) could descend and ascend. Unfortunately, we have no specific descriptions of the scenery, other than the fact that it contained Danae's tower-prison, nor any indication of what sort of device transformed her into a star.

Nor can we be sure about the amount of music or dancing involved. The text mentions specifically only the instrumental music that closed the acts and the hymn of praise sung by the nymphs. Other sections may have been sung, however. Gian Christoforo Romano was famous for his beautiful voice, and it seems plausible that this talent would have been employed in the play. Furthermore, since Apollo descends with a lyre, it would seem likely that he also sang the closing passage of the play. Dance may well have been limited to that of the nymphs approaching Jupiter, for no other scenes of the play would logically have called for dancing.

DANCE AND THE PROGRAMS OF POWER: ANDROMEDA AND PERSEUS IN FRANCE

While dance was an accessory to Taccone's *Danae*, it was central to several court appearances of Perseus in France. The centrality of the dance in France was primarily due to aesthetic preferences for that art form, reinforced by the appeal of the visual demonstration of harmony and order in courts besieged by religious strife and a rebellious nobility. The conjunction of artistic and political programs in the French court ballet has been well illustrated by researchers such as McGowan, Christout, and Isherwood. Under such circumstances, we should not be surprised that French ballets focused almost exclusively on the heroic rescue episode of the Perseus-Andromeda story.

That episode afforded the material for the movement from images of danger to rescue and celebration in the "Ballet d'Andromède exposée au monstre marin," danced during the last years of Henri IV and repeated, at least in part, at the beginning of Louis XIII's reign.[8] Unfortunately, no details about the performance have survived, and if the surviving text constitutes the original in its entirety, it is an extreme example of the "minceur des livrets" of the court ballet (Christout 3), for it consists of only ten stanzas of five lines each. The ballet in no way attempts to recount the story in full but focuses instead on the pathos of the beautiful Andromeda attached naked to the rock as she awaits, tearful and fainting, the arrival of the monster. The ninth stanza brings on both the monster and Perseus, and the tenth anticipates a joyful wedding ceremony. The length of the text may have had little relation to the performance time, however; the music for the "Ballet d'Andromède dansé l'an 1608" consisted of three entries and a final grand ballet.[9] One might presume that the first entry portrayed the suffering Andromeda, the second the approach of the monster, and the third the arrival of Perseus, while a final "grand ballet" representing the wedding celebration could easily have opened into a great ball for the assembled spectators. Another reason for believing that the dance considerably elaborated the text is that Perseus's arrival merits only two lines: "Quand un jeune Mars arrive / Qui de la mort la defend." McGowan (69) says that the ballets of the end of Henri IV's reign, when the civil war was over, were primarily drawn from the chivalric romances. They were ideal because they centered on the theme of deliverance that "se prêtait bien aux intentions politiques de l'inventeur. Il exige un libérateur, rôle qui convenait admirablement au roi quand on voulait mettre en relief sa gloire" (72). As noted above, the Perseus story offers the same advantage, and we can therefore presume that his heroic action would have been portrayed at some length in the dance if not in the text.[10]

In the absence of documents, we can only speculate on the staging of this ballet. It seems likely, however, that the scenic highlight was some sort of turbulent sea scene, a favorite effect in court spectacles as Sabbattini's manual demonstrated and one that was used in a number of other court ballets. Such effects were central to the staging of the Andromeda-Perseus story as an *intermède* in Nantes in 1596, as described by Rousset: " 'Sur le théâtre parut une mer agitée, et les pentagones changeant de face parurent portant des grotesques et rochers, à l'un desquel, dont le pied se baignait dans les flots de la mer, parut Andromède attachée.' Persée descend du ciel sur un cheval ailé. 'A l'instant sortit le monstre de la mer, avec un haut bruit et jaillisements de flots' " (238).

What must certainly have been one of the most spectacular of all dramatizations of the Andromeda-Perseus story required no illusionistic water, for it was an extremely elaborate fireworks display staged on the Seine in 1628, to celebrate Louis XIII's reentry to Paris after the taking of the Huguenot stronghold La Rochelle. Its organizer was neither poet nor stage architect but the king's commissioner of artillery, Morel.[11] In front of the Louvre, a rock was built in the

Seine, to which Andromeda was chained. Around her danced nymphs carrying torches and declaiming lugubrious verses, when a monster suddenly appeared from beneath the water, spouting flames. The current carried it to the rock, but just as it was on the point of seizing Andromeda, Perseus appeared astride Pegasus, flying toward her from the Tower of Nesles (thanks to a rope stretched across the Seine). At this point, all the participants, the rock, and the tower lit up with fireworks, and eight men spouting fireworks danced a ballet of happiness on a floating platform. The whole fiery spectacle lasted several hours, culminating with a display in the sky of Louis's name accompaned by "des sentences glorieuses et triomphales" and the name of the conquered village, all ablaze in the sky.[12] As Christout summarizes the significance of this spectacular event, "Sous la voile transparente de la fiction, Andromède symbolise la Religion catholique attaquée par le monstre huguenot et sauvée par Persée—Louis XIII" ("Les Feux d'artifices" 252).

ANDROMEDA AND PERSEUS AND THE BIRTH OF OPERA

While in France Andromeda and Perseus learned to dance, in Italy they were taught to sing with the expressiveness of the new recitative. If the sponsors of the Italian melodramma had a political program, it was generally less overt than that of the French court ballet and has not been emphasized by historians of the form.[13] The latter have concerned themselves primarily with the relationship of the melodramma to the development of opera and with the rivalry between the cultivation of the expressive potential of the human voice and the appeal of the marvelous in the form of visual spectacle.

During Carnival 1610, a melodramma entitled *Andromeda. Tragedia. Da recitarsi in Musica* was performed in Bologna as the first "opera" performance in the Theatro del Pubblico of the Palazzo del Podestà. Ridolfo Campeggi wrote the poetry, and the music (now lost) was by Girolamo Giacobbi, one of the first composers outside Florence to write in the new "monodic" style (Smith). No details of the performance are available, and the music has been lost, but the libretto indicates that it was "fatta recitare in musica di stile rappresentativo . . . con apparato magnifico." A few years earlier, Giacobbi had composed the music for four interludes for the pastoral play *Filarmindo*. This score, published under the title *Dramatodia*, is characterized by recitatives in an intense pathetic style, alternating with short ensembles and strophic choruses (Smith). In the surviving libretto for the *Andromeda,* emotionally charged individual speeches in a variety of moods—lament, rejoicing, and infernal fury—also alternate with strophic choral commentary written in an interesting variety of metrical forms.

Campeggi's plot for this five-act piece follows the general structure of the Ovidian account, including its division into two nearly independent units, the first climaxing with Perseus's rescue of Andromeda, the second centering on the jealous attack of her previous fiancé, Phineus.[14] This rupture in the Ovidian account presented a problem for dramatic unity that was not fully resolved in any version prior to Calderón's. Following a prologue recited by the Sun, Campeggi's Act I opens with King Cepheus lamenting to his counselor the destruction wreaked on his kingdom by a formidable monster from the sea. They decide the only hope is prayer to the gods, and a chorus of citizens goes off to beseech Jove to close the jaws of the infamous monster, who regularly collects tribute in the form of innocent lives. Cassiopea then bewails her vanity, which brought on this curse.[15] A messenger arrives, returning from Libia where he had gone "ad apportare al saggio Amonio Dio/Le publiche querele" (f.7), and a melodramatic exchange follows, as he leads up to telling the king that the price for ridding the kingdom of the scourge from the sea is the life of his daughter Andromeda:

MES: Lugubre, miserabile, e mortale.
CEF: Oime, chi fia ch'un tanto danno apporte?
MES: Una sola ben sì, ma fiera morte.
CEF: Eccoti il cor, se chiede i mio morire,
MES: Altra Morte, altro sangue, altro martire,
CEF: Plachisi il Ciel, ch'io soffirò ogni doglia,
MES: Pur che de l'altrui duolo (ah) non ti doglia,
CEF: Salvisi il Regno con l'altrui ruine.
MES: Così de la tua figlia hor chiedi il fine,
CEF: Oime, che mesci tù l'amata figlia,
     Spirito de i mei conforti;
     Fra il sangue, e fra la Morti?
MES: Perche sola può dar con la sua vita
     A questa terra aita.
CEF: Che parli o lingua audace?
MES: Que che Gioue parlò, quanto al Ciel piace (f.7).

When the messenger tells him that Andromeda must be bound to a rock to feed the beast, Cepheus is anguished:

     Ahi crudeli parole
     Parole no, flagelli,
     Flagelli no, coltelli
     che mi passate il core (f.8).

Cepheus decides to refer the matter to the Senate and with further laments by him, Cassiopea, and the chorus of citizens, the act ends.

Act II opens with a lovely pastoral scene of Andromeda and her ladies-in-waiting that makes evident Campeggi's indebtedness not only to the Ovidian

37

account but also to the pastoral tradition. Andromeda recounts a dream of a shining knight, her lover and liberator, and the ladies then dance a musical ballet whose refrain refers to a kissing contest reminiscent of that in which Mirtillo wins laurels from Amarilli in *El pastor fido*. The counselor arrives to stop the happy scene by announcing her death sentence: Jove commands that her beautiful nude body appease the hunger of the monster, and her parents and the Senate have reluctantly acquiesced. After a brief lament, Andromeda accepts her fate bravely and bids a touching farewell to her damsels; a lament by the chorus of citizens again closes the act.

The lamenting Cepheus spies the approach of Perseus at the beginning of Act III and immediately recognizes him as a "semideo"; Perseus says he has been moved by the sight of "la bella ignuda" and offers to kill the monster if the reward is his marriage to Andromeda. Cepheus promptly accepts, and Perseus goes off to slay the sea dragon. Meanwhile, the chorus begs for pity on Ethiopia and its royal damsel, and Pallas Athena arrives to announce the return of peace and the victory of the son of Jove. After a celebration by Cepheus, the chorus of citizens, and lengthy songs by choruses of "fanciulli" and "donzelles," Perseus reappears to declare his love to Andromeda, and she assures him it is reciprocated. The chorus of citizens again closes the act, but on happier notes.

The dark mood returns with the opening of the fourth act as Nereus surfaces to protest the insult of the murder of Orca (the monster) in his realm and the added injury of praise for his slayer.[16] He calls Envy and Jealousy from their work of tormenting souls in Hell and sets them the task of inciting Phineus to start a quarrel. They accede happily, and Jealousy promises to make a river of blood run as a tribute to the sea. Phineus is Andromeda's fiancé and, as brother to the king, her uncle. When he appears, lamenting that he didn't make his body a shield for Andromeda's defenseless body, to die or be liberated with her, a citizen informs him that his niece is not only alive and free but betrothed to Perseus, and Envy and Jealousy provoke him to a furious harangue. Eventually Mercury arrives and chases that pair of demons back to the "pitiless realm," and a messenger tells briefly how Perseus first fought bravely against Phineus and his many allies, and then unveiled the Gorgon's head to turn them to stone. The citizens bring down the curtain with a didactic chorus warning that those who do not restrain their senses with reason plunge toward a precipice. Act V consists of the thankful prayers to Jove of the protagonists—Cefeo, Cassiopea, Perseo, and Andromeda—and a variety of choruses (priests, damsels and citizens) capped by the (surely airborne) appearance of Jove himself and a grand finale of all the choruses.

With its overall fidelity to the Ovidian account, Campeggi's libretto includes most of the plot elements that we will see repeated in subsequent versions of the Perseus-Andromeda story. Furthermore, the Campeggi-Giacobbi production is characteristic of the modification of the tale as it advanced from court to court, adapting to local artistic trends—in this case, the development of the new recitative style and the influence of Ariosto and pastoral drama.

The spread of wholly sung drama in the new style did not mean the immediate disappearance of the intermedi, which retained an important place on the court stage in the early seventeenth century. Shortly after the Campeggi work, Jacopo Cicognini wrote another Italian version of the Andromeda story that he called a "favola marittima," performed as six intermedi accompanying a five-act pastoral play. Domenico Belli's music for the "favola" has been lost, but the text survives in manuscript, as well as a letter Caccini wrote to the secretary of the Grand Duke of Tuscany on 10 March 1618, the day after a performance of the work in the home of "Rinaldi miei vicini." This must have been a repeat performance since the manuscript says that it was performed in 1617 in the Rinaldi palace in the presence of Archduke Leopoldo of Austria. In 1611, Cicognini had written a first version of the libretto (now in the Archivo Secreto Vaticano) "indebted both to the intermedio tradition and to a familiarity with operatic practice" (Fenlon 166), which he later adapted for performance as intermedi (Fenlon 166–167, Solerti 127 n.2).

Caccini has high praise for the whole performance, but his first honors go to the architect of the scenery and machinery, the same Cosimo Lotti who would later take the new stage techniques to Spain. Having learned from the example of previous productions in similar circumstances, says Caccini, Lotti's effort was their equal in beauty, richness, and invention.[17] For each act of the favola, the scene changed to that of a beautiful seascape, and a new machine effect appeared: first the chariot carrying Venus and Cupid; then the sea monster who was to devour Andromeda; then a dolphin bearing Amphitrite "con molti Tritoni"; then Perseus in armor on a winged horse; and a ship carrying a singing fisherman. This may not have exhausted the effects employed, for Caccini says he does not recount all the details. He does state emphatically that all these effects were exquisitely staged and congratulates Pietro Bonsi for the fact that the whole performance was accomplished in four hours and did not become tedious. He also applauds Belli's music, which by its variety avoided the tedium that often plagued the favola, however expertly it was performed. In this case, however, "questo ha auto tanto di varietà per l'invenzione e la dolcezza dell'armonia sempre accompagnata da varietà di strumenti, che realmente M.ʳ Domenico Belli autor di essa può gloriarsi di aver mostrato quanto possa l'arte della musica accompagnata col giudizio" (qtd Solerti 128). Belli, in fact, earned a reputation as one of the most radical monodists of the early seventeenth century for his harmonic and formal daring. He seems to have been somewhat in advance of public taste or singers' training, for in 1616 he had written a letter to Ferdinando Gonzaga, duke of Mantua, in which he indicated that his arias were considered "difficult and unsingable" because of the number of quavers in their basses. He asked the duke to have them sung in Mantua to correct this unfortunate reputation (Strainchamps 444). Since Caccini also speaks glowingly about the singers' execution of their parts, this problem seems to have been resolved for the *Andromeda* performance. The one negative note in the whole evening, by Caccini's report, was that because so many women had been invited and some ill-bred men (plebeians and foreigners) occupied the low seats reserved for them, many of the women had to stand most uncomfortably.

Between 1618 and 1620, Monteverdi himself composed music for another version of the Andromeda story. The book was by Ercole Marigliani, secretary to the duke of Mantua, and a daughter of Giulio Caccini was promised the title role. First planned for 1618, the performance was twice postponed and finally took place in 1620. The music has been lost, but the vicissitudes of its composition are chronicled in Monteverdi's letters. He protested regularly that other demands kept him from working on it, that he should not be asked to compose music without having seen the entire libretto, and that neither his composition nor rehearsal time should be hurried lest the work suffer:

> But just as I am having to do a bad job through being obliged to finish it in a hurry, so too I am thinking that it will be badly performed and badly played because of the acute shortage of time. I am also greatly surprised that Signor Marigliani wishes to involve himself in such a dubious enterprise, since even if it had been begun before Christmas, there would hardly be time to rehearse it, let alone learn it.
>
> . . . What do you think can be done when more than four hundred lines, which have to be set to music, are still lacking? I can envisage no other result than bad singing of the poetry, bad playing of the instruments, and bad musical ensemble. These are not things to be done hastily, as it were; and you know from *Arianna* that after it was finished and learned by heart, five months of strenuous rehearsal took place (160).

Monteverdi's slow progress may have been due less to worries over musical quality, however, than to a lack of enthusiasm for the project as a whole. Scholars have speculated that he might have found Marigliani's text uninspiring, but that libretto long thought lost, has recently been found (Rosenthal 1), and Fenlon, who has seen it, discounts the quality of the libretto as the reason for Monteverdi's delay. Fenlon describes it as a major work, written with a prologue but without division into acts, which, whatever its defects, "does not seem markedly less appealing than any number of other occasional stage pieces which Monteverdi set from time to time. And, with its frequent use of chorus work and obvious structural devices, *Andromeda* can hardly have seemed daunting to a composer of Monteverdi's operatic experience" (164). Fenlon attributes his reluctance to devote his time to this project to personal reasons, unhappy memories connected with his years as court composer in Mantua, and his less than cordial relations with the current duke, Ferdinando Gonzaga, who preferred Florentine music. Marigliani was closer to Prince Vincenzo Gonzaga than to Duke Ferdinando, and it was Vincenzo who urged the completion of the project, which was finally accomplished just two weeks before its performance in the carnival festivities (Fenlon 168–171). A curious footnote to the history of Andromeda and Perseus is Stevens's (Monteverdi 162) observation that those mythic figures at one point had literally taken on flesh in Mantuan court circles: "The prince's father, Duke Vicenzo, had reveled in a youthful and passionate affair with Hippolita Torelli, a noble lady of Reggio, and their letters . . . reveal that the names they used for each other were Perseus and Andromeda."

Andromeda was also the heroine of a 1637 opera in Venice, written by Benedetto Ferrari with music by Francesco Manelli. In strict terms, this work is not a court spectacle, for it was the opening work in what became the first "public" opera house in republican Venice where wealthy families maintained theatres to which they admitted the public on a paying basis (Donington 215). However, themes and performance styles passed back and forth between courtly and "commercial" opera in seventeenth-century Italy, so they cannot be considered in isolation.[18] Although the Ferrari opera was designed to allow for an economical production suited to its conditions of patronage and performance, visual effects were nevertheless central to it. Both Ferrari and Manelli were Romans and brought with them a Roman style that relied heavily on spectacular brilliance. Ferrari describes in elaborate detail and glowing pride the rapid changes of perspective scenery, rich costumes, and airborne appearances of chariots and gods, on clouds or flying solo supported only by an "invisible" harness. In the three-act libretto, Ferrari reduces the Perseus-Andromeda story to its basic elements, the divine decree that Andromeda be sacrificed to the sea monster and Perseus's rescue of the innocent maiden. At the same time, he surrounds the heroes with a panoply of gods: Juno, Jove, Mercury, Neptune, Proteus, Astrea, and Venus. In his version, Cassiopea has offended Juno herself by claiming to outdo her in beauty, and it is the queen of heaven who decrees Andromeda's death and sends Mercury to Neptune and Proteus to call up a fearsome sea monster. A jealous and menacing Juno will also figure in Corneille's and Calderón's version of the story, but her fury will be directed instead toward Perseus, as the product of Jove's dalliance with Danae. While Ferrari's Juno calls up a monster, his Andromeda plans a campaign with her damsels against another beast, a wild boar; this scene and that which opens Act II with a celebration of their successful hunt would seem to reflect a Venetian version of the pastoral tradition, perhaps related to a "tragedia boschereccia" on Andromeda performed in that city in 1587. Astrea and Venus appear to intercede on Andromeda's behalf, pleading respectively for justice and pity; Jove also takes up her case against an adamant Juno, but their threatened power struggle evaporates after Perseo rescues Andromeda. In the climactic scene, the heavens open to reveal Jove and Juno in glory with other gods, and in a machine effect that anticipates Calderón's finale, "scese questo gran machinone in terra, accompagnato da un Concerto di voci, e di stromenti, veramente di Paradiso" (12). The two heroes then ascend with the gods to heaven.

This Venetian *Andromeda* was sung by seven musicians and a chorus, including Manelli, who sang the roles of Neptuno and the magician Astarco, and his wife Maddalena, who sang the prologue as Aurora as well as the role of Andromeda. (The other singers were Francesco Angeletti, from Assisi, singing Juno; Annibale Graselli, from Citta di Castello, as Mercurio, Perseo, and Ascala, a knight of Andromeda's court; Giovanni Battista Bisucci, from Bologna, as Proteus and Jove; Girolamo Medici, a Roman, as Astrea; and Anselmo Marconi, another Roman, as Venus.) The first two acts ended with madrigals "a più voci concertato con istrumento diversi," and there were danced intermedi choreographed by a Venetian, Giovanni Battista Balbi. Ferrari played theorbo in the orchestra. Enthusiastic public acceptance of the work inspired a series of operas and the dedication of other theatres to operatic performances.

As the Andromeda story was adapted for a new paying public in republican Venice, it conformed to a strong aristocratic preference for chivalric display in a fascinating performance in Ferrara in 1638. The title page of the libretto published the following year called it "L'Andromeda di D. Ascanio Pio di Savoia cantata, e combattuta in Ferrara il carnevale dell'anno 1638," and the description is accurate, for it was both sung and "fought."[19] On the death without a male heir of Alfonso II d'Este, Ferrara had passed to the effective domain of the church in 1598 (Walker, "Echi Estense" 1). At least partially to fill the political and cultural vacuum left by the absence of Este patronage, the Accademia degli Intrepidi was founded in 1600 to provide a valid institutional framework for cultural activity by a nobility still wedded to chivalric exercises (Walker, "Echi Estense" 8–9). Their activities included "ogni genere di amena letteratura, e tutte le arti che diconsi cavalleresche cioè, scherma, ballo, e musica . . . [and] grandiosi spettacoli, e rappresentazioni, e torneamenti, e giostre, e melodrammi &c" (G. Baruffaldi, qtd in Walker, "Echi Estense" 9). The second motto of the Academy was in fact "Litteris armata, et armis erudita" (Walker, "Echi Estense" 9).

The *Andromeda* was performed for a dual celebration, a noble wedding and the arrival of Cardinal Ciriacco Rocci; accordingly, the libretto emphasizes the joy of love and marriage, and the inevitable triumph of the brave and virtuous man who follows heaven's plan. In general terms, the libretto follows the Ovidian account, probably through Campeggi's model. The music was composed by Michelangelo Rossi, and Walker ("Echi Estense" 14) judges from the libretto that it was closely akin to Venetian operas of the same period. The scenery and stage machinery, designed by Francesco Giutti, were elaborate indeed; so many deities fly in on clouds and chariots that airborne activity seems to rival that on the stage itself.

The real novelty of the work, however, is the incorporation of a chivalric tournament within the dramatic structure. The pretext is indeed provided by the second part of the Ovidian account in which the discarded fiancé-uncle Fineo attacks Perseo and King Cefeo for awarding Andromeda to her rescuers.[20] To avoid generalized bloodshed, Cefeo and Fineo agree to entrust the combat to their seven best knights. At this point, the whole hall becomes brilliantly lit, and the Cardinal and some two hundred honored guests occupying the seats of honor on a central platform in the center of the hall are astonished as the whole platform slowly moves back to clear the central space for a joust (10, 97). The knights descend a majestic staircase from the stage to the hall, where they are met by their "Padrini."[21] After making their bows to the Cardinal, they meet in combat, first singly, using a series of weapons from pikes to daggers, then in groups, forming a kind of military ballet "choreographed" by Marquis Pio Enea Obizzi with mathematically beautiful figures "che forse non fu mai dallo stesso Euclide imaginata" (103–104).[22] Peace is restored by Iris, descending on a rainbow; she is followed by an airborne Imeneo who comes to bless Perseo and Andromeda's wedding and finally Jove himself, seated on an eagle, who arrives to praise the three honored guests. The same nobles who had performed the theatrical tournament demonstrate their versatility (and endurance) by dancing the finale of the event. Since its score was lost, we cannot evaluate it for musical quality; the poetic text is pedestrian but relatively coherent dramatically; in terms of imaginative staging, however, this performance surely rivaled the fiery French rendition on the Seine.

THE NATURALIZATION OF ANDROMEDA AND PERSEUS IN SPAIN: LOPE DE VEGA AND THE *COMEDIA NUEVA*

The story of Andromeda and Perseus made its debut on the Spanish stage with Lope de Vega's *La fábula de Perseo, o la bella Andrómeda*, commissioned by the duke of Lerma and apparently first performed at his estate in 1613.[23] It seems possible that Cicognini provided the inspiration for its introduction at that time, since his first version preceded Lope's by only two years and he is said to have corresponded with Lope, whom he acknowledged in his *Trionfo di David* as a source of inspiration for his own creations ("Cicognini" 390).[24] Lope is not likely to have seen Cicognini's text, which today exists only in manuscript form, but Cicognini might have written, telling him of his dramatization of the story and describing some of the effects, as Caccini did in his letter. Such a description could account for one significant Lopean alteration of the myth: Lope, like Cicognini, sends Perseus off to rescue Andromeda on Pegasus rather than the winged sandals lent by Mercury. Lope's Jupiter also makes a reference to the story of Amphitryon and Alcmena, an unrelated and anachronistic detour that might have been suggested by the similarity in name to the Amphitrite who rode a machine-dolphin in Cicognini's piece.[25]

Lope could also have derived the use of Pegasus from his basic source materials, which were, as McGaha points out (10–16), Jorge de Bustamante's free adaptation of the *Metamorphoses* (1543) and the mythological dictionary of Juan Pérez de Moya, *Philosofía secreta* (1585). Certainly he took from Bustamante the idea of Pegasus as a horse "con alas de mil colores" (line 1762), and Pérez de Moya also puts Perseus astride this steed.[26] Not all Lope's potential sources were literary, however. Two prized paintings in the royal collection were Titian's *Danae* (1549–1550) and *Perseus and Andromeda* (1554–1556).[27] The first shows Danae reclining on a couch as a golden rain descends from a cloud and her old servant holds her apron to catch it. Lope's play recalls this scene as Danae's maid Elisa exclaims, "Ay, señora, coger quiero / estas auríferas perlas!" (ll. 349–350).

To begin talking of Lope's play by discussing sources is in a sense to take on the entire literary tradition, for this work can best be described as something midway between a dramatized epic and a literary grab bag.[28] In his *Arte nuevo*, Lope said that the Spanish playgoer wanted to see everything from the Creation to the Last Judgment; in his *Perseo*, he attempts to satisfy that demand. With characteristic ambition, he presents in straight-line time the entire story, from Danae's enclosure in the tower to Perseo's marriage to Andrómeda. Tongue certainly in cheek, Lope even calls the allegorical figure Tiempo on stage in Act I and has him advance the calendar nine months so that Perseo can be born within the act assigned to his genesis. Each of the three acts becomes a separate episode in the story, complete with its own love triangle and other subplots. An act per episode is logical, given Lope's scope, but one unfortunate result is that the heroine never appears on stage until Act III.

A number of Lope's additions were probably intended to "naturalize" this strange mythic material for an audience accustomed to the standard comedia. For example, in the first act, Lope introduces the standard *galán* in the figure of Lisardo, a young and wealthy prince in love with Danae but prevented from seeing her by a father suspicious of all male intentions.[29] In Act II, in which Perseo slays Medusa, Lope familiarizes the "monstro horrendo" by depicting her as the sort of tempting sorceress common in the novels of chivalry and sometimes transferred to the stage. On the one hand, she is capable of turning men to stone with her gaze and lives in an enchanted place beyond the rule of law; on the other, she is the oldest, most beautiful, and wisest daughter of King Floro, who like any comedia princess, falls in love with Perseo and is jealous of Fineo's praise of Andrómeda's beauty.

In Act III, in which Perseo rescues Andrómeda, the heroine makes her first appearance with a speech characteristic of the familiar "mujer esquiva" who is untouched by love. In this same act, Lope gives the viewer not only the love triangle Fineo-Andrómeda-Perseo, but also the standard love-disdain chain between Andrómeda, Fineo, and Laura, Andrómeda's companion, who loves the suitor Andrómeda rejects. Furthermore, Lope introduces a gracioso-type figure in Celio, who accompanies Perseo on his adventures and provides a number of comic touches. For example, when Perseo advances to attack Medusa, Celio, with the classic cowardice of the *gracioso*, balances the shame of fleeing against the disadvantages of being turned to stone:

> Soy leal y bien nacido.
> Si me voy sin él de aquí,
> ¿qué dirá el mundo de mí
> y donde soy conocido?
> Mas también, ¿qué es lo que medra
> de ser un hombre de bien
> piedra, y que ocasión le den
> y calle como una piedra?
> Si estoy en algún zaguán,
> sentaránse sobre mí;
> y si me labran aquí,
> ¿qué golpes no me darán?
> Si soy dintel de una puerta,
> ¿qué lluvias no han de caer
> sobre mí? . . . (ll. 1569–1583)

Lope also provided other bridges into the mythic world for his public, in the form of citations of popular "wisdom" and current happenings in court. Regarding the sisters who guard Medusa, Celio says that it is a good idea that they share one eye because they can't see so many things to covet, but he suggests it would be even better were they to share one tongue (ll. 1275–1286). Lope's Mercurio speaks of his "privanza" to Júpiter, thus linking himself to Lerma, who offered the play to Felipe III. The playwright also provides a happy ending for the play in a double wedding of Andrómeda to Perseo and Laura to Fineo (transformed by the magic of Perseo's shield from disdain to love for that lady). Such weddings are the traditional comedia resolution and an ideal occasional reference to the double engagement of the future Felipe IV and his sister Ana to Louis XIII and his sister Elizabeth. This engagement, announced in 1612, was considered "a triumph of Lerma's diplomacy" (Vega Carpio, *Perseo* 4).

While those court references fit easily into the structure of the story, two more extended sections of direct address to the court audience severely disrupt the logical progress of the play. First, Lope includes as a "justa poética" between three shepherds three sonnets about a woman ordered to cut her hair as a remedy

45

for a malady of the eyes. The sonnets had been his contribution to a 1611 literary academy in memory of Queen Margarita, who had recently died. As well as giving a wider circulation to his poems, Lope probably wanted to remind the king of his previous service to royalty; he then closes the act with a thinly veiled appeal by one of his shepherd-poets that he be given the post of official court chronicler.[30]

The second episode tailored for the court audience is the most spectacularly staged scene of the play.[31] Just past the midpoint of the work, Perseo slays Medusa and holds up her head on which the hair has turned into snakes. Then the winged Pégaso emerges from beneath the stage and ascends to the top of Mt. Parnaso. His hoof brings forth a fountain, circled by musicians and laurel-crowned poets. After an explanatory song, Virgil appears to say that he would prefer to have been born in Spain to praise Felipe and the house of Lerma with verses that would bring him even greater fame than the *Aeneid*:

> Virgilio soy, que quisiera
> no haber nacido en Italia,
> por loar, siendo español,
> los claros reyes de España;
> al soberano Filipo,
> a quien los siglos aguardan
> para corona del mundo
> y sol de la esfera de Austria;
> a sus prendas, que han de ser
> gloria de España y de Francia,
> porque coman sus leones
> flores de lises doradas.[32]
> De la casa Sandoval
> dijera grandezas tantas
> que más que la dulce *Eneida*
> me dieran gloriosa fama. (ll. 1797–1812)

The musicians then sing a final quatrain predicting that the future will produce new Virgils to sing the praises of those eminences—another Lopean self-promotion (ll. 1812–1816). McGaha considers this passage the climax of the event, and viewing it purely as court spectacle, he is probably right; judged by the criteria of dramatic coherence, however, it is also the nadir of the play.

Lope throws in for good measure elements more at home in sixteenth-century novels of chivalry. His Fineo goes mad from Andrómeda's rejection and his grief over her proximate sacrifice to the monster. He plays a comic "Orlando furioso" for extended scenes—breaking trees, proposing to a peasant girl he thinks is Andrómeda, threatening suicide, and challenging Perseo.[33] Lope not only constructed figurative bridges for his audience; he also lowered a literal bridge from Medusa's castle, and across it charged four allegorical knights, Envy,

Flattery, Ingratitude, and Jealousy. Perseo's magic shield tricks them into blindly battling each other and exercises similar power over the giant, Competition, who next emerges.[34]

How this dramatic potpourri was staged is something of a puzzle. From a letter of Lope to the duke of Sessa we can be reasonably certain that it was performed in the gardens of the duke's estate, although Lope considered the gardens an unsatisfactory location and says that continual rains threatened to swamp the whole production.[35] It was an amateur production, played by "caballeros del Duque," which probably explains the enormous list of characters, forty-eight in all. A number of the smaller roles are totally superfluous and may have been introduced to give courtiers manageably small appearances. Lope's actress-mistress, Jerónima de Burgos, accompanied him to Ventosilla, and McGaha (Vega Carpio, *Perseo* 9) speculates that she may have played Andrómeda. If this was a mixed production like the 1622 masques, professional actors would certainly have played the parts of Perseo and Fineo as well.

The stage effects employed, clearly spelled out in the stage directions, are strategically distributed through the three acts to maintain audience interest. In Act I, Apolo is revealed in his temple, "en una grada con un rostro dorado y cercado de rayos, y en un arco por encima pintados los doce signos" (st.d. following l. 70). In their first appearance, Júpiter and Mercurio seem to have walked on stage like ordinary mortals rather than descending visibly on machines, and exit with the same simplicity. Then the golden cloud is made to appear "por lo alto, que abriéndose lloverá en el teatro muchos pedazos de oro hechos de oropel cortado" (st.d. l. 352). Some sort of movable ship "sailed" on stage carrying Danae and the infant Perseo near the end of the act. In Act II, Mercurio and Palas do stage a machine descent to bring their gifts to Perseo: "Baja, con dos tornos, Mercurio con una espada, y Palas con un escudo, y en medio dél un espejo" (st.d. l. 1410). A bridge is laid down for the four allegorical knights: "Echan una puente que estará asida con sus cadenas, y con barandas pintadas, de una y otra parte, a la puerta del castillo, y saldrán por ella cuatro caballeros armados" (st.d. l. 1479). Then Medusa's snaky head is displayed to the audience, followed by the spectacular appearance of Pegaso and Mt. Parnaso. Since the directions speak of the mountain as already present on stage and covered by a curtain at the end of the scene, this mountain probably was hidden in a backstage curtained space like that which in the corrales doubled as a tiring room and discovery space.[36] The subsequent transformation of Atlante (Atlas) into a mountain is handled in a rudimentary fashion, the actor hidden behind a cloth panel that rises to represent a man-mountain: "Póngase detrás de un lienzo, y levanten con artificio un monte de lienzo en forma de hombre" (st.d. l. 1931).

The discovery space serves again in Act III to reveal Andrómeda fastened to the boulder: "Descúbrese Andrómeda atada a una peña, vestida de velo de plata y los cabellos tendidos" (st.d. l. 2598). Perseo then appears astride Pegaso, apparently on some sort of beam attached to a counterweight in the tiring room so that he could be moved up and down to simulate attacking the fire-breathing dragon that "burst out of a feigned sea":

> Perseo aparezca en el Pegaso, con lanza y escudo y el caballo. Adviértase que esté con la invención que llaman el pozo, que es la viga con el peso dentro del vestuario (st.d. l. 2798).
>
> Por un pedazo de mar que se finja, salga una ballena con la boca abierta, por donde venga echando fuego, y tocándose dentro cajas y trompetas, baje Perseo en el caballo y con la lanza le dé por la boca, y afirmando en tierra, salte del caballo al suelo y suba por el monte, desatando a Andrómeda (st.d. l. 2830).

Just how this sea and other scenic backgrounds were represented is extremely problematic. Other than the discoveries, Lope's text makes no specific mention of scenery except to say that the bridge was "at the door of the castle." If the sea and the castle were really present in some way more concrete than word-painting, it seems most likely that some system of painted cloth backdrops was used. The use of painted *lienzos* to transform Atlante into a mountain would have fitted well in such a scenic design.

However the scenery was constituted, it is clear that the crowd-pleasing power of machinery and scenic effects took priority over dramatic coherence in this event. Despite Lope's repeated complaints that such innovations detracted from audience attention to his poetry,[37] for him the heart and soul of drama, he yielded here to the prevailing taste in court spectacles. Some of his effects are logical in the development of the story, although he uses them inconsistently; Mercury sometimes walks on and off stage like a mortal, sometimes descends from heaven. Other effects, such as the charge across the bridge of the allegorical knights, are gratuitous. The appearance of Mt. Parnaso, while a surefire success with a court audience, totally disrupts dramatic continuity.

We cannot know whether all this visual display did indeed close the audience's ears to his poetry as he feared. If it did, such deafness was their loss, for despite its structural weaknesses, the *Fábula de Perseo* is a pleasure to read for the graceful variety of its poetry. With the exception of the Mt. Parnaso show-stopper, music seems to have played no great role in the play beyond hiding machine noise and announcing battle scenes. Yet Lope's poetry itself constitutes a kind of music. In a virtuoso display that McGaha rightly calls a "prodigious demonstration of Lope's mastery of the technique of versification," he employs thirteen metric forms. A full quarter of the text is in Italianate verse, much more than the limited passages in other comedias: sonnets, *liras, tercetos*, and other forms. For pure virtuosity, the high point is perhaps an unrhymed *canción* in which Lope poetically underlines King Acrisius' pompous and ill-founded concept of his own importance by piling up a total of twenty-seven lines, all ending in *esdrújulos* (proparoxytones).

The play displays a certain degree of thematic consistency in the recurring commentary on the capacity of gold to buy power and love. McGaha argues that it also presents a potentially subversive history of the abuse of power. While this is technically true, I think the fragmentation of the plot into numerous short actions and the disruptive use of spectacular effect would have diminished the impact of this potential message virtually to the vanishing point. Furthermore, Lope, who quite clearly used this play to promote his own pretensions to a court post, was in no position to make it a clearly critical vehicle.[38] If, despite Lope's expressed misgivings, the machinery worked relatively smoothly, he surely offered Felipe III, Lerma, and the court audience a most entertaining evening.[39] It would be better described, however, as a sort of spectacular variety show than a work of thematic complexity or dramatic coherence.

COHERENT, CUMULATIVE SPECTACLE:
CORNEILLE'S *ANDROMÈDE*

When Pierre Corneille took on the Perseus and Andromeda story, his most notable advance over previous treatments was precisely a much tighter and more logical structure. Throughout, the work revolves around the alternation and dangerous combination of human and divine jealousy. Although Corneille follows the Ovidian narrative quite closely, his *Andromède* (written 1647, staged 1650) eliminates the lead-in episodes of Perseus's slaying of Medusa and his encounter with Atlas. Both are mentioned at appropriate moments but in passing references that presume an acquaintance of the audience with those adventures and the history of Danae and Jupiter. Corneille also brings Phinée on stage at the beginning of the play and sets up the rivalry between him and Persée from the outset, thus avoiding the rupture into two discrete episodes that occurs in Ovid's tale. To give psychological plausibility to the instant love affair, his Persée has already been in Céphée's court for a month. The mysterious stranger has in that time fallen in love with the beautiful princess and attracted the interest of many young women, including the already-betrothed Andromède. Whereas Lope led his audience through a variety of dramatic detours to sustain their interest in the familiar story, Corneille maintains dramatic tension in the first part by counterposing two ambiguous oracular declarations and in the second by holding out a threat of combined human and divine revenge against Persée for his slaughter of the monster and his conquest of Andromède.

Corneille prefaces the text of the play with a summary of Ovid's story and explains his alterations in such a way that he appears to have drawn only on Ovid and his own imagination. In fact, a number of his "innovations" had already been introduced in previous texts that he seems to have known.[40] He quite clearly drew on Lope's text, as he had on other Spanish plays.[41] Corneille goes to some length to justify having placed Persée astride Pégase—which Lope (and Cicognini) had already done—and having Cassiope boast of her daughter's

49

beauty rather than her own, a change Lope had also made. Corneille also explains that he makes Phinée Andromède's cousin rather than uncle (as in Ovid) to make their engagement more plausible; Lope had silently done away with any blood relationship. He claims to have invented the idea of the periodic sacrifice of beautiful maidens to the monster, but as we have seen, it had already appeared in Ariosto and Campeggi. Corneille also believes the spectacular apotheosis with which he ends his drama to be a unique inspiration. In Corneille's play, Jupiter descends on a golden throne and raises Andromède and Persée, Cassiope and Céphée, to become gods who by day will feast on nectar and ambrosia and by night will be stars whose light mortals will worship. It is doubtful that Corneille knew that Taccone and da Vinci had anticipated his ending in their *Danae* some 150 years before but probable that he had read of the elevation of the four to the heavens in Boccaccio's *Genealogia* (Chapter 25) or a derivative of it.[42]

To recognize that Corneille drew on a tradition of court spectacle is not to diminish the artistry of his creation. His prologue, for example, is reminiscent of that of Campeggi in the centrality of the figure of the Sun. It also bears some likeness to Lope's inserted paean to Felipe III, for Corneille stages the prologue over a mountain that a subsequent description likens to Mont Parnasse and says that the muses foresee great deeds for Louis XIV that will furnish material for more than one *Iliad* and *Aeneid*.[43] Whereas Lope interrupted his drama to offer Felipe the obligatory homage and made his self-promotion painfully obvious, Corneille confined his celebration of the monarch to the opening and closing of the event and was much more artful in underlining the service of the dramatist to his king.

Corneille specifically comments on the cumulative nature of this court spectacle, as Melpomène, the muse of tragedy, says she has brought together all that is most beautiful in France and Italy, and her sisters have beautified it with all their arts. Melpomène flies through the air to meet the chariot of the Sun and asks him to pause in his course to lend his light to perfect the event, thus subtly pointing out the fact that it is the presence of the royal spectator that completes the court fiesta. The Sun says he is saving the miracle of a halt in his inexorable path for the time when he can employ it to admire the first victory of this "Monarque des Lys" who will outdo the achievements of Pompey, Alexander, Caesar, and even his father and grandfather. He invites her instead to join him in his chariot as he makes his heavenly orbit; together, then:

> Nous fassions résonner sur la Terre et sur l'Onde
> Qu'il est et le plus jeune et le plus grand des Rois. (ll. 71–72)

As a choir of music repeats and elaborates this refrain, the two fly off rapidly together, a dramatic demonstration of the mutual support of art and power.

Corneille seems to have had a somewhat ambivalent attitude toward the role of the sister arts that Melpomène summoned to her assistance. In the prologue, he says: "De tous leurs Arts mes sœurs l'ont embellie" (l. 7) as if their contribution were decorative rather than constitutive. In the preface, he also praises the Andromeda and Perseus story because it is "un sujet capable de tant d'ornements extérieurs"; yet in the same paragraph, he also states proudly that in *his* play, the stage machines are not "agréments détachés" but are essential to the heart of the drama. This is not an idle boast because all but the machines of the prologue and the final apotheosis are vital to the plot as Corneille has constructed it, and those two machine scenes effectively complete the laudatory purposes of the court spectacle. In all their appearances, the deities descend or arise from their appropriate heavenly or marine abodes. In Act I, Vénus descends on her star to announce that the victim for the monster will be chosen for the last time that day and that Andromède's delayed wedding should be readied for her marriage that evening to "l'illustre époux / Qui seul est digne d'elle et dont seule elle est digne" (ll. 358–359). Although the Vénus role is Corneille's addition to the story, this doubly ambiguous announcement not only maintains dramatic tension but also counterposes the forces of love and marriage to those of jealousy, fate, and death.[44] In Act II, a clap of thunder proclaims the anger of the gods at Phinée, who sacrilegiously rails against the sacrifice of Andromède, whose beautiful eyes he swears to be: "Et mes uniques Rois, et mes uniques Dieux" (ll. 741, 753). Then Eole descends with eight winds, who perform an involved aerial maneuver and carry off Andromède to attach her to the sacrificial rock. Again the introduced effect is functional, for as Delmas points out (66 n.1), it relieves Céphée of the cruel act of giving final consent to his daughter's awful death.

Corneille promised and delivered one machine per act except in the third, which has a number of other engineering feats in addition to the standard battle between the sea monster and the airborne Persée (mounted on Pégase). After his victory, at Persée's command, the winds reappear to untie Andromède and carry her back to safety. Barely giving the audience time to enjoy the apparent security of the heroine, Corneille then raises three Nereids from the waves and brings on Neptune in a chariot drawn by two sea horses. They announce the outrage of the marine deities at Jupiter's profanation of their realm and their planned revenge against his son, Persée. Junon reinforces this menace in the fourth act. She appears in "a superb chariot" drawn by two peacocks that moves from right to left repeatedly as she assures Phinée that he has her support against her faithless husband's son and that of Neptune and of Pluton, who has loosed an infernal horde to assist in his revenge. The value of this addition to the story is debatable because Corneille never convincingly demonstrates how and why this triple threat is dissolved; it therefore contributes effectively to heightening dramatic tension but not to the overall credibility that he also seeks. With this one reservation, however, Corneille speaks accurately when he says of the machines in his work, "elles en font le nœud, et le dénouement, et y sont si nécessaires, que vous n'en sauriez retrancher aucune, que vous ne fassiez tomber l'édifice" (12).

If we can fairly judge from black-and-white reproductions, however, the same cannot be said for the scenery.[45] Like the machines, the sets were those created for the 1647 production of Luigi Rossi's *Orfeo*, but revamped and reconditioned by Torelli at considerable expense (xxxiv–xxxv). Six sets were used— one for the prologue and each of the five acts. The first depicted a mountain strangely tunneled out to reveal a distant maritime scene, the second a public plaza, the third a formal garden, the fourth a rocky coastline, the fifth a royal palace, and the last a temple. In fact, however, the obvious delight in presenting extreme distances through a stylized use of perspective makes most of the scenes look quite similar. They consist in general of a central arch of some sort (a triumphal arch, a temple door, joined ranks of trees, or even the hollowed-out mountain) framing a distant scene carried to the vanishing point. On each side of the stage, a row of tall, slender shapes of gradually diminishing size leads the eye back and inward toward the central arch. These shapes could be trees, columns, statuary, or even bizarre-shaped rocks. A major drawback to this essentially Serlian type of scenery was that the exaggerated use of perspective made all but the front part of the stage unusable because actors were out of proportion with the scenery farther back; this was obviously the way Torelli's sets were used, as all the drawings depict action occuring at the front of the set. One interesting exception is the last set, of which Corneille says that through the central door of the temple, "on y verrait Céphée sacrifiant à Jupiter pour le mariage de sa fille" (109). Precisely how this sacrifice could be accomplished is a puzzle, for if the drawing is at all accurate, normal-size human figures could not possibly have been used in this reduced space. Corneille then continues with regard to this sacrifice scene: "n'était que l'attention que les spectateurs prê-teraient à ce sacrifice les détournerait de celle qu'ils doivent à ce qui se passe dans le parvis, que représente le Théâtre" (109). The problem was obviously that of finding a way to employ stage sets so that they would heighten dramatic effect without distracting from the action on stage. D'Aubignac gave voice to this concern in his 1657 *Pratique du Théâtre*:

> Que quand les Spectacles sont de Choses, c'est-à-dire d'objets permanents, il faut, s'il est possible, qu'ils paraissent dès l'ouverture du Théâtre, afin que le murmure du peuple qui s'émeut toujours en ces apparitions, soit fini avant que les Acteurs commencent le Récit; Ou s'il faut faire quelque changement de Décoration dans la suite de la Pièce, que ce soit dans l'in-tervalle d'un Acte, afin que les Ouvriers prennent tout le temps nécessaire pour remuer les machines, et que le Personnage qui doit ouvrir l'Acte, laisse passer le bruit que ce nouvel ornement aura excité. Et si par la néces-sité du Sujet, il fallait faire paraître quelque grande nouveauté dans le milieu d'un Acte, qu'il se souvienne de composer les discours de ses Acteurs en

telle sorte, qu'ils disent en ce moment fort peu de paroles, soit d'admiration, d'étonnement, de douleur ou de joie, pour donner quelque loisir à
l'émotion des Regardants qu'on ne peut éviter (qtd in Corneille 138–139).

Although D'Aubignac found nothing to criticize in Corneille's work in
this regard since all set changes were made between acts, he did criticize the sets
for being external to the action:

C'est en quoi je trouve un assez notable défaut dans l'*Andromède*, où l'on
avait mis dans le premier et quatrième Actes deux grands et superbes Édi-
fices de différente Architecture, sans qu'il en soit dit une seule parole dans
les vers; car ces deux Actes pourraient être joués avec les Décorations de tel
des trois autres qu'on voudrait choisir, sans blesser l'intention du Poète, et
sans contredire aucun incident, ni aucune action de la Pièce. On en pour-
rait presque dire autant du second Acte, sinon qu'au commencement il y
a deux ou trois paroles de Guirlandes et de Fleurs, qui semblent avoir
quelque rapport à un Jardin présent. . . . (138)

With the exception of the rocky maritime set for the battle of Persée and the
monster, these sets are in fact "agréments détachés" that could have contributed
little more than a decorative sumptuousness to the theatrical event.

The effective integration of music also presented a problem for Corneille.
Significantly, he did not mention in his preface the name of his musician,
Charles Dassoucy, although he does accord extensive praise to Torelli's machines. Music is used quite extensively in the work, primarily in the form of
choruses that sing hymns of praise or prayer to the deities while they ascend or
descend on machines. Although Mazarin's support had given Italian opera a
fresh resurgence in Paris since his accession to power in 1643 (Pitou 4), no
French adaptation of recitative had yet been achieved, and the traditional
French division of labor between actors and musicians still prevailed (Corneille
xxvii–xxxi). Given these facts as well as Corneille's overriding concern for clarity of diction, music had necessarily to be confined to an accessory role. No
major figure sings; when Phinée courts Andromède, it is his page who sings
offstage, and it is Andromède's Liriope who sings in answer. Corneille states
explicity in his preface that he has used music just to satisfy the spectator's ear
while a machine ascends or descends or otherwise distracts attention and that he
has no essential verses sung, lest meaning be lost: "Mais je me suis bien gardé de
faire rien chanter qui fût nécessaire à l'intelligence de la Pièce, parce que com-
munément les paroles qui se chantent étant mal entendues des auditeurs, pour la
confusion qu'y apporte la diversité des voix qui les prononcent ensemble, elles
auraient fait une grande obscurité dans le corps de l'ouvrage, si elles avaient eu
à instruire l'Auditeur de quelque chose d'important" (11–12).

Music, then, was an accessory element that was to decorate but never compete with the poetic text.[46] The reverse was true of the stage machines, which

Corneille considered the heart of the court spectacle, taking precedence over the poetry itself in this piece that is primarily for the eyes. In a statement that could have served as a model for Menéndez y Pelayo's judgment of Calderón's myth plays, he apologizes—unnecessarily—for the scarcity of beautiful verse, saying that his principal goal has been to satisfy the eye with the brilliance and diversity of the spectacle, not to touch the spirit through the power of its reasoning (*raissonnement*) or the heart by the delicacy of its passions (12–13). In Corneille's mind, then, meaningful verse, music, and machines were all legitimate but necessarily discrete elements of the spectacle play that must be used successively rather than simultaneously lest the force of one detract from the other.

THE CALDERONIAN SYNTHESIS

Calderón's technique is precisely the opposite, as he consciously acknowledges in his preface to the first edition of his *autos* (42): "Parecerán tibios algunos trozos; respeto de que el papel no puede dar de sí ni lo sonoro de la música, ni lo aparatoso de las tramoyas, . . . si ya no es que el que lea haga en su imaginación composición de lugares. . . . " The "composición de lugares" to which Calderón refers is a visualization technique that St. Ignatius de Loyola prescribed for meditation in his *Spiritual Exercises*, by which the meditator was instructed to re-create through the "ojos de la imaginación" the scene he or she would contemplate, employing all five senses to constitute in the imagination with fully plastic vividness the sight, sound, smell, touch, and taste of scenes such as Christ's crucifixion or the suffering of the damned in hell (23, 40–41).[47] In appealing to the reader to perform a similar "composición de lugares," Calderón asks him or her to accompany reading of the text with a mental reconstruction of the music and scenic pomp that enriched and completed its meaning.

If Calderón's caution to the reader is valid for the autos, it is even more important for the court plays. With a masterful sense of theatre, he used music, dance, scenery, and machines to enhance rather than compete with his poetic text. Music is not just something to fill gaps or hide machine noise but an integral part of the dramatic structure. The appearance of a tramoya does not stop the stage dialogue but is effectively integrated to heighten it. Significantly, Calderón presents his conception of the appropriate composition of the court spectacle not in a prose preface like Corneille's but in a dramatic prologue that explains its procedure in moving images, music, and dance.[48]

In the spring of 1653, the Infanta María Teresa (Felipe's fourteen-year-old daughter and future bride of Louis XIV) commissioned Calderón's play *Las fortunas de Andrómeda y Perseo* as the high point of a series of festivities to celebrate the recovery of the seventeen-year-old Queen Mariana from "un achaque grave," apparently smallpox. For this production, Calderón had the assistance of the able stage architect Baccio del Bianco, who had been sent to Spain at Felipe IV's request by Fernando II de'Medici in 1651.[49] Various popular accounts show

Figure 1. Baccio del Bianco, *Andrómeda y Perseo*, Prologue.

that the play was a great success,[50] and Mariana was apparently equally pleased, for she ordered Baccio to make a series of drawings to send with the text and music as a gift to her father, Ferdinand III, emperor of Austria and holy roman emperor (Massar 367). That set of eleven drawings, with the musical score, a complete text of the play, and a contemporary description of the event, which has come to rest in the Houghton Library at Harvard, is a gift to us as well, for it greatly facilitates our task of "composición de lugares."[51]

For the occasion, a handsome stage curtain was prepared, decorated with the names of Felipe, Mariana and María Teresa, and a "geroglífico":

Pintóse un sol, con algunas nubecillas, que ni le deslucían ni afeauan; y a merced de sus rayos, un país de varias flores, en cuyo primer término, eran de mayor tamaño, un laurel y un rosal. En la parte superior del cielo, que sobre él se terminaua, decía la letra latina GENERAT OMNIA. Y en la inferior la castellana.

> Vive tú, vivirá todo,
> Que no ay distancia, entre
> padecer, a padecer.

55

The sun is Mariana, the laurel Felipe IV, and the *rosal* María Teresa; the "nubecillas," which are described as not detracting from the beauty of the sun, would seem to be a reference to the queen's smallpox scars. Felipe was fond of jokingly calling them her "costurones" (a rough seam or stitches that leave a prominent scar).[52] The equation of Mariana with the sun on which all life depends is characteristically hyperbolic but also extremely appropriate, for the future of Spain under the Hapsburg monarchs depended on the young queen's capacity to produce a male heir.

A first prologue, which constitutes Calderón's poetics of the court spectacle, is played in front of this curtain. To the strains of a chorus of instruments, a handsome blue and silver cloud appears on high, bearing a nymph on a golden throne, who represents the art of music. She descends majestically to the stage, and taking up the refrain depicted on the curtain, explains in song that all the plants (i.e., subjects) of the country suffered from the eclipse of their sun's rays, but most of all the majesty of the laurel and the tender rose, both deities themselves. In happiness at seeing the recovery of the queen and therefore of the king as well, María has ordered a fiesta. In a brief and veiled moment of self-referentiality, Calderón has Música say: "Y quien le obedece, á ella [María], / me encarga a mi el parabién." In other words, María Teresa has commissioned Calderón, and he in turn has employed the "liberal art of music." While affirming her own capacities, she calls for assistance in celebrating the occasion and is answered by Poesía and Pintura, represented by two more richly clad nymphs, also cloud-borne and carrying symbols of their arts.[53] In what constitutes our closest approximation to a theoretical statement of the procedures of such spectaculars, the three discuss the artistic goal each must achieve. Painting offers the illusionistic pleasure of perspective scenery:

> El arte de la Pintura
> soy; que te vengo a ofrecer
> en vistosas perspectivas
> oy, quantos primores sé
>   Pues en los visos, y lexos
> de mi dibuxo, has de ver
> al parecer de los ojos
> desmentido el parecer.

Música adds to the obligations of Pintura those of absolute novelty and variety:

> advierte Pintura tú
> que siempre tan varia estés
> que lo que una vez se ha visto
> no vuelva a verse otra vez.

Música in turns promises to provide an appropriate form of harmony for the gods because "no es bien / que hablen los Dioses, como / los mortales." In effect, this meant the Spanish version of recitative, introduced the previous year in Calderón's first mature spectacle play, *La fiera, el rayo y la piedra* (Stein, "Music" 214–216). Finally, in a pledge that recalls Jonson's definition of the masque, Poesía says she will provide both the subject and the soul of the celebration:

> Pues yo soy la Poesía
> en mis números daré
> a tus coros, y a tus líneas
> el alma que han de tener.
> Las fortunas de Perseo
> serán asunto; . . .[54]

Since we are fortunate enough in the case of this drama to have a presentation copy including music, we know how music contributed to it in practice as well as in theory. Música enters singing the refrain "Vive tú, vivirá todo . . . ," which decorated the stage curtain, as a "short solo air in triple meter" (Stein, "Music" 223). When Poesía and Pintura enter, they sing the refrain as a duet, and as they join forces to raise the curtain, the three figures repeat it as a trio. The intervening sections in which they explain their roles in the fiesta are in "duple-meter coplas, characterized by smoothly moving eighth notes [that] allowed for efficient declamation" of the text (Stein, "Music" 223).

Having thus described their individual contributions, the three figures, Música, Poesía, and Pintura, unite in a marvelously dramatic demonstration of the artistic unity that Calderón sought and achieved:

> En tanto que las tres hasta aquí introducidas, igualmente diestras y suaves representavan, cantando este raçonamiento . . . las nubes de los lados, se fueron açercando a la de en medio, y uniéndose con ella, compusieron de los tres pedaços, un cuerpo tan primoroso; que estando cada uno de por sí perfectamente acauado, pareció que solo se havían fabricado, para verse juntos (ff.6–6v).

With their forces thus united, they rise together, carrying the stage curtain up with them. Just as painting, music, and poetry together constitute the fiesta, so poetry, machines, and music raise the curtain. Corneille had only Melpomène climb into the chariot of the Sun (the king) to sing his praises; Calderón both figuratively and literally enlists a trio of arts in that cause.[55]

Calderón almost certainly drew the idea for this dramatized poetics from the prologue with which Cardinal Giulio Rospigliosi prefaced his libretto for the opera *Il palazzo incantato* (1642; music by Luigi Rossi, stage architect Andrea Sacchi).[56] Rospigliosi, later Pope Clement IX, was the most important librettist of his day for Roman opera and the creator of sacred operas. He was the papal nuncio at the court of Felipe IV from 1644 to 1653 and was clearly in close contact with the Spanish theatre world during his residence there as he wrote two comic operas based on Calderonian plays, *Dal male il bene* (1654, based on *Peor está que estaba*) and *Le armi e gli amori* (1656, from *Los empeños de un acaso*) (Murata 1–11, 50). He also played an important role in the introduction of recitative in Spain. Baccio del Bianco said in a 1652 letter to Florence that Rospigliosi had written "una favola" to demonstrate to the king and unbelieving gentlemen of the Spanish court "che si possa parlar cantando" (qtd in Stein, "Music" 215).

In this prologue to *Il palazzo incantato*, the three figures, Pittura, Poesia, and Musica, boast of their own powers, quarrel, and threaten to go their own ways because Pittura complains they are hurrying her, but are finally brought into line by the arrival of a fourth figure, Magia. She could be considered a rough equivalent to stage effects, for she has the power to "uolger' gl'elementi; / E dare a'i Boschi il moto, e torlo a i venti."[57] Magia agrees to use her powers to ready the scene but insists on choosing the plot. When they agree to her right to do so, she causes the Palace of Atlante to appear. The machine opera that follows involves no less than seven love stories, organized around Atlante's attempt to imprison all of Ariosto's noble lovers in his enchanted palace.

As a *Gesamtkunstwerk*, this machine opera was far from the integrated form Calderón achieved; Murata describes it as "Baroque theater at its narrative and dramatic loosest," "a sort of Disneyland revue built around a few incidents to keep the characters coming onstage." Furthermore, its spectacle does not extend much beyond the painted backdrops, and the dancing and choral scenes are rarely more than ornamental additions (Murata 43, 45, 302–303). The poetry and dramatic coherence of the prologue also leave a good deal to be desired, but the basic idea served Calderón well for his dramatized *poética*.[58]

Calderón could not devote his entire prologue to an explanation of his techniques. Since the primary purpose of the loa to a court spectacular was its celebration of the royal spectators, he put his trio to work in the second half of the prologue in a display guaranteed to please the young queen. The curtain rose to reveal an enormous figure of Atlante dressed in royal purple and gold but bent under the weight of a globe. About the globe hovered twelve nymphs carrying torches and attired as the twelve signs of the zodiac. Atlante sang in a "sonorous, grave and low" voice, in dialogue with the twelve signs, who picked up his bass fragments and expanded on them in song (Stein, "Music" 225). Together they explained that he has been bowed not by supporting the universe but by the weight of a new suffering, the illness of Mariana. The automaton that represented Atlante then announced in music that as that new weight had doubled him over, so a new joy, the news of her recovery, uplifted him. As he sang, he straightened up to gigantic proportions (f.10r). At the same time, the twelve

Figure 2. Baccio del Bianco, *Andrómeda y Perseo*, Loa.

signs of the zodiac descended to the stage and took up and wove into a dance Atlante's melody, which had sustained them musically as he supported them physically (Stein, "Music" 227). Thus Calderón offered to Mariana a doubly flattering spectacle: Not only did she see that her recovery restored to his full mythic stature the giant pillar of the universe, who figured her husband, but also her recovery brought to earth the harmonious movement of the heavens.[59]

Baccio del Bianco was less than satisfied with the real-life harmony of the scene. He was not attuned to the Spanish tradition that called for the onstage accompaniment of guitarists (dressed in black capes) during danced interludes. When Baccio tried to eliminate this "barbarous custom," which by his lights destroyed the precision and refinement of the scene, the "nymphs" reacted violently: "Poco meno che non me crocifiggono" (qtd in Stein, "Music" 228 n.33).

To work with Calderón producing court spectacles, Baccio also had to accept a number of other features of the comedia tradition. Like Lope, Calderón used many elements from the public theatre to make the strange world of myth familiar and acceptable to his audience; unlike Lope, he made those traditions work to organize the material into a coherent drama. Furthermore, he did so without excising any significant material, as Corneille had done. With the exception of

Figure 3. Baccio del Bianco, *Andrómeda y Perseo*, Perseo, Palas, and Mercurio.

the episode of Atlas, which he employs only in the loa and in passing references, Calderón puts on stage the entire story from the rape of Danae to the death of Phineus (Fineo), including a number of additions drawn from Lope and Corneille, and he even finds ways of setting before his public segments, such as the slaying of Medusa, that most dramatists only reported as occurring offstage.

In structuring this volume of material, the comedia traditions that served Calderón well were the multiple plot, the free use of time and space, and the mixture of rustic figures with kings and comedy with high drama. Calderón weaves together stories of heavenly and terrestial rivalries and events in three lands: the Acaya, which sheltered Danae and Perseo; an African kingdom terrorized by Medusa; and Trinacria, which he makes Andrómeda's home. Through the creative use of time, he consolidates the episodic plot to bring all the major characters on stage in the first act and literally rearranges space to draw them together for the grand finale. Furthermore, he opens the play with shepherds in a rustic setting and after moving his characters from heaven to hell, brings peasant girls back to dance with the nine muses in the ending celebration of earthly and heavenly harmony.

Calderón unifies all these strands by the extensive use of parallelism. To the love triangle of Perseo, Andrómeda, and Fineo he adds a subordinate love inter-

Figure 4. Baccio del Bianco, *Andrómeda y Perseo*, Inferno.

est involving Lidoro, Danae, Júpiter, and Polítides. His version has two monsters—the sea dragon, whose venemous plague ravages the land of Andrómeda
and Fineo, and the land-based *fiera* Medusa, who terrorizes Lidoro's kingdom.
The two monsters are the ferocious creations of an offended goddess: Casiopea's
boast that Andrómeda is fairer than the Nereydas has enraged Venus (rather than
Neptune) in Calderón's story, and Minerba has turned Medusa from a beautiful
woman to a snake-haired beast because the river god Nereo raped her in Minerba's temple. As Andrómeda is to be chained to a rock to feed the sea monster,
Bato is to be tied to a tree to lure Medusa. Fineo and Lidoro arrive simultaneously in Acaya, which houses the shrine of Júpiter, to bring prayers for relief on
behalf of their countrymen. The oracles that Júpiter pronounces link the fates of
their two realms in a way that Fineo and Lidoro interpret as meaning that only
the blood of Medusa can slay the sea dragon; eventually, the oracle will prove to
have meant that Perseo will be the remedy for both. It is Lidoro who initiates the
chain of events by pressing his suit for Danae despite the enmity of her father,
who then locks her up out of jealousy, and it is Lidoro who brings it to a full
close by killing Fineo. As he does so, he compares himself to Perseo, for if Perseo
has slain a monster with serpents in her hair, he has killed one who carried the
asp of jealousy in his heart.

Calderón also reordered the basic narrative to unify his drama. His Perseo at the outset is a young man living as a humble shepherd in ignorance of his origin. *Humble* describes only his condition, not his character, however, for his innate belief that he was meant for higher pursuits has made this arrogant youth intolerable to his fellow shepherds. The play opens with a comic scene as three *villanos*, Gilote, Ergasto, and Riselo, hold Perseo down while the gracioso Bato tells him the "truth" about his background. The four are convinced that knowing that he was born in some shame will put a halt to his presumptuous commanding ways. When he springs up to attack Bato furiously for having told such a tale of misfortune to his face, Bato says, "I must have forgotten something in the story, because he's still hitting me" (f.17–17v).[60]

As well as providing a comic and familiar-sounding introduction, this device enabled Calderón to recount Perseo's history to his audience as the youth himself learns it, and the dramatist therefore needs to presume no previous knowledge on the part of his audience. Furthermore, his recounting of it humanizes the tale and brings it alive with several affective touches. The first is Bato's proud claim that he should be the one to tell Perseo because he was an eyewitness. He tells how he saw the little storm-battered boat with no mast or rudder that "no causó más nouedad, / que la lástima de verlo" (f.15v). Fishermen "fleeing the wrath of Neptune" chanced to hear a pitiful human voice from the boat, says Bato, and when the storm died down, he and curious neighbors rowed out to see if there were people in it. Bato is pleased to report that he was one of the first to see the pathetic sight of

> . . . vna muger dentro,
> con vn infante en los braços;
> que abrigándole en el pecho
> sin tenerle ella, le daua
> el calor, y el alimento (f.16v).

No human figure could reveal to Perseo the circumstances of his conception, however, for that is known only to Danae and the gods, and in Calderón's version, fear of the wrath of Juno seals Danae's lips. In a masterfully designed scene, Calderón shows Perseo and the audience the golden rain as a flashback that Perseo dreams. His half-brother and half-sister, Mercurio and Palas, have arranged this dream as the most diplomatic way of informing him of his divine origins and consoling him without awakening Juno's vengeance. To lure Perseo into the grotto of Morfeo, who stages the dream, they conjure up a vision of Andrómeda as the most beautiful object that "truth can lend to fiction" (f.24). This maneuver not only takes Perseo into the grotto but also brings the heroine on the stage in the first act, effectively solving the structural problem of her late entrance in the narrative. It also presents the occasion for some humor when he encounters her later and Bato laughs at his use of the old I've-seen-you-before gambit.

Now, the coincidences and supernatural interventions Calderón uses to bring all the characters on stage in the first act would obviously not be acceptable to nineteenth-century realism, but they fit comfortably within the conventions of verisimilitude of court mythological drama. Furthermore, he makes effective use of the gracioso Bato as a mediative bridge for the audience as the gracioso resists and then enters this unfamiliar world.[61] For example, having accompanied Fineo and Lidoro to the temple of Júpiter, Bato is the first to return, complaining:

> Yo no entiendo aquestos Dioses
> que andan siempre con mosotros,
> en oráculos habrando
> allá por sus circumloquios,
> que nadie ay que los entienda.

He prefers Momo (the god of sarcasm), he says, because he talks more than he should (f.48). Bato himself then delivers to Danae and Perseo an equally oracular report, which is not only comic but also builds suspense by postponing the revelation:

DANAE:	Dime a mí qué hubo en el templo,
	que bueluen tan tristes todos?
BATO:	Que hicieron sus sacrificios
	los dos; y a vno, y al otro
	Iúpiter respondió.
LOS DOS:	¿Qué?
BATO:	Dos casos bien espantosos.
LOS DOS:	¿Qué son?
BATO:	De vno no me acuerdo,
	pero del otro, tampoco:
	y pues ya aquí los he dicho,
	voy a decirlos a otros;
	que no ay cosa como andarse
	con sus nueuas de retorno
	vno, informando a otros tantos
	a otros tintos, y a otros tontos (f.48–48v).

Just before the climactic scene, when Lidoro rushes in to report that a temple is flying through the air, Bato remarks, "Y habrá algún bobo despúes, / que piense que es verdad esto?" (f.97). However, as it lands, he joins the crowd, exclaiming "¡Qué prodigio!" (f.97v), and when his friends Gilote, Ergasto, and Riselo descend from it, he accepts the miracle as not only true but absolutely appropriate to the occasion:

> Aunque me espanto de veros,
> no me espanto de que haga
> Iúpiter tales estremos:
> porque por grande que sea
> vn padre, no puede menos
> de hacer fiestas viendo vn hijo
> que le ha puesto en paz dos Reynos (f.99).[62]

Calderón also uses the comic Bato to explain the use of recitative, a relative novelty on the Spanish stage as we shall see, and Bato's comments heighten and extend spectacular effects. For example, when Perseo attacks Medusa, she flees offstage from her reflection in Perseo's shield; from within she says that it is poisoning and weakening her so that "tropeçando en mi sombra / soy de mi mesma cadáuer." As she speaks of tripping, a statue dressed like her is thrown on stage, and Perseo, entering behind, cuts off "her" head, which apparently bounces about on the stage. Bato first says he would have killed her himself if he had known it would be so easy, but as her head jumps toward him, he scurries away, saying:

> Salte acia otra parte usted
> sora cabeça, y no salte
> acia mí se lo supplico.

The commentary that accompanies the manuscript reports that "fue . . . admirable la tropelía de la cabeça; pues llegando Perseo y cortándola, hiço pauor y gusto: y más al ver los miedos de Bato, viéndola saltar en el tablado" (f.83). His part in this scene was apparently so memorable that Baccio drew him into his sketch, far off downstage left (thus literally mediating between the action and the audience) and labeled "Juan Rana" (Figure 5).

By so doing, Baccio helps us again to "componer lugares" and understand both the extensive role which Calderón wrote for Bato and the delight it afforded the audience.[63] Juan Rana was the stage name of the comic actor Cosme Pérez whom Asensio calls the "monarca de la graciosidad" (169). He had played the *entremés* role of Juan Rana so repeatedly and to such popular acclaim that even in legal documents he was called either Cosme Pérez or Juan Rana. As Felipe IV's frequent mentions of him in his letters to Sor Luisa attest, he was a great favorite with the royal family, and soon after Felipe's marriage to Mariana, the king bestowed on him a lifelong royal pension (Bergman 67–68). He is the only Golden Age actor of whom we have a portrait, perhaps ordered by the royal family since it is unlikely that even such a famous actor could have afforded such a luxury (Bergman 70–71).[64] We can be sure, then, that he was a substantial

Figure 5. Baccio del Bianco, *Andrómeda y Perseo*, Triumph of Perseo over Medusa, with Bato (Juan Rana).

bridge into this mythic world, not only because he was a fat little man but also because he was a consummate comic and a great favorite of the court whose presence was obligatory on all special occasions.

Calderón used other techniques as well as comedy to draw worlds together. As he used a flashback to tell Danae's story, he used overlapping scenes to indicate simultaneity of action in the human and divine realms. For example, in Act I, Perseo prays to Júpiter for some sort of explanation of why he feels convinced that he is more than a base-born person. Offstage, a mysterious divine chorus begins to sing him a Sibylline answer. While he puzzles over this new development, he also hears a confusion of human voices from within, some calling hunting dogs, others those of the arriving Fineo and Lidoro. They stay within while Palas and Mercury appear on clouds to discuss what they will do to help their half-brother. As they complete their scene and fly away, the confusion of human voices within is repeated, and one at a time, the three parties they represent (King Politides on a hunt, Fineo, and Lidoro) emerge on their differing quests. Thus Calderón demonstrates that forces from heaven and various points on the globe are coming together and operating at the same time to lift Perseo from obscurity.

In building this dramatic work, Calderón took advantage not only of the comedia formula in general but of Lope's *Fabula de Perseo* in particular. Without so much as a name change, he adopted Lope's Laura as a *dama* of Danae and Lidoro as her would-be suitor. He situates Danae in Acaya but transforms Tiro into Piro and makes it Danae's homeland rather than Andrómeda's. Like Lope, he has Casiopea brag about her daughter's beauty rather than her own and has Palas give to Perseo a "cristalino espejo" that will defeat Medusa by reflecting her fatal vision. Calderón's Andrómeda, like Lope's, despises Fineo but expresses a selfless concern for Perseo when he appears on Pegaso to rescue her. He also takes up and improves upon Lope's idea of using a portrait to introduce the heroine early in the play.

Other material from Lope he incorporates much more subtly. For example, the Lopean idea that Medusa was the daughter of a king is repeated not in words but in a set that shows a princely country house as her abode. Lope's Lidoro worries about whether he should use his gold to bribe the guards, but Calderón's Júpiter says blatantly that he has done so, and the group of damas that accompany Danae scurry for the gold pieces, then leave her to Júpiter's pleasure, exulting over what their gold will buy them: new furniture, a seigniorial residence, even a higher-class husband[65]—a conversation that surely drew a laugh from a court audience that lived with the ambitions of ladies-in-waiting. He also turns Lope's climactic scene of the appearance of Mt. Parnaso into a joke about the poverty of poets, describing the first flight of Pegaso over it and the crystalline spring his hoof brings forth. Bato immediately identifies it as the fountain of poets because it satisfies thirst but not hunger. There is even a faint reminiscence of Lope's *justa poética* about Clori's beautiful hair in the Gongorine comparison of Medusa's hair to the sun:

> . . . cuyas hebras
> yló el sol entre sus rayos,
> siendo su frente vna esphera,
> que trençada anochecía;
> por que amaneciesse suelta (f.32).

While it seems that Calderón may have been subtly making fun of some of Lope's extraneous inspirations, he took more seriously what he drew from Corneille.[66] In general, the nature of Calderón's borrowings from Corneille suggests that he had read Corneille's play, or at least seen a detailed plot summary, for the sorts of details he follows are not those that would be described in a diplomatic report or popular newsletter. His borrowing is most evident in relation to the character Fineo, who in Calderón as in Corneille is Andrómeda's cousin. Like Corneille, Calderón has Fineo aver that all her countrymen should die rather than sacrificing Andrómeda. But while Corneille's Phinée rants sacrilegiously against the gods, Calderón's is more cautious and conscious of his dilemma, in

Calderón that of deciding whether to inform his countrymen honestly of what the oracle has said:

> Si al oráculo no creo,
> el sacrilegio no ignoro;
> y si le creo, trofeo
> de vn monstro hago a la que adoro.
> Desuerte, que a un tiempo me hallo
> entre creello, y dudallo,
> fiel de vno y otro castigo;
> pues muere ella, si lo digo
> y ella, y todos si lo callo (f.49)

In both versions, a month elapses between Perseus's acquaintance with Andrómeda and his rescue of her, with the difference that in the Spanish version the month transpires within the dramatic action while in the French it precedes it. At the end of each rescue scene, Perseus humbly places himself at Andromeda's feet. Calderón also follows Corneille in introducing a jealous Juno, but in Calderón she becomes a much more important figure who repeatedly underlines her rage at Júpiter's infidelities.[67] She enlists her ally Discordia to conspire against Perseo in heaven, on earth, and in hell, and to send Fineo and the Furies against him as well. In this play and in other Calderonian works, Discordia is regularly described as the bastard daughter of Plutón, who is also depicted in Corneille as having unleashed the infernal hordes against Perseo.

Unlike Lope and Corneille, Calderón makes no attempt at an artificially even distribution of scenery and stage effects. Rather, he allows the structure of the plot to determine change of scenery and keys the use of stage effects to the pace of the action. He uses only one set in the first act, five in the second, and three in the third; from two aerial effects in the first act he quickens the pace with six effects in the second and some nine or ten in the final act. The whole first act is set in Acaya before a set of rustic snow-covered huts in a rough, hilly, and wooded setting. As the opening scene demonstrates, D'Aubignac could not have criticized Calderón for a divorce between stage set and action, for Riselo, Gilote, Ergasto, and Bato come running in looking for a place to hide from the angry Perseo and name varieties of trees, probably those painted in the set, that will shelter them.[68] (Bato, with a characteristic gracioso taste for wine, chooses grapevines.)

Similarly, Calderón integrates the arriving machine effects in the text. Perseo anticipates the arrival of the clouds bearing Mercury and Palas in the densely constructed scene of overlapping voices earlier described. Discarding the possibility that the mysterious music promises divine assistance, he says:

> . . . apenas pequeña nube,
> se descubre en todos ellos;

Figure 6. Baccio del Bianco, *Andrómeda y Perseo*, Fall of Discordia.

que boreal carro triunfal
sea del sagrado dueño
de la voz; pues vna sola
que allá en el perfil postrero
del oriçonte, es apenas
fingida garça del viento,
no es capaz, trono de hermosa
deidad. . . . (f.21–21v)

Thus he underlines the delight in the feigned distances of the perspective scenery and offers the audience the pleasure of a mobile dramatic irony, for the "pequeña nube" that Perseo discounted grows larger as he speaks (thanks to mechanical arms that could fold in and out), and as Perseo leaves the stage, it disappears, revealing behind it "otro bello nubarrón de oro coronado de rayos, que a manera de trono sustentaua en la vltima de sus gradas, las dos Deidades de Palas, y Mercurio" (f.22).

Calderón's stage effects do not interrupt the action as in most spectaculars; they are integrated to reinforce the dramatic power of the text. For example, the second effect in Act I is the airborne struggle between Palas and Discordia.[69] Discordia wants to tell Juno that Mercurio is about to reveal to Perseo that he is Júpiter's son, which will publicize her husband's infidelities and lack of respect for her. To keep Discordia from informing on them, Palas literally pushes her out of the heavens, and Discordia falls "desde la más alta punta de vna parte del teatro, hasta esconderse en lo más inferior de la otra" (f.38v) in less time than it takes her to cry out her last line, "Ay, infelice de mí!" (f.37v)—a bang-up ending for Act I. According to the description, it produced first shock in the audience, then applause: "[el] arrebatado mouimiento quitaua con el susto, mucha parte del agrado. Pero asegurado del peligro lo vno, y lo otro, pagaua en admiraciones el aplauso: con que dio fin el primer acto" (f.38).[70]

At this point in his account, the unknown describer of the event calls attention to the fact that the score of the songs accompanies the text and suggests that performance of the music should complement the reading. And well he might, for music in this work is not merely decorative but a constitutive element in the structure of meaning. In the first place, Calderón employs it to distinguish between deities and mortals. As his figure Música had stated in the prologue, the gods have "otra armonía en la voz" (f.6) because they participate in the celestial harmony of Pythagorean-Platonic theory. When Palas and Mercurio appear on their cloud, therefore, they do not speak as earthly men and women but in recitative,[71] as the manuscript description tells us: "Empeçaron su plática, a diferencia de los humanos, en vn estilo recitatibo, que siendo vn compuesto de representación, y música, ni bien era música, ni bien representación, sino vna entonada consonancia, a quien acompañaua el coro de los instrumentos . . ." (f.22v). In a lovely dialogue between two graciosos, Calderón described his system a few years later in *El laurel de Apolo*:

BATA: Los dioses, aun disfrazados
            dan de quién son señas craras,
            que no habran como mosotros.
RÚSTICO: Pues, ¿de qué manera habran?
BATA: Con tan dulce melodía,
            tan suave consonancia,
            que siempre suena su voz
            como música en el alma:
            y así, en oyéndole que hace
            gorgoritas de garganta,
            cátale dios.
RÚSTICO: El sabello
            es bien, porque todos hagan
            esta distinción: Mas dime
            ¿todo lo que dicen cantan?
BATA: Cuando habran entre sí,
            ¿qué sé yo lo que les pasa? (2179a)

Stein offers a precise and innovative analysis of the conjunction between musical setting and text in this play, and its relationship to better-known Italian models. Although I summarize certain of her findings for the nonspecialist, I recommend direct consultation of her work for a full analysis with technical examples.[72] The form of recitative developed in Italy to imitate in song the natural inflections of speech was characteristically in duple meter, with small notes to facilitate delivery of text in a syllabic style over a static bass line. The unknown musician of *Las fortuna de Andrómeda y Perseo* follows this paradigm, but with one important difference: The recitative is in triple meter and employs almost none of the expressive devices commonly used in Italian recitative. The explanation for the difference, says Stein, is that in the Calderonian play, "the structure of the musical setting is governed exclusively by the text" and functions as a rhetorical support for declaiming his long expository texts in an appropriately harmonic form. The careful syllabic setting preserves the text accents, while simple melodic and rhythmic devices emphasize important words. "In Palas' first recitative, for example, the word *montes* (mountains) is set as an upward leap of an octave; later, the words *muriendo* (dying) and *lamentos* (laments) are set as suspensions in a stylized hemiola pattern. . . . The triple meter allows for the fluent passage from repetitive, syllabic declamation into brief instances of text painting or lyrical ornamentation, although these occur mainly at the ends of sections as part of extended cadential figures" (Stein, "Music" 232–233).

Besides this practical advantage in serving the text, Stein believes that it has a theoretical base in the concept of divinity as a triune being, extended from the Christian divinity to these pagan gods, who were considered to be pagan prefigurations of Christian truth. Representatives of the divine speak in "perfect" triple time. "This would also explain the heavily triadic orientation of the melodic lines. Divine harmony and divine rhythm would both be perfect, triple, and triadic. All the recitative scenes of act I are in triple meter, and they take place in the heavens, the realm of the deities, the point of emanation of celestial harmony." It also explains the peculiar nature of the second musical section, the struggle between Palas and Discordia. "In this scene, the recitative is again in triple meter, but only Palas sings in recitative. Discordia, the 'false goddess' (*mentida deidad*) speaks, 'sounding without harmony' (*sonando sin consonancia*). Discordia does not sing because discord is the antithesis of musical consonance" ("Music" 234). Furthermore, she is a bastard deity, the daughter of Plutón, whose infernal domain is the origin and center of discord.

Although the instrumental score is not included with the vocal music in the manuscript and has not survived, we know from the description that instrumental music also served to heighten the dramatic impact of the text. For example, the struggle between Palas and Discordia is accompanied by "vna batalla que tocauan los violones" (f.36v) and "out-of-tune drums" and "shrill trumpets" played as Andrómeda was led to the sacrificial rock (Stein, "Music" 243–245). Stein concludes that "dramatic situation and textual content dictated the specific choice of a musical setting and of instrumental accompaniment. . . .

Each section of vocal music, solo, or ensemble, is intricately linked to a specific text and to a special dramatic context or situation. The music does not detract from the tightly-knit Calderonian drama, but strongly supports the themes and the plot, so that it is not a superfluous element of spectacle, but intrinsic to the success of the play" ("Music" 245–246).

A similarly dense orchestration of scenery, stage effects, text, and music prevails throughout this play. For the most part, the kind of scenery and stage effects employed are not unique; rather, it is Calderón's close integration of them into the overall structure of the drama that distinguishes his work. Therefore, I will not describe all the staging but only particularly imaginative uses.

The continuity between text and scenery even carries over between acts. In the first act, Lidoro describes Medusa's residence exactly as it will appear in the third act: "casa de campo a vna parte; / y a otra vna intrincada selua" (f.31v). In the next-to-last scene of Act I, the illusionistic Andrómeda goes offstage, saying, "Búscame si hallarme quieres en esta gruta," and Perseo follows her, observing, "Aunque veo / que a la gruta de Morfeo / ha entrado, tras ella voy" (f.36–36v). Discordia attempted in vain to prevent this meeting, and Act II opens with the "fingida sombra de Andrómeda" running out to the set of the grotto of Morfeo,

Figure 7. Baccio del Bianco, *Andrómeda y Perseo*, Grotto of Morfeo.

Figure 8. Baccio del Bianco, *Andrómeda y Perseo*, Seduction of Danae.

with Perseo close behind. She quickly disappears, saying, "Aquí me hallarás, Perseo, / rayo y sombra en humo y polbo" (f.40). Morfeo takes command and first sings Perseo into a somnolent state with a gentle song in a lyrical triple-meter arioso style, then changes to a declamatory style strongly reminiscent of Palas' first recitative as he conjures up the dream she had planned (Stein, "Music" 235).

The dream sequence that follows contains Calderón's most imaginative use of scenery. As Morfeo leaves the stage, the scene changes from his gloomy grotto to the sumptuously furnished chamber of Danae and her damas, the scene of Perseo's dream. As Varey points out, the drawing shows by the proportion of the human figures that this was not a full-size set with receding bastidores.[73] Rather, it appears to have been some sort of prosceniumlike frame with a flat behind it, painted in perspective to create the effect of distance through receding doorways.

Varey believes this to have been a drop-in set placed in front of the grotto of Morfeo; however, it is possible that it was in some way hidden behind the grotto scenery, which was either partially or entirely removed to reveal it, because the description speaks of Danae and her damas as already present when the scene is revealed and the text has no indication of their entry.[74] In any case, Perseo was also still on stage, to one side, perhaps in front of part of the scenery of the grotto of Morfeo. He exclaims at the scene:

> Mi madre entre tantas reales
> pompas, palacios, y adornos;
> qué es esto cielos?

Danae asks her ladies to sing to alleviate her sadness, and they respond with a four-part setting of the refrain "Ya no les pienso pedir / más lágrimas a mis ojos," and Danae then takes up the theme and its tune, and elaborates on it as a solo. Stein observes that this was a well-known tune, the sort of song used for "realistic" purposes in the simple comedia. With what Stein calls a "sort of twisted verisimilitude," Calderón had Danae lament her "real" past misfortunes with a preexistent song that is a legacy from the real past.[75] Danae's musical conversation with her damas is interrupted by an offstage "divine" chorus that signals the beginning of the golden rain. The damas scoop it up and leave Danae alone as Perseo comments from the sidelines: "Qué dulce sueño me tiene, / aun más que dormido absorto" (f.44v).

A certain space was apparently left between the prosceniumlike frame and the painted flat, and through it now descends Júpiter on an eagle dressed as Cupid. (For the significance of this surprising attire, see Chapter 4.) He does not return by the same route; instead, after disclosing to Danae his identity and his passion for her, he pursues her as she flees offstage, leaving the audience to imagine the outcome. As they exit, the dream set disappears, revealing again the first set of rustic huts.

This return to the first scene is a violation of the code of the court spectacle, specifically enunciated in the prologue, that no set should be repeated. It is, however, the mark of a dramatic genius who knows when to break the rules, as the description explains: "Cuya Scena repetida, disculpó despertando, el confuso ademán de Perseo; pues no pudiera de otra manera, significarse más viuamente, hauer sido todo ilusión y fantasía, que voluiendo a hallarse en el mismo lugar, donde le asaltó la sombra de la sombra de la fingida Andrómeda" (f.46).

Calderón has used stage sets to display the workings of the human mind, for he has put on stage both the sleeping Perseo and the dream. Since in dreams we regularly transcend spatial and chronological limits, he can employ this scene to concentrate and unify the story without violating psychological truth.

Where appropriate, Calderón also counterposed two effects, such as machines and music. When the Ninfas leave Andrómeda chained to the rock, the anguished girl asks the stars if there is any consolation, any hope. In response, offstage "heavenly" echoes pick up one by one the last syllable of her lines to form the ambiguous refrain "Vna ventura ay segura" (f.93v). At the same time, the sea monster appears in the distance, small at first but growing larger with each writhing turn in the waves. Andrómeda despairs, thinking the echoing song is nothing but the projection of her own desperate imagination. As the monster reaches its full size in front of her, Perseo comes to the rescue on Pegaso.

With all his mastery at integrating scenery, stage effects, and music, however, Calderón did not neglect the poetic text. In this sacrifice scene, for example, he provided a showpiece for the actress who portrayed Andrómeda. A gloating Discordia describes the pathetic scene as she is lead out crying, dressed in mourning, to the accompaniment of out-of-tune drums, harsh trumpets, and a crowd shouting, "¡Muera Andrómeda!" "¡Viua Trinacria!" (f.86–86v).[76] She argues with the human chorus that condemns her to death, then curses "ears that will not hear, hearers who will not listen" and pleads with the very mountains of Trinacria to open a grave for her lest her tomb be the bowels of the monster.

When the Ninfas of Nereo emerge from the waves to claim her as payment for the injury to Venus, Andrómeda delivers a plea worthy of the best defense lawyer. She appeals to the bond of their shared heritage as children of Trinacria and to their friendship, to the days when they danced together on this very beach. She calls on their sense of honor: Divinity reveals itself best in compassion. She humbles herself before them and argues that all mothers, even those of scaly wrinkled snakes, see their offspring as beautiful. Should the children be blamed for that blind love? Is the sun offended if someone thinks its rays are dark? On her knees, she pleads that they, like the sun, forbear vengeance and cruelty.

Responding only by telling her be quiet, not to flatter them with false humility, they begin to strip her jewels and clothes before dragging her to the boulder to which they will chain her. Angry and proud, Andrómeda shakes them off, strips her own mourning garb, and climbs unassisted to the rock, which will better hear her lament than they, she says:

> Y hauiendo de llorar [a] alguien,
> llore a aquestas peñas rudas,
> antes que a vosotras; pues
> menos toscas, menos brutas
> son las que ostentan el serlo,
> que las que lo disimulan (f.92v).

She then cries for comfort or hope from whatever feeble tremulous star might be hers, but when Perseo appears to confront the monster, she selflessly warns him away, saying that she would rather die than see him risk his life for hers. The mechanisms that powered the monster and Pegaso would have had to be most impressive not to seem anticlimactic after this melodramatic performance.

To surpass it, Calderón brings his full dramatic universe together for the grand finale. Lidoro rushes in to bring news of the flying temple, and a chorus "en lo alto" proclaims that Júpiter, patron of Perseo's victory, is transporting his temple from Acaya to Trinacria. Seated on identical clouds, Juno and Discordia appear above the stage on one side, Mercurio and Palas on the other, for one last quarrel. While the scene changes to that of a royal palace, a temple appears on high, carrying on its steps the heavenly chorus that has been singing. It descends to the

Figure 9. Baccio del Bianco, *Andrómeda y Perseo*, Perseo rescuing Andrómeda.

Figure 10. Baccio del Bianco, *Andrómeda y Perseo*, Final Celebration.

stage, and from it emerge Polidites, Danae, Cardenio, the shepherds, and others. Their scene of betrothal and celebration is rudely interrupted by Fineo's attempt to kill Perseo. Lidoro sends an arrow through his jealousy-ridden heart, and Andrómeda proclaims that now that love is safe, hatred should die, while Discordia and Juno complain that even this last-ditch effort has failed them. Finally, the skies open above the temple to reveal Júpiter seated amid a choir of gods, who sing:

> Viua, viua la gala del gran Perseo,
> que de Júpiter hijo merece serlo
>   Quando a padre tan grande
>   ponen sus hechos
>   con dos monstruos vencidos
>   en paz dos Reynos.

While Júpiter and the choir of gods sing above, another choir and its accompaniment join in from one side, a third choir with rustic instruments from the other. Two companies of dancers come in from opposite sides, the first composed of the nine muses who sponsor music and poetry, the other of gods dressed in peasant attire in honor of Perseo, the divine hero who was once a shepherd. The residents of Acaya return to their temple, which rises into the air and disappears as the gods sing above and the two companies dance below. Music and verse, peasants and gods, join in song and dance to celebrate the reestablishment of peace and harmony in the heavens and on earth.

But has harmony been securely reestablished? Juno and Discordia have been defeated but not banished from the stage. Calderón leaves them, angry and unrepentant, securely seated on their cloud in opposition to Palas and Mercurio. In another chapter we will consider the structures of meaning that Calderón erected in this play and their relationship to its audience, assembled in a hierarchy very like that which faced it on the stage.

What I hope to have demonstrated with this survey is Calderón's remarkable mastery of the ensemble of components that make up the court spectacle.[77] Calderón demonstrated himself to be a consummate playwright in the concentrated exploitation of the density of theatrical sign systems, effectively integrating music, dance, elaborate scenery, and stage machinery to intensify the dramatic power of his poetic text. In the figures of Música, Pintura, and Poesía (with the silent partnership of "Maquinaria") he dramatized the polyphony of the theatrical idiom in the prologue of *Las fortunas de Andrómeda y Perseo*. Throughout the work that followed he blended their operation in close harmony, making this court spectacle truly a "play of power."

THREE

Power at Play: *El mayor encanto, amor*

By PERFORMING with *Las fortunas de Andrómeda y Perseo* the "composición de lugares" that Calderón requested of his readers,[1] we can see the falsity of the first charge leveled against his court spectacles—that they were mere shows dominated by scenic carpenters, to the detriment of dramatic coherence. If subsequent readers have been unable to perceive the theatrical power of these works, it is because they have reduced the polyphony of Calderón's dramatic idiom to the monody of a printed page.

We must now deal with the second charge brought against these plays—that they were at best frivolous spectacle and at worst servile flattery designed for the pleasure of a decadent monarchy. To counter this misunderstanding will necessitate an equally active reading, for it requires that the twentieth-century reader envision the plays in the political situation of their creation and the unique physical circumstances of their performance.

Born in 1600, Calderón lived and worked in a century characterized in Castille by an increasingly acute sense of the decline of the Spanish monarchy.[2] The populace was beset by economic hardships and the ravages of plague and war, and a series of generally unpopular royal favorites presided over a massive, cumbersome, and often corrupt government bureaucracy. Calderón wrote his first court-spectacular play, based on the Circe myth, in 1635 when war had just been renewed with France and the young Felipe IV's subjects worried that his sensual passions distracted his attention from affairs of state and criticized the ascendancy over the king of his favorite, Count-Duke Olivares (Brown and Elliott 32–33, 232–238). He wrote his last play in 1680, in the shadow of his death and that of the Hapsburg dynasty in Spain as the country was left in the hands of the mentally and physically feeble Carlos II.

In an attempt to reverse this trend, Olivares had launched an ambitious program of fiscal, institutional, and moral reform in 1623 with twenty-three "articles of reformation," augmented in 1626 by a project called the Union of Arms that would have increased the integration of the various kingdoms of the monarchy and distributed more evenly the economic and manpower costs of defense with which Castille was overburdened.[3] His reform program met with very little success, however, partly because the numerous military campaigns to maintain the extensive Hapsburg domains doomed the reforms urgently needed at home.[4]

Olivares was more successful in another campaign—royal image making. Felipe, with a natural grace and dignity, and a fascination for ceremony and etiquette, proved an ideal pupil.[5] Olivares groomed Felipe IV to be "el rey planeta," the fourth planet or sun around which a glittering social and cultural life would revolve. We have already seen the flurry of court theatrical activity that followed his accession and the importation of Cosimo Lotti to augment its brilliance in 1626.

A key piece in this project was the construction of the Palace of the Buen Retiro, begun as a simple expansion of the Royal Apartment adjoined to the Church of San Jerónimo in 1630 and vastly expanded into a royal pleasure palace after 1633, at a cost of perhaps some 2.5 million to 3 million ducats.[6] The ceremonial center of this edifice was the Hall of Realms, the throne room in which the king presided over court ceremonies and entertainments. This magnificent room, so well described and explained by Brown and Elliott, was decorated with paintings of recent Spanish victories, interspersed with ten canvases by Zurbarán depicting the labors of Hercules along the side walls, while in the vaults above the windows were painted the escutcheons of the twenty-four kingdoms of the Spanish monarchy.

The Hercules paintings symbolically represented the kings of Spain as conquerors of religious and political discord, "the triumph of the just sovereign over domestic and foreign enemies" (161), and these victories were also figured in a more immediate way in the battle paintings. The Maino painting of the recapture of Bahía is particularly fascinating as a political statement subtly presented through art, in which Felipe is depicted crushing Heresy, Discord, and Treachery, "better known in those days as the Dutch, the English, and the French" (188). The conquering general, Don Fadrique de Toledo, who had earned the enmity of Olivares, is reduced to a subordinate position, while the conde-duque is painted into the picture, standing behind the king with a sword and olive branch, joining with Minerva to crown the king with the laurel wreath of victory. In the Brown and Elliott interpretation, this painting, linked with the choice of the other battles depicted and the escutcheons over the windows, demonstrates that Olivares had planned the hall not only to exalt the monarch he served but also to promote his own importance and that of the Union of Arms he espoused. Overseeing the room from either end were five Velázquez equestrian portraits of Felipe III and Felipe IV, their queens and the Crown Prince Baltasar Carlos, clearly designed to "represent the immediate past, present and future of the Habsburgs and assert the legitimate rights and continuity of the dynasty" (156).

It was for a celebration of the completion of this Hall of Realms that Calderón wrote his first mythological court spectacle, *El mayor encanto, amor*. The play was to be performed for the king on the Noche de San Juan (Midsummer Night's Eve, 23 June) of 1635, with performances on three subsequent nights for (1) members of the Councils, (2) members of the Cortes; and (3) the general public, who paid for admission.[7] For such an occasion, Olivares clearly expected a drama that would publish the standard message of the court spectacle, the glory and power of the monarch. As we have seen, one purported object of this play was that of impressing the French enemy with the depth of the royal Spanish coffers. How could a play designed for such circumstances be anything but a celebratory ritual, perhaps verging on servile flattery?

Recent critics who have attempted to consider Calderón's court plays in their historical context have continued to be discomfited by the incongruity of the obligatory "text of royal power" with the political realities of the Hapsburg court. Cascardi summarizes the essential political facts of the era, then concludes that in these plays Calderón devoted his technical mastery to "wholly uncritical ends," to shoring up threatened collective social values viewed through the royal optic, and to congratulating the ineffective kings Felipe IV and Carlos II. Sebastian Neumeister, though recognizing the importance of reading the plays in context, follows the traditional line of reading them as religious allegories (137–200) and/or as solipsistic structures dedicated to flattering the royal family and affording them a narcissistic escape from harsh political realities (268–283). He discounts the possibility of any sort of critical address in a drama commissioned for the entertainment of an absolutist court.

Yet the possibility of if not "loyal opposition," at least "loyal criticism" was not excluded in the court of Felipe IV; rather, particularly as the consciousness of crisis deepened with the advancing century, it was considered by some to be an *obligation*, however delicate, of true friends of the royalty. A faithful correspondent of Felipe IV, the nun María de Agreda, referred to the king as an "enfermo" and to herself as his "médico," and commented in her correspondence with Don Fernando de Borja and his son that "Al Rey todos le engañan. Señor, esta Monarquía se va acabando, y quien no lo remedie arderá en los infiernos" (Pérez Villanueva 11–12). Sor María was more circumspect in her direct address to the king, but not all others were so discreet. A bold peasant was reported to have planted himself before the king and delivered virtually the identical verdict in June 1640 (Kamen, *Sociedad* 370). Furthermore, the chronicler Barrionuevo recounts several instances in which priests delivered sermons containing harsh criticisms in the presence of the king. Such action was not considered prudent for ambitious men. Barrionuevo comments on the appointment of one Francisco de Aranda as preacher to the king, saying, "Harálo muy bien, que es docto, y no le dirá pesares, porque desea medrar" (2:67).[8] On the other hand, Felipe did not punish these plainspeakers for treason. When it was suggested to the king that he exile several such preachers, he reportedly responded: " '*Haréme más odioso con todos si lo hago'. Dejadlos decir, que ellos se cansarán* '"[emphasis in original] (2:71).

Overall, seventeenth-century Spain was characterized by a noteworthy freedom of expression in the political arena according to Kamen's analysis (*Sociedad* 368–375). Although some pamphlets critical of government policies did circulate, the most common forms of critical printed expression were satirical sheets, or *pasquines*, pasted to city walls or even on the doors of the palace according to Maura Gamazo (*Carlos II y su corte*, 1:21). Another standard feature of the era were the *arbitristas*, men who wrote treatises analyzing the causes of national decline and presenting their remedies for the problem—some as sensible as the construction of a good system of roads and canals or the development of import-replacement manufacturing, others so bizarre that they in turn became the object of satirical treatment by Cervantes and other writers. More than 165 such *arbitrios* were published between 1598 and 1665 (Kamen, *Sociedad* 372), and many others circulated less formally.

The importance of maintaining this freedom to voice the truth to the monarch was upheld by writers whose political philosophies were as diverse as those of Juan de Mariana and Quevedo. The Jesuit Mariana, in his influential work *De Rege et Regis Institutione* (1599), maintained that the source of the monarch's right to rule was a compact by which society, composed of individuals who came together for their own protection, transferred governing power to one man. Their transfer of power was not total and irreversible, however; it was limited by laws and by the community's residual authority to defend itself against a king turned tyrant. Mariana says that one of the characteristic actions of the tyrant is abolition of freedom of speech: "He forbids the citizens to congregate, to come together in political meetings and societies, and to talk at all about public business; this he accomplishes by secret inquisitions, and by taking away the means of speaking and hearing freely, which is the height of servitude. He does not even allow them the freedom of complaint in such bad conditions" (140).

This equation of tyranny and limitation of speech may explain Felipe's reluctance to silence critical priests. By Mariana's standards, the king is also obligated to make himself accessible to all: "He makes himself available to all in every duty of life; no one in his helplessness, no one in his loneliness is kept away, not only from his office, but not even from his dwelling and court. His ears are open to the complaints of all" (136). Not only must he listen to all complaints; he must also resist the temptation to self-delusion encouraged by flatterers who flock around him (118–119) and gather about him the most honest and forthright men in the kingdom:

> After he has driven the flatterers far away, he will summon the best men from every province. These he will use as his eyes and ears, but they will be upright and uncorrupted by defects. Let him give them access to himself for reporting not only the truth, but everything that is said about him, even the vain and empty gossip of the crowd. His objective of public service and the safety of the province as a whole will balance the grief that he feels because of these rumors and this frankness. Truth's roots are bitter; its fruits, most sweet (138).

Quevedo's view of man and government was much more pessimistic and conservative, yet he too argued for the importance of speaking the truth to the king, in his *Política de Dios*. He sees the imposition of monarchy as a punishment for man's sin and inability to govern himself; the restraint on the monarch's power derives not from the residual sovereignty of the people but from the king's subordination to divine law. The only free and perfect king was Christ; all others must strive to imitate his example and prepare to answer for their actions at the final judgment. As Christ invited the weak and suffering to come to him, so must the king: "El Rey es persona pública, su Corona son las necessidades de su Reyno, el reynar no es entretenimiento, sino tarea; mal Rey el que goza sus estados, y bueno el que los sirue. Rey que se esconde a las quexas, y que tiene porteros para los agrauiados, y no para quien los agrauia, esse retírase de su oficio y obligación, y cree que los ojos de Dios no entran en su retiramiento, y está de par en par a la perdición, y al castigo del Señor, de quien no quiere aprender a ser Rey" (100). Furthermore, his ears must be open to the opinions of all: "La libertad de la conciencia respira inquiriendo, y los Reyes deuen saber lo que les conuiene, y no se han de contentar de saber lo que otros quieren que sepan: vna cosa es oír a los que assisten a los Príncipes, otra a los que, o sufren, o padecen, a essos tales. Sepa, Señor, el Monarca lo que dizen del sus gentes, y los que le siruen" (85).

Saavedra Fajardo, in his important book of political emblems, *Idea de un príncipe político-cristiano representada en cien empresas*, dedicates a chapter to the value of "murmuración" (roughly speaking, "critical gossip"), which although bad in itself, is nevertheless good for the republic, even essential to its liberty, because fear of such criticism is the most effective restraint on the excesses of the prince.[9] He also provides us with the explanation for Felipe's reaction to another outspoken preacher, Fray Nicolas Bautista. Barrionuevo recounts one of Bautista's sermons in detail and reports that he was not told to be silent, only more discreet: "Hanle mandado, según se dice, al padre fray Nicolás Bautista, que *no predique* al rey *tan claro*, ni en el púlpito se arroje a decir verdades, sino que pues tiene audiencia a todas horas, se las diga en secreto, que lo demás es dar ocasión al pueblo de sentimientos y mover sediciones" (2:172).

Saavedra Fajardo maintains that the secret is in the way one presents truths to the king. He roundly condemns servile flattery, which he considers equivalent to poison for the monarch, and recommends "sugar-coated" honesty.[10] His disquisition on Emblem 48, "Sub lvce lves" (443–456), could function as a theoretical explanation of Calderón's procedure in the mythological plays. After a long disquisition on the dangers of flattery, he suggests the preferred method of revealing unpleasant truths to kings who do not like to hear them but will prefer truth to flattery if it is delivered gently, at the right time and in the right way:

Aun Dios las [verdades] manifestó con recato a los Príncipes, pues aunque pudo por Ioseph, y por Daniel notificar a Pharaón, y a Nebucodonosor algunas verdades de calamidades futuras, se las representó por sueños, quando estavan enagenados los sentidos, y dormida la Magestad, y *aun entonzes no claramente, sino en figuras, y geroglíficos*, para que interpusiese tiempo en la interpretación. . . . Conténtese el Ministro, conque las llegue a conozer el Príncipe, *y si pudiere por señas, no vse de palabras"* (452–453).

Calderón demonstrates the advantages of this discretion in *Fortunas de Andrómeda y Perseo*. Bato and his companions hold Perseo down to tell him of his dubious origins; Perseo listens transfixed but at the end becomes more violent than ever and attacks them ferociously for having the effrontery to tell him such ugly facts directly to his face. In contrast, Mercurio and Palas, in their divine wisdom, stage an elaborate dream to inform Perseo of his mother's seduction by Júpiter in such a way that he will "saberlo sin saberlo," as the mysterious offstage voices sing repeatedly. They want him to know of his illustrious ancestry so that he will be inspired to properly heroic action, but without a direct and public declaration that could be dangerous to Perseo and others.[11]

Carballo, in his poetics, *Cisne de Apolo*, published in 1602, names essentially the same need for discretion and a sweetened pill as a major reason for poets' use of figures and fables to present unpleasant truth not just to the prince but to the public at large (1:114–115). He adds another point important to the use of mythical figures in the court plays: "Fue otra razón el procurar huyr el odio y aborrecimiento, que como no ay ninguno que naturalme[n]te no le pese de que le digan sus vicios, y faltas, [los poetas] vsaron de representárnoslas en otras personas para que viendo las agenas costumbres, cayéssemos en cuenta de las nuestras" (1:118).

The difficulty of satisfying these contradictory demands (for laudatory yet truthful speech) is evident in the work of other poets of court spectacles, both Spanish and non-Spanish, in which references to the ruling monarch, explicit or implied, are almost universally celebratory.[12] Calderón, however, succeeded in creating such a polyvalent discourse. He did so by incorporating the context of the court play into the text of the event and by taking advantage of the conventional forms of the Spanish dramatic tradition in which the theatrical event was made up of several semi-independent pieces. These pieces could work both with and in opposition to the central play to create a polysemous total work proffering its contemporary spectators a minimum of three "texts" or readings of the total event. For the sake of convenience, I will call these the *text of royal power*, the *political text*, and the *particular text*, and will consider only the first two texts at this point, leaving discussion of the third for a subsequent chapter.

The text of royal power, the text fundamental to all court spectacles, was conveyed in two ways, the first the physical disposition of the theatre itself. Wherever the plays were presented, in the Coliseo of the Buen Retiro, the Salón Dorado of the Alcázar, or the open air, the viewing area was arranged so that the play on stage was one pole of the spectacle, while the royalty, seated on an elevated, well-lighted platform at the opposite end of the hall, constituted the other pole. The royal party occupied the spot where the perspective scenery created its most perfect illusion of reality. Other spectators were arranged hierarchically, the most notable closest to the king, and in such a manner that both poles of the spectacle were visible to them. As Orgel points out, what they took in was not simply the drama on stage but the more complex spectacle of observing the king watch the drama on stage, "and their response would not have been simply to the drama, but to the relationship between the drama and its primary audience, the royal spectator" (9).

Figures 11 and 12 show the seating for performance in two royal theatres. The type of arrangement shown in Figure 11 is described for a 1637 *particular*, or private performance, of a standard comedia. For the observer who describes it, the royal "box" is the primary spectacle and is in fact called a *teatro*, while the play represented on stage is an "accessory":

Tienen sus Magestades dos días en la semana, como de tabla, comedia en el Salón, a cuyo festejo se combida a su Alteza [la Princesa de Carignano], y a mí la ocasión de noticiar a las naciones, la Magestad y grandeza de respetos con que venera España sus Reyes, aun en lo retirado, y más doméstica atención de entretenimiento. Fórmase pues vn teatro, en cuyo frontispicio haziéndole espaldas dos biombos, se pone el sitial a su[s] Magestades, silla al Rey, y cuatro almohadas, a la mano izquierda a la Reyna, pusieron a su Alteza dos, si bien dentro dél, con reconocimiento el asiento,

Figure 11. Audience Arrangement in the Salón Dorado of the Alcázar.

83

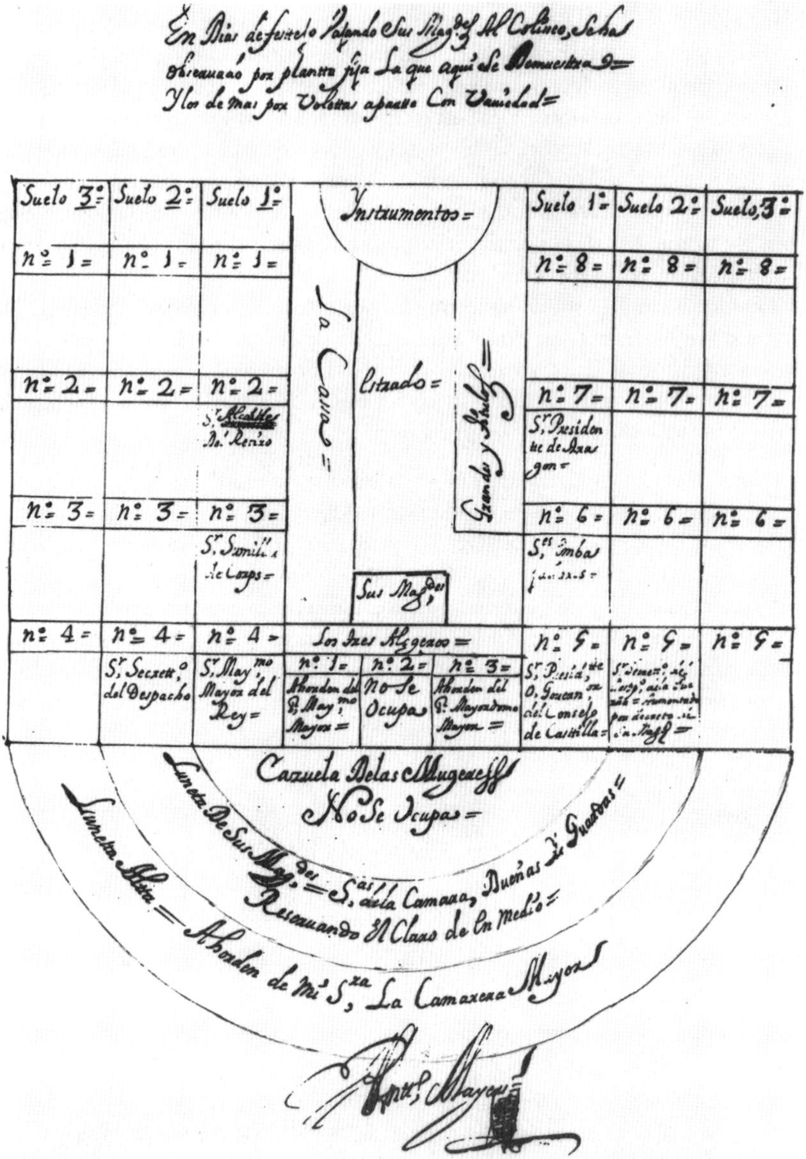

En Dias de ferreto Tofando Sus Magd: Al Coliseo, Se ha
de acauao por planta fija La que aqui se Demuestra =
Ylos de mas por Voletas aparte Con Vaniedad =

Suelo 3?	Suelo 2?	Suelo 1?	Instrumentos =		Suelo 1?	Suelo 2?	Suelo 3?
n? 1 =	n? 1 =	n? 1 =			n? 8 =	n? 8 =	n? 8 =
n? 2 =	n? 2 =	n? 2 = Sr. Alcalde No. Retiro	Citado =		n? 7 = Sr. Presiden te de Ara gon =	n? 7 =	n? 7 =
n? 3 =	n? 3 =	n? 3 = Sr. Semill de Corps =	Sus Magd		n? 6 = Srs. Emba jadores =	n? 6 =	n? 6 =
n? 4 =	n? 4 = Sr. Secreto del Despacho	n? 4 = Sr. Mayo Mayor del Rey =	Los Ires Algeaco =		n? 5 = Sr. Presie O. Gouan del Consejo de Castilla =	n? 5 = S. dimen ? de S. dimen ?	n? 5 =

Cazuela Delas Mugeres
No Se Ocupa =

Figure 12. Drawing of Seating in the Coliseo of the Buen Retiro.

84

que pudiesse ver su Alteza como en idea en los Reyes la representación, y por acessorio lo representado de la comedia. En los remates, que ya hazen espaldas al Real assiento tienen su lugar sus mayordomos mayores en pie, y por Grandes (que siempre lo son) cubiertos. La Camarera mayor en almohada, sin ella la Guarda mayor, y Dueñas de honor fuera del teatro, dentro dé diuididals [sic; dél divididas] a dos coros en orden sucessiuo, adornan los dos lados: las Damas y meninas galanteadas de Grandes, Títulos, Señores, y Caualleros de entrada, que por parte de afuera coronan el teatro en pie, y cubiertos los Grandes. En la fachada los Mayordomos tócandole al de semana las órdenes, despejo y entrada. . . .[13]

Most of Calderón's court-spectacle plays were performed in the Coliseo of the Buen Retiro, a theatre specially designed for machine plays, begun in 1638 and finished in 1640. As Figure 12 (a drawing from the end of the seventeenth-century) demonstrates, it was a horseshoe-shaped theater, with three tiers of boxes all the way around.[14] Although a special box had been constructed for the royal party on the second level opposite the stage, they sat instead on a raised and richly canopied platform farther forward in the horseshoe, the best point for viewing the perspective scenery. The description of the performance of *Hado y divisa de Leonido y Marfisa* depicts the sumptuous appointment of the royal dais. "Este se cubrió de riquísimas alfombras, que felices lograron mantener un camón de brocado encarnado, fundadas sus puertas en doradas molduras, cuyos cuatro lados terminaban ramilleteros de oro, prosiguiendo la techumbre con diminución de las propias molduras y brocado, y rematando en un bellísimo florón de oro. Estaba cubierta esta luciente esfera de una brillante nube: que con razón se puede llamar así a vista de la luz que había de tener dentro" (356). Other nobles and diplomats were arranged in the surrounding boxes or stood along the sides, as the diagram indicates.

The importance of the monarchs was further accentuated by the solemn and elaborate ceremonial accompanying entry to and exit from the performances. Numerous spectators described the ceremony; the following is a description by François Bertaut of the royal presence at a performance in the Buen Retiro in 1659:

> Le Roi, la Reine & l'Infante sont entrez après une de ces Dames, qui portoit un Flambeau. En entrant il ôta son Chapeau a toutes ces Dames, & puis il s'est assis contre un paravant, la Reine à sa main gauche, & l'Infante aussi à la gauche de la Reine. Pendant toute la Comédie, hormis une parole qu'il a dite à la Reine, il n'a pas branlé ni des piés, ni des mains, ni de la tête; tournant seulement les yeux quelques fois d'un côté & d'autre, & n'aiant personne auprès de lui qu'un Nain. Au sortir de la Comédie, toutes ces Dames se sont levées, & puis après sont parties une à une de chaque côté, & se joignant au milieu comme des Chanoines, que quittent leurs Chaises

quand ils ont fait l'Office. Elles se sont prises par la main & ont fait leur
Révérences, qui durent un demi quart d'heure & les unes après les autres,
sont sorties, pendant que le Roi a été toujours decouvert.

A la fin il s'est levé, & a fait lui-même une Révérence raisonnable à la
Reine en a fait une à l'Infante, & se prenant aussi, ce me semble, par la
main, elles s'en sont allées (qtd in Varey, "L'Auditoire" 90).

This entry ceremony also required careful advance stipulation of which doors
were to be used by which household officials.[15] This elaborate theatrical entry
focused all eyes on the royal spectators and constituted, in effect, the first "act"
of the spectacle.

Both royal and nonroyal spectators were greeted by a handsome stage curtain
that intertwined symbols of gods of classical myth with others representing the
Spanish monarchy and the names of the royal spectators. The curtain for *Fieras
afemina Amor* featured Mercury, Hercules, and Cupid, along with a lion and a
tiger signifying "el valor y la osadía," "courage and daring" (529); on that for *Las
fortunas de Andrómeda y Perseo*, the names of Felipe, Mariana, and María Teresa
were written in large silver letters, interspersed between "florones coronadas"
under a figure of the sun and the motto GENERAT OMNIA. The curtain for *Hado
y divisa de Leonido y Marfisa* displayed the motto AD NULLIUS PAVET OCCURSUM
above a medallion figuring in gold the Spanish coat of arms, a lion resting on a
globe, with a cross, scepter, and sword, and around his neck, the golden fleece,
symbol of the Hapsburg monarchs. On a banner below the medallion the names
of the royal newlyweds, Carlos II and Marie Louise d'Orléans, were woven
about with flowers and cupids (356).

The loa that opened the onstage action raised the celebration of the royal
family to a new pitch, as elaborately costumed actors and actresses, often flying
in on stage machinery, proclaimed the centrality of the monarchs to the kingdom and to the entire universe. The queen was the sun whose light was essential
to all life in the kingdom, from delicate flowers to her human subjects (*Andrómeda y Perseo* ff.2–5); Felipe IV was "el cuarto planeta," "Apolo destos valles,"
(*El golfo de las sirenas* 618); or Atlas carrying the weight of the world on his
shoulders (*Andrómeda y Perseo* ff.7–10). Mariana is again central to the loa for
Fieras afemina Amor, which consists primarily of a musical competition between
the twelve months of the year, with their associated zodiacal signs, for the title
of most important month. Since the occasion for the performance was her 22
December birthday, December wins the laurels because its generally sunless days
saw the birth of the royal sun, Mariana, "a suplir del sol la ausencia" (531). The
message proclaimed by this and other loas for court plays is that of an entire
universe, and/or all time, come to pay homage to the reigning Hapsburg kings.

Thus the ceremonial framework of the Calderonian court spectacular publishes the text of royal power, glorifying the monarchs by linking them to divin-

ities. Heroic or divine genealogies can be a two-edged weapon, however, as Judith Shklar has pointed out. Divine ancestors or associates are the ultimate source of honor; conversely, vulgar ones are a source of disgrace, as the common language of insults reveals. "It is because origins can glorify that they can also defame. . . . Since Hesiod's day the myth of origins has been a typical form of questioning and condemning the established order, divine and human, ethical and political" (Shklar 129–130). The central text of Calderón's play can therefore reverse the king-god equation and construct the two- or three-act drama on the very human frailties of those divinities, failings that not so coincidentally are also characteristic of the royal spectators.

In the case of Calderón's first extant court spectacle, *El mayor encanto, amor,* we cannot give the specifics of the glorifying framework because we have neither the loa nor a detailed ex post facto description of the performance. What has survived, however, is an undated memorandum in which Cosimo Lotti proposed the subject and plot, and described the scenery and machinery to be employed.[16] Having seen this proposal, Calderón wrote a letter on 30 April 1635 (Rouanet), rejecting the plot as outlined by Lotti (see Chapter 1). Since Calderón did employ in one form or another a substantial number of the effects Lotti proposed, particularly at the opening of the play, we may use his memorandum as at least a foundation for speculation.

The play was performed on an island built in the middle of the large lake in the Buen Retiro gardens.[17] Under the circumstances, the opening ceremony would certainly have taken advantage of the marine environment, so it may have followed Lotti's suggestion that the festivities open with the arrival on the lake of a large silver chariot carrying the goddess Agua from whose head and dress and an urn she carried ran a variety of water fountains. The chariot was to be pulled by two giant fish spouting water from their mouths and accompanied by a chorus of twenty nymphs who were to come barefoot, singing and playing, over the surface of the water. As this procession drew nearer, the lights on the theatre were to go up until the whole machine came to a halt before the royal couple and the goddess Agua opened the loa. This concluded, the musical aquatic procession was to leave as it had entered.[18] The play then opens, in Lotti's memorandum and Calderón's text, with the arrival by ship of Ulises and his companions.

The basic plot of the play is that of Ulises' relationship with Circe: While his men are converted to animals, he first overcomes her magic, then succumbs to love for her, and finally, reluctantly responds to the call of his martial duty and leaves the island. She, in fury, destroys her sumptuous palace, which sinks below the stage, and in its place springs up a flame-throwing volcano.[19] Calderón adds to the basic story a double subplot in the form of Arsidas, a prince of Trinacria also in love with Circe, and a pair of faithful lovers, Flérida and Lísidas, whom Circe has turned into trees but returns to their human form at Ulises' request;

they thereafter serve to complicate the plot, as the proud Circe charges Flérida to court Ulises in her stead and Lísidas becomes predictably jealous. The play is pleasing and logical in its development, with spectacular effects well integrated into the story line, and seasoned with a good deal of humor in the antics of two graciosos, Lebrel and Clarín.[20] When read out of its historical context, however, it can seem strangely flat, as Calderón presents the issue of Ulises' enchantment by Circe without apparently developing its moral implications with the profundity he demonstrated in his *auto* on the same story, *Los encantos de la culpa.*[21] Several years ago, I speculated that this apparent superficiality was due to Calderón's reluctance to develop the issues precisely because of the contemporary criticism of Felipe IV for his multiple love affairs (*Prometeo* 172). Recently, however, De Armas (*Astrea*) has collected historical data that enable us to see that Calderón was in fact quite daringly pointed in his application of the story to the political situation of the moment.[22]

Calderón's play is in a number of ways closely matched to its particular moment: It is a story about the enchantment of love, written for Midsummer Night's Eve, traditionally associated with lovers; the play, set in the magnificent palace and gardens of Circe, was performed in the gardens surrounding the controversial new Buen Retiro palace; and the drama ends with Circe's palace destroyed and replaced by flames, recalling spectacularly the bonfires traditionally built on St. John's Day to ward off dragons, witches, and evil spirits (De Armas, *Astrea* 141).

The link between royalty and Circe's enchantment is made in the first scene. Exploring the strange woods of the island, Ulises and Clarín encounter a "squadron of wild beasts," who to their amazement kneel at the men's feet and attempt to warn them to put back out to sea immediately. Significantly, the "king" of this enchanted pack is a "crowned" lion:

> el rey de todos ellos
> El león, coronado de cabellos,
> En pie puesto, una vez hacia las peñas,
> Y otra hacia el mar, cortés nos hace señas.
> ¡Oh generoso bruto,
> Rey de tanta república absoluto!
> ¿Qué me quieres decir cuando a la playa
> Señalas? Que me vaya,
> Y que no tale más el bosque donde
> Tienes tu imperio? A todo me responde,
> Inclinada la testa,
> Con halagos firmando la respuesta.
> Creamos pues al hado;
> Que un bruto no mintiera coronado (391).

The lion is not only the traditional king of beasts but also central to the coat of arms of the Spanish monarchy and, as we have seen, a standard symbol for the king on the curtain and in the loa of court performances. Even what Jonson called a "thick-eyed" spectator could therefore be expected to make the connection between this enchanted animal, kings in general, and Felipe in particular.

The more telling connections, however, are those between Circe's gardens and palace and the Buen Retiro, and between Felipe and Ulises. Even without the linking framework of the loa, which may have provided more clues, contemporary residents of Madrid would surely have seen the parallels.[23] Had the spectators not made the connection between the new royal pleasure palace and Circe's abode when the text and scenery first presented it, they were nudged toward that association by Circe's reference to "el retiro / de mi palacio," which she promises will be for Ulises:

> Selva si de Amor y Venus,
> Deleitoso paraíso,
> Donde sea todo gusto,
> Todo aplauso, todo alivio (394).

Shortly before the performance of the play, satirical pieces had been circulating in Madrid criticizing the king for luxuriating in entertainments when the country was at war.[24] One spoke mordantly of the king of France on campaign and the king of Spain in retreat ("en el Retiro") (De Armas, *Astrea* 142; Brown and Elliott 196). Another uses the same pun on "retreat/Retiro" to say the king should instead be doing solitary penance for the sins that have turned heaven against his country and brought on such disasters (Deleito y Piñuela 199). The association between Felipe and Ulises would therefore be made clear as the musicians sang:

> Olvidado de su patria
> en los palacios de Circe
> vive el más valiente griego
> si quien vive amando, vive (402).

Antistes, the one soldier from Ulises' troop who escaped Circe's spell, laments his leader's frivolous occupation in terms similar to the satirical pieces':

> Ulises, pues, sin recelo
> sólo de sus gustos trata
> siempre en los brazos de Circe
> y asistido de sus damas
> en academias de amores,
> saraos, festines y danzas (404).

The spectators witness Ulises' loss of will and moral strength. In the first act, he is a resolute leader who defeats Circe's first charmed potion with the help of magic flowers sent by Juno and lingers in her realm only to rescue other victims of her magic;[25] by the second, he has entered into the sophist debates of the "academia de amor" on such topics as whether it is more difficult to feign love or affect disdain. These debates were regular features of pastoral literature, and to judge by their frequency in the comedia, they were apparently well received on stage too. But in other court dramas, such as *Eco y Narciso*, Calderón assigns them to minor characters whose role as rejected suitors makes them pathetic if not comic figures. To see Ulises participating in such debates certainly lessens his heroic stature, even before he succumbs to his own argumentation (he has taken up Circe's command that he feign love for her) and falls in love with the sorceress. By Act III, when Circe's love prevents Ulises from responding to a call to arms, the specter of Aquiles hurls the ultimate insult at him, "afeminado griego" (409).

The issue of the moral conduct of the monarch was not viewed as a trivial or personal question but as a matter of importance to the state. Seventeenth-century Spaniards attributed the perceived decline of the empire to one of two causes: the natural cycle of growth and decline of all organisms, including powerful states; or divine will. By the second explanation, the repeated disasters befalling Spain were evidence of God's displeasure, and the only remedy was moral regeneration of the nation, beginning with the court. As Elliott puts it: "This direct equation between national morality and national fortune was one that weighed heavily on the rulers of Spain, who had been taught to consider themselves personally responsible for the defeats and the sufferings of the peoples committed to their charge" ("Self-Perception" 47). Felipe himself, as he confessed repeatedly in letters to Sor María (*Cartas*), felt that the rebellion of subject territories, the deaths of his legitimate heirs, the dearth of good political and military leaders, and other disasters were divine punishment for his sins. Emblem 60 of Saavedra Fajardo (601–602) names "incontinence and lust" of the monarch as the worst illness for the republic and the origin of sedition, dynastic changes, and the downfall of princes.

The "political text" available in the play is not limited, however, to a critical parallel between the enslavement to pleasures and passion of Ulises and Felipe IV. A corollary concern in Spain was Felipe's surrender of effective control of the nation's affairs to his *privado*. It was believed that Olivares deliberately provided the king with unending rounds of entertainment to distract his attention from affairs of state; furthermore, Olivares was said to encourage the king's weakness for women and even to prowl the streets of Madrid with him at night in pursuit of new romantic adventures (Brown and Elliott 32). The new palace of the Buen Retiro was facetiously referred to as the "gallinero" (Brown and Elliott 59–60) not only because it had previously been the site of Olivares's aviary but also because of the number of nonfeathered beauties it was reputed to house for the king's pleasure.

Furthermore, popular opinion held Olivares guilty of employing sorcery to increase his sway over Felipe.

> The president of the Royal Council investigated in . . . [1622] the claims of a Leonorilla that certain philters she was selling were "los mismos que el conde de Olivares daba al rey para conservar su privanza" "the same ones that the Count of Olivares gave to the king to preserve his position."[26] According to some, Olivares had no need for philters. His magic powers were derived from a spirit in the *muletilla* [cane] he always carried with him because of his gout (De Armas, *Astrea* 144).

Olivares's use of the occult appears in at least two other plays, and he is satirically linked to Circe in Quevedo's *La hora de todos* (De Armas, *Astrea* 144). Since the construction of the Retiro was a pet project of Olivares's, a court audience could be expected to link Circe's palace with that built by the conde-duque, and the mythical sorceress with the political one, particularly when in the play a foreign invasion is announced and Circe's first concern is to keep Ulises in ignorance of the event:

> Calla, calla, no prosigas
> ni lleguen ecos marciales
> a los oídos de Ulises:
> Aquí tengo de dejarle
> sepultado en blando sueño
> porque el belicoso alarde
> no pueda de mi amor nunca
> dividirle ni olvidarle (407).

Calderón's desire to link Circe's palace and the Buen Retiro is as tellingly evidenced in what he omits from the play as in what he includes, as De Armas points out (*Astrea* 142–143). Lotti's memorandum included an old giant dressed as a hermit, who was to personify the Buen Retiro (because it was built on the grounds of the monastery of San Jerónimo and included several small hermitages in its gardens). Ulises was to embrace this figure, signifying his choice of virtue over lust—and clearly separating Circe's palace from that of the conde-duque. Calderón uses the giant figure, but in a very different way.[27] The giant Bruta-monte is a creature in Circe's orbit whom she sends to torment Clarín for his insults to her. He says of Circe, "su obediencia / Atadas mis manos tiene" (399). The huge if somewhat ramshackle Buen Retiro was developed as the royal pleasure palace in large part because it was a site Olivares could have directly under his control. Other possible sites had disadvantages, as Brown and Elliott demonstrate (55–62): the lovely Palace of Aranjuez, thirty miles to the south, was too far away from the capital to serve as a showcase for the king; the nearby Pardo was valuable primarily as excellent hunting country, which would be ruined by other uses; the gardens of the Casa de Campo were associated with the previous privado, Lerma, whose family held its governorship in perpetuity. In the early 1630s, Olivares's program for royal patronage of the arts was beginning to bear fruit, but too many of the festivities were taking place in someone else's garden. When the expansion of the Royal Apartment at San Jerónimo began,[28] Olivares secured for himself and his successors the governorship of the "house and gardens and other things that might be added to the site for recreational purposes" (qtd in Brown and Elliott 57). The public in general considered the Retiro the conde-duque's palace, a device for bewitching the king, and they opposed the Retiro not only for the vast expense of its construction but because it symbolized the Olivares government. The audience could not have appreciated the significance of Calderón's Brutamonte since only the few palace officials who had seen Lotti's memorandum could know that Calderón transformed the giant symbolizing the Buen Retiro to a slave of Circe-Olivares. For subsequent readers who can juxtapose the two uses of the giant, however, this metamorphosis is a telling indication of the dramatist's intentions.

Contemporary spectators could appreciate, however, a comic parallel insistently repeated in the play by which Calderón links Circe's control over the gracioso Clarín with her enslavement of Ulises. She turns the comic lackey into a monkey, and in the last lines of the scene, Clarín comments: "¡Hombres monas! Presto habrá / otro más de vuestra especie" (1617). Clarín exits, to be replaced immediately by Ulises, who follows Circe's command to feign love for her, only to find to his dismay that his love for her is no pretense. Clarín coins a new word for his own state, calling himself "enmonado," "made a monkey."[29] Only two letters separate his condition from that of Ulises, who is "enamorado," "in love." Calderón underlines the link by closely juxtaposing the appearances of the "enmonado" and the "enamorado," and cements it by the following exchange between Ulises' and Clarín's closest friends, Antistes and Lebrel:

ANTISTES: Dime, Lebrel, ¿dónde está? . . .
LEBREL: ¿La mona? No sé: ¡ay de mí!
ANTISTES: Ulises, te digo (1629).

Clarín regains his human form when he sees himself in a mirror. This symbolic instrument of self-knowledge serves to cure various forms of bestiality in Calderón's myth plays: to free Mars of his passion for Venus in *La púrpura de la rosa* (2209); to kill Medusa in *Fortunas de Andrómeda y Perseo* (f.81); and to demonstrate his savage appearance to Hercules in *Fieras afemina Amor* (2069). The "mirror" that rouses Ulises from his bestial enslavement to passion is the sight of Aquiles' arms and the latter's command that Ulises remember his duty.

Before resorting to this mirror, Ulises' loyal follower Antistes has tried several stratagems. First, he tries sounding the trumpet of war, which touches Ulises' soul and arouses him to the call to duty; but Circe's siren song of love has an even more powerful hold on him. Antistes then tries direct speech:

ANTISTES: (*Ap.* Aunque me cueste la vida,
　　　　　Tengo de hablar claramente.)
　　　　　Ulises, invicto griego,
　　　　　¿Cómo cuando así te llama
　　　　　La trompeta de la fama,
　　　　　En delicioso sosiego,
　　　　　Sordo yaces? ¿Cuánto yerra,
　　　　　No sabes, el que rendido
　　　　　A su amor, labra su olvido?
　　　　　¡Oye esta voz!
GRIEGOS (*dentro*):　　¡Guerra, guerra!

When Ulises fails to respond to this feigned call of war and to a subsequent real invasion (turned back by the women), his followers leave Aquiles' arms before the sleeping "enamorado" in the hopes that "Quien no creyó la voz, crea / Las insignias del valor" (408). Another soldier speaks to the arms (and also to Felipe IV) as he exits:

　　　　　Volved por vos, y entre viles
　　　　　Amores no os permitáis
　　　　　Empañar, pues aun guardáis
　　　　　El muerto calor de Aquiles (408).

As Ulises awakens and sees the arms, he says they have come too late; then, amid drums, trumpets and flames, the ground opens and spits forth a sepulchre, on which sits the veiled shadow of Aquiles. He pulls back the veil and tells Ulises why he has come:

　　　　　A cobrar vengo mis armas,
　　　　　Porque el amor no las juzgue
　　　　　Ya de su templo despojo,
　　　　　Torpe, olvidado é inutil;

　　　　　. . . . .

　　　　　Y tú, afeminado griego,
　　　　　Que entre las delicias dulces
　　　　　Del amor, de negras sombras
　　　　　Tantos esplendores cubres;
　　　　　No entre amorosos encantos

CHAPTER THREE

> Las tengas y las deslustres;
> Sino rompiendo de amor
> Las mágicas inquietudes,
> Sal de Trinacria. . . . (409)

Aquiles then sinks from sight, warning Ulises that if he does not follow the martial destiny the gods appointed for him, he will have to answer to another judgment that will come in lightning, thunder, and ashes.

Ulises does respond and prepares to flee as Lebrel comes out lamenting the disappearance of the monkey, thus underlining one more time the "enmonado-enamorado" parallel. Lebrel asks Ulises what he is fleeing, and he says, "de mi mismo;" "que hoy / Es huir acción ilustre, / Pues los encantos de amor / Los vence aquél que los huye" (409).

Circe, citing again the beneficent but limited protective power of the flowers sent by Juno (quite possibly a figure for Queen Isabel), charges the marine gods to sink Ulises' departing ship, but Galatea arrives in a dolphin-pulled chariot to calm the seas,[30] and Circe destroys herself, sinking the palace in flames and freeing all the captive spirits. The six-hour spectacle ended at one in the morning with a dance signifying the restoration of harmony on land and sea.[31]

Calderón's staging of this story provides an interesting contrast with *Le Balet comique de la Roine* of Beaujoyeulx, a 1581 landmark in the development of the ballet de cour which also employs the Circe myth. As both Figure 13 (Figure de la Salle) and Beaujoyeulx's description make clear, this ballet involved the king in the performance as one pole of the conflict, both physically and dramatically. Evil and disorder were personified on stage by Circe, while Henri III at the opposite end of the hall represented the order and good of a strong monarch. Circe, who controls all change in the universe and all human desire for change, fears only one adversary, the king of France, "possessor of all virtuous attributes" (21). The movable action takes place at various points around the hall, and when the defeated Circe comes to surrender her wand and sit at Henri's feet at the end of the drama, it clearly symbolizes that he has prevailed in the battlefield that is France.[32]

Calderón's play also puts the king figuratively on stage—not as one pole of the dramatic conflict but as the battlefield itself. If Aquiles' arms served to awaken Ulises to his duty, what was to serve as the mirror to recall Felipe IV from amorous pursuits to active control of the affairs of state? The play itself, which clearly publishes the popular criticism of the king's degradation, but does so in the most palatable form, coating the criticism with generous doses of humor and spectacular brilliance.[33]

Figure 13. Baltasar de Beaujoyeulx. *Balet comique de la Roine.*
Figure de la Salle.

FOUR

The Problem of Don Juan José

THE MAJORITY of Calderón's court spectaculars date from the 1650s and 1660s, by which time the concern for Felipe's subordination to Olivares had disappeared with the conde-duque's downfall in 1643 and subsequent death. The results of the king's love life remained, however, very much present in the person of Don Juan José de Austria. Felipe's illegitimate son was variously considered a major problem for the monarchy or its best hope for salvation, and we find him in both roles in Calderonian court plays.

Felipe IV, unfamiliar with genetic explanations of the effect of inbreeding, considered it a punishment for his sins that almost all of his legitimate offspring died within months or hours of birth, while numerous royal bastards thrived.[1] The only one of these children whom Felipe officially recognized was Don Juan José, born in April of 1629 to the actress María Calderón, then Felipe's mistress. "La Calderona," as she was generally known, entered a convent soon after her son's birth. Don Juan was baptized as "Juan hijo de la tierra" and brought up away from the court, in Ocaña, by able guardians and tutors.[2] Inheriting his mother's dark curly hair and his father's blue eyes, he was a handsome, energetic, and intelligent individual, and Felipe recognized him as his illegitimate son in May 1642, giving him the title Serenidad. Capdet and Flecniakoska suggest that it was no coincidence that in that same year, two comedias appeared about his famous precedesor, Don Juan of Austria, hero of the battle of Lepanto:[3] "Le bâtard royal élevé, lui aussi en secret, . . . sera-t-il le sauveur d'une cause nationale à venir? A dire vrai l'Espagne de 1642, et depuis un certain temps déjà, a bien besoin de redorer son blason militaire, fut-ce par l'action d'un bâtard: elle a pratiquement abandonné les Flandres, elle a perdu le Portugal en 1640 et cette même année 1642 elle est amputée du Roussillon. Un bâtard royal vaudrait mieux qu'un favori comme le Conde Duque de Olivares" (130). He was made a knight of the ecclesiastical order of San Juan the following year, with the title of Gran Prior of the order in Castilla and León, which had its seat in Consuegra, south of Toledo.

Never given to underestimating his own talents, Don Juan José surely aspired to equal the successes of his predecessor when he embarked on a military career at age eighteen. In 1647, he was named "Príncipe de la Mar," and in April sailed from Cádiz to Barcelona, capturing a French ship en route. Later that year, he took command of the fleet headed for Naples to put down an uprising in Mas-

Figure 14. Anonymous Spanish artist, seventeenth century. *Don Juan de Austria*. Monasterio de San Lorenzo de El Escorial.

saniello. Succeeding in this, he remained in Sicily as viceroy from 1648 to 1651. In 1650, he was named to the Consejo de Estado. On his return from Sicily in 1651, he assumed command of the campaign to end the Catalan separatist movement and brought it to a successful conclusion both militarily and politically as Kamen describes: "On 10 October 1652 the Conseller en cap of Barcelona came to offer the city's submission and prostrated himself at the general's feet. Don Juan refused to let him kneel and raised him up. It was a symbol of the generosity that was to win him the constant support of the Catalans" (Kamen,

97

Spain 330). He was subsequently named viceroy of Cataluña and consolidated a base of popularity in that territory that was to serve him well in later years.

Negotiation of the end of the twelve-year Catalan rebellion and the return of that important realm to the Spanish monarchy was a major accomplishment; Calderón one year later concluded *Las fortunas de Andrómeda y Perseo* with the refrain:

> Viua, viua la gala del gran Perseo
> que de Júpiter hijo merece serlo,
> Quando a padre tan grande
> ponen sus hechos
> con dos monstruos vencidos
> en paz dos Reynos (f.101).

The miraculous celebration is first explained by Bato, the comic bridge between the play and its audience, who says on seeing his friends emerge from the temple:

> Aunque me espanto de veros
> no me espanto de que haga
> Júpiter tales estremos:
> porque por grande que sea
> vn padre, no puede menos
> de hacer fiestas, viendo vn hijo
> que le ha puesto en paz dos Reynos (f.99).

The refrain is then sung by a heavenly chorus and repeated three more times by terrestial singers; the spectacle concludes, as we have observed, with a dance of rustically attired goddesses, celebrating the reestablishment of harmony on earth. Ending the drama with such a "peace treaty" is an alteration to the myth unique to Calderón and not one that could be construed to grow naturally from the story. Under the circumstances, it seems reasonably clear that Calderón intended to parallel Perseo's accomplishments with those of Don Juan José—and his royal father—in securing peace in Cataluña.

This figuring of Felipe and Don Juan José in Júpiter and Perseo may also explain another Calderonian alteration to the story—having Júpiter descend from heaven disguised as Cupid. This seems a rather superfluous innovation unless we remember that our first recorded instance of the appearance of the future Felipe IV (in this case, bodily, not figuratively) in a court spectacle took place in 1614, in Lope's *El premio de la hermosura*, when he was lowered on a cloud dressed as Cupid. Granted, nearly forty years had intervened, but if this royal theatrical debut was still common knowledge among courtly theatregoers, it would explain the use of the Cupid disguise in this play and the fact that

Calderón has him revert to this attire for his final celestial appearance. Júpiter himself explains the appearance as follows:

> Yo el festiuo parabien,
> de vuestro aplauso agradezco.
> Y en el trage de Cupido
> que fue mi disfraz primero,
> le recibo; por hacer
> de mis fineças acuerdo:
> como al fin primera causa
> de tan gloriosos efectos (f.101).

Júpiter points out that he has been "first cause" of "glorious effects," and this play does end with a spectacularly joyful celebration of heroism and harmony, only lightly qualified by the continued threatening presence of Discordia at Juno's side in the heavens. The immediate effects of Júpiter's amorous escapade were extremely theatening, however, as it unleashed a wave of jealousy that created a devastating monster in the form of Juno's jealousy. As Don Juan José (like Don Juan before him), Perseo was brought up in the country, and his paternity was silenced not to arouse the divine queen's wrath. Mercurio explains the case of their brother Perseo to Palas:

> . . . de Júpiter diuino
> hijo el infeliz Perseo
> hermano es nuestro. Y ya sabes,
> que por temor de los celos
> de Juno, no le declara:
> obligando sus despechos,
> a que en rústicos sayales
> le dege viuir muriendo (f.23–23v).

Any mention or support of him reminds her of the "dorada trayción" of her "adúltero esposo" (f.55v) and sets her ally Discordia at war against Mercurio and Palas because

> Por declarar el vastardo
> hijo de Iúpiter andan
> en oprobio de tus celos:
> pues si vna vez le declaran,
> sabrá el mundo que no estima
> tu mérito el que te agrauia (f.37v).

Mercurio and Palas call Juno their "madrasta," and Mercurio says that it was her pride, her "altibeces" (f.23v), that gave the infernal being Discordia a seat in their heavenly realm and keeps her there, "a pesar de todo el Cielo" (f.24). Felipe IV's first queen, Isabel, had resented Don Juan José at his birth, which preceded that of her son Baltasar Carlos by six months (Davies 68), and Mariana was later the prime source of opposition to him, not only from personal antipathy toward this handsome and popular royal bastard, but also because she saw him as a threat to her own sons, Felipe Próspero, born in 1657, and Carlos II, born in 1661 just five days after the death of his brother.

Although Calderón gives Juno's jealousy center stage, he also makes jealousy the universally active and destructive force in all threads of the action, even those not precipitated by Júpiter's lust for Danae. Danae says that her father Acrisio locked her up, not because of an oracle that had forecast his death at the hands of her son, as in the traditional story, but because he is "celoso" of Lidoro's love for her (f.43v).

The monster that would devour Andrómeda is also the product of divine jealousy, created by Nereo in response to the protest of the Nereydas and Venus, offended by Casiopea's boast that her daughter was more beautiful:

> Ofendiéronse las ninfas;
> que en tocando a esta materia,
> de más hermosa soy yo,
> no ay deidad que no lo sienta (f.28v).

The horror Medusa wreaks on the countryside is also the result of envy, jealousy, and lust. Calderón describes Neptune's first attraction to Medusa in a lovely Gongorine image of her combing her hair:

> . . . pues
> vn día que a la ribera
> del mar, a peynar salió
> el rubio ofir de sus trenças,
> embidioso al ver Neptuno
> que el ayre en su espacio tenga
> más bello golfo de ondas,
> (cuyos pielagos nauegan
> en vageles de marfil
> conchas de nácar y perlas,)
> pasó su embidia a deseo,
> si ya no a codicia necia,
> de presumir que podía
> enrriquecer su soberuia,
> con el oro de otras Indias
> más ricas, quanto más cerca.
> Amante pues suyo, no

> se valió de las fineças
> de rendido; que el amor
> de vn poderoso no ruega,
> quando puede la caricia
> valerse de la violencia (f.32–32v).

To have Medusa, he flooded Minerba's temple, and that goddess, offended by the sacrilege against her temple and honor yet frustrated because she could not take revenge against him, let her wrath fall on Medusa:

> no pudiendo dél vengarse,
> dispuso vengarse en ella:
> Que vn rencor que en el culpado
> no se satisface, queda
> siempre rencor hasta que
> en el que puede se venga (f.33).

This displacement of rancor was clearly applicable to the situation between the wandering Felipe IV, his wives, and his bastard children. In the traditional myth, Perseo's valor and skill, with the assistance of subordinate divinities, were sufficient to overcome the devastating effects of jealousy. And in 1653, in the wake of Don Juan José's success in Cataluña, the parallel could be celebrated with wholehearted rejoicing. Yet Calderón knew, and coming years would prove, that the underlying problem had not been resolved, and he left Discordia at Juno's side in the heavens, still injecting into the chorus of celebration their characteristic notes: *Juno*: "Qué rabia"; *Discordia*: "Qué tormento" (f.102v).

The power of their voices should not be overemphasized, however. Calderón in this play offers the audience a much more thoroughly positive outcome than in many of his later court spectacles, in which the requisite "happy ending" for a court drama is an obvious distortion of an otherwise tragic tale. Here the warning voice is at the end no more than a cautionary note in the happy celebration. Furthermore, Calderón blurs the allegorical reference to soften its pointedness and employs a tactful "divine" method of insinuation. His method of hinting at dangerous facts is akin to that of Mercury and Palas, who teach Perseo through a dream to "decirlo, sin decirlo" (f.21), rather than that of Bato, whose tactless barrage of truth about Perseo's origins earns the gracioso only a beating.

To lighten the weight of the implicit Juno-Mariana parallel, Calderón suggests in the flattering loa that even she, like Andrómeda, has suffered the effect of divine jealousy. The signs of the zodiac explain in song that the "accidente" (Mariana's illness) was the result of "alguna / Embidia . . . al ver /Aún más que nuestras estrellas / Las suyas resplandecer" (f.9v). Mariana can see herself portrayed therefore both as the victim of jealousy and its wellspring. Similarly, the dramatist draws in the loa a Perseo-Felipe link flattering to both members of the royal couple:

> Las fortunas de Perseo
> serán asunto, porque
> son afectos de vn amante
> que en riesgo a su dama ve (f.5v).

He is in fact careful to remove any negative king figures from the story. Acrisio never appears on stage, and Politides sends Perseo to fight the monster for his own benefit and that of his country, not so that the beast might dispose of him, as in the standard myth:

> . . . mi amor te ofrece
> darte exércitos y armadas
> con que vengues tus agrauios,
> y restituyas tu patria (f.53).

On the one hand, we might consider this blurring of reference points a politic discretion in the court's preferred dramatist. In more general terms, however, it is characteristic of his mature technique in the court spectacular. Correspondence between stage and court figures is rarely as precise as in *El mayor encanto, amor*, which was, after all, Calderón's first court play. His subsequent plays do not offer simplistic political allegory in which a mythic figure personifies a single vice or virtue and points at a particular figure in the court. Rather, in his most successful dramas he constructs actions that have a general fidelity to human nature and inserts clues that would tactfully steer a court audience toward certain political readings while maintaining a breadth of reference that prevents the drama's applicability from being anchored to one time and place.[4]

To understand this interpretative procedure, we can look to the semiotics of theatre for help in explaining how spectators make sense of what they see. Although the creation and communication of meaning in theatrical performances have yet to be satisfactorily described, we can state at least one basic fact: Even in the most realistic performances, the audience sees the stage action with a special kind of double vision that accepts and denies its reality. It accepts the actions on stage as a possible reality—not the actual experience of the actors playing the roles, who have their own existence as John Gielgud or Cosme Pérez, but of another "possible world," "a spacio-temporal *elsewhere* represented as if actually present for the audience" (Elam 99). The possible world of the drama is made accessible to the spectator by its overlap with his actual world (Eco, "Possible Worlds"; Elam 104); hence, the nature of this other possible world is necessarily conditioned by the particular experience of the spectators in whose minds it is constructed (Eco, "Semiotics" 115–117). In the specific context of a court representation, it is directly influenced by the conspicuous presence of the ruling figures, which, given the appropriate cues in the drama, would encourage a political interpretation as one possible world construct suggested by the action on stage. In the gardens of the newly constructed Buen Retiro, for example, Circe's palace clearly points toward Olivares's showplace, and in 1653, the story of a bastard son who had won popular acclaim for bringing "peace to two realms" suggests Don Juan José's recent successes.

Although we do not have a contemporary report making these readings explicit, we do have scattered evidence over the seventeenth century that the Spanish public identified fictional characters with court figures. Gómez de Liaño and Infantes have recently found in the Biblioteca Pública of Toledo a manuscript of a comedia by Diego Ximénez de Enciso, *Fábula de Criselio y Cleón*, which they believe was commissioned by the conde-duque (to whom it is dedicated) to justify the deaths in suspicious circumstances of the conde de Villamediana and don Baltazar de Zúñiga. It was generally believed that Felipe IV had ordered the assassination of Villamediana out of jealousy and offended honor, either because the latter was enamoured of the queen, Isabel de Bourbón, and had dared to declare his love publicly, or because the king and the count were competing for the attentions of a captivating Portuguese lady-in-waiting, Francisca de Tabora.[5] In the *Fábula*, "los nombres vagamente legendarios con que los personajes salen a escena no son más que un culto y alegórico revestimiento que apenas oculta a los personajes reales a que se refieren" (Gómez de Liaño and Infantes 490); should any doubt about their identity remain, however, the copyist of this manuscript entered by the list of characters not the actors who were to portray them but the initials of the court personalities they represented. Those figured in the play included: Júpiter–Felipe III; Criselio–Felipe IV; Cleón–conde-duque de Olivares; Alcino–conde de Villamediana; Glauco–don Luis de Haro; Amphílico–don Baltasar de Zúñiga; Nerea (whom both Criselio and Alcino loved)–doña Francisca de Tavara; Niove–doña María de Coutiño; and several others either left blank or not definitely identified by Gómez de Liaño and Infantes (490–491).

Although the luxuriant growth of legends around the life, loves, and death of Villamediana makes the separation of fact from fiction difficult if not impossible,[6] his fellow poets left a number of poetic epitaphs which attributed to his brazenly free speech in life his sudden, violent, and nearly speechless death, which left him time only to gasp, "Esto es hecho." Along with other daring acts and verses, he was thought to have courted danger with the spectacular "invención" *La gloria de Niquea*, which he wrote and financed (see Chapter 1). In this amateur piece played by the queen, the infanta, and ladies of the court, Villamediana cast the queen as Venus, the goddess of beauty, to whom he directed extravagant praise. He also lavished praise on Francisca de Tabora, the only participant who played two important roles, and the suggestion of her relationship with the young king is quite bold. Describing her first splendid appearance as the month of April, he says she was so beautiful that "la juzgaron los ojos por la Donzella Europa, amante robo del trasformado Iúpiter" (Villamediana 7). Her second appearance is as Lurcano, accused of faithlessness by Alvida (probably as an inside joke on Francisca de Tabora's reputed coquetry); Lurcano, a fickle Orfeo, ceases following his beloved into the flames of hell and instead falls in love with a beautiful deity, repeatedly referred to as a being far above Lurcano's station, a "Sol," or as some other figure that suggests the royal connection.

In the closing decades of the seventeenth century, Bances Candamo explicitly declares the political intentionality of his court plays, as Quintero (37) points out. Bances, a follower of the Calderonian model of theatre whom Wilson and Moir classify as the last important playwright of the century, was named official court dramatist in 1687, apparently the only dramatist accorded this honor in the seventeenth century (138). In his treatise on the theatre, *Theatro de los Theatros de los passados y presentes siglos*, he defines both his position and his didactic intention: "Me hallo elegido de su Magestad por su Real decreto para escribir unicamente sus festejos, y con renta asignada por ello, he juzgado tocarme por muchos títulos estudiar ex profeso cuanto pudiese conducir a hacer arte áulica y política la de festejar a tan gran Rei, cuios oídos se me entregan aquellas tres horas, siendo ésta una de las maiores confianzas que se pueden hacer de una doctrina" (qtd in Quintero 40). His most popular play, *Por su rey y por su dama*, uses a conveniently modified historical plot to urge Spanish cession of the Netherlands, while three other plays, *El esclavo en grillos de oro, Cómo se curan los celos y Orlando furioso*, and *La piedra filosofal*, allude clearly to the pressing problem of succession (Wilson and Moir 140–141). In his treatise, Bances spells out how he uses historical or pseudohistorical stories to teach a political lesson to his royal audience: "Son las comedias de los Reyes unas historias vivas que, sin hablar con ellos, les han de instruir con tal respeto que sea su misma razón quien de lo que ve tome las advertencias, y no el ingenio quien se las diga. Para este decir sin decir, quien dudará sea menester gran arte" (qtd in Quintero 42). Calderón's Mercurio and Palas in *Las fortunas de Andrómeda y Perseo* use virtually the same words, "a decirlo, sin decirlo" (f.21, 25), to describe the diplomatic art of discussing controversial truths; as Bances says, the idea was to set the message before the powerful in such a sweetened or veiled form that they would embrace it through their own reasoning processes and not focus resentment on the author of the political allegory. This was the method of political counsel that Calderón modeled in his court spectacles for his successor on the court stage, Bances Candamo.[7]

Even in plays not written with a specifically political intent, audiences of the period were known to construct political readings in suggestive circumstances. In 1668, the audiences in the public theatres in Cataluña (a stronghold of support for Don Juan José in his campaign for power after the death of Felipe IV) applauded with great vigor performances of a mediocre play, *Lo que merece un soldado*, about a heroic illegitimate son who earns a throne with his sword. They celebrated in particular the passages that resembled Don Juan José's situation and redoubled their applause on one afternoon when he and his party attended the performance (Maura, *Corte* 1:388).

Outside of Cataluña, however, the acclaim for Don Juan was by the 1660s far from unanimous. From 1661 to 1664 he was commander in chief of the forces attempting to end the Portuguese rebellion, and his lack of success in that campaign diminished his father's enthusiasm for this bastard son, and that of significant sectors of the public. A substantial portion of the nobility in particular had resented his sudden elevation and were further exasperated by instances of pretentious behavior and his insistence that he be accorded courtesies due to legitimate royal sons.[8] While Don Juan pressed for further recognition and greater power, Felipe denied his petitions and kept him away from the court. When he returned to Spain from Flanders to prepare the Portuguese campaign in 1661, he was not allowed to reside in Madrid but at a more discreet distance in El Escorial (Maura, *Corte* 1:185). In 1663, he threatened to resign his command of the Portuguese effort unless he was granted the title Infante, made first minister, and given the right of free access to the king, but after consultation with his ministers, Felipe denied the request, explaining privately that "el dictamen en que estoy es el empacho que me causaría el tener a D. Juan cerca de mi persona, manifestándose así más con ello las travesuras de mi mocedad. Pero esto no es para que él lo entienda, sino para que lo reservéis en vos y quedéis respondido en este punto."[9] After Felipe's death, the Junta de Gobierno, left in charge again, denied Don Juan the right to live in Madrid because his presence would be the cause of "conflicts and competition" and his previous pretensions had exhibited his "genio ambicioso y audaces pensamientos" (Maura, *Corte* 1: 232). Whereas Don Juan had left for Portugal supported by the hopes of all, the sympathy of the majority and the praise of poets, the Almirante de Castilla subsequently penned a less flattering portrait:

> Sólo tiene una señal
> de nuestro Rey soberano:
> que en nada pone la mano,
> que no le suceda mal.
> Acá perdió á Portugal;
> en las Dunas su arrogancia;
> dió tantos triunfos á Francia,
> que es cosa de admiración
> el dar tanta perdición
> en un hijo de ganancia (qtd in Maura, *Corte* 1:187).

The myths on which Calderón founded his linked plays *Apolo y Climene* and *El hijo del sol, Faetón* offered him an excellent vehicle for dramatizing the problem of Don Juan. As Ovid tells the story, when both were adolescents,

105

Epaphus, son of Jupiter and Io, challenged the boastful Phaeton's story that Apollo was his father. In order to prove his parentage, Phaeton persuaded a reluctant Apollo to allow him to drive the chariot of the sun for one day. He flew too close to earth, causing conflagration there, then mounted too high in the heavens, whereupon Jupiter struck him down with a lightning bolt, and he fell into the river Eridanus. From Garcilaso on, the story became a virtual cliché in Spanish poetry and drama for the dangers posed by excessive ambition, and Pérez de Moya in his *Philosofía secreta* had already interpreted the myth as a poetic metaphor for the need for experience in government and the relationship between fathers and sons:[10]

> Que los grandes imperios, y administraciones, y república, no se han de encargar a moços, ni a hombres de poco saber, mas a sabios y experimentados. Amonéstanos también que los hijos no menosprecien los consejos de los padres, si no quieren auer mal fin (f.85v).[11]

Furthermore, the scene of the fall of Faetón had recently been painted on a ceiling in the king's quarters in the Alcázar. In 1658, the painters Angel Colonna and Agustín Mitelli were brought from Italy to redecorate parts of that palace, and they decorated the three rooms of the *cuarto del verano* with scenes of Night, Aurora, and the fall of Faetón. Surviving drawings of the paintings indicate that the central scene on the ceiling would have been one of Apolo watching Faetón's fall from his chariot and that other episodes of the story were depicted in smaller lateral spaces, the first probably being that of Faetón kneeling before his father's throne as he makes his fatal request (Torrijos 296–297; Orso 70). Felipe was so fascinated with the work in progress and the *quadratura* technique of fresco painting that he climbed the painters' scaffolding to observe the work as closely as possible (Orso 70). With respect to paintings of another Apollo story, that of the punishment of the satyr Marsyas, Torrijos suggests that Felipe liked to see represented the just punishment of pride, the arrogance of the subject who would pretend to equal his lord (302).

By 1662, when these plays were produced, Don Juan's most recent activities did not lend themselves to a celebratory finale like that of *Las fortunas de Andrómeda y Perseo*.[12] Hernández-Araico has reason to describe the plays as a "tragic diptych," for Apolo's return to his throne in *Apolo y Climene* ends that play in "divorce" rather than marriage, as the gracioso points out, and *Faetón* concludes with the death of the hero, the conflagration of his country, and the marriage of the rival Epafo to his beloved Tetis. An early critic of the plays, Pierre Paris, found no tragic spirit in them, however. Sharing Menéndez y Pelayo's opinion of the mythological plays as "pièces qui sont évidemment d'ordre secondaire" (557), he thinks they are more like a fairy tale or opera, or perhaps even a parody, than comedy or true drama. He complains that Calderón's alterations of the myth demonstrate that he either did not know or did not sufficiently respect classical material. That Calderón did not take these works seriously or expect his audience to do so is proved, says Paris, by the fact that the gracioso concludes *El hijo del sol, Faetón* with the words "con que los bobos lo creerán" (570). Paris misrepresents both the complexity of Calderón's ambiguous ending of the play and the seriousness of his intentions in the work. As Tetis and Amaltea report how the grieving Climene and the náyades (Faetón's sisters) are turning into white poplars weeping tears of amber, Batillo says to the audience:

> Con que los bobos
> Lo creerán, y los discretos
> Sacarán cuan peligroso
> Es desvanecerse, dando
> Fin *Faetón, hijo de Apolo* (198).

Parker, in contrast to Paris, found in the plays a moving and richly symbolic dramatization of the tragedy of human life, which aspires toward divinity and perfect love but is condemned to failure by the materiality of the body ("Metáfora" 153–160). And Hernández-Araico in her recent article comes to the conclusion that in addition to the universal validity of their symbolism, these dramas offered the king a veiled lesson in the art of government.

Calderón's alterations to the classical myth, which Paris attributed either to ignorance or frivolity, are better explained as changes made to increase both the dramatic power of the story and its applicability to the problem of Don Juan José. Like Perseo, Calderón's Faetón has been brought up in the country in ignorance of his parentage, cared for by a guardian, the old Erídano, who found the cast-off child as a baby and gave him his own name, Erídano.[13] Amaltea, the flower goddess whose love Faetón rejects, constantly throws in his face both his illegitimacy and his pride. She criticizes old Erídano's upbringing of Faetón because

> . . . encontrándote sin más
> Padres que la desnudez
> De hijo espurio de los hados,
> Piadosamente cruel
> Te crió con tantas alas,
> Como dicen la esquivez
> Con que desdeñas deidad,
> A quien Júpiter después,
> Del imperio de las flores
> Dio la copa.

Don Juan was baptized as "Juan hijo de la tierra"; Faetón is, more poetically, "de las flores fruto," and as such he predicts the sudden elevation that both he and Don Juan receive as adolescents:

FAETÓN: Y pues de las flores fruto
              Somos los dos, yo al nacer
              Y tú al vivir, aprendamos
              Dellas. . . .
AMALTEA: ¿Qué hemos de aprender?
FAETÓN: Yo, que pueden ser mañana
              Pompas las que hoy sombras ves;
              Y tú, que hoy puedes ver sombras
              Las que eran pompas ayer.

The curse Amaltea then hurls after him foreshadows the tragic end of the play:

AMALTEA: ¡Oh plegue al cielo, cruel
             Falso, fementido, aleve,
             Sin lustre, honor, fama y ser,
             Villano al fin, mal nacido,
             Que esa soberbia altivez
             De tu presunción castigue
             Tu mismo espíritu! y que
             Della despeñado, digas. . . .
ADMETO (*dentro*): ¡Ay de mi infeliz! (177)

Erídano adopted another abandoned child, Epafo, who has grown up with Faetón as his "opuesto hermano" (175). Their rivalry has been intensified by the fact that they are both in love with Neptune's daughter Tetis. It is brought to a boiling point with the arrival of Admeto, king of Tesalia, who is hunting a "fiera" known to inhabit the surrounding woods. Faetón saves Admeto by stopping his runaway horse and protects Tetis from the "fiera," but fate conspires against him so that the credit for both feats goes to Epafo, and a chorus sings the ambiguous refrain:

             Los casos dificultosos
             Con razón son envidiados
             Inténtanlos los osados
             Y acábanlos los dichosos (180).

When Epafo, feeling guilty for having unduly received credit, comes to try to make peace with Faetón, that proud and hypersensitive youth refuses his offer with an explosion of bravado:

             No prosigas; que no quiero
             De ti hidalguía ninguna;
             Y antes, que goces, me alegro,
             Estos desperdicios míos.
             Y adelante, te aconsejo

> Que no me pierdas de vista,
> Para que, como yo haciendo
> Vaya heroicos hechos, tú
> Te vayas honrando dellos (181).

The two come to blows, Faetón seizes a dagger that Erídano carries, and when King Admeto sees it, he recognizes Epafo as his son and heir.

Don Juan José knew well the anger of seeing his accomplishments disputed. The conde de Oñate distributed publications claiming all credit for the pacification of Naples, and writers of other newsletters of the period also attributed it to that viceroy rather than Don Juan (Maura, *Corte* 1:180 n.2). Others said that his success in Cataluña was due more to luck and good timing than skill. As already noted, Don Juan was, like Faetón, both extremely ambitious and hypersensitive to any real or imagined slight. In Maura Gamazo's words:

> Aquel escrupuloso velar por las más menudas prerrogativas de su rango; . . . aquel perseguir el éxito, por el éxito mismo, sin ponderar el esfuerzo requerido ni el provecho posible; aquella ambición, no tanto de mando como de lucimiento, ni de ostentación tanto como de fama; aquel rodearse de astrólogos que desvelaran el porvenir ignoto; aquel continuo reclamar más títulos pomposos que substanciosos favores, síntomas fueron de la inquietud de su espíritu, afligido por la obsesión punzante de la mácula originaria, siempre en acecho del insulto en la omisión inocente, del desdén en la réplica cortés, de la ironía en el exagerado respeto, del retorno a la obscuridad de la infancia . . . (*Corte* 1:182).

In Flanders, he devoted considerable energy to securing preeminence in official acts and documents over the prince of Condé (serving Spain since the defeat of the Fronde), whom he considered his inferior because that Bourbon prince was less directly linked by blood to the throne. Condé retaliated by bestowing on Don Juan the nickname "Don Juanísimo." More serious was the fact that his sensitivity and desire for glory might push him, like Faetón, into ill-advised battles. Mazarin predicted in 1656 that "es de presumir que el Príncipe [de Condé] use de toda su habilidad para impulsar a D. Juan a presentar batalla cuantas veces pueda; y verosímil parece también que D. Juan consienta en ello, por la sed de renombre que le domina. La prudencia no le permite aún reflexionar sobre las desastrosas consecuencias que acarrearía a Flandes una derrota" (qtd in Maura, *Corte* 1:183). Calderón's Faetón similarly shows a proud sensitivity that makes a verbal insult outweigh a good turn. Epafo attempts to return the favor he owed Faetón by telling Admeto that Faetón has captured the "fiera," but all Faetón can hear is the aside in which Epafo addresses him as "villano" (188).

The *fiera* turns out to be Climene, who for her sin against Diana, the goddess of chastity, must live outside society in a cave from which she emerges only for food and water.[14] Although it seems rash to say that Calderón intended to draw a parallel between her and "La Calderona," who took refuge in a convent after the birth of Don Juan José, whether created with a conscious intent or not, the number of connections between their experiences are striking.[15] An Italian biographer of Don Juan José, Gregorio Leti, recounts the meeting of Felipe IV and María Calderón as follows:

> Studiando sempre più il Conte [de Olivares], di tenere il Re ingolfato nè vezzi e piaceri del senso, haveva dato ordine che si formasse in Madrid, una banda di comici delli più esquisiti della Spagna, per representar comedie alla presenza del Rè, e nel anno 1627, sendo venuta una compagnia di comedianti e trovandosi tra queste una comica di mediocre bellezza ma di rezzo singularisimo e d'una parola così grata e gratiosa, che teneva sospesi tutti i cuori di quelli, che l'ascoltano, onde non si tosto fu vista da Filippo su la scena questa comediante, detta la Calderona, che invaghitto delle sue fattezze, ordinò che se gli conducesse in camera, sotto pretesto di sentirla discorrere più da vicino; ed il Conte intesa la volontà reale, ne comandó l'essecutione, che successe di notte tempo, essendo stata condotta in secreto nella camera del Rè, di dove non si partì, che il giorno seguente (qtd in Maura, *Corte* 1:170 n.1).

Climene says Apolo first saw her "en este templo," which literally refers to the temple of Diana in which the scene is set; but the "templo" is in reality the stage of a royal theatre, as was that on which Felipe first saw La Calderona.[16] Apolo's sight of her led to feelings, feelings to sighs, and thence to plans, and, says Climene, to a man who would "inquirir / medios, ¿a quién le faltaron / tercero, noche y jardín?" By Leti's account, Felipe also availed himself of a "tercero" and cover of night. Leti makes the conde-duque instrumental in facilitating the affair to maintain his control of the king; in Calderón's drama, the facilitator who gives shelter to Climene is Fitón, akin to the Circe who earlier served to figure Olivares as a proud and manipulative magician. In *Apolo y Climene*, Fitón is a patently diabolical figure who encourages Climene not to fear Apolo's love because, he says, the fatal prophecy for her son can be averted; he then reveals to the audience that his assurances to her were a lie and that he is really using her affair with Apolo to confirm his own power over the universe.

Climene, pleading the shame of what she must say, exclaims: "¡Oh, si hubiera algún sutil / ingenio inventado frase / para decir sin decir!" Which is, of course, precisely what Calderón is doing. With a peculiar phraseology that would seem on the surface contrary to logic, Climene says that when Diana learned of the birth of Faetón, "me dio la investidura . . . / de su imperio, destinada / no sólo a ser desde allí / fiera, mas fiera de las fieras (190). Now, that Diana would punish a love affair of one of her followers is logical, but that she would do so by giving her "investidura" over her realm is not, unless Calderón meant it to suggest another sort of "investidura," that is, the habit and vow of chastity that La Calderona took after the birth of Don Juan José. Given the habit by the papal nuncio Pamfili, who later became Clemente X, she entered the convent of the Valle de Utande, in the Alcarria (Maura G, *Corte* 1: 180), and lived to be not "fiera de las fieras" in a forest but, according to Davies, "abadesa en un monas-terio de un apartado rincón de España" (68).[17]

On the baptismal certificate of "Juan, hijo de la tierra," neither the name of his mother nor his father appeared. And Climene, even when obliged to reveal the story of her relationship with Apolo, refuses to reveal that her son is Faetón (or Erídano, as he is then called) because "El dia que él sepa de sí / y quién es, será del mundo / la ruina, el estrago, el fin" (191). Faetón, who has already added up clues and realized that Climene and Apolo were his parents, protests in private to his mother that her silence is unfair to him, even in the face of such a threat, because the menace of the prophecy hangs over him whether or not his parentage is recognized and it is therefore unjust that he should be deprived of the honors due him: "¿No será injuria / vivir sujeto á sus sañas / sin sus ho-nores?" Climene still refuses on the grounds that recognition of his status affects not only him, but others: "No está / solo en ti la circunstancia, / sino en los demás" (192).

The question of Don Juan's recognition and consequent position in the power structure and relationship to the throne obviously affected the Spanish nation as a whole. There was a group more immediately affected by his rec-ognition, however, that is also recognized in this play. In a society in which the nobility had been quite effectively reduced to dependence on court favor, every post that went to Don Juan left a number of resentful aspirants in the courtyards of the palace. In Maura Gamazo's words: "Debía conocer él, ó sospechar al menos, las antípatias que entre los aspirantes desahuciados le granjeó su desig-nación para cada cual de los cargos obtenidos; pudo maliciar que, en el hormi-guero de codicias cortesanas, su inesperada presencia y su voracidad calificábanse de fraude, y que su posición ante el tablero político se asemejaba á la de un jugador de ventaja" (*Corte* 1:191). In *El hijo del sol, Faetón*, the principal prize in dispute is the favor of Tetis, who prefers Faetón, and Batillo suggests to Epafo, despairing after another rejection by her, that he buy an "esperanza." When Epafo says that would be good advice if there were a market for them, Batillo answers:

> ¿Luego no la hay? Tome y vaya
> Al terrero de palacio,

Verá cuán de lance la halla;
Que allí a cualquiera le sobra,
Porque ninguno la gasta.

Epafo, in anger, strikes Batillo, who passes the blow along to his companion Silvia and suggests that she in turn hit a tree because as he says, "Cada uno da donde puede / en descargo de su alma" (194). Disappointed nobles could do nothing against Felipe IV, but they could turn their resentment over Don Juan José's advancement against the bastard and his supporters, causing tensions and violence which would redound against all. Mazarin had earlier recognized the weakening of Spanish forces in Flanders by the rivalry between Don Juan and other generals, and events after Felipe's death would prove the full divisive force of his presence. In Calderón's play, Epafo, after hitting Batillo, goes on to plot with Amaltea a scheme for taking Tetis by force since he cannot have her any other way, and it is this kidnapping attempt that precipitates the final disaster for Faetón and Tesalia.

The resentment of the nobility was further aggravated by Don Juan's arrogance, as Barrionuevo reported:

Tiénese por cierto que [Don Juan] deja muy desafectos en esta Corte a todos los señores, por haberlos tratado con mucha superioridad, tanto, que porque no se cubriesen en su presencia los grandes de Castilla, los oía el señor Don Juan descubierto, y de aquí se hizo muy célebre una acción del señor duque de Cardona: que visitando a Su Alteza y viendo que no se cubría, le hizo ademán de que se cubriese y dándose Su Alteza por desentendido, Su Excelencia se cubrió y prosiguió la visita cubierto, y descubierto Su Alteza. Divulgóse el caso en la Corte y fue muy aplaudido de todo género de personas, diciendo con mucha gracia Su Excelencia a los demás señores grandes: "Vosotros sois grandes del Rey, y yo sólo soy el grande del señor Don Juan de Austria" (2:291).

Comments on Faetón's pride are constantly reiterated in the play, even by those most in his favor. Tetis calls him "Ignorado hijo del viento / (que sólo a tanta soberbia / él pudiera dar las alas)" (185). As Faetón puzzles over why he, "nacido en tanta miseria," should have a spirit so arrogant as to love that goddess, Batillo comments that it stems from "Poca vergüenza, / que es lo que tienen los que / como nacen no se acuerdan" (187). When he announces his discovery that he is "hijo del Sol," he is literally cast out of society, pushed out of the valley with cries of "Vaya el loco" (191).

Like Don Juan, Calderón's Faetón planned to turn to military service as a path to fortune, leaving with bitter words the homeland that spurned him:

Ingrata patria, decía,
Que fuiste cuna primera

De quien apenas nació
De ti, cuando nació a penas. . . .

. . . .

Si espurio aborto del hado
Me arrojaron a las puertas
De quien piadoso me dio
De hijo el nombre, sin que sepa
De mí más de que nací;
En cuya fortuna mesma
Naciendo Epafo, la dicha
Halló en un puñal envuelta,
Y tan grande, que admirada
Lo oyó Tetis en su esfera,
Pues ya príncipe Peleo,
Le da el reino la obediencia;
¿Qué mucho que yo, mirando
Mi suerte a la suya opuesta,
Ya que no la tengo hallada,
Buscada intente tenerla (185).

Faetón's search for his fortune finally takes him not on a military campaign but into the heavens where he is brought to the throne of Apolo himself. As he departs on his quest, however, Tetis calls "oracular" the voices of the unseen graciosos as they pronounce:

SILVIA (*dentro*):   ¡Mal haya
          Ambición, diré mil veces,
          Que a más de lo que es se ensalza!

          . . . .

BATILLO (*dentro*): Quien no sabe lo que pide,
          ¿Qué mucho, Silvia, que caiga
          O tarde o nunca en la cuenta? (193)

Apolo, with the ill-advised indulgence of parents who feel they have neglected their children, promises to grant whatever his son requests. Faetón asks of course to drive the chariot of the sun:[18]

Pues déjame que su carro
Hoy rija, para que triunfe
Tan de todos de una vez,
Que todos de mí se alumbren.

. . . .

Que hijo tuyo me acredita

113

Tu mismo esplendor, y suple
Tu persona la mía. . . (195)

This was precisely the ambition Don Juan's opponents feared: nothing less than driving the "chariot of state" as prime minister and perhaps even occupying the throne after his father's death.

Apolo tries to back out of his promise, warning Faetón that he is too inexperienced for the task, that the splendor will blind him, and that should he fail, "Todo el orden de la tierra / viviera contra costumbre / y al descender presumieras / que todo el cielo se hunde" (195). Unwilling to break his oath, however, Apolo finally yields control of the chariot, and Faetón comments: "A él y a tus plantas me eleva / más la ambición que la nube" (196). Yet as he crosses the heavens proving to all that he is indeed the son of Apolo, the prize Faetón most covets, Tetis, is kidnapped by his rival Epafo, now the Príncipe Peleo. Faetón sets the world ablaze in his attempt to reclaim her, and Júpiter strikes him from the chariot with a bolt of lighting. In a spectacularly staged scene of burning trees and huts, probably accompanied by the sound of thunder, Faetón falls from the chariot to earth, and the drama ends with the marriage of Tetis and Epafo, the contentment of his father, the earthly king figure Admeto, mourning by Galatea, the nayades, and Climene, and Batillo's final moral about the dangers of excessive ambition.

The lesson for Felipe IV was obvious: A similarly lenient concession to the exorbitant demands for status and power by Don Juan José might bring disaster to him and to the nation as a whole. Calderón provided a sweetener to this warning, however, in his additions to the role of Epafo. Paris scorned as superfluous fancy his baptism of this character with the name Peleo, traditionally considered the father of Achilles; in fact, it is Calderón's way of balancing the heroic stature of Faetón with an unvoiced prediction of future glory for his "opuesto hermano." While Faetón is, as Parker has pointed out, a very sympathetic figure in this play,[19] his rival is never painted as a repellant villain, only a rather weak young man subject to normal human failings and temptations who resorts to the violent and ignoble action of kidnapping Tetis when he cannot otherwise obtain her. This "newly born" prince stands in line to inherit the throne of Tesalia, as the four-month-old Carlos would that of Spain. His appearance is cause for great celebration among his future subjects. As Admeto leads the shouts of "¡Viva el príncipe Peleo!" Batillo explains to Silvia that "un príncipe basta a ser / alborozo de su reino" (183).[20] She then leads a chorus of dancing shepherds in a musical adoration:

El Príncipe nuestro
Es con su presencia
Lustre de los montes,

Honor de las selvas.
Venga norabuena.

Todos estos montes
Le den la obediencia
Y ciña de rosas
Su frente Amaltea.
Venga norabuena (186).

The loa Calderón penned for this performance also highlighted the hopes for the "tierno jazmín," Carlos.[21] This prologue, in which Calderón equates his service with a pen to that of a soldier with his sword, celebrates both the recovery of Felipe IV from illness and the recent arrival of the new prince. In structure, the loa is very similar to that with which he prefaced his last play, *Hado y divisa de Leonido y Marfisa*, as its second part centers on a genealogy of the royal couple focused on an onstage gallery of portraits of their ancestors. Historia and Poesía call up a variety of allegorical figures—Fe, Hermosura, Guerra, Prudencia, and so on, who point out the virtues of these royal forebears, joined in the union of Felipe and Mariana and their son Carlos whose name Fama is asked to write in bronze. She promises to do so, along with the good tidings "que crezca su tierna infancia / tan feliz como linda / de todas esas virtudes, / que heredero le apellidan" (329).

The loa begins and ends with a refrain whose royal referent is interestingly ambiguous. A hidden chorus, joined by Historia and Poesía, sings:

A la sombra del laurel
no temas, vasalla flor
del cierzo el soplo cruel
que presto vendrá el favor
del austro que inspira en él (317, 331).

The refrain is applied most directly to the "laurel,"[22] Felipe IV, whose health had been failing since 1658 when a severe chill he suffered while hunting in Aranjuez apparently led to the paralysis of his right foot and leg, and a first attack of the kidney trouble that plagued him with increasing frequency in following years.[23] The "cierzo" thus refers to the cold north wind thought to precipitate such attacks. It also provides the audience with the pleasure of a reference to local conditions because the play was performed in February when bone-chilling winds prevail in Madrid.[24]

Who is, then, the "vasalla flor" and what the saving "austro"? In the first instance, members of the royal family are personified as flowers: Queen Mariana as "la rosa, que invicta / reina es del prado," the ten-year-old Margarita María as "la bella azucena peregrina," and the pale and fragile newborn Carlos as a "tierno jazmín" (321). More generally, all Felipe's subjects are referred to as flowers. When the chill north wind attacked the royal laurel, all the flowers who live in his protective shadow trembled:

> No sólo hasta las divinas
> hermosuras que del valle
> o ya sean maravillas
> o ya siempre vivas son,
> nobleza de su familia,
> pero hasta las más humildes
> desechadas clavellinas,
> que, plebe del bosque, apenas
> tienen nombre con que vivan (321).

This hyperbolic language had a basis in reality, for the prospect of the death of Felipe IV was not one Spaniards could face with equanimity in 1662. The health of the newborn Carlos was considered extremely precarious. After the 1657 birth of Felipe Próspero, the infanta María Teresa had been married to Louis XIV in 1660, with a provision in the marriage agreement renouncing any claim to the Spanish throne for their succession. But Felipe Próspero had died, and it was common knowledge that Louis and his ministers had no intention of respecting that renunciation.[25]

Literally speaking, the "austro" is the warm south wind that revived the royal laurel and his subject flowers. It also suggested, however, an "Austrian" current en route to protect the "vasalla flor."[26] This would appear to be a diplomatic reference to the tentative Madrid-Vienna agreement on the marriage of Margarita María to Leopold I of Austria. In order to further strengthen its ties to the Spanish branch of the Hapsburg family and to secure its claim to the throne in the case of the death of Felipe IV without a male heir, the Austrian house had earlier sought the hand of María Teresa.

Disappointed by Felipe's choice of a French marriage for her after the birth of Felipe Próspero, Leopold had been happy to accept the prospect of marriage to Margarita María. Felipe IV had agreed verbally to the match in May of 1660, but 1661 and 1662 passed without a formal agreement (Pribam lv–lvi). The able Count von Pötting was dispatched to Madrid in late 1662 (Pribam xli) and secured a ceremonious approval of the marriage in December, but departure of the princess for Vienna was delayed for three more years, despite the reiterated insistence of Leopold through his ambassador. A variety of reasons and pretexts for the delay were offered, including Margarita's youth, but an underlying concern was that in the case of the premature death of Carlos, Margarita might better be married to a consort who would live in Spain (Maura, *Corte* 1:86–87).[27] Official confirmation of this match would also offer consolation to another "vasalla flor," Mariana, who was anxious to solidify relations with her homeland against any French claims to the throne, or worse, the threat of heightened stature and power for Don Juan José.[28]

HAVING progressed in reverse from *El hijo del sol, Faetón* to the loa that prefaced it, I would like to continue in that direction toward a consideration of the possible political text(s) in *Apolo y Climene*. The reason for this procedure is that the political text of the second play is very clear, but that of the first is more subtle and debatable. The second and closely related problem is the relationship between the two plays, rather like a marriage in which each element invites completion by linkage with the other yet contains characteristics that make a perfectly harmonious union impossible.

The end of the second play is foreshadowed early in *Apolo y Climene* by Climene's vision that the chariot of the sun is falling, burning her and all her world, and the first play ends with an announcement of its sequel. Similarly, *El hijo del sol, Faetón* frequently refers back to events that had transpired in the previous play. But significant details do not match. In *Apolo y Climene*, the heroine's father is Admeto, king of Etiopía, and old Erídano is the *mayoral* or head shepherd for Admeto's flocks, a minor character not even listed in the cast of characters in the first edition. In *El hijo del sol, Faetón*, Erídano is Climene's father and a priest of Diana, Admeto is king of Tesalia and father to Epafo-Peleo.

The usual explanation for these discrepancies is simply that Calderón was careless. Hernández-Araico adds to this the hypothesis that a number of years intervened between the writing of the two plays, so that Calderón forgot what he had written earlier. She postulates that *Apolo y Climene* was contemporary with *La aurora en Copacabana*, variously dated between 1649 and 1661, on the grounds that (1) a variant of the same refrain, "Mejor sol amanece / con mejor alba," is used in both works; (2) a "pescante" (device for rapidly lowering or raising one character), cloud mechanisms, and a boulder that opens are used in both works; and (3) a stage direction specifies in one passage " 'Representa Apolo, repite la Música, y bailan todos. . . . ,' " which she believes indicates an early date when the public was not accustomed to sung performances (79 and 84–85, n.20).

The first two similarities, however, prove nothing. Calderón reused the same songs in works from very different periods. For example, the song "Sólo el silencio testigo ha de ser" appears in *El mayor encanto, amor* in 1635 and in *Eco y Narciso* in 1661.[29] The "pescante," rising clouds, and opening boulders were extremely common devices in European court spectaculars, and Calderón used them throughout his court plays. With regard to the third point, Hernández-Araico has apparently misinterpreted the meaning of "representa," which does not mean that Apolo sings but specifically points out that he does *not* sing but recites, and the chorus repeats his phrases in music.[30] Apolo cannot sing in this play because he has been expelled from heaven by Júpiter, and as he points out in his first speech, appears "En traje y persona humano, / Negado a todas las ciencias / Que me acreditaron dios" (153). As a human being, he speaks throughout the play rather than singing in recitative, and it is precisely the lack of this divine harmony he laments in the speech just prior to that stage direction and for which he hopes to compensate with the musical accompaniment: "Pero porque disimule / mi mal estilo sus faltas, / de la música el concento / siga mi voz con la blanda / armonía, porque suplan / mis yerros sus consonancias" (159). In fact, this stage direction points precisely in the opposite direction, toward a later performance, probably in the 1660s, when performers and the public were accustomed to the convention that gods sang while mortals recited, and the anomaly of a speaking Apolo therefore needed explanation.

Unless further evidence for an early date is discovered, therefore, it seems most logical to assume that the plays were conceived as a pair and written and performed in fairly close succession.[31] This does not rule out the possibility of carelessness on Calderón's part. However, previous experience with this cerebral dramatist has proven that it is precisely the unraveling of puzzling aspects of his plays that provides insights valuable to their interpretation. A minor example would be his choice of the name Peleo for Epafo, which Paris labeled arbitrary if not ridiculous. In fact, recognizing that this name was meant to heighten the stature of the "newborn" prince is crucial to understanding why Faetón's antagonist prevails at the end of the drama.[32] Calderón has in effect offered Felipe two regal father figures in the drama: Apolo and Admeto. As Apolo, he should keep his son Faetón away from the chariot of state; as Admeto, he should ensure that his son Peleo will not have to resort to violence to secure it.

We cannot use such alterations in the basic myth as keys to understanding Calderón's purpose in *Apolo y Climene*, for the story is almost completely his invention. Ovid provided no details about the affair between the sun–god and the nymph; Calderón has therefore imagined it occurring when Jupiter punished Apollo for killing his cyclops by banishing him from heaven and sentencing him to serve as a shepherd to Admeto. The rest is Calderón's fabrication. Climene is Admeto's only daughter and inheritor of his kingdom of Etiopía. Hoping to avert the fearful prophecy that her son Faetón, or "lightning bolt," would engulf Etiopía in flames, turning the land and its people black, he seals her up in a palace-fortress with the company of Clicie, Flora, and two other damas. Apolo falls from heaven into the tunnel Céfiro has dug under the walls to see Flora just as Climene has discovered Céfiro in her garden at night, summoned the guards, and raised the cry of treason against the ladies who accompany her confinement in the *alcázar*, as her prison-palace is labeled in the opening line.

The opening scene unfolds as a series of accusations, counteraccusations, and deceits between Climene and her damas and among the maids themselves, two of whom prove to be covering up clandestine love affairs, while the nervous reactions of the other two make their innocence questionable as well. The following two acts compound this situation as the various lovers mistake each other's signals, and jealousies and recriminations multiply. The audience in all likelihood recognized a similarity to another Alcázar, the official palace in Madrid, which in Felipe IV's reign, and particularly since the arrival of Mariana, had become crowded with ladies-in-waiting and their maidservants, to the extent that it was described as an "hormiguero de mujeres no necesarias" who divided into political factions, burdened the palace budget, and occasioned continual scandals. A paper written to Mariana a few years later described the situation as follows:

> Es constante y notorio a V. M. que cuanto mayor es el número de las Damas tanto menos bien se halla V. M. servida . . . Apenas recibidas, luego admiten, y, lo que es peor, solicitan galanteos, y ¡ay dolor! con hombres casados. De estos galanteos se originan grandísimas ofensas a Dios, como son: escándalos públicos; pecados contra la ley del santo matrimonio; señas y contraseñas, hasta en la misma Capilla real y delante del Santísimo Sacramento; inquietudes de ánimos, perturbaciones de las conciencias; . . . dolor y aflicción a sus padres y parientes; desdoro al sagrado del real Palacio; ruidos y voceríos en los corredores dél; inquietudes nocturnas; afán y trabajo intolerable a los guardas; pérdida del debido respeto a la persona y casa real; indecencias innumerables con increíble sentimiento de todos los buenos y temerosos de Dios y amantes de lo decoroso y honesto (qtd in Maura, *Corte* 1:293).

Desperate to protect their own complicity, Céfiro, Flora, and Clicie finally accuse Climene of having an affair herself, and as Admeto threatens to kill her, Apolo steals her away across the river Erídano to the abode of the magician Fitón. He hides the pair from their pursuers and says that Climene has died, then duplicitously reassures Climene that Apolo's love for her will not bring disastrous consequences. After she yields to his love, Apolo returns to the heavens, leaving her sequestered in another prison-palace, that of Fitón.

Although a plot summary and the presence of a diabolically controlling magician facilitating the love affair that led to the procreation of Faetón might suggest superficially that the political text in this play involved a critical view of Felipe's affair with La Calderona, I do not believe this to be the case. The love between Apolo and Climene is presented very sympathetically as a natural attraction between two appealing young people, both resentful of the injustice of their controlling fathers.[33] Furthermore, there would have been no point to such a critique by 1662; if the painful guilt for such conduct that Felipe revealed in his letters to Sor María had not curbed his passions, his increasingly poor health was an effective bar. Rather, the theme this play suggests through its wealth of symbols is that love is a natural and inevitable process; it is as natural for Céfiro to seek out Flora as it is for the gentle west wind to caress spring flowers and for them to bend to its breath. If young women are unnaturally imprisoned, love will find a way to tunnel under the walls.

If the focus of *El hijo del sol, Faetón* is toward the heavens, the chariot of the sun and man's aspiration to climb toward glory, that of *Apolo and Climene* is subterranean. Its primary symbol is the tunnel, and the action centers around the grotto and *escotillón* (trapdoor) that represent its openings inside and outside the walls of the Alcázar. As the mesh of confusions and deceits surrounding the young people weaves ever tighter, Apolo comments:

> Más fácil es de argüir
> Que hay en el humano ser
> Tropiezo para caer
> Que escalón para subir (163).

He appeals to Venus, "madre de amor," for assistance in helping him find the opening of the tunnel that will lead him back to Climene, and a boulder miraculously opens to offer him access to her garden. For those with a weaker claim on divine powers, there are always human means to undermine walls. The gracioso Sátiro, who had been a gardener within the walls and is now a shepherd outside, says that the double temptations of gossip and greed led him to reveal to Céfiro the water conduits under the walls.[34] So channels built to carry water, the liquid of life, now conduct lovers back and forth.

Why have the young people resorted to deceits and subterranean routes? If we trace the chain of causality backward, we find that it leads us to Admeto, who, like Basilio in *La vida es sueño*, has unwisely attempted to control the course of fate and human nature by imprisoning his daughter.[35] His motives were legitimate, for he wanted to protect his daughter and his kingdom, but his methods were not, for he does not have the right to deny liberty to an innocent human being. In an impassioned plea for liberty similar to Segismundo's famous monologue, Climene cries out to Admeto that even a bird in a golden cage longs for its natural freedom. Furthermore, she points out that his very attempt to avert danger is precipitating it: "Llegas a ver cuán violentos / los peligros de allá fuera / saben buscarme acá dentro" (157). Admeto recognizes the legitimacy of her argument as he says:

> ¡Ay cielos!
> Cuán en vano solicita
> El corto discurso nuestro
> Enmendar de las estrellas
> Los influjos, pues los medios
> Que pone para impedirlos
> Le sirven para atraerlos! (157)

His illegitimate imprisonment of Climene has exposed her to the very passions he wished to exclude, as Apolo underlines in a fascinating elaboration of the tunnel symbol. He fell, he tells Climene,

en la sima
Que a tus jardines conduce
Ajeno amor. ¿Quién creerá
Que equivocando arcaduces,
De minas que fueron de agua,
Minas de fuego resulten? (171)

Calderón has employed a variety of synonyms throughout the play to portray the tunnel as the route of passions that undermine the most solidly laid human constructions. By using the term *arcaduces* at the moment when Apolo and Fitón are convincing Climene to yield to Apolo's love, Calderón adds a new richness of meaning to the symbol. While *arcaduz* literally signifies a water pipe, the *Diccionario de Autoridades* adds several metaphorical meanings. It is the "conducto o la parte por donde el alma se explica, y da a entender sus afectos" and also "el chismoso, el lisongero y el alcahuete." Both of these are variants of the tunnel as the route of human passions. More importantly, *arcaduz* also means "el medio por donde se consigue o se entabla algun negocio o pretensión." This tunnel of passion is also the route of a "pretensión" that will become a "mina de fuego"—a foreshadowing of the fiery end of the second drama.

From the mid-1650s to 1665 there was a potential Climene within the walls of the real-life Alcázar of Madrid in the persons of María Teresa and then Margarita. We have already seen how and why Margarita's departure was delayed; for the same reason, the marriage of María Teresa had been postponed even longer, until the survival of Felipe Próspero seemed relatively sure. When she was finally married to Louis XIV in 1660, she was twenty-one years old, an advanced age for a royal princess; three years earlier, Barrionuevo had reported that "la señora Infanta está sangrada dos veces, pero mejor. Todo su achaque es el no ser casada, que ya está de sazón" (2:110). The problem of the future of these princesses was of course that lacking a male heir, their children could (and did) claim the Spanish throne, bringing to an end the reign of the Spanish Hapsburg dynasty.

There was another pretender to their hands in the wings. During his government in Flanders (1656–1658), according to an anonymous publication entitled *Razón de la sinrazón*, "había inquirido D. Juan de los teólogos de Lovaina si la salvación de una Monarquía, sería razón bastante poderosa a obtener del Pontífice dispensa para un matrimonio entre hermanos. . . . Meditaba entonces el suyo con María Teresa, única heredera del Trono después de muerto Baltasar Carlos, y por eso le contrarió sobremanera el nacimiento de Felipe Próspero, negándose a autorizar las colgaduras y luminarias de costumbre" (qtd in Maura, *Corte* 1:192–193, n. 2). Frustrated in his first hopes, Don Juan José himself employed the tactful but powerful medium of artistic representation to make a bolder proposal of his marriage to Margarita as Maura Gamazo reports:

En la primavera de 1665, durante la jornada de Aranjuez, pidió y obtuvo venia para saludar al Monarca, y, en el curso de la entrevista, le mostró una miniatura, que dijo haber concebido y pintado. Representaba ella al anciano Saturno, sonriendo complaciente a los incestuosos amores de Júpiter y Juno, pero se advertía bien, que el pincel del artista copió, con atinado parecido, en los rostros de las figuras mitológicas, las facciones del Rey, D. Juan y la Infanta Margarita. Airado volvió Felipe la espalda al audaz pintor, y no quiso verle ya más en la tierra (1:192–193).[36]

Despite Don Juan's repeated efforts, Felipe refused to see him, even on his deathbed several months later, and since no other explanations for his refusal have been forthcoming, we may plausibly attribute it to his lingering anger at this Faetón's attempt to secure the hand of Tetis.

Based on surviving information, Parker ("Father-Son Conflict") has postulated that an element in Calderón's unhappy family history was a love relationship between an unrecognized half-brother who lived with the family and a sister who was dispatched to a convent at an unusually young age. If Parker's deduction is accurate, any circulating rumors of Don Juan's pretensions to the role of consort to the future queen, his half-sister, would understandably raise a powerful response in the dramatist. In *La devoción de la cruz*, Calderón lays the blame for the development of a potentially incestuous love not on the young people but on the injustice of their father, Curcio. Admeto is not guilty of the cruelty of Curcio (if only because Erídano stops his hand when he would kill Climene), but he is similar in that his unjust action has given rise to the ensuing disaster. Reports from the 1650s and 1660s indicate that various counselors of Felipe IV considered inadvisable the continuance of his marriageable daughters within the walls of the Alcázar, which could subject them and the realm to undermining political passions of the epoch.[37] In fleshing out the story of Apolo and Climene, Calderón shaped it into a pertinent case history to set before Felipe IV. The faces of the participants were not clearly identifiable, as in the cameo that Don Juan José is supposed to have painted, but the parallels were suggestive.

By his "careless" alteration of the father between *Apolo y Climene* and *El hijo del sol, Faetón*, then, Calderón has underlined for Felipe IV the relevance of both stories to his own situation as a royal father, to his governance of all four of his surviving recognized children. While such a political text is only one among a number of likely readings of these richly symbolic dramas, its recovery shows again that as Calderón entertained the court, he also offered it object lessons in the consequences of human passions that were clearly pertinent not only to the dilemma of mankind in general but to that of the royal family in particular.

FIVE

An Optimistic Answer: *La estatua*
de Prometeo

BECAUSE the neglect of Calderón's court plays was founded on the idea that they were empty spectacle, I have first concentrated on demonstrating his mastery therein of the polyphony of the dramatic idiom. Since a corollary misconception held the plays to be at best escapist entertainment and at worst servile flattery, I have next concentrated on pointing out the complex tension between the celebratory "text of royal power" and the critical "political text" that we can recover by performing a historical "composición de lugares," re-creating as best we can the specific political climate in which they were first performed. By foregrounding these texts I do not wish to imply, however, that all possible meanings in these dramas are linked to questions of public power. It would be reductionist in the extreme to suggest that the richly symbolic world Calderón constructs in *Apolo y Climene* and *El hijo del sol, Faetón* is concerned only with the position in the power structure of Don Juan José de Austria. I would like to illustrate through one of Calderón's masterpieces, *La estatua de Prometeo*, the coexistence of the three basic texts—the *text of royal power*, the *political text*, and a *particular text*.

This terminology is advanced only to facilitate discussion, not with a defining intention. Certainly the text of royal power is also a political text, and the political text in turn is a sort of particular text when we view it as if through the king's eyes; that is, it is an individual's appropriation of the structures of meaning of the dramatic world to his own experience. *Particular* is an inadequate word that I use only as the least objectionable term to point to a construction of meaning that is not anchored in the specific framework of political issues in the Spanish Hapsburg court. The more traditional term, *universal*, carries imperialistic overtones of authorially determined, universally and eternally valid meaning, which do not seem to describe how diverse readers, over time, experience literary texts. In actual fact, the range of "particular" interpretations may be quite narrow at any given time since its boundaries are set by inscribed authorial structures and common cultural and literary traditions.[1] For example, the interpretations of *La estatua de Prometeo* presented in this chapter, all by twentieth-century American critics, evidence both a clear kinship and significant differences. In proposing that Calderón deliberately created a polysemic structure, I do not suggest that he intended to write an "open" text in the twentieth-century sense of total relativism, but one constructed on a hermeneutic tradition of bounded pluralism.

We have seen in Chapter 2 how the conspicuous presence of the ruling figures in the theatre conditioned the "possible world" construction of the audience in such a way as to produce the political reading as one text of the drama. Even in the court setting, however, most spectators would not define themselves solely in reference to the monarchs, nor are the possible worlds they might construct in response to the stage action limited to classically political issues. In his best court dramas, Calderón has sufficiently abstracted—or to use the term of Jerome Bruner (24–43), "subjunctivized"—the *fabula* so that each reader-spectator can extrapolate from it a possible world built in the shape of his own experiences and concerns.[2]

The main point to be made with this triad of texts is that they are not mutually exclusive but simultaneously present; the fundamental structure of meaning of these plays is polysemic. For the seventeenth-century spectator, the text of royal power, the local political reading, and a particular construction of meaning could coexist. How, given the well-discussed difficulty of reconstructing the horizon of expectations of a distant era, can we know this? Such pluralistic interpretative practices have their obvious attractions in the world of academic fashion and contemporary interpretive trends, but to what extent can we legitimately attribute them to Calderón and his contemporary readers and spectators?[3] Hermeneutic practices of his era, particularly as applied to mythology, yield clear evidence of a bounded pluralism.

When classical myth burgeoned to new literary life in Renaissance Europe, the justification for reading and re-creating these pagan tales in the Christian era was that they contained pre-Christian intuitions of truths to be revealed with the coming of Christ.[4] They were, therefore, often subjected to the fourfold exegesis applied to the Old Testament, in which the stories were read as having simultaneously a literal, moral, allegorical, and anagogical sense. Thus, the story of Jonah represented concurrently (1) the tale of a historical figure who spent three days in the belly of a whale; (2) a figure of Christ's resurrection on the third day; (3) a moral example to human beings never to give up hope; and (4) a pointer toward resurrection in the afterlife (Hollander 24–26).

Compilers of mythological dictionaries from Boccaccio on, appropriated this fourfold system in the explanation of the mythic stories, although their definition of the four senses was far from rigorous and the applications often overlapped. Carballo (1:84–104), for example, uses a lengthy discussion of the four senses in defending poets against the charge of the ignorant that they are liars. He includes the virtually obligatory rhyme in which medieval treatises encapsulated the four meanings, albeit transformed from a couplet to a four-line stanza:

> Littera gesta docet,
> Quid credas alegoria
> Moralis quid agas
> Quo tendas anagogia.

His subsequent amplification, however, bears little resemblance to the senses defined by Aquinas; only the example he gives for the moral sense really fits the classic definition of the theologians, while his illustrations for the anagogical and even the literal senses are often simple personification allegories, in which the poet begins with an abstract idea and then casts it in a concrete form. Despite such theoretical confusion, nevertheless, the currency of the fourfold interpretive method both encouraged and justified the multiple interpretations the mythographers offered of each tale. Pérez de Moya, who compiled the *Philosofía secreta* that served as an important source for Spanish poets, including Calderón, gives a charming explanation of such multiple readings. He says the ancients expressed themselves in myths because "el poco papel y recaudo para escriuir que tenían en aquel tiempo les deuió necesitar a vsar de las fábulas para declarar muchas cosas con pocas palabras" (f.2–2v).

Following such practices, Prometheus was portrayed in Pérez de Moya's mythological dictionary as at once a historical ruler in Egypt; the second creator of the human race, either as first sculptor of clay or as bringer of learning and civilization to man; a model of the man who consumes himself in study and the prudent man who elevates himself through devotion to learning; and a figure of God, who created humans from nothing. Calderón's basic source for details of the Prometheus story, like those of his other mythological dramas, appears to have been Pérez de Moya's dictionary;[5] he thus had before him a model of pluralistic interpretation.

SOURCES

Although we may identify Pérez de Moya as Calderón's source for *La estatua de Prometeo*, that does not answer the interesting question of how this story came to be chosen for a court play. Ovid barely mentions Prometheus in passing, and while many other mythical figures drawn from poetic models in Ovid, Virgil, and Horace came to populate the poetry of the Renaissance, no important work was dedicated to Prometheus, in Spain or elsewhere, until the end of the seventeenth century.[6] In Spain, a few poets used Prometheus either as a metaphor for the lover's ever-renewed pain, as a symbol of the creative artist, or, more pessimistically, as a culprit in bringing an end to the golden age through his formation of men and Pandora's release of evils on earth. However, Prometheus was a minor mythological figure in Spanish poetry prior to Calderón's drama.

Pandora and Prometheus did take an important place in the decorative scheme of the Alcázar Palace in midcentury, however. Beginning in 1659, in the same redecoration that used Apolo and Faetón to decorate the king's quarters, the ceiling of the Hall of Mirrors, the principal receiving salon of the palace, was decorated with a series of frescoes depicting the story of Pandora. Velázquez supervised the work, which was carried out by Agostino Mitelli and Angelo Colonna, two Bolognese fresco painters recruited by Velázquez on his second trip to Italy, and two Spanish painters, Francisco Carreño and Francisco Rizi (Panofsky 75; Orso 67–69). The paintings were all destroyed in the 1734 fire that gutted the palace, but ten years before the fire, Antonio Palomino had published an extensive description of them.

Velázquez drew up a plan that divided the ceiling into five episodes of the Pandora story. In the first scene, Vulcan showed the statue of Pandora to Jupiter, who had ordered him to make it, while the Cyclopes worked in Vulcan's forge and shop in the background. The second scene, and principal picture, which occupied the center of the slightly concave ceiling, showed the various gods seated on thrones of clouds, bestowing their gifts on Pandora. The Panofskys (182) believe this scene to have been derived from an engraving by Callot, either directly or through the related engraving of Cornelius Bloemaert (see Figures 15 and 16). In the third fresco, Jupiter gave Pandora a golden vase. In the fourth, Prometheus rejected Pandora's advances while Hymen, the god of marriage, and a small Cupid left the scene in defeat. The fifth scene showed the marriage of Pandora and Epimetheus (Orso 68–69). Interestingly, the sequence did not include the climactic episode of Pandora opening the urn and releasing the cloud of evils. The Panofskys offer a humorous speculation concerning its absence: "Podremos presumir que Velázquez consideraba que la humanidad ya estaba suficientemente castigada con las 'aflicciones y desconsuelos' del matrimonio?" (182).

Orso's explanation of the series is more serious but not fully convincing. After surveying all the paintings in the hall, an assortment of regal portraits and pictures of both biblical and mythological stories, Orso concludes that the plan was that of exalting the Spanish kings from Carlos I to Felipe IV (Carlos II being added later) as defenders of the Christian faith. Of the central Pandora fresco, he says:

> It, too, enhanced the presentation of the Spanish Habsburgs as heroic proponents of Catholicism. According to her myth it was Pandora who released into the world all the evils that afflict mankind when she opened the vessel that Jupiter had given her as a dowry. The patristic tradition that equated her with Eve, who brought about the Fall of Man, had been revived in the sixteenth century. Because one of the subsidiary scenes in the fresco showed Prometheus rejecting Pandora's advances, it is certain that she was meant to be seen in a negative light. The implication of the fresco for the overall program was that the evils that Pandora had released into the world were opposed by the Spanish Habsburgs, Christian princes all (104–105).

This was, says Orso, the intended "long-range" meaning of the sequence. He proposes that it had a quite different "short-range" message—celebrating the marriage of María Teresa to Louis XIV in 1660. Orso suggests that Velázquez

Figure 15. Jacques Callot. *Pandora*. J. Lieure, *Jacques Callot*, 2d part, vol. 2, plate 568.

Figure 16. Cornelis Bloemaert. *Pandora*.
Michel de Marolles, *Tableaux du temple des Muses*
(Paris, 1736).

anticipated that the marriage ceremony would be performed in the Hall of Mirrors, since 1650 the salon where the king received distinguished visitors. Therefore, the final scene of the Pandora sequence was omitted. "Instead, the dominant image overhead at the ceremony was the central oval in which the Olympian gods bestowed their gifts of beauty, grace, and refinement upon Pandora. On that day the scene alluded to the many virtues of the bride-to-be, María Teresa, while the negative aspects of the myth were discreetly ignored" (106). Thereafter, says Orso, "the perceived significance of the fresco reverted to its more conventional meaning" (107).

There are several problems with this interpretation of the significance of the frescoes. The first is the somewhat schizophrenic perception it demands of seventeenth-century Spanish and French courtiers, who are required to read the same series of images as totally positive or totally negative, as the occasion requires. It would also seem to be rather dangerous diplomatically. The Spanish court was to know the "true story" of Pandora and to perceive her as a danger to the Christian prince, even in the absence of a picture of the final episode; yet those same Spaniards would be assuming that the French court was sufficiently innocent or ignorant of the full story to accept her as a bounteous gift.

Furthermore, while we may accept that some of the mythological paintings in the hall were chosen as warning of the dangers to Christian princes, it seems doubtful that such a negative image would occupy the central ceiling position in the hall, or that such a position would be occupied by a story that reduced the allegorical equivalent of the king (Prometheus = Spanish king) to that of a secondary figure participating in only one of the five scenes.

Third, and perhaps most importantly, we cannot assume that seventeenth-century viewers would automatically perceive Pandora as a negative figure, as a pagan Eve. The Panofskys give only two examples of the Pandora-Eve association, at the same time pointing out an equal number of parallels between Christ and Pandora, inasmuch as she denotes the perfect union of all things. Biblical figures aside, the Panofskys also describe another tradition in which Pandora (whose name means "all-gifted," as Calderón points out in his play) represents a positive good for mankind. For some scholars, she represented human acquisition (through the discovery of fire) of the arts, the skills and techniques necessary for the development of a civilized style of life. More importantly, in the Neoplatonic schemes of Plotinus and Ficino, she represented the incarnation of divine beauty in material form.[7] Such a positive evaluation coordinates with Boccaccio's suggestion, repeated by Pérez de Moya, of a second Prometheus whose creation of Pandora represents the "re-creation" of man as a civilized being.

The beautiful Pandora surrounded by gods on the ceiling of the Hall of Mirrors probably was meant to represent—in the long and short run, to the Spaniards and French—not the first temptress, whose lures were to be shunned, but the "all-gifted" creature of beauty, the perfection of earthly civilization somehow associated with Spanish Hapsburg rule. The omission of the final episode of the story was not a sort of diplomatic ruse but a logical decision to ensure a favorable perception of the meaning of the story.

We know that Mariana, along with Felipe IV, followed the painting of the frescoes with great interest, for Palomino's account tells us that Felipe went every day to observe their progress and that Mariana and the infantas often accompanied him (Orso 69). The fresco's depiction of a woman as a central figure in human civilization would certainly have pleased Mariana and may have been a factor in the selection of the Prometheus-Pandora story for the celebration of her birthday with one of the first court spectacles of the interregnum.[8]

The more immediate inspiration for its dramatization, however, probably came from Vienna. The Vienna court was closely linked to that of Madrid, culturally and politically because of Margarita's marriage to Leopold I and because Ambassador von Pötting was an enthusiast of Spanish theatre. As soon as the young empress reached Vienna in late 1666, requests began returning to Madrid for copies of Spanish music and plays, and texts of court theatrical productions in Vienna were sent back to Madrid.[9] To celebrate Mariana's birthday, Leopold and Margarita offered a performance in 1669 of an opera entitled *Benche vinto, vince amore. ò il Prometeo*, with a libretto in Spanish and music probably by Antonio Draghi. In a letter of 5 February 1670 from Emperor Leopold I to von Pötting, he says he is sending nine copies of the opera presented for the Queen Mother's birthday and requests that von Pötting give her four and dispose of the other five as he pleases. Given the previous infrequency of the Prometheus story in Spanish poetry and drama, it seems likely that it was the arrival of this opera that led to Calderón's creation, probably at the request of the Queen Mother, and that he wrote his play in the year of the opera's arrival in Madrid, 1670. If this speculative chain is accurate, however, Calderón took little more than the idea from the opera; one would hope that work justified its existence by the beauty of its music, for the libretto is best described as a mythological fruit salad.[10]

THE PARTICULAR TEXT

The dramatic coherence so conspicuously lacking in the libretto of the Vienna opera is amply supplied in Calderón's compact drama.[11] The central issue of *La estatua de Prometeo* is the duality of human existence: the inherent tension within man and the ambiguity of his position in the traditionally conceived hierarchy of the universe. Virtually all its critics have perceived the importance of dualism in the play because the insistent polarization of the primary characters with which Calderón structures the plot creates a pattern of countervailing forces that seems to represent an archetypal human experience. Since readers, like spectators, draw on their own experience as well as the "on-page" word-world, those critics' identifications of the axis of tension have differed.[12] For example, Chapman (64), one of the first modern critics to recognize merit in the mythological plays, sees it as a conflict between reason and passions, while Mujica (279, 286) reads it as reason against will or force. Pasero (111) labels it an opposition between male and female principles, and terHorst (67–68) considers the basic structural tension that between nature and culture.

The following reading of the particular text is a conservative one that describes the plot in terms of the dualism most repeatedly seen as fundamental to human existence in Calderón's era: the mind-body dualism, variously labeled as spirit or soul against body. Within Thomistic psychology, the axis of tension could be more precisely labeled as the rational versus the sensory faculties of man, and within those categories, the *appetitus sensitivus*, the mechanisms of desire we would call the emotions, against the *intellectus* (Brennan, 261–266, 432). The same basic dualism continues in Ficino's Neoplatonic cosmos, and Ficino makes Prometheus the figure of reason's eternal torment, caged within a mortal body and endlessly seeking to ascend to its divine source.[13]

Calderón created a delightful comic treatment of this dualism that only death can resolve in the *mojiganga Las visiones de la muerte*.[14] A group of actors have to travel in costume, like the players Don Quixote met, and the actress dressed as Alma gets the best seat in the wagon "porque el alma es lo primero" (374). Cuerpo is her husband, but the autor de comedias does not want them to sit together because they always fight, and he therefore designates Muerte as the appropriate one to sit between them. The wagon overturns, and Alma is pinned underneath. A passerby, Caminante, hears her cries that she is being crushed to death and voices the wish that "¡No tuviera el alma cuerpo!" (377). But in this case, Cuerpo comes to rescue her and urges her to drink wine from the Caminante's *bota*. When she and the figure Angel finish off the "divine liquor," however, the conciliatory mood ends, and Cuerpo and Alma come to blows again with such ferocity that not even Demonio can stop them. Muerte is the only one who can stop their quarrel by separating them: "Baste estar yo de por medio" (382).

Calderón makes dualism central to the court play through his major innovation in the interpretation of the Prometheus myth: the linking of Prometheus and Epimetheus as twin brothers and the doubling of the single goddess Minerva as twin goddesses, Minerba and Palas. Prometeo, whose Greek name means "forethought," is portrayed by Calderón as a man of reason who seeks understanding and endeavors to bring the fruits of his learning to his uncivilized countrymen. Epimeteo, "afterthought" in Greek, is the man of passion and force whose rivalry with Prometeo threatens all with destruction. By drawing the two together as twin brothers, the dramatist indicates to us that he considers them not separate types within the human race but competing elements within one being: man as a creature divided against himself.[15] They are as inseparable as two sides of a coin. The counterpoised splitting of the goddess into Minerba as the goddess of wisdom and Palas as the deity of war suggests a parallel competition between countervailing forces at a determinative celestial level in the nature of life as it is given to man. By his equally unique introduction of Discordia as a major character in the play, Calderón reinforces this image of a bipolar universe. As Apolo is the god of light and life, so Plutón reigns over darkness and death. Although Plutón does not appear himself to measure forces with Apolo, Calderón specifically links Discordia with him, as he had in *Las fortunas de Andrómeda y Perseo*, calling her "bastarda Deydad . . . hija de Plutón" (III, 586–587). Up to the final scene, the play appears to present a virtually Manichean universe in which every good impulse is counteracted by a corresponding evil, and terHorst goes so far as to describe Calderón as a "Manichean fusionist" (68).

Calderón is not unique in his presentation of human dualism or in its externalization in linked human figures. Its universality can be seen in tales as disparate as the Mesopotamian myth of Gilgamesh and his ill-fated double Enkidu and Robert L. Stevenson's Dr. Jekyll and Mr. Hyde. The dualistic perception has yielded some of the greatest figures of Spanish literature: witness the beloved Don Quixote and Sancho Panza; Critilo and Andrenio of Gracián's *El Criticón*; or in a twentieth-century masterpiece, the two shoemakers of Pérez de Ayala's *Belarmino y Apolonio*. This idea of the internal warfare within man and his universe, a much-repeated topic in Golden Age Spain (Green 2:52–63), was one of Critilo's early lessons for Andrenio:

> Todo este universo se compone de contrarios y se concierta de desconciertos: . . . Los elementos, que llevan la vanguardia, comiençan a batallar entre sí; . . . los mismos astros guerrean y se vencen, y aunque entre sí no se dañan a fuer de príncipes, viene a parar su contienda en daño de los sublunares vassallos. . . . En la edad, se oponen los viejos a los moços; . . . en el estado, los ricos a los pobres; en la región, los españoles a los franceses. . . . Pero qué mucho, si dentro del mismo hombre, de las puertas adentro de su terrena casa, está más encendida esta discordia.
> —¡Qué dizes?, ¡un hombre contra sí mismo?
> —Sí, que por lo que tiene de mundo, aunque pequeño, todo él se compone de contrarios. Los humores comiençan la pelea. . . . La parte inferior está siempre de ceño con la superior y a la razón se le atreve el apetito, y tal vez la atropella. El mismo inmortal espíritu no está essento desta tan general discordia, pues combaten entre sí, y en él, muy vivas las passiones: el temor las ha contra el valor, la tristeza contra la alegría; ya apetece, ya aborrece; la irascible se baraxa con la concupiscible; ya vencen los vicios, ya triunfan las virtudes, todo es arma y todo guerra. De suerte, que la vida del hombre no es otro que una milicia sobre la haz de la tierra" (90–91).

To present externally the internal conflict of "un hombre contra sí mismo" poses a problem for the dramatist. Calderón solves it by the device of twins, a refinement of a technique he used in the comedia *El gran príncipe de Fez*, written

131

shortly before the *Prometeo* in 1669, to solve the problem of presenting dramatically the internal conflict within a man. In this story of the conversion of Baltasar de Loyola to Christianity, Calderón creates two characters, Buen Genio and Mal Genio, and has Buen Genio state explicitly the reason for their existence:

> Representando los dos
> de su Buen Genio y Mal Genio
> exteriormente la lid
> que arde interior en su pecho (1412).

The distribution of good and evil in *La estatua de Prometeo* is much more complex than in *El gran príncipe de Fez*—and more intriguing. Epimeteo and Prometeo are not simply negative and positive figures but two mutually dependent and inherently antagonic elements congenital in man, with the effect, as Prometeo puts it, that the crib becomes "en vez de primer abrigo, campaña de primer lucha" (I, 63–64).

Calderón's Prometeo and Epimeteo are personifications of the war of man against himself and of the suffering that afflicts "los sublunares vassallos" because the very stars that direct his existence "guerrean y se vencen." The conflictive stars in his play are the twin goddesses Minerba and Palas, who were born equal in power and beauty but opposed in their inclinations, with Palas "auxiliando lides / dictando ella [Minerba] ciencias" (II, 660). Not only are they twins, but Calderón alters traditional mythical genealogy to make them sisters of Apolo. The sun-god is the giver of life; as Minerba says, "el sol y el hombre / dan la vida" (II, 337–339), and his ray brings Pandora to life in the play. By making Minerba and Palas sisters of Apolo, Calderón indicates symbolically that reason and violence are genetically and inextricably linked to the gift of life itself; they are the positive and negative forces ever competing within and without man for control of his existence. The sister deities appropriate the twin brothers as their respective subjects in a competition to see which star pupil can achieve the greater stature—Prometeo, with Minerba's gift of intelligence and learning, or Epimeteo, with the force of arms.

Epimeteo has become the embodiment of man as the supreme hunter, the nemesis of every wild bird or beast in the forest. His accomplishments, as recounted by Prometeo, take on a negative coloration as Calderón borrows Góngora's imagery to link him with the brute Polifemo. Epimeteo is the epitome of the man who controls his environment by the use of force. Prometeo disdains this "comerço de la bruta" (I, 84) as demeaning to the noble nature of man: he has chosen to develop instead his specifically human capacity for reason because, as he says:

> Este anhelo de saber,
> . . . es el que al hombre le ylustra
> más que otro alguno (supuesto

> que aquella distançia mucha
> que ay del hombre al bruto, ay
> del hombre al hombre, si junta
> la comferençia tal vez
> al que ygnora y al que estudia) (I, 97–103).

Not only does the use of reason distinguish man from animals but, says Prometeo, it also links him with the gods:

> Viendo, pues, en vna parte
> cuanto los hombres repudian
> la enseñanza, y viendo en otra
> cuanto los Dioses la ylustran,
> a su alto conoçimiento
> elebé la mente. . . . (I, 207–212)

Along with immortality, deities are characterized in Calderonian drama by their total understanding.[16] In *Apolo y Climene*, Apolo complains that his banishment from the heavens is not only a physical but an intellectual exile, for he finds himself "negado a todas las ciencias / que me acreditaron Dios" (1868). The pursuit of knowledge, then, separates man from beast and raises him toward the gods.

Scholarly figures, frequent protagonists in Calderón's dramas, generally fall into one of two categories: (1) those who study in order to understand and (2) those who learn in order to control. Calderón always presents the first group in a positive light—for example, Cide Hamete (Baltasar de Loyola) of *El gran príncipe de Fez*, Licanoro of *Las cadenas del demonio*, or Carlos of *De una causa dos efectos*. He paints a dark picture of characters who employ knowledge for negative, controlling uses, as do many figures in the mythological plays—Medea in *Los tres mayores prodigios*, Circe in *El mayor encanto amor*, Liríope in *Eco y Narciso*, Fitón in *Apolo y Climene,* and the devil figure in various religious plays. On the border between the two groups are a number of human figures whose original motivations for study may have been laudable but who, either from pride in their learning (e.g., Basilio of *La vida es sueño*), diabolical influence (e.g., Cipriano in *El mágico prodigioso*), or simple misjudgment (e.g., Admeto in *Apolo y Climene*) have attempted to play a Godlike role that impinges unjustly on the liberty of other human beings. Valbuena Briones (Calderón, *Prometeo* 1065) places Prometeo in the first group and calls the play "una exaltación del intelectualismo," while O'Connor ("Reason's Impasse" 229) makes him a borderline case who represents not only reason's powers but also its limitations.

Prometeo's study begins with a laudatory quest for understanding. He leaves his homeland to study in Syria, "la más çelebrada curia de artes y çienzias" (I, 108–109) and devotes himself particularly to the study of astrology with the Chaldeans, for whom the heavenly bodies were gods who rule the destinies of men and empires.[17] As he searches for an explanation of how brothers born under the same star could be so differently disposed, Prometeo questions how one cause could have diverse effects, a part of the inquiry into cause and effect that, as Calderón points out, was central to Scholastic philosophy.[18] Prometeo answers his question in astrological terms, attributing the differences between himself and Epimeteo to the rapid revolutions of the heavens, which are such that although twins are born under the same planet, their births may occur under different constellations.[19] As Calderón develops the tale, the differences between Prometeo and Epimeteo result from their subjection to the influences of Minerba and Palas, the contradictory goddesses who are sisters of Apolo, the life-giver.

Viewed in the context of the play as a whole, this explanation is not an answer to the cause of human difference and strife but a begging of the question. Palas will subsequently say that she and Minerba are

> . . . vna cosa mesma.
> Pero aunque en deydad, en solio,
> en magestad y grandeza,
> naçimos las dos comformes,
> crezimos las dos opuestas
> en los diuididos genios
> de nuestras dos ymfluencias (I, 652–658).

Calderón leaves ambiguous whether these "dos ymfluencias" are the effects the twin sisters exercise on their subjects or two contrary powers that shaped the divine beings themselves. What, then, is the first cause of this dualism? An old story tells of an Eastern prophet who preached that the universe rests on the back of an elephant, which in turn rests on the back of another elephant. When queried regarding the support of the second elephant, he said, "There are elephants all the way down" (cited in Booth 242). Does Prometeo's universe, then, consist of contrary pairs "all the way up"? In this work, Calderón provides no explanation of the first cause of dualism, beyond the symbolic sisterhood of Minerba and Palas with Apolo.

Prometeo, however, accepted the astrological explanation, and feeling an obligation to make use of his newly acquired knowledge, he then returned to the Cáucaso, hoping to apply the fruits of his learning to civilize his barbarous homeland through the application of "político gobierno."[20] His efforts were a total failure. The populace rebelled, seeing him as an ambitious tyrant, and Prometeo retreated into solitude. Throughout the play, Calderón presents his man of reason as a solitary hero, divorced from the populace he aspires to lead. The play opens with Prometeo alone on a hidden peak the people find difficult to reach, even when they attempt to answer his summons. Seeing his reforms rejected, the offended Prometeo had withdrawn into himself, symbolically retreating to a "melancólica espelunca" because "no ay / compañía más segura / que la soledad a quien / no encuentra con lo que gusta" (I, 185–188). He later repeats the pattern of defeat and retreat, and when the populace divides into warring factions, his band is much smaller than that of his brother.

Epimeteo, in contrast, emerges as a natural leader. He first appears as the leader who instructs the populace to follow Prometeo's voice and then organizes the "desmandadas cuadrillas" of the "tropel," uniting them "en seguimiento mío" (I, 38–40). When the people are astonished by the beauty of the statue of Minerba that Prometeo has created, Epimeteo says, "Yo responderé por todos" (I, 315), and it is he whom the mob follows in the scenes of trial and punishment. From the outset, then, Calderón suggests that Prometeo as a reasoning man is ineffective in communicating the fruits of his knowledge to the populace, which is more easily led by Epimeteo's passionate, forceful approach.

Calderón underlines the potentially isolating effect of reason by a fascinating symbolic device. He has Minerba appear disguised as a fiera. Such a wild figure frequently appears in the mythological dramas, as a sign of the threat to civilized society posed by the savagery and wildness that exists either just beyond its limits, or, more often, hidden in the antisocial passions of its members. Calderón has the goddess of wisdom herself don a beastly disguise to draw Prometeo from the populace where she can speak to him alone. The symbolic inference is that not only brutish passions but reason itself can, at will, separate man from his society.

It was precisely his withdrawal from a hostile society that led Prometeo to his worship of Minerba. Prometeo describes his relationship with the goddess as a somewhat peculiar version of the mystical path of union with God, as related in Spanish mystical literature of the late sixteenth century.[21] He has undertaken a variety of recollection, withdrawing physically from the world and meditating first on the wonders of nature. This leads him to elevate his mind to speculating on the dominion of the gods. Finding himself particularly blessed with Minerba's gifts of wisdom, he dedicates to her an "ynterior culto" like the contemplative silent prayer described by Santa Teresa: "Tenía este modo de oración, que como no podía discurrir con el entendimiento procuraba representar a Cristo dentro de mí" (147). Prometeo describes similarly the process by which he brought Minerba to life in his "fantasía," so vividly that he experiences an all-encompassing involuntary vision of her akin to those some mystics describe as part of the *via illuminativa*. He sees it even in the darkness of the "noche siempre obscura," which in this context must surely be considered a multiple reference to the physical darkness of a world never illuminated by the light of fire, or understanding, and to the dark night of the soul to which San Juan de la Cruz refers in his poem "Noche obscura." His vision is illuminated by a "vibo fuego," which can similarly be associated with the light of understanding that mystics describe experiencing as they feel themselves close to God. Rather than following the mystics in persevering to the final stage of the soul's true union with God, in which imaginary visions cease, Prometeo tries to dominate his vision by giving it corporeal existence in the statue he shapes in its image. He has come to worship wisdom, yet at the same time, he tries to control it, as he had earlier tried to use his knowledge to direct the populace of the Cáucaso. In effect, Prometeo attempts to use reason to control the universe, as Epimeteo tries to dominate his environment by force.

There is a narcissistic element in his worship of Minerba, however, for he had been drawn to it by seeing "cuanto en mí las [the gifts of wisdom] distribuía" (I, 232). Furthermore, his exclusive attention to her is ill-advised. It is not only Minerba's jealous twin Palas who may be offended at his total devotion to her; Prometeo calls Minerba "de las çiençias / la ynspirazión absoluta" (I, 229–230) and says that he dedicated his worship primarily to this deity, "oféndanse o no se ofendan / las demás" (I, 235–236). According to Christian theology, God is the ultimate source of true wisdom, which cannot be reached by purely human reasoning powers. Human reason is a good, but Prometeo's self-absorbed worship of it as an end in itself is a defect in the purity of that good, which makes it vulnerable to domination by self-centered passions. Prometeo's single-minded devotion to reason will trigger a countervailing effort by his "irrational" twin to redress the balance of power.

The immediate fruit of Prometeo's worship of reason is a positive one, however, as his intellectually inspired artistry yields a divinely beautiful creation. TerHorst (24) calls art "the resurrectionary principle" in Calderón, which triumphs over its hostile twin, nature, the "death-force." The inspired artist is for Calderón endowed with semidivine powers, capable of a creation like Prometeo's statue, which is "algo menos que viba / con algo más que difunta" (I, 325–326). Of Pigmaleon's artistry, he says in *La fiera, el rayo y la piedra* that he shares Júpiter's creative power, and in the auto *El pintor de su deshonra*, the artist who creates Naturaleza Humana is God himself. In Calderón's theocentric theory of art, God is the supreme artist who shaped the beauty of the universe from chaos and portrayed man in his own image. The artist who creates lifelike forms from "nothing," from the simple elements of nature, imitates the divine creativity.[22]

Seeing the beautiful product of Prometeo's reason, Epimeteo finds himself instinctively and passionately drawn to it. He appoints himself spokesman for the populace and vows to build her a temple that will challenge the domain of the heavens as a demonstration that "açepta lo sacro, quien lo político renunçia" (I, 338–340). The implication is that since the mass of men will not follow the dictates of reason, they are better governed by religion than law.[23] As the embodiment of the emotional aspect of humanity, Epimeteo leads in the establishment of the rites and temples for the new "goddess."

As he does so, he shows himself to be a proud, selfish, and dissembling creature in a series of impassioned asides that reveal the constant tug-of-war between his public and private faces.[24] On seeing the marvelously lifelike statue, Epimeteo says with bravado, "Nothing scares me," only to whisper immediately, "Mal dije, que quizá a ellos / admira, y a mí me ofusca" (I, 317–318). Then he proclaims altruistically that the statue should be left in the grotto until the temple can be built, lest "familiarity breed contempt," but admits privately that his true motivation is a selfish desire to keep it safely in his own view (I, 349–350). Epimeteo's false bravado does not hide physical cowardice, however, for when Timantes announces the approach of a fearsome monster (Minerba in disguise), he immediately sets out to conquer the "fiera" with the force of his arms, as an offering to the new "goddess." Prometeo follows, vowing to prove that it is not true "que se embotan los aceros / en el corte de las plumas" (I, 427–428), thus initiating as a contest between "armas y letras" the first phase of the brotherly competition to honor the new creation.

The contrasting attitudes of the twin brothers are demonstrated as each has his first encounter with the goddess that has inspired his development. Prometeo says factually that he will penetrate "al más paboroso centro" "desta bárbara montaña" (I, 469, 468) and quickly encounters the goddess of reason, who removes her fierce disguise to reveal her true "aspeto amable" (I, 485). Epimeteo, in contrast, struggles fruitlessly to follow where Prometeo has led and is overcome with terror at the same surroundings. His lengthy description of them abounds in images of monsters, darkness, and tombs, which, as Maurin pointed out, Calderón intertwines to suggest the death-in-life of a man whose passions dominate his reason. When he finally penetrates the tomblike cave, he encounters not a beautiful goddess disguised as a beast, as had Prometeo, but another kind of monster, the goddess of force, whose beautiful exterior conflicts with her monstrous, threatening nature (I, 636–637, 643–644). While a grateful Minerba had descended to earth to reward Prometeo with a heavenly gift for his adoration of her, Palas comes inspired by jealousy, with threats of dire punishment for Epimeteo's faithlessness. Appropriately, it is the envious goddess Palas who tells the story of the competition initiated by the divine twins. Calderón's poetry effectively underlines the contrast between the two goddesses, as he assigns a graceful lyrical meter to Minerba and a heavy pounding one to Palas. He also employs both the illusionistic scenery and the *tramoyas* of the court spectacle to effect a symbolic and superbly dramatic presentation of their divergent influences. While Minerba takes Prometeo soaring upward to choose whatever he would from the heavens as a reward for his pursuit of knowledge,[25] Palas draws Epimeteo into a black cave of fear, the end of those who follow the road of passion and force. The goddess of reason inspires creation. The goddess of force offers only destruction. A creature divided against himself, man's pursuit of knowledge leads him toward the heavens, while his selfish passions pull him down into a hell on earth.

Prometeo reacts with pride to Minerba's offer of any gift he chooses, saying that he already has the greatest gift the earth can offer in the knowledge she has bestowed on him. Therefore, his ambition leads him to aspire to enter the heavenly realm. He says self-confidently that he who travels with the goddess of reason will venture anything, and with her, he dares to "climb the wind." Despite this pride and ambition, Calderón's Prometeo is not the defiantly rebellious hero beloved of the romantic period.[26] He does not rail against the unjust division of goods and power between humans and the gods. His animosity is directed downward, toward earth, rather than upward against the heavens, and his rebellion, if such it should be called, is against the brutish condition in which human beings live and their resistance to improvement. He chooses to steal a ray of Apolo's life-giving light not to redress the balance of power but because it will be useful to humanity and will serve as a demonstration of the value of the gifts of reason, "pues moralmente se biera / que quien da luz a las gentes / es quien da a las gentes çiençia" (I, 852–854). He does not seek to challenge the power of the gods, only to improve humanity.

Epimeteo, on the other hand, is left in torment by Palas's threat. He is torn between a positive passion, his attraction toward the beauty of the statue he loves, and a negative passion, his fear of the vengeance of Palas. He decides to "fingir," to kidnap the statue and hide it for himself, but finding it animated by Prometeo's flame, he is terrified and blinded by the dazzling light, and flees to look for someone to explain the enigma to him (II, 269–280). Despite his bravado, this supreme hunter is not truly brave; he possesses physical courage but is frightened by what he does not understand, and blinded and put to flight by the concentrated flame of knowledge.

Prometeo, in contrast, possesses mental as well as physical courage, for his reasoning powers enable him to reach an understanding of what is an enigma to his twin. When he finds the "statue" (now called Pandora) animated, he first thinks it is Minerba herself, who, offended for some reason, no longer speaks to him in the harmonies characteristic of deities but in an ordinary mortal speaking voice. He is not frightened, however, and between the two, they reason that it is the torch that has brought her to life. He does not take personal credit for the flame but prefers to let the populace accept it as a gift of Minerba, his ideal goddess of reason.

The true source of the animating fire, however, is kept deliberately vague. When Epimeteo asks who gave life to the statue, offstage music like a divine chorus answers with the refrain:

> Quien triumpha para enseñanza
> de que quien da çiençias, da
> voz al barro y luz al alma. (II, 236–238)

The action in this first half of the drama thus establishes the basic human dichotomy between man as a reasoning being seeking knowledge and a passionate beast acting on his instincts—between the philosopher and the hunter. The philosopher first tried to civilize humanity by the introduction of reason, ruling directly through a rational code of law. When that failed, he created instead a beautiful image, which men accept, for the positive role played by the passions is their instinctive attraction toward the beautiful, the perceived good. Pandora represents not the inevitable doom of mankind but its potential salvation. Prometeo created her from all the beauty that nature offers, shaped by all the creative artistry that reason inspires in man; the result is

> la más perfecta hermosura
> que el arte y naturaleza
> en sus dos primores juntan. (I, 34–36)

Pandora is "la providencia del tiempo"—animated by the divine fire, "quien supla la falta / del sol para los comerçios de la noche" (II, 441–443); she is civilization, a product of reason refining itself away from the bestial element of humanity and seeking to dwell with the gods, stealing from them the light of understanding that gives them control over their existence, over night and day, over life and death. Yet the animal nature of man persists, and its desire to possess the new life for its own selfish ends brings the threat of her destruction.

No sooner do the villanos begin to celebrate the miraculous life of Prometeo's creation than they are interrupted by drums and trumpets and shouts of "¡Guerra, guerra, al arma, al arma! (II, 447). This time, Epimeteo's egocentric reaction is right, as he interprets the shouts as that which "en baldón de Minerba, / es el enojo de Palas contra mí" (II, 450–452). The scene continues as a duel between the threatening war cries and the music celebrating "que quien da las çiençias, da / voz al barro y luz al alma." Minerba/Pandora concludes that:

> . . . el ver mezclados
> horrores y voçes blandas
> geroglífico es que diga
> que pacífica, esta llama
> será alhago, será alibio,
> será gozo, será graçia
> y colérica, será
> ynçendio, yra, estrago, y rabia;
> y así, temed y adorad
> al fuego cuando le exparza,
> o afable, o sañudo, a toda
> la naturaleza humana
> la estatua de Prometeo. (II, 460–472)

The flame of civilization is as ambivalent in its effects as the mankind that employs it—the truth of which is only too evident in our nuclear age.

While the concrete action of the play depicts Prometeo and Epimeteo as the human playthings of Minerba and Palas, its complex symbolism suggests that the goddesses may also be read as creatures of human manufacture, as the embodiment of the disparate strivings of the contrary facets of humanity. When Minerba removes her fierce disguise, she appears dressed exactly like the statue Prometeo has created, a copy of his imagination. Similarly, the terror-stricken Epimeteo plunges through the underbrush and encounters exactly what he feared, a threatening, all-powerful monster.

Reading this way, we can see in Discordia's arrival the embodiment of the conflict about to explode between man the philosopher and man the hunter. This infernal goddess is in Calderón's dramas the inherent and indispensable ally of war, for neither war nor discord can accomplish their ends without the assistance of the other. Palas says that she has summoned Discordia because war requires not only weapons but also the "vmanos desabenençias" and "corazones opuestos" that are Discordia's specialty.[27] Discordia's powers have a diabolical origin: Minerba calls her "bastarda Deydad . . . hija de Plutón" (III, 586–587), and she describes herself as "aborted daughter of the first rebellion" in the auto *El lirio y la azucena* (916, 919). As Mujica (291) points out, she is capable of divine song and human speech because she exists among men and among gods, at an earthly and an eternal level. Like her progenitor, she can assume a variety of deceiving and alluring disguises. In the auto, Discordia explains that the two human weaknesses that give her free rein in the world are pride and envy—the self-assertive pride of Lucifer's rebellion and the envy caused by inequality—which lead men to violate the two precepts of natural law: loving God and loving their neighbors. *La estatua de Prometeo* does not rely on the theological explanations of the auto, but Calderón has built into Prometeo and Epimeteo the same psychological foundations for the operation of Discordia, giving her fertile ground for the implantation of jealousy, her "última sedición." Thus the second act ends dramatically with the joined threats of Discordia and Palas ringing over the background music of the peasants celebrating their new goddess.

As the brothers argue and threaten to proceed from words to swords in Act III, Discordia is present but silent. This is in keeping with the role played by the more familiar god Cupido and his brother Anteros in other Calderonian mythological plays; although the characters protest that they are helpless against such divine powers, the divine magic is generally only accentuating inclinations the characters have already betrayed. The internal friction inherent in man's dual composition allows the demonic Discordia to take charge of humanity.

Hoping to cut off their dispute, Pandora innocently prepares to open the golden urn the disguised Discordia had given her and to distribute the wealth of gifts it purportedly contains. As she opens the urn, a cloud of smoke emerges, blocking the sun, blinding everyone, and turning the relationship between Epimeteo, Pandora, and Prometeo into a classic love-hate triangle, while the populace divides into opposing factions and nature repeats the human tumult with lightning, thunder, and an earthquake. Henceforth, the earthly characters live in the confusion of misunderstanding and strife so characteristic of the social world of the cape-and-sword dramas, as Epimeteo and Prometeo try to discern which is the divine Minerba and which her human image, Pandora, and struggle to understand their own illogical emotions. When Pandora protests Prometeo's abhorrence of her, this previously rational being can give her no logical explanation, but can only say:

> ¿Cómo puedo, sin saberlo,
> deçirlo tampoco yo?
> pues si Deydad te contemplo,
> te adoro; si hermosa, te amo;
> si discreta, te venero;
> si prodijiosa, te admiro;
> y si todo, te aborrezco;
> que ay otro yo que sin mí
> manda en mí más que yo mesmo (III, 848–856).

Dramatically speaking, the "otro yo" is Discordia, the demon dispatched by Palas to overcome the man of reason, twisting all his judgments to her ends. The characters regain clear perception and harmony only in the final resolution when Apolo, as the representative of Júpiter's supreme wisdom and justice, banishes Discordia.

Psychologically speaking, and focusing on Prometeo and Epimeteo as two aspects of a single being, the metaphor of internal discord works equally well. Prometeo, as the human reasoning capacity, disappointed in the corporeal reality of the image he had created of his ideal and horrified at the prospect of the destruction his ambitious theft had brought about, retreats into a deathlike isolation (III, 554–564). His retreat leaves Epimeteo in virtual control of the "battlefield," in this case man himself, dramatically illustrating the cliché of the man whose reason is blinded by his passions.

The earthly civil war is paralleled by a celestial quarrel as Palas condemns Prometeo's theft before Apolo and Minerba comes to his defense. This debate is absolutely central to both the "particular" text and its political counterpart, as Apolo's ray symbolizes the wisdom of God and the power of the king. For the second axis of tension in this play is that between man and the divine and temporal powers that rule over him. Man's dilemma is not only that he is divided against himself but also that he exists in an ambiguous position, between heaven and earth, between god and animal. His reason rebels against the limitations imposed by his rude physical composition and leads him to aspire to divine understanding and power. The issue thus raised is whether his reasoning powers give him the right to control ever-increasing spheres of his own existence or whether such accretions to human power represent punishable treason toward God and king, the previous sole possessors of such powers. Prometeo's theft of Apolo's ray raises precisely the same issue as the Adamic eating of the fruit of the tree of knowledge—whether man may rightly acquire "divine" wisdom or whether his attempts to do so represent a sinful attempt to be "like God," a challenge to the supreme authority.

Once advised of the theft by Palas, Apolo is angry not only with Prometeo but with the populace as a whole:

> . . . en mi yndignación
> todos son
> cómpliçes del robo el día
> que a nueba Deydad, con nueba alegría
> sabiendo que es hurto, le admiten por don (III, 313–317).

By accepting his gift, they have incriminated themselves in his crime against divine power. Calderón spelled out in his version of the Prometeo myth exactly the ambiguity since pointed out by Donoghue: "A gift of any kind starts a cycle of obligation. . . . But a gift which has been stolen is a much more complex matter because it cannot release itself from its origin in violence, risk, and guilt; the receiver is incriminated in the donor's crime." Donoghue considers the story essentially an account of the origin of human consciousness and finds that "the interest of the myth consists in the ambiguity with which it surrounds the lucidity of knowledge, the moral darkness from which its brightness came" (17–18).

As Calderón's gods and goddesses debate the question, Palas emphasizes the moral darkness, arguing that Prometeo's appropriation of the ray was robbery and that robbery is always wrong. Minerba defends the lucidity, saying that stealing to do good is not a crime and that the loss of such a tiny ray did not diminish Apolo's power but rather perfected its goodness by extending it to a needy humanity while preserving Apolo's dignity as the essential source of its power. Palas counters with the charge of treason, maintaining that it was solely Apolo's right to distribute his powers, if and when he should choose to do so. Apolo finds both his sisters' arguments convincing and finally chooses neutrality, leaving reason and force to decide the issue on the human battlefield. Theoretically speaking, Apolo's neutrality is consistent with the doctrine of free will, which reserves for man the obligation of electing the path between good and evil. However, in this episode drawn quite directly from Lucian's account of the Prometheus story, Calderón dramatizes Apolo's indecision not as a well-considered good for mankind but as a weakness in the sun-god on whom all life depends.

The opposing forces are now aligned on earth. Prometeo has emerged from hiding, saying that he would hide to avoid a fight from starting but will not flee as a coward from leading his followers once a fight is imminent. His band is smaller but confident that with Minerba—reason—on their side, they are stronger. Epimeteo criticizes the elderly Timantes for following Prometeo in opposing the goddess of war, and Timantes says that he prefers the risk of destruction in defense of Prometeo's honorable cause—bringing the ray that enlightens and warms humanity—to the dishonorable victory of Epimeteo's ingratitude. Epimeteo says that any possible good from Prometeo's accomplishment has been negated by the threat of Apolo's punishment. Timantes, the voice of wisdom acquired through experience, answers with a fascinating scientific metaphor:

> Los metheoros del ayre
> sin esa causa los vemos
> en condensados vapores
> conjelarse (III, 909–912).

In other words, he says that it is not Apolo who keeps flaming meteors from reaching earth; we do not understand completely the ways of nature or the gods and cannot be sure that Apolo will punish Prometeo's theft. Fear of possible retribution by higher powers should not deter man from securing a certain good for humanity.

Epimeteo reacts impatiently to Timantes' reasoning and urges his followers to battle. Discordia, unsure that even her larger force will enable her to prevail over Minerba's intelligence, intervenes again, disguising herself as an ambassadress of Júpiter, who she claims requires either the sacrifice of the two principal offenders, Pandora by fire and Prometeo by his traditional punishment, or the destruction of the whole Cáucaso. At this second, explicit threat, Timantes and the remaining members of Prometeo's band desert him. When he accuses them of treason, they reply that obedience to divine decrees is not treason, and they aid Epimeteo in taking the two prisoner, covering their faces to deny all possibility of appeal or compassion. The man of reason has now been blindfolded literally as well as figuratively by his passionate brother, to prevent any possibility of his communicating with the rest of humanity or appealing for his right to exist.

Prometeo has reached his nadir. Deserted by all his supporters, he and his creation seem totally at the mercy of the passions of his vengeful brother and a populace fearful of jealous deities. As O'Connor has said, the drama speaks as much of the limitation of unaided human reason as its triumph.

Yet tragedy is averted.[28] As Epimeteo leads his brother and Pandora to prison, Minerba appears to sing an appeal for justice to Júpiter that Prometeo's robbery, if such it is, was no crime compared to Discordia's treasonous theft of his voice and falsification of his decrees. When Palas descends to prevent Minerba from personally taking her appeal directly to Júpiter, the goddess of reason and the goddess of force lock in battle. Minerba emerges triumphant and leaves to take her claim to the highest court, proclaiming:

> . . . mortales,
> ved si entre yngenio y valor
> más que la fuerza del brazo
> vale la de la razón (III, 1075–1078).[29]

Calderón described Discordia in *El lirio y la azucena* as the bastard offspring of Lucifer's rebellion, who flourishes in the world by reason of her introduction of inequalities and the resultant violation of the two precepts of Natural Law: loving God and loving one's neighbor. According to Thomistic philosophy (*Summa* Part 2, 1, Art. 1–2), the principal roots of sin are pride, which causes human beings to turn away from God, and covetousness. The obvious villains in *La estatua de Prometeo* are those who embody the second of these two sins, the jealous Palas and her protegé, Epimeteo. Yet it is Prometeo, not Epimeteo, who must change to reassert his leadership and avert disaster. The defect in Calderón's philosopher Prometeo is a proud self-involvement that leads him to worship reason as an end in itself. As Minerba, in one sense a projection of Prometeo's aspiration, carries her appeal to Júpiter, she represents the recognition of final dependence on the supreme god as the ultimate source of wisdom and justice, a sign of humanity's return to obedience to the first precept of Natural Law as defined by Calderón. Prometeo manifests his beginning compliance with the second precept, that of loving his neighbor, when Epimeteo removes the blindfold and Prometeo, viewing Pandora, truly sees the suffering of another human being and learns compassion.

That Calderón has Epimeteo first tie and then remove the blindfold is not a gratuitous detail but a symbol vital to the structure of the play. Calderón has throughout depicted Prometeo as a solitary figure unable to relate to other human beings, while the passionate Epimeteo is eminently capable of such bonds. His blindfolding of Prometeo symbolizes the negative effect of passion when it dominates reason. That it is his removal of the blindfold that triggers Prometeo's love for Pandora and awakens the sympathies of all onlookers dramatizes the positive role that human emotions play in binding man to those with whom he shares the earth.

Apolo thereupon intervenes to convey Júpiter's inevitable pardon, to banish Discordia, and thereby to restore in all "razón y sentido / sentido y razón" (III, 1188–1189), and the twin brothers are restored to harmonious unity. Thus the final redemption of Prometeo is not a totally arbitrary intervention by a *deus ex machina* but a response to modification within Prometeo himself—or rather within the complex protagonist, Prometeo-Epimeteo. That it is depicted as an unexpected and largely unearned event is in accord with the theological doctrine repeatedly dramatized by Calderón in the autos—that human salvation is a free gift from God that occurs only when human beings come to recognize dependence on the mercy of the supreme authority. Significantly, however,

Calderón never depicts an active involvement by the supreme god to avert the tragedy, only a realignment of the lower deities (and their dependent human subjects) acting on their concept of Júpiter's code of justice. Taken in conjunction with Timantes' comment that earth is not protected from meteors by Apolo's intervention, this suggests that it is not direct intervention of a supreme authority that governs human events but the human conception of the possibility of such an intervention.

The "particular text" in *La estatua de Prometeo* is, then, a glorification of human reason *and* a recognition of reason's limitations. The progress of the individual and of human society depends on the creative and civilizing powers of human reason, in ascendancy over egocentric and potentially destructive passion. Yet precisely because he is not an angel but a human being, living in society with other human beings, man cannot deny or divorce himself from the emotional component of his dual nature but must incorporate, under the guidance of reason, the positive bonding capacity the passions contribute to human existence. If this delicate balance is maintained, man's attempts to perfect his condition are not punishable by death or expulsion from paradise like Adam but merit the highest reward—marriage to the "semidivine" beauty of his creation so that a new civilized society may people the earth.

THE POLITICAL TEXT

Since analysis of the defects of political society tended to focus, in the seventeenth as in the twentieth century, on the villain in the system, we can best approach the political text of this play through its central villain, Discordia. She was a familiar figure in the Hapsburg court of the 1670s, both literally and figuratively. In *El lirio y la azucena,* the frankly political auto that celebrated the peace concluded between France and Spain in 1659, Calderón called the court her natural habitat, as Discordia says to her partner Guerra:

> Aunque en el fin uno no más seamos,
> somos dos en las sendas que pisamos,
> pues cuando hacia las cortes van mis sañas,
> van tus furores hacia las campañas: (916)

She had long since become a familiar figure in the iconography of court-commissioned art, and looms large in the ten-picture Hercules cycle painted by Zurbarán for the Hall of Realms of the Buen Retiro, as Brown and Elliott point out:

Religious and political struggles of this period, and the divided loyalty of a sovereign's subjects, made the threat of discord loom large over the times.

The extension of the Herculean metaphor to include the power to stifle rebellion was almost inevitable, and by the mid-sixteenth century the usual form for the symbol showed Hercules vanquishing a monster. By the time that Cesare Ripa published his influential encyclopedia of emblems *Iconologia* (1603), the identification between monster and Discordia was universally understood. Discordia, he writes, is a woman in the form of an infernal demon, *furia infernale,* dressed in multicolored clothes, with snakes in her hair (160).

Six of the ten pictures of the cycle show Hercules defeating various monsters, "feats which were understood to symbolize the triumph of the just sovereign over his domestic and foreign enemies" (161).

Furthermore, Discordia is one of the "unholy triumvirate" crushed by Felipe IV and Olivares in Maino's *Recapture of Bahía* in the same hall. "At the king's feet lie in defeat the personifications of his enemies—Heresy, holding a broken cross in its hands and mouth; Discord, the *"furia infernale,"* with snakes in her hair; and Treachery, or Fraud, a two-faced creature, with left and right hands reversed, who offers peace and then stabs in the back" (188). Ironically, while Heresy lies under Felipe's feet, it is Olivares whose foot crushes Discordia's neck. While this was the image he surely wished to project, that valido was certainly more cause than cure for discord during most of his tenure.

With no strong foot to crush her, Discordia (or factional struggle) grew to truly monstrous proportions in the Spanish court after Felipe IV died in 1665, leaving his widow Mariana and a junta of ministers to rule for his retarded four-year-old son Carlos. In a decade, the Spanish governmental system, which was designed to function around the person of a mature monarch, degenerated from one of the most stable and orderly in Europe to one of the most chaotic and vacillating, and pure politics filled the vacuum left by the absence of an effective sovereign (Stradling 147). At the center of this struggle stood Don Juan José, whom Kamen calls "the most powerful personality in the kingdom and one of the most significant figures in the history of Habsburg Spain" (329). Stradling describes his role as follows:

> The single most significant political fact during the subsequent decade was the existence of the new king's adult halfbrother, Don Juan José. Even whilst his father had lived, this prince has made no secret of his claim to share power, and now publicly advanced a cause which amounted to a demand for the regency itself. The politics of this period were dominated by his campaign, and the faction fighting which it encouraged in Madrid. By the late 1660s, Don Juan provided an alternative centre of allegiance for many individuals and sectional interests, like the "court" of the Prince of Wales in Hanoverian England (147).

Don Juan José was not only a political and military leader but also the principal patron of the introduction of new scientific information in Spain. José María López Piñero, in his study of scientific renovation in Spain, maintains that it did not begin with Feijóo, as is commonly thought, but had its roots in the late seventeenth century, despite the common image of the reign of Carlos II as Spain's period of greatest cultural decadence. During the last twenty-five or thirty years of the seventeenth century, the first really modern Spanish scientists appeared and began the process of breaking with traditional principles and introducing modern science, earning in the process the negative title *novatores* from their traditional opponents (8–9, 12, 34). Don Juan José was a vital patron of this group, as López Piñero points out:

> Al no tener prácticamente cabida en las instituciones existentes, los *novatores* tuvieron que depender de la protección de nobles y clérigos de mentalidad preilustrada, y agruparse en "tertulias" independientes o en torno a sus mecenas. Entre estos últimos destaca, por su importancia y sobre todo por su prioridad cronológica, el varias veces citado Juan José de Austria. Si se tiene en cuenta su papel dentro de la historia política española, resulta extraordinariamente ilustrativo conocer su interés por la ciencia moderna. Seguía con gran atención la producción astronómica y física de su tiempo, manejaba con gran destreza los instrumentos de observación astronómica, y era un gran aficionado a la mecánica, llegando a construir personalmente varios aparatos. Su postura acerca de la aplicación de los nuevos conocimientos y técnicas a la resolución de los problemas colectivos, se refleja en dos significativas dedicatorias a su persona: la del *Discurso físico y político* (1679) de Juan Bautista Juanini, primer texto español en el que se utilizan los saberes médicos y químicos "modernos" para enfrentarse con un problema de higiene pública, y la *Arquitectura civil, recta y oblicua* (1678) de Juan Caramuel, fundamentación matemática al día de las técnicas de construcción. Su apoyo es, sin duda, una de las claves explicativas de la pujanza del grupo de novatores y tradicionalistas moderados de Zaragoza (42).

Six years after the death of Don Juan in 1679, Juanini, who had been his personal physician for six years, wrote in glowing praise of his intellectual interests and talents:

> No he hallado otro Príncipe que como su Alteza tuviesse talentos tan universales y eminentes. . . . El tiempo que le sobrava de los manejos públicos, no lo entregava al descanso del cuerpo, lo aplicava al divertimiento honesto y erudito del espíritu. . . . En todas las partes de Mathemática era versadísimo; conocía y manejava con gran destreza y acierto los Instrumentos. . . . Distinguía las doctrinas de todos con incomparable claridad, y lo

bueno, dudoso y Religioso de ellas, dando a Aristóteles, Ptholomeo, Thico Brahe, Copérnico, Galileo y otros lo que les tocava. En la Geometría, Geographía, Cosmografía, hablava y obrava con la misma excelencia. Y como el mando del Mar era el primer empleo a que le destinó la prudente atención del Señor Rey su Padre, tenía el Arte Náutica tan sabida que el Padre Lasalle de la Compañía de Jesús dixo al Rey: no sabía ya qué enseñarle. . . . (qtd in Kamen, *Spain* 546)

Don Juan José, benefiting from his experience in governing Cataluña in particular, was also the proponent of substantial economic and political reforms; those that were actually initiated during his brief tenure as prime minister between 1677 and 1679 include monetary reforms aimed at producing a stable Spanish currency; limiting the growth of ecclesiastical orders; and the establishment of a Junta de Comercio, which worked toward the modernization of the industrial system by breaking down the ancient guild system, increasing trade, and declaring nobility compatible with participation in industry (Kamen, *Spain* 103, 130, 272–273).

Despite his talents, preparation, and widespread popular support, nevertheless, Don Juan remained in an anomalous position when Felipe IV died on 17 September 1665, refusing on his deathbed to grant an audience to his illegitimate son. As Kamen puts it: "By the end of his father's reign, Don Juan was in the curious position of being his country's most distinguished general, yet denied any political honours suited to his status. Philip IV's refusal to legitimise him effectively blocked his way to any higher dignities. The most obvious candidate as acting head of state, he was nevertheless excluded from the Committee of Government" (330).

The center of opposition to Don Juan, after Felipe IV's death as before, was Mariana, who saw him as a threat to her own authority and to the future rule of her pathetic son Carlos, who at four years of age could not yet walk and had only recently been weaned, who at nine still seemed incapable of learning to read and write (Kamen, *Spain* 21). Lacking the intellectual gifts or political acumen to rule herself, Mariana sought a strong man to rely on, but her two choices of valido were almost universally unpopular. Her first choice was her confessor, Juan Everardo Nithard, an Austrian Jesuit who had accompanied her to Madrid when she married Felipe IV in 1649. Mariana maneuvered to have him naturalized in 1666 because her husband's will had specified that no foreigner could hold office in the councils of state. Succeeding in that, she arranged for his appointment as inquisitor general on 22 September 1666. Kamen describes the result: "The appointment of an obscure foreigner to the highest offices in the state was the direct cause of the constitutional crises of the next two years. But the spark that ignited the flame was the chafing impatience of Don Juan, waiting at Consuegra for the call that did not come" (331).

Mariana and Nithard arranged to have Don Juan appointed commander of the forces in Flanders, to remove him from the center of power. But alleging various difficulties, he refused the post. In August 1668, he was exiled to Consuegra and forbidden to come within twenty leagues of Madrid. Alerted to an attempt by Don Juan's secretary to kidnap Nithard, the Junta de Gobierno voted on 19 October 1668 to arrest him, but he escaped and eventually fled to Cataluña, a stronghold of support for him dating from the days of his viceroyalty. From there, he began a war of pamphlets and letters, seeking to use public opinion to control the country. As the various councils of state turned toward support of Don Juan, he began a triumphant march from Barcelona toward Madrid in early 1669, with a troop of four hundred cavalrymen he claimed to need as a personal escort. He entered incognito and as a private person in Zaragoza, yet received a tumultuous welcome from the crowd, and excited students burned the effigy of a Jesuit in front of the Jesuit residence (Kamen, *Spain* 331–334). Don Juan's approach, even with this small force, threatened civil war, and with it he achieved "what may perhaps be called the first *pronunciamiento* in modern Spanish history: a military coup against Madrid with the aid of the provinces. It was completely bloodless" (Kamen, *Spain* 336). The Junta de Gobierno at last met all his demands: Nithard left for Rome; a Junta de Alivios was created to carry out reforms; all recent legislation against Don Juan was removed from the records; and Don Juan, unable to achieve more, accepted the post of vicar general of the Crown of Aragón.

Mariana's subsequent choice for valido was Fernando Valenzuela, a member of the lesser nobility who rose to power through his charm and marriage to one of the queen's ladies-in-waiting. As the queen appointed him to ever more honored posts, the resentment of the old nobility increased. The tension reached a climax in November 1675 when Carlos reached his majority at fourteen. According to his father's will, the Junta de Gobierno was to be suspended automatically on his birthday, but the young king was obviously incapable of ruling alone, and Don Juan's cause was raised again. The secretary of the junta presented Carlos with a decree continuing its powers another two years, but Carlos refused to sign and informed his mother on 5 November that he had summoned Don Juan.

That morning the prince drove through the cheering crowds to the royal Alcázar; he was greeted as an Infante of Spain, and ushered into the king's presence at the appointed hour; the brothers embraced each other and Charles assured Don Juan of his protection. After mass and a Te Deum, the prince went to the Buen Retiro and the king went to visit his mother.

Charles was closeted with Mariana for two hours, and emerged with tears in his eyes. . . . It took several hours to put pressure successfully on the king. Shortly after six the duke of Medinaceli came to Don Juan at the

Buen Retiro, with a handwritten order from the king to leave for Italy at once. . . .

Don Juan left Madrid that evening. In a letter of 8 November to the Diputación and city of Saragossa, accounting for the sudden change of events, and published openly as all the prince's letters were, Don Juan explained that he had withdrawn in order to avoid a confrontation. To rescue "His Majesty from the situation he is in" he would have needed the help of the aristocracy, but a minority of them had been hostile (Kamen, *Spain* 337–338).

Valenzuela was also ordered out of Madrid, being made captain general of the kingdom of Granada, but he returned in April of 1676 with the support of the queen, who appointed him caballerizo mayor, a post supposedly reserved for the highest nobility. The majority of the nobility went on strike and circulated a public petition demanding the permanent separation of the queen from her son, the imprisonment of Valenzuela, and the designation of Don Juan as "colaborador inmediato" of the king. Valenzuela began gathering troops in the capital, and armed conflict threatened again. As Don Juan marched from Zaragoza to Madrid, volunteers from Valencia, Cataluña, and Aragón swelled his forces, which came to number more than fifteen thousand men, including "eighteen grandees of Castile, the flower of the Aragonese aristocracy, and several other nobles; it was possibly the biggest force ever collected in Spain in peacetime" (Kamen, *Spain* 340). The king sent troops to arrest Valenzuela, who had fled to El Escorial, and at 6:00 A.M. 23 January 1677, Don Juan entered the Buen Retiro palace, had the king awakened, and offered him his services.

The events of January 1677, were, as Kamen says, more than a pronunciamiento: "They were also a *coup d'état*, the first to occur in modern Spanish history. But unlike many later coups, this one had the overwhelming support of both the ruling classes and the people of Spain. In contrast to Valenzuela, who was a petty favourite of no historical importance, Don Juan was supremely significant as the first real national leader in Spain's history. From every side he was looked up to as the savior of Spain" (*Spain* 340). The savior proved disappointing. Don Juan found the obstacles to reform even more intractable than the obstacles he had overcome on his way to power. His own authority was dependent on the continued favor of the king, on whom Mariana continued to apply pressure against the prince. In the end, his tenure proved too brief to effect any real change. He died in September 1679 at the age of fifty.

We cannot be sure of the exact year in which Calderón wrote *La estatua de Prometeo*, only that it was sometime between 1669 and 1674. As the preceding account demonstrates, in any one of those years, the principal issue in the court at Madrid was the power struggle between the factions supporting and opposing

Don Juan José. When Calderón wrote a play about a contest between "los dos nobles caudillos del pueblo" and their heavenly patronesses, its local relevance would be apparent.

It is also likely that the audience would relate Don Juan with Prometeo, whom Calderón draws as the man of reason, the student of science, who had studied abroad and returned to institute a new rule of law in his country. He creates Pandora, civilization (in political terms, a new Spain), a beautiful product of human rationality that he brings to life with power stolen from Apolo—ever the symbol of the king. When Prometeo, representative of "forethought" or progressive forces, has created the new Spain, his brother Epimeteo, representing "afterthought" or memory, the reactionary leader who had led the populace to reject rational new laws for the simple old ways, becomes enamored of the new creation and wishes to possess it. Pandora rejects his advances and follows Prometeo, whereupon the jealous conservative leader turns his vengeance on her "galán," the progressive leader, and threatens to destroy both him and his new Spain.

Whether Calderón intended his audience to identify Epimeteo with any specific opponent of Don Juan is questionable. While certain features of characterization might suggest certain figures, the political text Calderón constructed was both more subtle and more universal than such a simplistic, one-to-one allegorical message, limited by specific identification of Epimeteo with Don Juan's current opponent.[30] Rather, Calderón structured the drama to convey the idea that as each individual is divided by the discord between his reason and passion, every country is torn by the strife between progressives and conservatives, and every political movement by the contest between reason and force. This broader structuring makes the myth applicable to an almost infinite variety of conflictive political situations. Aubrun (vii) mentioned three: the 1669 peace between Spain and Portugal; the struggle between Don Juan and Valenzuela; and that between Carlos II and Louis XIV of France. The list could be expanded well beyond the seventeenth century, and beyond the borders of Spain. Certainly this story of the contest between progressives and conservatives, between reason and force, is equally applicable three centuries later to the problems faced by Spain after the death of Franco. Rather than a straightforward political allegory anchored to specific personalities, Calderón created situations in which the central issue reflected current political dilemmas, as De Armas points out: "It is the allusiveness of his *comedias* that attracts the reader or spectator. The relevance of Calderón's images and plots to contemporary situations captures the attention of the spectator who, in his attempt to unravel a series of indirect references, enters into an emotional and intellectual exchange with the dialogic actions being presented. Ideas, images, and concepts lead to contemporary historical events and vice versa" (*Astrea* 176).

Certain aspects of the dominant political figure of the period, Don Juan José, would lead spectators to Prometeo, while Epimeteo possessed traits identifiable in his opponents; yet Don Juan José can also be viewed as a compound of Prometeo and Epimeteo—he is every man divided between reason and passion, and his pursuit of power reflects both the positive use of human reason and the negative threat of force. Both were clearly applicable to Don Juan, who was at once the patron of science and modernization, and the focus for the threat of civil war. Calderón provides a similar double personality for the second crucial figure of the period, Mariana. As Don Juan José can be read as both Prometeo and Epimeteo, so Mariana can be related to the twin goddesses in her controlling influence over the fate of "earthly" *caudillos* and their followers. In Minerba and Palas Calderón created for her two powerful female models, obviously suggesting Minerba as the preferable image of the two. Nor is Mariana the only one whom Calderón is tactfully counseling with his play. Tragedy is averted at the end of the drama because Prometeo has learned humility and compassion for humankind. He is then rewarded by marriage to Pandora, so that in the product of their union the new civilization might continue. The inferred lesson is that the dominant political leader should justify his ascendancy by demonstrating not a proud or possessive self-assertion but a genuine concern for the people he governs.

The peculiarly vacillating role of Apolo in the play also becomes understandable in the reading of the political myth. The sun-god is the traditional symbol of kingship, both human and divine. Calderón underlines this symbolism emphatically in *La estatua de Prometeo*, calling Apolo

> . . . *árbitro* del día y la noche,
> *monarca* de los planetas,
> *rey* de los signos, y *dueño*
> de luzeros y de estrellas,
> vida es de frutos y flores,
> y alma de montes y selbas (I, 837–843; emphasis mine).

In the play, civil war threatens because the indecisive Apolo cannot choose to side with either sister. As Stradling pointed out, the basic political problem of the time was the lack of a decisive mature king in a system designed to function around such a figure. We can therefore presume that a contemporary audience would have recognized the validity of the Apolo scenario, even before they witnessed the dramatic spectacle in November 1675 of Carlos II pulled back and forth between his half-brother and his mother.

Calderón's play addresses in two symbolic actions the issue of the threat Don Juan's bid for power represented to the authority of Carlos and Mariana. The first is the end of the first act, in which the audience saw Apolo crossing the stage singing while Prometeo stole a ray of his light:

No temas, no, desçender,
que si en todo es de sentir
que naçe para morir,
tú mueres para naçer (I, 877–885).

Felipe IV, "el cuarto planeta," was the king most regularly identified with the sun-god, but the image of the sun setting only to be reborn was a standard motif in the funerary art of other Hapsburg kings. The idea thus suggested is that the transference of power is not the "death" of the Hapsburg monarchy but only its regeneration through the natural process of periodic renewal.[31]

Calderón treats the more immediate and more eternal issue—whether Prometeo's theft of regal authority is a praiseworthy advance for mankind or a damnable act of treason—through Apolo's actions at the end of the drama. After Minerba appeals to Júpiter and Prometeo demonstrates compassion for Pandora, Apolo intervenes to pardon Prometeo and thus banish the villainous Discordia. Apolo justifies his last-minute decision to intervene by saying that he wants to be the bringer of the pardon he knows Júpiter will grant:

. . . al ver que Minerba
al solio subió
de Júpiter, donde
pide su perdón,
y que el conçederle
es preçisa acçión,
porque nunca niega
piedades vn dios,
venir e querido
a traerle yo;
débanmele a mí
y a Júpiter no (III, 1162–1173).

His action accords with the theory of the divine right of kings: They are the representatives through whom God's wisdom and justice are dispensed on earth. As Calderón phrases this speech, the process works not because the supreme god actually orders earthly affairs through a regal intermediary but because the king's conception of Júpiter's ultimate goodness makes him eventually act in accord with his understanding of that goodness.

Significantly, Júpiter never actively intervenes. The final verdict is not dictated by a *deus ex machina* in the classic sense of a supreme being who swings in on stage machinery to arrange human affairs but by invocation of a supreme authority who remains totally outside the works. Apolo is, of course, a machine-born god, but as he had earlier abjured his regal authority to settle the dispute between Minerba-Prometeo and Palas-Epimeteo, so now he invokes not his own authority but his conception of an invisible supreme being. The king figure, who had first refused to act, now acts only as an intermediary for an absent authority principle whose presumed judgment Apolo explains only in the flat, unrevealing, and unsatisfying phrase "nunca niega / piedades vn dios" (III, 1168–1169).

In the end, Calderón's Prometeo is not condemned to either divine or regal punishment for his usurpation of power or expelled from paradise like Adam. Instead, he emerges a wise, triumphant figure, rewarded with marriage to Pandora and once again in ascendancy over his contrary brother, who is restored to allegiance to him. The accretion of regal or "divine" power to the human sphere of control is, then, if properly motivated and guided, not to be condemned but generously applauded.

How does this redistribution of power accord with the theory of Maravall that Golden Age theatre, while superficially modern, was in ultimate intent and effect an important force toward immobilization and the maintenance of an authoritarian status quo? Maravall states:

> Shakespeare o Ben Jonson no representan una cultura que hiciera imposible la revolución industrial. Racine o Molière tal vez contribuyeron a preparar los espíritus para la fase renovadora del colbertismo. Pero de las condiciones en que se produjo el teatro de Lope o el de Calderón y que en sus obras se reflejaron—con no dejar de ser ellos modernos—, no se podría salir, sin embargo, hacia un mundo definitivamente moderno, rompiendo el inmovilismo de la estructura social en que el teatro de uno y otro se apoyaban—a pesar de lo mucho que para la primera aparición de una modernidad contribuyeran. Tan sólo cuando, a pesar de todo, entran en la Península Descartes o Galileo, y con ellos la ciencia moderna, se pueden descubrir algunas novedades en el pensamiento que, no obstante la noble polémica que representa la Illustración dieciochesca, no lograrían tampoco triunfar (*Barroco* 77).

For Maravall, Golden Age theatre assists in undermining the drive toward human liberty set in motion by the Renaissance. For terHorst, on the other hand, the expression of that force provides the life of Calderonian drama:

> A departure from orthodoxy . . . is . . . of absolutely fundamental and crucial importance to the life and function of Calderonian drama. To rise up in rebellion against the mandates of governing powers, paternal and divine, is an essential role which man constantly creates for himself, in contradistinction to the part that God or one's father would have one passively play. In this sense, though an oversimplification, it might help to say that the pressures toward paternalistic conformism are the medieval dogmatic continuum in Calderón's theatre, while the irrepressible urge of the gifted man

to fashion his own fate constitutes a Renaissance corollary. Both impulses are required. They engage each other so as to give voice to the contrapuntal melody of struggle that always informs Calderón's plays. Disobedience, there, can be original, creative, and can ultimately be reconciled to the world harmonic (58).

Both these statements are at least partially valid with regard to other works of Calderón; neither, however, adequately describes the fundamental attitude toward authority embodied in the structure of *La estatua de Prometeo*.

TerHorst's interpretation is subconsciously influenced by the rebellious Prometheus of Aeschylus and romantic writers. As pointed out above, Calderón's Prometeo is not driven by a rebellious attitude toward superior authority. He complains of being limited not by the restrictive pressure of divine beings but by the ignorant and conservative barbarity of those below him. He expresses boundless admiration for the gods (I, 207–230) and commits his theft under the tutelage of a goddess; when he thinks that Apolo threatens retribution, he first withdraws from conflict and then joins the fray only in self-defense, when the battle has become inevitable.

On the other hand, and in contradiction to Maravall's views (in the case of *La estatua de Prometeo*, based on a superficial reading of the play), Calderón's hero in this work neither advocates nor yields to the status quo. In this play it is the "villains"—Discordia, Epimeteo, and Palas—who advocate the maintenance of the status quo and constantly raise the spectre of divine retribution for human acquisition of knowledge and power. Prometeo, in contrast, is an outspoken advocate for political change and new scientific knowledge. In a key exchange, Timantes, the voice of experience, supports Prometeo precisely because he has brought the invaluable gift of fire to his people. When Epimeteo objects that Apolo's punishment will negate that good, Timantes replies with the enigmatic metaphor that it is not Apolo who makes meteors dissolve before reaching earth. The implication is that given his lack of understanding of the relationship between natural phenomena and divine (or regal) will, man should not be deterred from a proven good by a fear of punishment.

In effect, the entire structure of the play demonstrates a fundamental uncertainty concerning the locus of power over human affairs. Calderón raised, then sidestepped, the issue of the cause of dualism by naming Minerba and Palas as the efficient causes of the divergence between Prometeo and his alter ego, but specifying no first cause for the split between the heavenly pair. When various characters ask who brought the statue to life, an offstage chorus answers enigmatically:

> Quien triumpha para enseñanza
> de que quien da çiençias, da
> voz al barro y luz al alma.

Minerba and Palas appeal their quarrel to Apolo, only to have him renounce his monarchical role and tell them to fight it out on earth. Lastly, the supreme authority, Júpiter, is an absent and ultimately unfathomable power who shapes the outcome only as a concept of final justice in the minds of his subjects.

In spite of the multiple deities involved in this drama, authority is notable in *La estatua de Prometeo* as much for its absence as for its presence. This reflects quite accurately the vacuum of royal authority that characterized Hapsburg Spain after the death of Felipe IV. In this situation, Calderón does not postulate as a model a return to immobility and absolutism but political change and the introduction of precisely the "ciencia moderna" whose lack Maravall laments. The artificial suddenness of the happy resolution Calderón gives to the Prometheus story we may perhaps attribute to the fact that for him, as for the rest of the late Hapsburg court, the destructive conflict caused by the dualism of human nature was a lived experience. In the absence of a strong authority and depending on decidedly human resources, the channeling of that conflict toward the path of peace and progress could be at best a hypothetical scenario. Calderón's play survives as a witness that even in those bitter years, the aging playwright could construct a scenario in which the power of true human wisdom might change the established order and build a better future.[32]

By underlining the "progressive" message of *La estatua de Prometeo*, and foregrounding the critical content in others of his court spectacles, I do not attempt to portray Calderón as a "closet democrat." His political views were generally conservative, although not immobile, as *La estatua de Prometeo* demonstrates, and his intent was to purify the monarchy to strengthen and preserve it, not to undermine it. But as Jameson has observed, the process of figural articulation in artistic and cultural productions may serve to foreground the contradictions and structural limitations of the ideological construction the author wishes to uphold.[33] In the case of *La estatua de Prometeo*, for example, the logical extension of sanctioning the redistribution of power whenever it results in the good of humanity could lead to the eventual end of monarchical authority. Legitimizing such a development was certainly not Calderón's intent, as we will see in his dramatization of the constitution of monarchy in his last court play (see Chapter 7).

This potentially contradictory effect of figuration is perhaps most characteristic of dramatic expression, which requires the author to create an oppositional discourse sufficiently strong to provide a credible dramatic conflict. In the dramatic tradition of the Spanish corrales, a sort of oppositional discourse had indeed become institutionalized in the short burlesque pieces played between acts of the dramatic mainstay. We shall see in the following chapter how Calderón put this tradition to work, as he had the introductory loa, to serve his complex of texts.

SIX

A Pessimistic View:
Fieras afemina Amor

ON THE PURELY literary quality of its central dramatic text, *Fieras afemina Amor* would not merit a lengthy discussion, for it is a work cluttered with a strange assortment of deities and a number of spectacular effects whose integration into a unified theme seems tenuous at best.[1] Its overall dramatic coherence is considerably below that of the plays treated in the preceding chapters. Nevertheless, *Fieras* is a fascinating work, for two reasons: (1) its dark vision of male-female relationships, and the equally negative text of the political realities of the interregnum that Calderón constructs around that relationship; (2) the wealth of information about the 1672 first performance that has survived, which makes possible a more complete "composición de lugares" than for Calderón's other court plays.[2] We have not only the text of the full dramatic event, including the loa, other minor pieces, and a description of the scenery and stage effects, but also the accounts for the costumes made for the play, with details as precise as the number of buttons for each costume and the width and quantity of lace used to trim each one.[3] Combining names of actors and actresses given in the text and the accounts, we can also construct most of the cast of the opening performance, performed by the troupe of Antonio de Escamilla, with additional actresses for the occasion.

The date of the first performance has usually been given as January 1670, but the costume accounts make it quite certain that the actual opening took place in 1672. It was written, like *La estatua de Prometeo*, for the celebration of Mariana's birthday on 22 December, but as the loa makes clear, performance was postponed until January also to honor the birthday of her only grandchild, Princess María Antonia, born in Vienna on 18 January 1669. Although the text in no way specifies her age, Cotarelo (*Calderón*, 324) assumed that meant the celebration of her *first* birthday in 1670, and subsequent scholars have followed his reasoning. However, the 1672 production was a lavish one, financed by the príncipe de Astillano, who spent 277,861 *reales* on costumes alone.[4] If the play had been lavishly performed in 1670, it is virtually inconceivable that it would have been repeated on this scale only two years later, and we can therefore assume that the 1672 performance was the first and that it honored María Antonia's third rather than first birthday. Maura (*Corte* 2:147) gives the date of the lavish 1672 performance as 29 January, and the costume accounts confirm that date. A few orders and payments for materials were submitted in late December, beginning with the costumes for Hércules and the actress Mariana Borja, but the largest number were dated 13 January, perhaps the date when full-scale rehearsals began. On 25 January, Bernarda Manuela, concerned that her attire might be less brilliant than that of others, sent a note to the príncipe, asking for twenty-five more *varas* of trim to complete her costume, and added: "Atrevo a suplicarle remedie esta necesidad mandando a un criado se las aga dar al portador porque el tiempo es breve." The authorization was dated 28 January. The last bill, which seems to refer to a performance not yet accomplished, is that of 29 January, an obviously last-minute miscellaneous order that includes ninety-nine varas of crimson ribbon to attach the actresses to the tramoyas.

Costume design seems to have been a collaborative venture, calmly begun well in advance of the performance. The príncipe de Astillano appears to have been responsible for the costume choice because his embroiderer, Francisco de Avila, submitted a bill for a variety of materials he used to make up samples for the príncipe.[5] A number of other people, including perhaps the actors and actresses themselves, apparently had a say in costume design. The account file contains, as a sort of supporting annex, forty separate orders for material for the individual actors' costumes, written in a variety of hands, sometimes on reused scraps of paper. Another hand later corrected parts of these orders, changing some colors, type of fabrics, or quantities, and specifying the kind of lace or other trim. In the end, however, costume making came down to a feverish race toward curtain time; sewing the costume of Manuela Escamilla "de bobo" cost extra because it was made in one night, as did that of the costumes of seventeen captives, which were made "el mismo día que se izo la comedia."

Without accounts for the scenery and stage machinery, we do not know if their assembly required a similar race with time.[6] All was apparently in order, however, by the time of the ceremonial entry of Mariana and the nine-year-old Carlos II. An elaborate frontispiece had been erected, featuring four columns painted to imitate "piedra lazuli" embossed with gold along the stems, bases, and cornices (see Plate 1). Other decorative motifs over the cornices came together in a central medallion in relief, which showed Mercury with helmet and winged sandals.[7] The lateral niches formed by the colonnade were occupied by statues (in imitation bronze) of a lion and a tiger signifying "el valor y la osadía" (58). The large central space was covered by a curtain that spelled out the theme of the production much more explicitly than usual. Central to it was a large figure of Hercules, club in hand, with monstrous beasts lying defeated at his feet and Cupid hovering overhead, readying the arrow that would make him the ultimate victor. Had any spectator been so "dim of eyes" as to miss the significance of this scene, it was explained by inscriptions "Fieras afemina Amor" and "Omnia vincit Amor" slanted across the space on either side of Hercules.

After the audience had had a few minutes to enjoy this sight, music began with a fanfare of shawms followed by "templados instrumentos" (59). Ushered in by these strains, from behind the medallion (in a space left between the frontispiece and the curtain) descended a gilded eagle (symbol of the house of Austria) wearing the imperial crown and bearing on its back a nymph singing in praise of Mariana:

> a los felices años
> del Aguila suprema,
> que más que en nuestras vidas
> en nuestras almas reina (59).

She was joined by two other nymphs borne in from each side on a feathered "court," a phoenix (symbolizing renewal through the fire of love) and a peacock (figure of royal vigilance). Their costumes heightened the elegance of the scene, for the three nymphs were attired in blue and silver, trimmed (as were virtually all the costumes) about the hem, bodice, and sleeves with rows of silver and gold lace.[8]

The Aguila invites the phoenix and peacock to a "dulce competencia" to see which is best qualified to honor her, which is "la que mira / al Sol desde más cerca" (60). Phoenix says she will summon the months of the year to celebrate the occasion, and the Peacock counters by calling in the signs of the zodiac. The Aguila, who represents Mariana, flies up, raising the curtain with the assistance of her feathered court and saying that as she draws back the clouds from the sun, so will she raise the curtain on this smaller theatre (63–64):

> . . . haré del aire
> retirar las nubes densas,
> corriendo al Sol la cortina,
> para que mejor se vea
> a un tiempo entrambos teatros (63).

The theatre is to be viewed, like the court, as a world centered around and controlled by Mariana. This idea is reinforced by the physical nature of the elaborate illusionistic scenery and stage machinery, which apparently presented on stage for all to see a total universe under human—more specifically, royal—control.

The first view of this theatrical universe was one of the heavens—perspective scenery of the sky with cutouts in the panels illuminated from behind to imitate the effect of twinkling stars.[9] Hovering in the air were twelve "nymphs," each holding in one hand a silvery shield figuring the sign of the zodiac she represented, and carrying a torch in the other from which flowed a "ray" of silvery gauze (see Plate 2). Visibly representing the concept of the influence of each sign

on earth, these rays descended to the months, twelve youths arranged in a geometric design, each placed below the sign to which his month corresponded. All
were attired in blue taffeta—the men with wide blue sleeves, the women with
oversleeves of silver and white. Certain musicians in costume were also on stage
in the background.[10]

Adulation of the royal family continues in the remainder of the loa, which
consists of a musical competition between the twelve signs and their associated
months for the title of the most important month. Since the primary occasion for
the performance was the 22 December birthday of Mariana, December wins the
laurels because its generally sunless days saw the birth of the royal sun, Mariana,
"A suplir del sol la ausencia" (377). As in the loas for other court plays, the
message proclaimed was that of an entire universe and of all time paying homage
to the Hapsburg rulers. Carballo said in his poetics that the term *loa* was derived
from its function, which was to "loar en el [*sic*] la comedia, al auditorio, o festi-
uidad en que se haze" and thereby "captar la beneuolencia y atención del auditorio" (2:22). The masterfully orchestrated adulation of this loa can hardly have
failed to capture Mariana's benevolence and attention.[11]

Having accomplished this, Calderón gently transforms the adulatory "dulce
competencia" of the loa into the very different sort of contest for power that
prevails in the play itself. No clear line is drawn between the celebratory framework and the central dramatic text;[12] rather, a cinematographic fade-out–fade-in
links the two as the musicians sing:

Ya que la Aguila plumas
dio a su guirnalda bella,
la tierra con sus flores
la adorne y la guarnezca,
las fuentes (y) instrumentos
en su aplauso prevengan
dulces cuerdas de plata,
a cítaras de perlas.
en sus ecos los montes
templadas cajas sean,
y en su espacio los aires
clarines y trompetas.
¡arma, arma, guerra, guerra!;
pero guerra amorosa,
que en paces se convierta,
¡arma, arma, guerra, guerra!

(A esta batalla música, respondió la militar de cajas y trompetas, con que
sonando de cajas y trompetas, con instrumentos y voces, y trocando lugares

Meses y Signos, desaparecieron unos por el aire y otros por la tierra, en cuya confusa disonancia festiva dio fin la loa, transformándose la escena en un ameno bosque, en cuya frondosa variedad, ya de vestidos troncos, y ya de desnudas peñas, empezó su primer jornada la comedia.) (74)

The play opens with voices crying, "¡Pastores, huid la fiera!" as the three Hespérides, Verusa, Egle, and Hesperia, and other nymphs hurry across the stage, trying to regain the sanctuary of their garden, which they call a "Real Retiro," again linking the world of the drama with that of the court.[13] The "fiera" they are ostensibly fleeing is a lion (the Nemean lion whose slaughter was one of Hercules' labors), but the real "beast" of the piece is Hércules himself. Although Calderón alters it drastically and conflates it with the story of Iole, the basic myth of *Fieras afemina Amor* is that of Hercules and Omphale, who reduced the mighty hero to spinning among the women and wearing women's clothes.[14]

Comic or negative treatments of Hercules have appeared through the centuries as a common variant on the heroic picture of Hercules as the possessor of all strengths and virtues (Galinsky, ch. 5). But that Calderón would so present him in this courtly context is striking, for Hercules was traditionally claimed to be the mythic founding father of Spain.[15] Fernández de Heredia, for example, in his chronology of the succession of the Spanish throne, names Hercules as the first king of Spain and then lists his descendants as a direct line to Carlos II, the 117th generation removed from Hercules. As a prodigious slayer of monstrous enemies, he also served as an ideal symbol of the Hapsburg monarchs. The most notable example, the Hall of Realms of the Buen Retiro, was organized around a ten-picture Hercules cycle painted by Zurbarán, showing the hero vanquishing a series of monsters; these were interspersed between portraits of the Hapsburg monarchs and pictures of notable Spanish victories. The intent was to link Hercules' feats with the triumph of the just sovereign over his domestic and foreign enemies (Brown and Elliott 159–161).

The Hercules motif also figured prominently in the iconography of the 1649 entry of Mariana into Madrid upon her marriage to Felipe IV. After the obvious figures of Hymenaeus and Cupid, Hercules was the most frequently represented deity, appearing in a variety of roles: a historical personage, a symbol of the power of the monarchy and of Felipe IV himself, dedicated to the arts and to love. In one particularly significant representation, Hercules appeared with the face of Felipe IV (López Torrijos 153–157, 352) receiving the weight of the world from Atlas. Beside him stood Mariana. As López Torrijos comments (154): "lo que se trataba era de ensalzar el poder y la responsabilidad del monarca hispano y la confianza puesta por los dioses en el monarca español que, fuerte como Hércules, debía gobernar el mundo a él confiado. Además, se señalaba la colaboración que había de prestar la reina en esta tarea, colocando su figura junto a Hércules. . . . y sobre ellos Himeneo y Cupido" (154). The inscription below the figures pointed out this symbolism, for both Hercules and Mariana, ending with verses that said that he was able to bear the weight of his responsibilities because

> Pues porque pueda sustentarla, el Cielo,
> Le da tan dulce Hermosa CONPANIA,
> Que ya con ella, es facil, i suave (López Torrijos 155).

Given this welcome to Madrid, it is understandable that Mariana should be partial to the Hercules motif, and in fact this was the only mythic theme used in royally commissioned art during the interregnum—the decoration by Claudio Coello and José Ximénez Donoso of the reconstructed Casa de Panadería. In this building, from which the royal family watched festivities in the Plaza Mayor, the center of the ceiling of the Salón de Reyes was occupied by the escutcheon of the Spanish Hapsburgs sustained by the four cardinal virtues and little groups of cupids, while the rest was adorned with medallions depicting a number of the labors of Hercules. These included several of the feats that Hercules performs or recounts in *Fieras afemina Amor*, most notably his struggle with the lion and his attacking the dragon of the garden of the Hespérides (López Torrijos 146–147).

In all these visions, Hercules is a predictably exemplary figure of moral and physical valor. However, Mariana probably was also familiar with one decidedly unheroic vision of Hercules. Among the paintings known to have hung in the Hall of Mirrors of the Alcázar Palace was *Hercules and Omphale*, painted by Artemisia Gentileschi, the Roman female painter, which showed an enamored Hercules meekly spinning among the women (Orso, "Presence" 55, 127).[16] While we have no documentation of her special liking for this painting, we do know that Mariana watched with interest the decoration of the ceiling of this same hall with the story of Prometheus and Pandora, central to *La estatua de Prometeo*. We also know that that vision of Pandora depicted her not as the bringer of a cloud of evils but rather as the "all-gifted" creature of beauty, the perfection of earthly civilization supposedly represented by Spanish Hapsburg rule. The coincidence of the presence in the Alcázar of both of these themes in which a woman exercises a powerful role, and of their utilization in the first two spectacular celebrations of Mariana's birthday during the interregnum, suggests strongly that she, or someone hoping to curry favor with her, chose the theme for the plays.

The central text of *Fieras afemina Amor*, however, represented a clear departure from the traditional symbolism of the Hercules myth in Spain—and anything but favorable evocations of the status quo under Hapsburg rule. Calderón shows Hercules, the heroic symbol of Spain and its monarchy, not in triumph but in ludicrous and well-deserved defeat.[17] Even before his first entrance on

Plate 1. *Fieras afemina Amor.* Prologue.

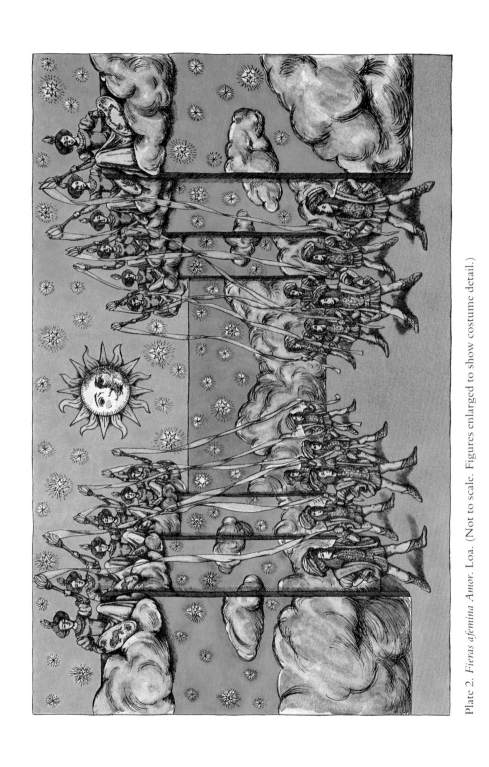

Plate 2. *Fieras afemina Amor.* Loa. (Not to scale. Figures enlarged to show costume detail.)

Plate 3. *Fieras afemina Amor.* Hércules and Yole. (Not to scale. Figures enlarged to show costume detail.)

stage, he has equated himself with a beast, saying as he comes to the rescue of the Hespérides,

> No huyáis, que ya el león que Africa asombra,
> Seguiros podrá en vano,
> Que si él es el nemeo, yo el tebano (75–76).

He behaves throughout almost the whole play as a complete brute, the incarnation of *soberbia*, boasting loudly of his absolute valor and prowess. For instance, defeating the dragon that guards the gardens of the Hespérides, he brags, "que oír de Hércules el nombre / más que la clava le ha muerto" (173). By his repeated admission, he is concerned only with his own fame, despises women, and is totally impervious to love, which he characterizes as "doméstica guerra" (878). In an initially rational analysis, he rejects the opportunity to secure from the garden of the Hespérides one of the golden apples that assures success in love (despite the temptation the challenge of danger and greater fame represent for him) because he recognizes that the human will must not be forced. He says,

> Que me ofendo
> de oír que haya hombre que pretenda
> que le merezca un hechizo
> lo que él por sí no merezca.
> ¡Qué bajo espíritu debe
> de tener quien se contenta
> con que lo que es voluntad
> lo haya de adquirir por fuerza!
> ¿Una mujer violentada
> es más, si se considera,
> que una estatua algo más viva,
> con alma algo menos muerta? (89–90)

Virtually in the same breath, however, he calls women vassals naturally subject to men, and when his pride is offended by Yole's rejection, he states repeatedly that he wants to make her his slave.

> ella, puesta a mis plantas,
> ha de ver no sólo que es
> mi esposa, sino mi esclava,
> mostrando que no hay tan soberana
> mujer que del hombre a serlo no nazca (132).

His rejection of women and the power of love of course precipitates the wrath of Venus and Cupid, who engineer the chain of revenge that leads to his eventual enslavement to Yole and the deities of love. (The involvement of those deities also provides the pretext for some spectacular effects, as the first act ends with Venus and Cupid flying over the stage enthroned on two white swans (see Plate 3). In the climactic final scene, a chorus of eight Muses herald the arrival of a golden chariot bearing the triumphant Venus and Cupid. Prostrated at their feet is the defeated Hércules, while seventeen "captives of love" follow in the wake of the chariot, struggling against the turning of its wheels.)[18]

If the leading man of this play is at best an antihero, does Calderón set against him an exemplary heroine in the role of Yole? O'Connor sees Calderón as an advance proponent of women's liberation in this play, which he says "afirma rotundamente la dignidad de la mujer y grita por su libertad" ("Hércules" 179). However anachronistic, this is fundamentally true, although I find Calderón's voice much less stridently in favor of that cause and more ambivalent because of his reliance on what we might call a "negative case history," which stages an example of the disaster that results from the unjust treatment of women rather than a positive model of the good that results from their freedom.

Yole is clearly presented as a victim in much of the play, not only of Hércules but her father and the social codes and power structures of a male-dominated society. Anteo describes her as suffering from "graves melancolías" of unexplained origin, and her first act as she appears on stage is to beg her father Euristio's pardon for arriving late. When Euristio tells her to give her hand to Hércules in a feigned ceremony of welcome, she answers with telling brevity: "Pues yo, ¿qúe voluntad tengo?" (107) After the king offers her to Hércules as part of a "package deal" for defending his kingdom, the scene figured in Plate 3, Yole sighs, "¡Ay, Anteo, / quién pudiera callar, no / dando a entender su tormento!" (110). We can imagine that María de Quiñones, who probably acted the part of Yole, would play her reticence not as passivity but as the enforced containment of emotion and resentment.[19] She is not permitted even to express a fleeting moment of happiness: when she has occasion to do so (her hurried marriage to Anteo, which the king has approved to spite Hércules), she says only, "Si lícito me fuera, / cúya es la dicha o mérito dijera" (134). The king cuts her off and orders the musicians to speak for her instead.

When Hércules interrupts the wedding celebration, however, she breaks out of the restraint of parental control and bravely takes upon herself the responsibility for the marriage to Anteo that Hércules threatens. Her speech to him postulates a woman's right to choose her own mate:

> Hércules, mi padre
> ofreció a tus esperanzas
> mi libertad, suponiendo
> mi gusto, pues cosa es clara
> que mi padre no querría
> que me casase forzada (135).

Whether she was convinced of the truth of that statement Calderón does not tell us, but Euristio has on no occasion showed any concern for his daughter's wishes. He had refused Aristeo's pretensions to her hand not because of her affection for Anteo but on political grounds; he did not want to allow a foreigner to rule the kingdom. Furthermore, he had seen Hércules in full monstrous attire when he promised Yole to him; any father genuinely concerned with his daughter's preferences would have known that this was not a match she would willingly accept. Nevertheless, Yole defends her father, knowing that she risks violent retribution from Hércules for so doing:

> no fue de mi padre,
> sino mía, la mudanza;
> a que me diese la muerte,
> resuelta y determinada,
> de Anteo amada, me atreví
> a decirle. . . . (136)

She is not mistaken, for the cry "¡Al arma! ¡Al arma!" interrupts her as Hércules initiates his campaign to take revenge not only on Yole, Anteo, and Euristio but on the whole kingdom of Libia. Yole attempts to answer violence with violence, demanding a horse and entering the battle alongside her father and Anteo, but this too proves futile as her father is killed and her horse (and perhaps her own fury) throws her over a cliff. Cupido, who wants to preserve her as an instrument of his revenge, saves her by catching her in midair and lowering her gently to earth.

Unable to protect her freedom either by forthright speech or violence, and having lost father, husband, and kingdom to Hércules' revenge, Yole tries to flee, preferring the "brutas fieras" of the forest to "una fiera humana" (177). This too proves impossible as Aristeo blocks her path, saying that although he sympathizes with her plight, his loyalty to Hércules prevents him from acceding to her request. Even in the absence of father and husband, the bonds of the male code of honor imprison the woman who would escape. Not even her female friends, the Hespérides, can hide her because Hércules has destroyed the dragon that guarded their garden and its miraculous tree. But they do have an alternate suggestion: using their talents to civilize Hércules, first by making him confront his ugly nature in a mirror, then by the power of song and reciting the example of heroic lovers. Yole is dubious about the outcome of such experiments and asks if there is no other remedy in case they fail. The unseen voices of Venus and Cupido sing the reply: "Fingir halago traidor" (181).

They have given her what proves to be woman's only remedy in this play, for Hércules is able to throw off the civilizing efforts of the Hespérides, but he cannot resist Yole's staged tears and protestations of love. With the repeated use of these weapons, she is able to charm him into declaring her queen, giving up his savage dress and pursuits for the luxury of palace life, and ignoring his duty to defend the Muses on Mt. Parnassus. Finally she sings him to sleep, and only the tactful intervention of Hesperia, who loves him, prevents Yole from stabbing Hércules to death. Instead she takes her revenge in humiliation, braiding his hair with ribbons and substituting a distaff for the club in his hand; then as he awakens, she holds up the mirror again and summons his soldiers to witness his disgrace and to tell all of Libia "si hay hombres que las agravian, / que hay mujeres que las vengan" (207).

Given Hércules' aggressive and brutal vengeance, Yole's use of any available method to secure his humiliation and/or death is psychologically understandable, even logically justifiable. Against his violence and the barriers of paternal control and a male-dominated social code, she breaks out of silent but resentful obedience to try first forthright honesty, then violence and flight, all to no avail. After one last experiment at restraining Hércules with the civilizing forces of beauty, music, and example, she resorts to the only weapon left to women in such a society—deceit and sexual wiles. Surely this can be read as a condemnation of the implicit and explicit violence of a system that forces women to resort to such tactics. Yole herself claims that her triumph is a victory for all women:

No dirás sino que Yole,
vengando en él sus ofensas,
vengó también la[s] de todas
las mujeres (208).

Yet does such a story make Yole an appealing protagonist? Wilson (37) finds the scenes of her enslavement of Hércules "painful reading. We cannot quite realize that Hércules has deserved this horrible humiliation. He is, after all, a hero." A feminist of our century would certainly react differently to these scenes. From his moderate stance, however, O'Connor does not argue that Yole is an exemplary figure, only that she is unjustly treated by Hércules in particular and by a society organized on the principle of the "myth of masculine superiority" in general. Probably most readers would agree that given the amount of her onstage time devoted to dissimulation, deceit, and crocodile tears culminating in a murder plot, only a consummate actress could make of Yole a truly sympathetic figure.[20]

The ambiguity of *Fieras afemina Amor* even extends to a kind of tension between the title and the text of the work, for Yole's triumph over Hércules is not really a victory of love over force, as the title might suggest, but the use of sexual wiles for control and revenge. As Wilson (39) pointed out, she is significantly absent from the triumphal car in which Hércules makes his final appearance at the feet of Venus and Cupid. Hércules concludes accurately when in his final speech he says, "traidora Yole, / sin amor al Amor venga" (213). O'Connor sees in the play a lesson that "love is the great civilizing force in society." "El triunfo de Cupido es una celebración de la capacidad que todo hombre posee: la de amar y respetar a su semejante en vez de su odio y dominación" (180).

166

This conclusion is a serious distortion of the love Calderón puts on stage in this play. The *amor* that triumphs in *Fieras* is not love with a small letter, in the Neoplatonic sense of the attraction of two souls or any positive sense of human understanding, but *Amor* with a capital A, the cunning and cruel god of sexual attraction. As Cupido explicitly states, he is not interested in a respectful, forgiving love but in revenge, in love as an instrument of domination and control. When Venus asks him why he relies on a feigned love, that of Yole, to secure Hércules' submission, he answers first by saying nobly that he does so in order that true love should become a prize rather than a punishment, but then goes on to explain his motives and plan in a way that totally negates that idealistic statement:

> Que él quiera y que no sea
> querido es lo que quiero:
> hállese más burlado
> cuanto más satisfecho.
> De amarle Yole, no
> pudiera lograr luego
> el que ella enamorada
> le ponga en el desprecio
> que le pondrá mañosa,
> cuando mi prisionero,
> trocando la acerada
> clava en vil instrumento,
> mi carro arrastre (182–183).

Despite its presence in the title and in the figures of Venus and Cupido hovering above the stage, real love is notable primarily for its absence in this work. Hércules blocks the fulfillment of the love between Anteo and Yole, and kills the former. The only case of love returned and rewarded in the drama is that of the secondary figure, Aristeo, the defeated suitor-king of Yole who merits the prize of Verusa's affection because of his loyalty to Hércules while all other principal figures devote themselves to deceit and revenge.

Deceit marks from the outset the interaction of all the interested parties in the succession to the throne of Libia. Our first view of Yole is a double deception, for it is not a true presence but a vision conjured up by Venus, one that "[para] develar sospechas / a los ardides de Venus" (98), pretends to warn Hércules against loving when her real function is to seduce him.[21] When Euristio offers Yole to Hércules in marriage, Hércules pretends to believe himself unworthy of the union until he has freed the country of the invading army of the rival suitor, Aristeo, although in truth he wants to avoid marriage altogether. Euristio responds to Hércules' pretended humility with even more self-serving duplicity:

167

> Aunque es fuerza haber sentido   *Aparte*
> tan necia respuesta, yo
> hasta servirme dél, no
> me daré por entendido.
> Es tan digna la atención
> que se funda en merecer,
> que la debo agradecer (105).

His immediate goal being that of having Hércules defeat Aristeo, Euristio instructs Yole to follow his example:

> Da licencia a Hércules que
> tu mano bese. (*Ap. a ella.*) Advirtiendo
> que es en él que te he hablado;
> Disimule sus desprecios   *Aparte*
> hasta mejor ocasión (107).

When Hércules returns with Aristeo in captivity to find not a hero's welcome but the celebration of Yole's marriage to Anteo, the prevailing mode of the drama changes from deceit to revenge: the revenge of Hércules against Euristio for breaking his promise of marriage to Yole and against Yole for her rejection of him; the revenge of Cibele against Hércules and against Parnaso for the death of her son Anteo; the revenge of Yole against Hércules, deflected from murder to humiliation only by the intervention of Hesperia; and the revenge of Venus and Cupid against Hércules for his defiance of their power. Various voices counsel against vengeance and in favor of forbearance and self-control. Calíope warns Hércules:

> No te vengues, si te quieres
> vengar de Yole, que vi
> muchas veces que el dejar
> alcanza más que el seguir (161).

He rejects her counsel, however, as the chorus intones over and over: "¡Ay de ti! / que vencer a las fieras no es vencerse a sí" (161). Yole herself pleads with Aristeo against revenge, saying: "que tomó mejor venganza / quien no se vengó pudiendo" (117)—a policy she clearly does not follow herself. Only the gentlemanly Aristeo truly considers the matter, and, coming to the conclusion that "lo vengativo infama" (117), forbears, although he knows that his restraint may be personally disastrous.

Despite the spectacular brilliance of this *tramoya*-packed production, then, the dramatic text itself conveys a dark, almost bitter vision of a society full of intrigue, deceit, and vengeance in which the real issue is not the triumph of love but the uses of power. Read as a self-enclosed text, the play seems a strange work at best; it becomes comprehensible, however, when read in reference to the political situation of its day. For example, Euristio's expressed motives for offering Iole to Hércules in marriage are a clear reflection of the dilemma of the Spanish Hapsburgs—assuring their continuance in power, given the physical and mental weakness of Carlos II, and the potential claims to the throne of Louis XIV and Leopold I of Austria through their wives, María Teresa and Margarita María, daughters of Felipe IV. (In effect, Leopold and Louis XIV had recently concluded a secret treaty of partition, dividing up the Spanish empire upon the probable death without issue of Carlos II.) Euristio says he offers Yole and the throne to Hércules

> porque no era justa ley
> que mi hija a otro reino fuera,
> y que sujeta quedara
> Libia a que la governara
> virrey que su rey no fuera (102).

The most obvious relevance of the central dramatic text to the political situation was of course the contest for power between Don Juan José and Mariana. Don Juan, like Hércules, had threatened to take power by force, and Mariana countered his efforts through political maneuvers and exertion of her maternal authority over Carlos II. She did not rely on these tactics alone, however. After Don Juan's first advance on Madrid with troops in 1669, she raised a special regiment in Madrid as her personal guard. This broke a long-standing tradition of the Spanish monarchy against such a practice and raised almost universal hostility in Madrid. While other European monarchs regularly maintained such a force, the argument was that the loyalty of the Spanish populace was such that their kings had no need of a special guard. On a more practical level, both the populace and all but the nobles closest to Mariana complained that the expense of maintaining it was an unnecessary burden on an already overtaxed people and that the presence of soldiers in the capital was in itself a threat to public order. Nevertheless, the regiment was formed in 1669, and because its colorful uniforms resembled those of the troops of the English general Schomberg in the Portuguese war, the soldiers became known as chambergos and the regiment itself La Chamberga (Maura, *Corte* 2:45–51).

As in *La estatua de Prometeo*, Calderón avoids the creation of a clear-cut political allegory based on one-to-one correspondence of characters. Certain aspects of Don Juan José's position link him with Hércules, but others might connect him with the unfortunate Anteo, who is twice described as a vile "hijo de la Tierra." There are also certain reminiscences in Anteo and Aristeo to the pretensions and problems of Mariana's two validos, Valenzuela and Nithard. And Hércules' final prostration at Mariana's feet was reminiscent of the position of both Don Juan José and Carlos II, the first because Mariana's stubborn resistence to his demands for power kept him confined in Aragón, the second because the ill-disciplined crown prince was becoming increasingly restive being confined in the palace to a world dominated by women. Maura Gamazo commented with regard to the attempt in 1673 to appoint a tutor for him: "Indecoroso pareció a propios y extraños mantener al Monarca español, cuya boda preocupaba ya a las Cancillerías, rodeado de servidumbre exclusivamente femenina, como a raíz del destete, cuando la desgobernada Majestad empuñaría el cetro en 1675, y sólo un ayo inteligente, dúctil y enérgico podría, en el escaso tiempo que aún quedaba, enmendar, en parte, omisiones y yerros" (*Corte,* 2:165). When this effort failed, predictably, because of political differences, a disgusted journalist commented:

> Si á los Príncipes que tuvieron padres tan atentos que celasen su educación, siempre se señalaron ayos que los adestrasen y enseñasen a todas horas, ¿quién podrá detener dentro del corazón las voces y suspiros para no formar quejas de los gobernadores que permitieron que el Rey Nuestro Señor tuviese por ayos las dueñas y damas de Palacio, por asistentes los truhanes y otros mancebos peligrosos, sin haber tenido comunicación alguna con persona que en todo el tiempo de su menor edad haya podido contribuir, no sólo a enseñarle las artes de reinar, pero ni a ver los primeros esbozos con que se adorna la crianza de un hidalgo? (qtd in Maura, *Corte* 2:168).

Wilson pointed out the possibility of interpreting the play as an allegory of the Don Juan José–Mariana contest for power: "The Queen Mother probably saw in Yole a compliment to her beauty and perhaps, too, to her skill in political intrigues. Did Hércules remind her and some of the spectators of the second Don John of Austria, her political enemy? If so, there can be no doubt about which camp the Royal Chaplain who wrote this play belonged to" (45). As the political text of plays such as *Las fortunas de Andrómeda y Perseo* and *La estatua de Prometeo* illustrate, however, Calderón was not an opponent of Don Juan José. Rather, I believe he served up a play that would please Mariana by displaying at face value the triumph of women and one that would delight Carlos II with a display of bravado (his favorite entertainments were *corridas de toros*) and spectacular brilliance. For the more critical spectator-reader, he offered a political text that flattered neither Don Juan José nor Mariana but dramatized the manner in which Spain itself was enslaved by their reliance on violence or the threat of violence and the pervasive climate of intrigue and deceit.

We do not have any written proof that contemporary spectators perceived this subtler text. Dramatic works did not regularly merit close commentary by anyone but the censors who approved them for the stage, and they were looking primarily for clear evidence of dogmatic error or licentiousness. Therefore, while we may demonstrate the political relevance of *Fieras* and other court plays, and offer related evidence such as the political interpretation evinced by the Catalán audience of *Lo que merece un soldado* (see Chapter 4), we cannot finally prove that Calderón's audiences perceived the political text we find in these works any more than we can prove that they saw the criticism of the honor code most modern readers find in such plays as *El médico de su honra*. Contemporary commentaries on court plays typically focus exclusively on their success as spectacles and the niceties of court etiquette involved in their presentation, and this production of *Fieras afemina Amor* received favorable reviews on both scores. An English lord wrote that

> Mr. Godolphin [English ambassador to Spain] está poco satisfecho en Madrid, aun cuando le ha tocado presenciar uno de los espectáculos más notables que se hayan visto en mucho tiempo: una comedia con escenas y máquinas, ofrecida en el Retiro por el príncipe de Astillano al Rey y a la Reina. Invitaron a los Embajadores, y por resolver la cuestión de precedencia, colocaron al Nuncio y a los demás en un palco a la derecha de los Reyes, y a nosotros solos en otro a la izquierda; de manera que los Embajadores de Francia y Alemania, que ceden el paso al Nuncio, no pudieron molestarse, ni nosotros tampoco. Escribo esto a V. E. para que vea cuánto ingenio derrocha esta gente en estas cosas, y no me extraña, pues aquí preocupan ellas más que en el resto del mundo (qtd in Maura, *Corte* 2:147–148 n. 2).

Not all reviews were favorable, however. The performance gave rise to an anonymous exchange of satirical poems, the first condemning and the second defending the production as a whole, which by their arguments implicitly prove the truth of the image of the political climate of the day that Calderón had presented. The author of the more coherent and better written critical poem refers to "Fiestas del odio compuestas / con emulaciones vanas" and concludes that "estas ocasiones / se deberán evitar, / porque pueden resultar / rencillas y disensiones." He rejects the whole production because of the self-interested motives of its sponsor, the príncipe de Astillano, who might better save his money to serve the royalty as a soldier than use court festivities as a route to becoming valido:[22]

> Entre lanzas y paveses
> se halla el honor adquirido,
> y aquí quiere ser Valido
> quien hace más entremeses.

Furthermore, the author dislikes the image of Spain the play presented, although he focuses not on the degradation of Hércules but on the replacement of that other symbol of Spanish heroism, the Cid, by the gracioso Juan Rana:

> La milicia castellana,
> para vencer en la lid,
> solía sacar al Cid,

> y ahora sale Juan Rana,
>   que después de sepultado
> a las cosas del honor,
> como al buen Cid Campeador,
> le tienen empapelado (Maura, *Corte* 2:503).

Both the critic and the defender of the event assumed that although the play celebrated Mariana's birthday, its real purpose was to entertain the young king. If Calderón was also working on this understanding, it might explain his prodigality with nonessential spectacular effects, but it was precisely this lavishness of which the critic complained:

> Yo no condeno la acción,
> que antes es muy justa ley
> el divertir a su Rey,
> pero con moderación.
>   Mas festejos con porfías,
> hechos a un Rey sin edad,
> no será temeridad
> el llamarlos niñerías.

The defender of the production is less than consistent in his arguments. On the one hand, he says that "juguetes" are appropriate ways to entertain a child-king and demonstrate one's love for him:

> El festejar con sainetes
> a su Rey un gran señor,
> no es mucho, que es niño amor
> y se vale de juguetes.
>   Que es bien hecho y justo, arguyo,
> divertir a un niño Rey,
> pues es adecuada ley
> dar al tiempo lo que es suyo.

At the same time, he upholds the serious purpose of such entertainments as both educative and demonstrative of royal power and splendor:

> que si el Rey comedias ve
> es cuando está en el Retiro.
>   Dellas la moralidad
> es provechosa a los Reyes,
> que allí se adornan las leyes,
> el poder y majestad.

Furthermore, with regard to the educative value of *Fieras afemina Amor*, the defender seems to have in mind the traditional portrayal of Hércules and to overlook its negative employment in this play, for he says, "De las españoles lides, / la bruta ferocidad / al Monarca en tierna edad / valor le infunden de Alcides" (Maura, *Corte* 2:504). Since this answering poem was clearly penned if not by the príncipe de Astillano himself by someone in his service, it is not surprising that he would wish to ignore the critical message in the play as Charles I of England had turned a blind eye to the message offered him by the Inns of Court in *The Triumph of Peace*.[23]

The full *Fieras* text does include, however, a fascinating entremés, the "Triunfo de Juan Rana," which dramatizes the necessity of "polysemic" reading of the court spectacle. Whether or not Calderón actually wrote this piece, performed after the first act, the *Sainete* that followed the second act, and the *Fin de fiesta*, is a matter of opinion. Rodríguez and Tordera (48–50) put it on a list of pieces of dubious attribution to Calderón, presumably on stylistic grounds and because they believe that it was not customary practice for a dramatist to write both the play and the minor pieces. Payment records do indicate that Calderón regularly wrote both play and loa, but do not specify payments for other minor pieces. On the other hand, D. W. Cruickshank and Cecilia Bainton feel that the thematic unity of the pieces with the central text in *Fieras* makes his authorship likely. (Calderón, *Fieras* 3–11). In any case, Calderón, whose primary control of his court festivals was demonstrated as early as 1635 when he vetoed Cosimo Lotti's list of stage effects for *El mayor encanto, amor*, would have had the final say on their appropriateness and inclusion, and we can therefore credit him with the dramatic appropriateness of the minor pieces.

In the framework of *Fieras afemina Amor*, as we have seen earlier, this production did exalt the Queen Mother as ruler of both the theatrical event and the world it evoked. No clear line was drawn between this framework and the central dramatic text; rather, the two worlds were joined by a sort of fade-in technique. This connection of stage fiction and royal presence was further reinforced in the minor pieces between acts and concluding the fiesta. The "Triunfo de Juan Rana" is particularly interesting in this regard because the baroque complexities of role-playing it celebrates reflect in a microcosm those that prevail in the total theatrical event.[24] In the Spanish dramatic tradition, the entremés often served to condense and subvert the conventions, both formal and thematic, of the main drama (Profeti, "Condensación" 2–3).[25]

The entremés opens with a parody of the adulatory function of the loa of the court fiesta.[26] Rather than the varieties of airborne nymphs who usually performed the first movement of the loa in front of the curtain, the entremés brings on two men who come to the rescue of Antonio de Escamilla, who has fallen off his donkey. He explains his hurry to his rescuers:

> Habéis de saber que hoy en el Retiro
> ha de haber una cosa
> tan nueva, tan terrible, tan grandiosa,

173

> tan mucha, tan horrenda,
> tan, tan, tan, tan, tan, tan, tan estupenda,
> que por verla, ese asno y yo en cuadrilla
> postas corrimos hoy desde la Villa,
> aunque tan recia la carrera ha sido
> que también por la posta hemos caído (114).

Trumpets and drums then play in the equivalent of a curtain-raising ceremony, and the aged and famous gracioso Cosme Pérez is carried on stage "en un
carro triunfal, con mucho accompañamiento, y (a)delante dos hombres, uno con
el sayo y otro con la vara." He is greeted by cries of

> ¡Viva Juan Rana!
> ¡Viva sin desvelo!
> ¡Viva hasta que la rana tenga pelo!

The shouts are repeated, interspersed with variants such as "¡Viva Juan Rana
más que vive Cribas!"[27] and the news that "hoy victorioso / le coronan por
máximo gracioso" (115). Eternal life is wished to this "monarca de la graciosidad" (Asensio 169) in a burlesque parody of the baroque conceits addressed to
Mariana at the opening of the loa:

> A los felices años
> que para dicha nuestra,
> ya en estatuas de bronce,
> ya en láminas de piedra,
> con luces cuente el fuego,
> el agua con arenas,
> con át[o]mos el aire
> y con flores la tierra;
> a los felices años
> del Aguila suprema,
> que más que en nuestra vidas
> en nuestras almas reina (59).

To his dismay, Juan Rana soon learns that the cries are not for Juan Rana
himself but for the statue of Juan Rana:

3		Pues es su estatua la que aquí triunfante
		viene, su nombre se publique y cante.
4		¡Viva Juan Rana!
TODOS:		¡Viva a cada paso!
JUAN RANA:	¡Ola! ¿Mi estatua aquí? ¡Notable caso!
ESCAMILLA:	¡Dure la estatua de Juan Rana eterna!
1		¡Dure sin que le falte brazo o pierna!

2   Pues en su casa vive retirado
      negado a aclamaciones del tablado
      ¡hoy en su estatua triunfe agradecido! (115)

Juan Rana, who was acting as early as 1617, had been officially retired for many years, living in his house on the Calle de "Cantarranas" where he died either in 1672 or 1673.[28] However, he was a great favorite with the royal household, as the repeated references to him in Felipe IV's letters to Sor Luisa make clear.[29] He had been granted a lifetime pension soon after the theatres reopened upon Felipe's marriage to Mariana, and his participation was obligatory on special occasions (Bergman 68).[30] The British traveler Lady Fanshawe saw him perform as late as 1665: "On January 5, 1665, here came, among other diversions of sports we had this Christmas, Juan Araña (*sic*), the famous comedian, who here acted about 2 hours, to the admiration of all who beheld him, considering that he was near upon 80 years of age" (qtd in Rennert 554).

The joke of Juan Rana being a statue was probably inspired by his advanced age; the entremés ends with the lines "que como es tan viejo / le sacan al Sol" (122). This close to death, perhaps he could do little more than be carried on stage. But it may also have been a comic reference to the stiffness required of true monarchs on occasions of state, who were expected to remain completely impassive, neither moving, smiling, nor laughing.[31] Felipe IV himself said in a 1653 letter to Sor Luisa that Juan Rana put this stricture to the test: "Muy buena a sido la comedia, y vuestro amigo Juan Rana a cumplido famosamente con sus obligaciones; bien creo que si le hubiérades visto, se atreviera la risa a inquietar la función" (Villanueva 200).

In *El toreador*, a marvelous entremés that Calderón definitely wrote, he had the gracioso break the picture frame of the stage, coming down from the stage and acting directly in front of the royal platform to draw the royal family into a joke about their solemnity. In order to please a woman he is courting, Juan Rana has reluctantly agreed to try his hand at bullfighting and is now "acting out" the salute to the royal spectators before combat:

(*Bájese del tablado y vase por el salón adonde está el Rey.*)
BERNARDA: Hacia el Rey va llegando, verle es vicio.
RANA: Señor, yo soy un toreador novicio, (*Al Rey.*)
     por la Pasión de Dios, que se dé traza
     para que me despejen de la plaza.
     Vos, Señora, rogádselo en secreto, (*A la Reina.*)
     porque al presente estoy en grande aprieto.
     ¿Calláis? Pues me remito
     a dalle un memorial al Principito. (*Al Príncipe.*)[32]
     ¿No me oye su merced? Pues mudo intento,
     que tanta majestad me infunde aliento.

Ea, reinas, levántense vusías,
y a tal señor, señoras cortesías.
(*Hace sus cortesías a los Reyes, y luego a las damas, y se sube al tablado.*)
(Calderón, *Entremeses* 197–198).

In the *Triunfo de Juan Rana*, as the monarchs are statuelike spectators, so the "monarca de la graciosidad" becomes a statue on stage. His subsequent comments emphasize to the audience that they, in contrast to the onstage beings, are to continue to see in him a human being, not just a fossilized hero that anyone may use to serve his own ends. The humor of the piece depends on the capacity of the spectator to maintain concurrently the triple reading of the figure as Cosme Pérez/Juan Rana/statue of Juan Rana. Gordon has pointed out that in English masques, in which the royalty themselves acted the parts of ancient or mythic heroes or allegorical qualities, the audience was intended to be simultaneously conscious of the king's two realities:

> The masque is a form in which the audience is required to be aware, consciously, all the time, of the performer beneath the role; to know that the king is king, and to take his various impersonations as translations of that basic, true identity. The roles he takes are real—as real as the role of king—because they are ways of defining his identity within the society; every role is true, in the sense that it is an abstraction, a personification of his qualities. The audience's participation is crucial; even if they do not join in the dance, they join in the play. They are bound together by their capacity to understand. . . . (21)

In the Spanish court spectaculars, performed by professional actors, the act of comprehension required of the audience became even more complex because they had to see in the figure on stage both the actor himself, the role he represented, and the "real-world" reality to which that role pointed. Thus in the condensation of theatrical conventions that this entremés represents, we have Cosme Pérez as himself, Juan Rana, and the statue of Juan Rana.

Furthermore, the entremés acknowledges that the reading of that real-world reality would in turn be plural. One can see it as a joke about Juan Rana's existence as the king of comedy and his advanced age, a play on the equivalent stiffness of the statuelike royal spectator, and/or a humorous piece of meta-theatre that makes fun of the conventions of court drama. The entremés spells out further its potential polysemy in the action that ensues after Juan Rana realizes he is not "himself" but a statue. The statue is claimed, in turn, by a man, to stand in the temple of fame; by a woman who is the messenger of the muses of Mt. Parnassus, whose usage of the statue suggests a blending of art and commerce; and finally by a soldier who claims him as a decoration for a fountain in the garden of the king, as a plaything of power.[33] Predictably, the latter claim prevails. That is, every spectator finds his own use for artistic representations, but even in this comic piece, the will of the most powerful takes precedence in the appropriation of the physical object.[34]

Traditionally, the freedom of the carnivalesque space the entremés represented was closed off at its end by some sort of statement saying, "This is just a joke," by *palos* (the pummeling of the transgressing figure), or by a dance that restored harmony.[35] In a variant of this practice appropriate to the occasion, the *Triunfo de Juan Rana* uses the very conventions of the loa to close off the potentially corrosive parody, converting itself back into adulation of the royalty. After a series of references to the play and its loa—to Juan Rana as Cupidillo, to the Aguila, the Fénix, and the month of December—Manuela de Escamilla comes out dressed as a more colorful version of Juan Rana to sing and dance the conclusion:[36]

> ¡A fuera! que el alma
> de Juan Rana soy,
> que este sayo, este cincho, este vara
> fueron siempre el alma de su buen humor;
> y vengo veloz
> a bailar en su nombre, porque
> su afecto este día celebre mejor.   *Repiten*
> Que alumbrando el mundo
> viva más que el Sol
> la bella María-Ana,
> no es admiración,
> no, no, no, no, no;
> que tiene más vida
> la luz que es mayor,   *Repiten*
> no, no, no, no, no.
> Que Carlos se lleve
> todo nuestro amor,
> siendo Rey y hermoso,
> no es admiración,
> no, no, no, no, no;
> que con tales gracias
> hiciéralo yo,   *Repiten*
> no, no, no, no, no.
> Que saquen a vista
> de nuestro Rey [hoy]
> al grande Juan Rana,
> no es admiración,
> no, no, no, no, no,

que como es tan viejo
le sacan al Sol,[37]   *Repiten*
no, no, no, no, no.   [*Vanse*] (121–122)

In its doubling of roles, the entremés parodies the conventions explicitly stated in the loa of *Fieras afemina Amor* and other Calderonian court plays, and implicit in the spectacle as a whole. In the entremés, the actor Cosme Pérez plays the role of a human being converted to a stone hero; in the loa, as the actors play gods, or other symbols of divine virtues that are incarnated in the royal family, the correspondence of the two roles is insistently underlined. As the loa fades into the central dramatic action, the audience has therefore been prepared to recognize in the divine fiction on stage an implicit correspondence to the royal counterparts present in the theatre. Should that linkage have slipped, the entremés reinforced it parodically after the first act, and the second sainete also ties together the celebratory framework and central text as it presents another competition, this time a courtly one between beauty and wit. It concludes with a flattering melodic curtsey to Mariana: "Que belleza y discreción / unido, es milagro, / que eso está escogido para Palacio" (170).[38] While the celebratory framework pieces presented courtly competitions that resolved in harmony, the "guerra amorosa" the audience witnessed in the central dramatic text of *Fieras afemina Amor* presented a story of war and intrigue but not of love, a model more to be avoided than praised or emulated.

SEVEN

The End of the Line: *Hado y divisa de Leonido y Marfisa*

THE DISCUSSIONS in the previous chapters leave two important questions unanswered. All the works considered thus far were based on plots drawn from classical mythology, which facilitated the construction of a polysemic text through an ambiguous identification of kings and gods. Not all Calderón's court-spectacle plays were mythological, however; in some, such as *Fineza contra fineza*, the gods were marginal characters who intervened briefly at critical points to shape human events. In others, such as *Hado y divisa de Leonido y Marfisa*, the classical gods were entirely absent.[1] The first question, then, is whether Calderón could create the same complex of texts in the absence of a panoply of classical deities whose intrigues paralleled those of the Hapsburg court.

The second problem is that of the king to be honored. Felipe IV, with all his defects as a ruler, was a man capable of playing the kingly role and eminently well groomed by Olivares to project that image. When Carlos II occupied the throne, however, Calderón clearly faced a severe test for a court poet who would serve and please his monarch without sacrificing his integrity. The king he was to honor was a poor specimen of a man. The sickly, mentally retarded product of royal inbreeding, Carlos II was not weaned until he was four and was not able to walk at that age because his legs were too weak to support him. At nine, he had not been able to learn to read and write, and although he did eventually become sufficiently lettered to sign royal decrees, he was never capable of actually governing. When he was twenty-five, the papal nuncio described him as follows: "No puede enderezar su cuerpo sino cuando camina, a menos de arrimarse a una pared, una mesa u otra cosa. Su cuerpo es tan débil como su mente. De vez en cuando da señales de inteligencia, de memoria y de cierta vivacidad, pero no ahora; por lo común tiene un aspecto lento e indiferente, torpe e indolente, pareciendo estupefacto. Se puede hacer con él lo que se desee, pues carece de voluntad propia" (qtd in Kamen, *Spain* 43).

During Carlos's minority, effective control was contested by the governing junta ordered by Felipe IV before his death and the Queen Mother, Mariana, with her unpopular advisors Nithard and Valenzuela. After the death of Don Juan José, the most powerful figure in government was either a privado such as Medinaceli or Oropesa or the secretary of the Despacho Universal, the king's private office. In the absence of a strong king, however, the privados were dependent on maintaining the support of the nobility through a system of patronage, which encouraged the growth of factionalism at court.[2] Meanwhile, other European powers argued and made secret treaties about the control of the Spanish monarchy and the divison of its territory when this feeble Hapsburg should meet the death that seemed imminent from the day of his birth. To celebrate such a monarch with both veracity and credibility was not an easy task, as is evident in the engraving by "P. Villafranca" that served as the cover of Pedro González de Salcedo's *De lege politico* in 1678 (see Figure 17). Rendering Carlos II with reasonable accuracy, Villafranca makes him an even more improbable king figure than Don Juan José as Atlas.

DON JUAN SOSTENIENDO AL MUNDO

Figure 17. P. Villafranca, *Don Juan sosteniendo al mundo*.
Don Juan José and Carlos II as Atlas and King.
Frontispiece for Pedro González de Salcedo,
De lege politico (Madrid, 1678).

180

Hado y divisa de Leonido y Marfisa was first performed in March 1680,[3] as part of the carnival festivities for that year and in celebration of the recent (November 1679) marriage of Carlos II to Marie-Louise d'Orléans, an event that held out the faint hope that he might not be the "end of the line" in biological terms. Calderón keyed the theatrical event to that occasion, from the opening curtain to the setting of the climactic scene in Act III. The curtain was decorated with garlands of flowers and cupids, the motto VULNERASTI COR MEUM, a blazing heart pierced by an arrow, and the explanation in Spanish: "Flechas que tan dulce hieren / Al llegar al corazón, / Flores, que no flechas son" (356). Such images expressed more than the rhetorical niceties of court fiestas, for by all reports, Carlos was much taken with the beauty and charm of his French wife, and to the relief of concerned observers, she seemed not dismayed with this less than ideal consort (Maura, *Corte* 1:342). A chorus sang the verses on the curtain as the opening lines of the loa, but Calderón then quickly moved from this occasional reference to the power of love to the topic of power itself.

The work was also the "end of the line" for Calderón, for it was the last comedia he wrote before his death the following year. Sebastian Neumeister (*Mythos* 283) thinks that under these adverse circumstances, the aging dramatist's art was infected by the decadence in the political sphere. Neumeister considers the court fiesta an essentially solipsistic event in which the monarchs could temporarily escape from the critical economic and political situation of the realm in viewing a dazzling representation of their own power and glory. He sees *Hado y divisa* as an extreme case of such royal narcissism, made explicit in the loa in which Carlos and Marie-Louise view their own portraits literally enthroned on stage, flanked by representations of their most noted royal ancestors. I believe, however, that if we look carefully at what Calderón says in explanation of this arrangement, we can see that he used this occasion to examine dramatically the question What is it that makes a man a king? On what is his authority grounded?

Calderón was evidently aware of the delicacy of his position and the difficulty of combining the required royal pomp with a reasonable degree of credibility. Two figures in the loa, Azucena and Clavel, avow the sincerity of their celebration of their royal referents, saying: "Y porque veáis que no / lisonjera los ensalzo . . ." and "Y porque no presumáis / que afectada los aplaudo . . ." Here we find no equations of the king with Apollo, Atlas, or Hercules, as Calderón had done for Felipe IV. Carlos is at most "el rey de las flores," or simply "Carlos el deseado."

Fortunately, a full manuscript text of *Hado y divisa* with all its minor pieces has survived, along with a description of the event apparently also written by Calderón himself.[4] An extensive set of accounts of expenses provides further details of the performance.[5] This wealth of documentation facilitates the modern reader's task of the "composición de lugares," both artistic and political, required to understand the full import of this court spectacle. Calderón (or whoever wrote the account) does a good deal of the work for the reader of his description as he presents the drama surrounded by a detailed description of its physical and ceremonial setting. He begins by describing the royal theater, praising the fact that it is designed so that when the primary spectator, the king, wishes to open his private festivities to a larger public, he can do so without compromising the dignity of the royal position: "Que cuando el cariño del Rey a sus vasallos dispone hacerles partícipes de sus festejos después de haberlos logrado, se puede unir el que los asientos del pueblo no impidan la decencia del monarca" (356).

The description then depicts in detail the splendor of that royal position, the first pole of the spectacle. It explains that the royal family, rather than occupying the box designed for them, had a special viewing platform erected at the perfect spot for enjoying the perspective scenery. There they had constructed a portable throne, surrounded with rich hangings and brilliantly lit.

> No ve en él [the royal box] las fiestas, porque por gozar del punto igual de la perspectiva, se forma abajo un sitial, levantado una vara del suelo. Este se cubrió de riquísimas alfombras, que felices lograron mantener un camón de brocado encarnado, fundadas sus puertas en doradas molduras, cuyos cuatro lados terminaban ramilleteros de oro, prosiguiendo la techumbre con diminución de las propias molduras y brocado, y rematando en un bellísimo florón de oro. Estaba cubierta esta luciente esfera de una brillante nube; que con razón se puede llamar así a vista de la luz que había de tener dentro (356).

The eye of the live spectator, as of the reader of the description, was to appreciate first the royal presence and then move on to the stage.

Considering the event as a whole, it is the framework surrounding *Hado y divisa* that is most interesting in understanding Calderón's conception of the relationship of art and power, and it is also the frontispiece, the onstage frame, that first reveals the solution to the problem of feting this monarch. That structure rested on four tall columns of "jaspe verde salpicado de diferentes colores" with elaborately decorated bases, cornices, and capitals. Between the columns in the side niches were statues of Pallas and Minerva, both in gleaming gold. This stage decor thus retained the unusual bifurcation of the goddess that Calderón had established in *La estatua de Prometeo*. On this occasion, however, Pallas had a positive value, signifying the power of armed force that joined with her sister Minerva's wisdom to constitute the two ideal bases of royal authority. On the columns rested a curved cornice, frieze, and architrave. The central feature of this superstructure, and of the frontispiece as a whole, was a medallion showing in relief a crowned lion resting on a globe, with a cross, sceptre, and sword, which the account calls "hieroglyphs of religion and power." Around his neck the lion wore the golden fleece, insignia of the Hapsburg monarch. The whole medallion was made of "the most brilliant gold, harmoniously uniting ferocity and splendor" (356).[6] Above the lion's head waved like a battle flag the motto AD NULLIUS PAVET OCCURSUM.[7] Around the medallion was a garland of laurel on a gold background, and outside that, another garland of children.[8] Woven in between the two garlands below the medallion was a placard bearing the names of the royal couple in large gold letters.[9]

The arrangement of the motifs in this key image (1) makes the statement that it is the *institution* of the Catholic monarchy, figured by the lion, with all the symbols of his power, that fears no adversary, and (2) associates Carlos and his bride with this institution. That is, rather than calling Carlos Apolo or depicting him as Atlas, as Calderón had Felipe IV, the images suggest Carlos's assimilation to the strength of the institution. Since this symbolic statement was placed on the frontispiece rather than the curtain, it would remain visible above the stage throughout the spectacle as a framework for interpreting the dramatic events that transpired below.

After thus setting the scene, the description recounts the opening ceremony. First the orchestra began playing the music for the royal entry: "empezó el número de instrumentos a imitar aquella sonora salva que el dulce murmurio de la aurora hace a la brillante venida del sol" (356). The lighting was raised to an almost blinding brilliance as the political "sun" entered his theatre, and with solemn ceremony, he and his wife and mother took their places on the theatrical throne. Reporting the placement of the most powerful nobility in relation to the royal family, the describer comments that "todos los señores estaban realzando su grandeza con el primor de su rendimiento, asistiendo como luces a la vista del sol de quien la recibían." He thus underlines for any grand nobles with ideas of exercising independent power (which in effect they did in the absence of a strong monarch) that their glory is only a reflection of that of the king, who is the center of their world and the source of all light (power) in the political universe. Therefore, in what would seem contrary to logic, it is only by hum-bling themselves to the king that they increase their own glory, which is only a reflection of the king's. At the same time, Calderón, or whoever penned the account, here recognizes implicitly that the power of the king is founded also on a willing recognition by the nobles of his might.[10]

The nobility who served as members of the royal households then took their places, "augmenting the dignity" of the occasion by their large number. Their presence constituted a statement of the financial power of a monarchy that could maintain such a household. Significantly, the describer mentions at this point the presence in their appointed balconies of the various foreign ambassadors, who were an important audience for this display of respect and power.

He concludes his description with another telling statement: "*Las bien aprendi-das y respetuosas etiquetas de la Casa Real redujeron a tanta brevedad el acomodarse todas estas jerarquías de personas* que en un punto se halló el coliseo sin más voz que la de la muda ansia con que esperaban la comedia" (357) [emphasis mine]. It is, he suggests, the strength of established institutions and respect for the hierarchical arrangement centered on the king that makes possible the efficient establishment and maintenance of order in a complex society.

In front of the curtain then appeared the two key figures of the loa, Historia and Poesía. Calderón had employed this same pair many years before in the loa for *El hijo del sol, Faetón*, in which he used these two allegorical figures to present to Felipe the argument that the poet serves the king as well as the soldier. That is an obvious application to the work of the court poet of the traditional *armas-letras* dispute. His employment of them in the *Hado y divisa* loa is both more complex and a more profound examination of the value of the dramatist's pen in the support of his monarch. Here Historia describes herself as "vida de la memoria," who has in her charge "la edad / del jaspe, el bronce y el mármol." She who represents the preserving and organizing force of memory and the most lasting elements of the physical world, such as jasper, marble, and bronze, preserves in her "doctos anales sabios" the might of past heroes. Poesía calls herself "alma de la fantasía" and says that she is in charge of "el resto de los aplausos." With the rhetorical force of her "numerosos ritmos" and the creative power of the imaginative faculty, she is what Madison Avenue would call an image maker.[11]

Combining their forces, Historia and Poesía call for the opening of the temple of Fame, and the curtain rises to display a throne room of "Corinthian architecture" with life-size "statues" of fourteen famous kings, seven French on one side and seven Spanish on the other. The converging lines they formed led to a central throne at "el medio de la perspectiva," thus exactly opposite the royal family seated at the other end of the Coliseo, at the perfect receiving point for the perspective. On the onstage throne, under a sumptuous dosser, hung portraits of Carlos and Marie-Louise, which Calderón describes as "imitados tan al vivo, que como estaban frente de sus originales pareció ser un espejo en que trasladaban sus peregrinas perfecciones; y el ansia que desea verlos en todas partes quisiera hallar más repetidas sus copias" (358).

Sebastian Neumeister asks what is surely the right question about this interesting arrangement: Why portraits? Why not a real mirror, or at least a representation of a mirror, as in Velázquez's *Las meninas*? After a series of interesting observations on the importance of the mirror as a symbol of self-knowledge and a puzzle for perspective in baroque literature and painting, Neumeister comes to what I think is an incomplete answer. He concludes that the loa represents an extreme example of the fundamentally narcissistic nature of the court play: "Los retratos de los reyes en la loa de *Hado y divisa de Leonido y Marfisa* muestran, aunque no se trata de espejos sino de pinturas accesibles para todos, el aislamiento perspectívico [*sic*] e incluso social del último Habsburgo español. La mirada del rey no alcanza a los demás porque está fijada únicamente en su propio retrato y a lo más en las estatuas de sus antepasados, los 14 reyes de la loa" ("Retratos" 89).

To say that the court fiesta was in its organization a narcissistic and escapist event is on a superficial level an obvious truth.[12] But such an evaluation ignores the more profound political function of the event and misses the perspicacity with which Calderón dramatizes that function in this loa. An important point generally overlooked is that, as the accounts make clear, the "statues" of the fourteen kings were in fact live men, each richly adorned with regal trappings as Calderón points out: "Eran figuras naturales adornadas con los aparatos regios de ricos mantos, cetros y coronas. Cargaban sobre unos orbes, teniendo cada uno por respaldo un pabellón en que se unía la purpura y el oro" (358). The first layer of ingenuity of this scene is that the "dead" and "absent" ancestral kings are represented by live figures, while the living and present monarchs are depicted in a still portrait which is at best "lifelike." Clavel, the flower who in another motif of the loa figures the young king, points out the wit and purpose of this scene in Fame's temple:

> Llamad y entrad en los ricos
> Salones de su palacio:
> Veréis en doradas orbes
> Sobre piras de alabastro
> Cómo en las *vivas estatuas*
> De *parecidos retratos*
> Conserva la Fama héroes
> De quien *participan ambos* (358; emphasis mine).

Through these living statues that seem to be portraits, joined with their own portraits on stage, the monarchs participate in the heroes who surround/preceded them.

Fame spells out the nature of this participation:

> En real joven, en real
> Esposa, el heredado
> Esplendor tira a un punto
> Las líneas de los años (358).

Carlos and Marie Louise are the "end of the line" in another, positive way. They are the combined inheritors of all the splendor of their illustrious predecessors, whom Historia and Poesía proceed to name and by this naming, says Fama, make "present past centuries."

What makes Carlos II a king? Calderón's dramatic answer is (1) institutional structures—the strength of the institutions behind him, the Hapsburg monarchy and the Catholic church; (2) history—not only heredity, as we think of inherited blood lines, but also the inherited glories of his royal ancestors, made present in him by (3) poetry, or the theatrical art, which can employ the richly polyphonic code of its medium toward transforming this feeble creature, both in his own and the public imagination, into the essential focal point of an absolutist state. In attributing this importance to his art, Calderón is doing much more than voicing a dramatist's illusions of grandeur. Stephen Greenblatt (13) has pointed out that in the theatricalized societies of sixteenth- and seventeenth-century European courts, power consisted largely of the capacity to impose one's fictions upon the world. And in his study *Le portrait du roi*, Louis Marin demonstrates how the power of representations not only undergirded but in fact constituted the absolute monarch.

Marin argues that to "re-present" is, in the first place, to fill an absence in time or space by presenting again or taking the place of something/someone past, gone, or dead. Secondly, it is to constitute a subject as one does by showing a passport—to authenticate one's existence.

> Premier effet du dispositif représentatif, premier pouvoir de la représentation; effet et pouvoir de présence au lieu de l'absence et de la mort; deuxième effet, deuxième pouvoir: effet de sujet, c'est-à-dire pouvoir d'institution, d'autorisation et de légitimation comme résultante du fonctionnement réfléchi du dispositif sur lui-même. Si donc la représentation en général a en effet un double pouvoir: celui de rendre à nouveau et imaginairement présent, voire vivant, l'absent et le mort, et celui de constituer son propre sujet légitime et autorisé en exhibant qualifications, justifications et titres du présent et du vivant à l'être, autrement dit, si la représentation non seulement reproduit en fait mais encore en droit les conditions qui rendent possibles sa reproduction, alors on comprend l'intérêt du pouvoir à se l'approprier. Représentation et pouvoir sont de même nature (10–11).

Power, Marin points out, rests initially on the capacity to dominate the other by force. The stronger party achieves a position of dominance over others in combat and, bringing an end to the conflict, effects institutional and political means of maintaining the position achieved through physical or mechanical means. In order that his power be transmitted to his succession without risking renewed conflict, he embodies it in legitimizing signs, the discourse of law; he thereby converts physical force into a representation that at the same time indicates its existence and reserves its physical employment (11, 45–46). For this essentially arbitrary discourse of the master to function effectively, to eliminate the need for recourse to physical force, it must be internalized as a discourse of obligatory belief in the imagination of his subjects. "Pouvoir du discours et discours du pouvoir, l'institution n'est que le moyen de conserver la force hors de son exercice dans la représentation de croyance" (46).

An inherent part of the desire on the part of the master for absolute power, for incomparable glory, takes the form of the abolition of time, and the representation of the king therefore frequently takes the form of a historical narrative that invokes a past to constitute it as an eternalized present (13, 91).

It is this "magic" force of representation that Calderón dramatizes on stage. In the medallion above the stage, he displays Carlos's "passport"—the institution that authorizes his exercise of power. He then calls upon history-memory and poetry-imagination to bring to life the glorious ancestors who contribute their heroic strength to the living monarch. The respect accorded to kings born of regal grandfathers and great-grandfathers gives strength, said Mariana (124–125), citing the case of a Moorish king who declined to fight Alfonso el Sabio because of his awe for that monarch's illustrious ancestors. That their grandeur and power remain "alive" in their descendents is dramatized in Calderón's loa by the use of live actors to represent the statues of the distinguished royal ancestors

This leads us also to the answer to the question Why portraits? In the real world, the achievement of truly absolute power is, like human perfection, an unattainable goal for any monarch. The only way this *imaginary* state can be achieved is precisely in images. Calderón speaks of the "peregrinas perfecciones" of the monarchs portrayed in the portraits, which his subjects would like to see repeated in many copies. Now, there is no questioning the truth of the latter part of the statement, for the Spanish empire urgently needed a strong monarchical presence throughout, as it needed biological "copies" of Carlos and Marie-Louise.[13] But one could speak of the "peregrinas perfecciones" of Carlos only in the presence of the idealized image that can be offered in a royal portrait, such as those which Carreño rendered of him (see Figures 18 and 19). Carlos is an extreme example, but the same theoretical gap existed between Louis XIV and his portrait, for the king can only see himself and project himself as a truly absolute monarch in the icons that so represent him, his "présence réelle," the efficacy of his signs. In his portrait, he is "le roi comme droit, le roi comme Etat, corps fictif symbolique du royaume dans sa tête et son âme. Ainsi le portrait comme corps sacramental du roi opère le corps historique représenté dans le corps symbolique politique et relève le corps historique de son absence et de son imaginaire dans la fiction symbolique du corps politique" (19). It is thus by assembling on stage the signs of Hapsburg law that Calderón represents Carlos in his portrait as a true king.

Such an amassing of the representation of power and the power of representation as that of the loa could constitute the external image of a king, which its organizers hoped would be internalized in the imagination of the spectators. Yet it remains a fictional image, as Pascal recognized in his tale of a shipwrecked man who finds himself enthroned because he resembles physically the islanders' lost monarch: To function, it depends on the desire of the subjects to fill the center left void by the disappearance of the monarch, as well as the chance proximity of the shipwrecked man to their image of the monarch and the ship-

Figure 18. Juan Carreño de Miranda. *Carlos II.*

Figure 19. Juan Carreño de Miranda. *Marie-Louise d'Orléans.*

wrecked man's willingness and capacity to assume the role offered him (Marin 263–290). In the central text of *Hado y divisa*, Calderón goes on to dramatize the *internal* qualities that make a man a king in fact as well as fiction.

We do not know whether Calderón himself or someone else selected the theme for the play, but the choice of subject matter was as significantly appropriate as that of strong female figures for Calderón's court spectacles during the interregnum. This was surely not the occasion to use mythic gods to discuss the failings of a recognized king, but one in which chivalric material might serve to inspire Carlos with a heroic example of how a man apparently overwhelmed by a conspiracy of adverse circumstances could overcome the odds to secure his kingship and bring peace to his realm. Furthermore, the chivalrous model of constancy in love was appealingly appropriate for a young newlywed king much enamored of his bride. In a more general sense, one might also see in the preference for a chivalric setting a response to the renewed strength of the aristocracy in the last decades of the century. After losing both economic and political power earlier in the century, the aristocracy benefited from both an economic upturn toward the end of the century and the power vacuum after Felipe IV's death that made validos from Nithard and Valenzuela to Medinaceli and Oropesa dependent on the support of the most powerful nobles.[14] An aristocratic audience, still theoretically and psychologically committed to the chivalric ethos (Lundelius 57; Yates 108–111), would certainly have found pleasure in the wish fulfillment of a chivalric romance that seemed to reaffirm those values. However, a close reading reveals a considerable use of irony in Calderón's presentation of chivalric themes.[15]

On the level of plot, *Hado y divisa* takes us into the fantastic, timeless world of the novels of chivalry, with a hero mysteriously born and brought up unaware of his royal blood or the existence of a twin sister—like him, abandoned at birth. The final scene reveals that Leonido is the lost son of King Casimiro of Chipre (Cyprus) and legitimate heir to the kingdom of Trinacria. As a young man, Casimiro had been a hostage in Trinacria and had secretly married the princess Mathilde. He was ransomed and left for Chipre; she died at the birth of the twins, and a shipwreck cast the babies on the shore of Toscana. Leonido was raised in the court of the gran duque de Toscana, who had found the infant at the mouth of a lioness' cave, wrapped in "ricos paños de oro" and wearing a mysterious medallion. In the opening scene, however, not only is his princely glory unrecognized, but his very existence is in imminent danger; he has killed Lisidante, the young ruler of Trinacria and brother of the beautiful Arminda, who inherits the kingdom and would move heaven and earth to avenge her brother's death with that of his mysterious assailant.

Leonido committed that deed not for such prosaic ends as securing political power or economic gain but for the noblest chivalric cause—the defense of his lady as the most beautiful on earth. He has fallen in love with a portrait of

Arminda, and when Arminda's brother Lisidante proclaimed his cousin Mitilene the supreme beauty, Leonido felt compelled to challenge that claim.[16] Furthermore, he has done so in the best chivalric tradition, downing Lisidante by jousting in a tournament he has entered in disguise, bearing the slogan "La sola hermosa es aquella / Que yo adoro y que no digo" (364). He is, as described by his lackey Merlin, the quintessential knight in armor, surpassing the best-known heroes:[17]

> Creció con tanta soberbia,
> Que todo es caballerías,
> Divisas, motes y empresas.
> El caballero del Febo
> Con él fue un mandria, una dueña
> Palmerín de Oliva, un zote
> Arturo de Ingalaterra,
> Y en fin, Amadís de Gaula
> Un muchacho de la escuela,
> Y un niño de la doctrina
> El gran Belianís de Grecia (360).

As in the novels of chivalry, a sorceress also plays an instrumental role. Megera conjures up a vision of distant actions and flies in on a serpent to darken the world and whisk Leonido's unknown twin sister Marfisa away from danger as a dramatic climax to the first act.[18] Megera concludes the second act even more spectacularly as she appears on a "horrorosa hidra" and stops a battle between Arminda and her cousin Mitilene by causing the volcano Etna to explode, throwing flaming boulders about the theatre.[19]

Yet this apparently timeless world of fantasy is also linked to the realities of Hapsburg Spain in 1680. In fact, a duality in the projection of time is characteristic of Calderón's court spectacles and even essential to the coexistence of the text of royal power and the political text. This is what Cascardi overlooks when he describes Calderón's court plays as "static," or as "self-contained, motionless lyric" (130). The creation of an atmosphere of stasis is a crucial element in the text of royal power; by linking the royalty to the classical gods, chivalry, or pastoral romance, all of which are in a sense outside our perceived chronological time, he ties the monarchy to that condition of permanence, of imperviousness to the passage of time. At the same time, he subtly undercuts this atmosphere with details vital to the political text, thereby tactfully reminding the monarchs that they are subject to the same forces and failings as the rest of humanity. Thus, Cascardi is right in pointing out the apparent stasis of the Arcadia of *Eco y Narciso*. Yet the very moment of creation of that pastoral world is linked with festivities in honor of the birthday of Eco, and this in turn with the ten-year-old Princess Margarita María for whose birthday celebration the play was written.

One of Eco's suitors offers not his congratulations but his condolences, for having a birthday shows that she is not immortal but one year closer to death:

> Pésames viene a daros mi tristeza
> de que la rara y singular belleza
> de Eco, desengañada de que ha sido
> inmortal, hoy un círculo ha cumplido
> de sus años; que aunque de dichas llenos,
> cada año más es una gracia menos (1957).

In the final scene of the play, when Eco vanishes into the air and Narciso is converted into a flower, the gracioso Bato contradicts the suggestion of immortality with his final lines "¡Y habrá bobos que lo crean!" (1990).[20]

The timelessness of the chivalric world also is subtly undermined early in *Hado y divisa* by an offstage chorus. Playing against the scenery of seaside boulders, as the beleagured Leonido comes ashore, the chorus intones repeatedly a well-known ballad with its theme of *desengaño*:

> Escollo armado de hiedra,
> Yo te conocí edificio.
> Ejemplo de lo que acaba
> La carrera de los siglos.
> De lo que fuiste primero,
> Estás tan desconocido
> Que de sí mismo olvidado,
> No se acuerda de sí mismo (362–365).[21]

Just two years after the peace of Nijmegen, which marked a further decline in Spain's international standing in the loss of a number of important towns in the Netherlands and the entire Franche-Comté, the relevance of this lament to the Spanish monarchy was obvious. As Elliott summarizes it,

> The empire that Charles V had governed was being shorn of its territories one by one, as Castile revealed itself too weak to come to their help. . . .
>
> It was in the years around 1680, between the death of Don Juan José and the fall of his mediocre successor, the Duke of Medinaceli, in 1685, that Castile's fortunes reached their nadir. The French envoy, the Marquis de Villars, was shocked at the change for the worse since his first mission to Madrid in 1668. Although "the power and the policy of the Spaniards" had been "diminishing constantly . . . since the beginning of the century," the change had "become so great in recent times that one can actually see it occurring from one year to the next" (Elliott, *Imperial Spain* 360).

The timeless chivalric world is also anchored to the Hapsburg court of 1680 in several more specific ways. *Hado y divisa* was part of the Carnestolendas celebration in that year, and the same pre-Lenten festivities occur in Arminda's court, as Merlín tells Polidoro:

> . . . como este es
> Tiempo de carnestolendas,
> Dando tregua a las contiendas
> De la guerra, como ves,
> De gala, máscara y fiesta
> Delante el concurso viene (384).

Much more significant and pointed than this standard occasional reference is a comment made by Arminda's aged counselor Aurelio. Her cousin Mitilene has challenged her right to the throne of Trinacria, and Arminda dispatches him with a bellicose reply for her cousin. After cautioning that it will surely mean war, Aurelio exits, saying to Arminda, "Guárdeos el cielo." But in an aside, he laments:

> ¡Ay, miserable Trinacria,
> ¡Qué de desdichas te esperan
> En castigo de la infausta
> Pérdida de tus dos hijos!
> Pues transversales[22] dos damas
> Te ponen en la ocasión. . . .
> Mas ¿qué digo? Lengua, calla,
> Que irremediables desdichas
> Mejor será no acordarlas (372).

The two "damas transversales" are of course Mitilene and Arminda, but this play mentions the death of only one "hijo," Arminda's brother. Aurelio's lament is clearly directed to the offstage world, to the deaths of Felipe Próspero and Baltasar Carlos that have left Spain menaced by war over the rival Austrian and French claims through two "damas transversales," María Teresa and Margarita María, should Carlos II die without an heir. The pointedness of this reference was quite daring, and Calderón therefore has Aurelio feign breaking off in mid-thought, although he has already said all that was necessary.

Aurelio's comment linked the onstage threat of war to that which hovered offstage; Calderón also ties the play's saving remedy to the event that was Hapsburg Spain's potential defense, the marriage of Carlos II and Marie-Louise. The play did this not with words but with the final stage set, which re-created the "set" for the public entry of Marie-Louise to Madrid two months earlier, on 13 January.[23] According to the description:

> Mudóse el teatro de jardín en uno que representaba la plaza de palacio de
> su Majestad, imitando la forma en que ha quedado con los adornos que en

ella se hicieron para la entrada de la Reina nuestra señora, que la han añadido grave variedad a la perfección con que antes se hallaba. Estaba la imitación dispuesta de suerte, que empezaba por el arco que da entrada a la plaza, siguiendo los bastidores la imitación de dos corredores que tiene de arcos, adornados de estatuas que significan los ríos y fuentes más celebrados de España, en que había diferentes tarjetas, en que se colocaron cifras, motes y versos a tan feliz asumpto. En el foro estaba el frontispicio del palacio, todo imitado con gran propiedad y hermosura (391).

This scenic device would clearly delight the new queen, whose still rudimentary Spanish would have kept her from understanding any but the visual aspects of the play; it also serves to link the royal couple with Leonido in his triumph over all obstacles, his marriage to his beloved, his recognition as legitimate king of Trinacria, and the aversion of the threat of war. The young Carlos is thus suggestively metamorphosed into a portrait of the ideal chivalric king.

If these two timely references are quite pointed, the drama also contains an ambiguous use of "time" that can be read as an explanatory apology for the utility of this play of fantasy. When Polidoro remarks on the improbable course of events, Leonido responds:

> Si esos
> Maravillosos, extraños,
> Raros y varios sucesos,
> Ya en verdaderas historias,
> Ya en fabulosos ejemplos,
> El tiempo no los labrara,
> ¡Qué ocioso estuviera el tiempo!

A straightforward meaning is that time is idle if it does not weave strange events into true histories or fictitious *exempla*. But *tiempo* also means "occasion," "oportunidad, ocasión, o coyuntura de hacer algo" (*DicAut*). Using this sense of *tiempo*, we can read this as a metatheatrical commentary on the exemplary use of the marvelous to make the court play more than just a pastime, an idle entertainment.

Along with the attachment of the timeless world of chivalry to a very contemporary time setting, other devices also link Leonido with the Spanish king. To begin with, the name of the hero is clearly meant to symbolize the Hapsburg monarchy, as does the lion of the medallion in the frontispiece. Marfisa is a familiar personage from the tales of Boiardo and Ariosto, but rather than using her brother Ruggiero, Calderón invented Leonido for the occasion. Secondly, that suggestive medallion remained visible throughout the performance and is alluded to in the text in ways that through dramatic irony, provide the audience with the satisfaction of knowing what his onstage associates do not—that Leonido is not only of royal blood but furthermore represents the Spanish monarchy. Merlin says that his master has "un león de oro por empresa / Orlada con el enigma / De las no entendidas letras" (360), an allusion to the Latin banner "Ad nullius pavet occursum" that waves above the lion's head in the medallion. The elderly magician Argante, who found Marfisa as an infant being nursed by a doe, recognizes the coat of arms on Leonido's shield and exclaims:

> Su divisa es un león
> Que de relieve esculpido
> Trae, y por orla unas letras
> Con los caracteres mismos
> De aquella lámina . . . ¡Oh hados!
> ¡Qué de cosas ha movido
> La memoria, reduciendo
> A un instante todo un siglo! (363)

In the final recognition scene, Casimiro reads the mysterious lámina Leonido wears as saying "Este hado y divisa / de quien soy te avisa" and proclaims it to mean that Leonido is his son and inheritor of the kingdom, and that "el hado fiero / ha mejorado la suerte" (392). Thus in his moment of triumph over adversity, this chivalric hero's identity is linked with the medallion and the symbolism of the loa that declared Carlos's biological and institutional legitimacy.

If we can assume that such reiterated symbolic links and contemporary references would have been comprehensible for most spectators of *Hado y divisa*, we can make no such assumption for the primary royal spectators because of Carlos's limited mental capacity and Marie-Louise's linguistic limitations. However, Calderón also provided purely visual devices that would have captured Carlos's attention and facilitated his identification and sympathy with the young hero. In each of his three entrances in Act I, Leonido finds himself in grave peril from nature, man, or beast. He first enters on a runaway horse "cuyos movimientos se ejecutaron con tal primor, que la atención engañada estaba temiéndole el despeño, según lo desbocado del bruto y lo fragoso del terreno" and falls down a "real" mountain, "no fingido en los bastidores, sino sacado al teatro" (350).[24] He next appears with Polidoro against a setting of a rocky coast, trying in vain to row a boat against the force of artificial waves and raising with each stroke of the oars "espumas que salpicaban sus congojas" (361). Then he and Polidoro emerge from the underbrush to face the drawn arrows of Mitilene and her company of damas and pastores (363–364). Leonido's life is at some point threatened by every character in the play, from his lackey to his sister and his beloved, with the single exception of his loyal friend Polidoro. The chivalric hero complains repeatedly that he is being overwhelmed by an accumulation of events beyond his control, a sentiment we presume Carlos could identify with, since his reported reaction to the mounting demands on a slim treasury was "¡Nunca he visto más necesidades y menos dinero con qué satisfacerlas! ¡Si las cosas siguen así, tendré que negarme a dar oídos a los acreedores!" (Davies 150).

As Leonidos's loyal friend and counselor Polidoro encourages him to persevere in the face of difficulty, Calderón departs from the stylized rhethoric of both the comedia and the romances of chivalry. In realistic language, Polidoro gives him advice that could be addressed to Carlos II as well as the onstage hero. He tells him in effect not to panic, to "dar tiempo al tiempo," letting time unravel the tangled web; he tells him to deal with his problems one at a time because

> Si juntas un hombre viera
> Todas las penalidades
> Que traen las adversidades,
> El más constante se diera
> Por vencido; pero si
> No juntas las considera,
> Y que le embistan espera
> Cada una de por sí,
> Bien podrá de cada una
> Defenderse, cuando no
> Pueda de todas

And finally, when the threat of death or dishonor is imminent and Leonido objects to the dangers of the daring remedy Polidoro proposes, the latter answers with a tellingly direct proverb: "Señor, quien se mira ahogar, / Se ase de desnuda espada" (384).

Calderón also presents with convincing psychological realism the truly close friendship between Leonido and Polidoro, who willingly shares all the hardships and dangers Leonido undergoes and is ever determined to risk his own life to shield that of his friend. Leonido has returned to Trinacria incognito, posing as an ordinary German soldier, and has there had occasion to save Arminda's life. Never having seen his face in the fatal tournament, she asks this valient "soldier" to publish a challenge to Leonido so that he will have to return to fight or lose his honor. Leonido thus finds himself in the dilemma of having to fight "himself" or lose his love and his honor. The "desnuda espada" that Leonido finally agrees to grasp is the remedy of allowing Polidoro to pose as himself (Leonido) in combat. This costs Polidoro his life, as Florante, a rival pretender to Arminda's hand, treacherously shoots him in the back before the meet. Although not in the intended fashion, Polidoro's sacrifice accomplishes the desired objective, for Marfisa in turn disguises herself as Leonido and takes to battle the impenetrable armor with the vital lion motif that signals his legitimacy as son of Casimiro and heir to Trinacria.

In this final battle of Leonido with "himself," there is, if not realism, a relevant psychological truth. Leaving aside all the other situations that threatened the young king and his country, within the setting of his marriage his final enemy was indeed himself, the biological degeneracy that made improbable his capacity to engender the desperately needed heir. It would require an almost superhuman effort for Carlos to overcome his deficient preparation and physical weakness to establish himself as an effective husband and ruler. In the play, Leonido was fortunate in the arrival of a strong father, Casimiro, to unsnarl the tangle by recognizing his lost son and daughter. Leonido is then married to his beloved Arminda and recognized as king, reestablishing peace between all contenders for power. Unfortunately, no such providential figure would appear to rescue Carlos.

In the denouement of *Hado y divisa,* however, there remains one discordant note, akin to the punishment of the rebel soldier in *La vida es sueño* in its psychological effect (at least on most modern readers) and harder to explain by reference to contemporary political philosophy:[25] the fate of Florante. This man, who had repeatedly accused Leonido of cowardice, disguised himself and his men as bandits to ambush Leonido, and murdered Polidoro by the decidedly unchivalrous means of a pistol shot in the back, is in no way chastized. While he does not secure Arminda's hand, he receives the valuable consolation of marriage to Mitilene. In an aside that underlines his unworthiness, he breathes a sigh of relief: "Pues mi delito en silencio / queda, venturoso he sido" (392).

Why would Calderón violate the principle of poetic justice in this way, rewarding the darkest blocking figure and destroying the hero's one ever-loyal friend? A comparison with Shakespeare's late romances may provide an answer. Heilman says, in an introduction to *Cymbeline*: "The convention of romance approaches life in terms of the ultimate reconcilability of desires and circumstances; though ambitions and needs may be great, they tend to fall within a realm of moral possibility; and circumstances, though they may be antagonistic for a long period, eventually yield to meritorious humanity" (1290). Yet as Traugott points out, in Shakespeare, "in the graciousness of romance there is inescapably hidden the corruption of violence, cruelty and destruction" (178), and there is at least one actual death in all Shakespeare's romances, except for *The Tempest* (Cohen 127), which certainly contains somber notes as well. While "meritorious humanity" does prevail in the end, it does not do so with the perfect felicity of comedy. Cohen (128–130) believes that this form in Shakespeare and Calderón is a response to a perception of an epoch of deepening crisis for the aristocracy, which failed to adapt to new political and economic circumstances in the era of Europe's transition from feudalism to capitalism. Referring particularly to *The Tempest* and *Hado y divisa,* Cohen says: "In each case, a dramatist at the end of an age found a way out of the persistent conflict of the present only in a utopian view of the future (391).[26]

Calderón did stage for the pleasure of king and court a utopian romance, but it was an imperfect utopia in which loyal supporters such as Polidoro may die and opponents such as Florante must sometimes be accommodated. In the political context of a dangerously weak king and a reassertive if not reinvigorated aristocracy, he did build this utopia on the aristocratic code of chivalry but tempered his presentation of this ethos with persistent touches of irony.[27] He did create in *Hado y divisa* a fantasy world, but one that blocked the escape route by repeated reference to the real world, one that would not be an "idle pastime" but aimed at weaving "marvelous events" into an "exemplary fantasy."

In the framework of this last work, Calderón put on stage for Carlos II and his court a demonstration of the forces that constitute a king externally. In the play itself, he offers that audience a model of a hero—a mortal man in an imperfect world—who, faced with apparently overwhelming adversity, prevails and secures peace for his kingdom and recognition as legitimate monarch. Rather than an example of solipsistic escapism, we should see in *Hado y divisa de Leonido y Marfisa* Calderón's use of the power of theater to convince Carlos II and the court that the Hapsburg monarchy had not in fact reached "the end of the line."[28] In his mythological court spectacles, Calderón had demonstrated that art can at the same time serve power by celebrating the glory of the monarch and strive to influence its course by tactfully illustrating the flaws in its operation. Explicitly, in his last work, he dramatizes the proposition that theatrical representation can not only support and guide but also generate the authority of the king; that the constitution of the central figure in the theatre of power depends, as it were, on the power of theatre.

EIGHT

Conclusion

DESPITE its traditional title, this conclusion does not pretend to be an ending, a summing up of an all-inclusive study of the the court-spectacle plays of Calderón de la Barca. I hope, rather, to have contributed to a beginning, an opening up of new and richer ways of reading this body of unduly neglected works. There are a number of fascinating plays I have barely mentioned that offer fertile material for a variety of critical approaches. For example, *El amor enamorado*, the story of Psyche and Cupid, is a complex and moving play, one that would make a good subject for a comparative treatment because that story was as common on court stages across Europe as that of Perseus and Andromeda. *Eco y Narciso* is an equally appealing drama, more easily comprehensible to modern readers than other Calderonian court spectacles; it problematizes discourse and the definition of self in ways that invite the application of a variety of poststructuralist approaches.[1] Using the story of Cephalus and Procris, Calderón wrote *Celos aun del aire matan*, his one full-length opera, which merits consideration in the context of the development of that musical tradition. Did he then write a sort of antidote to this grandiloquent treatment in *Céfalo y Procris*? A definitive answer to whether Calderón is really the author of this parodic mythological play has yet to be given; an affirmative answer would add another layer of complexity to Calderón's manipulation of the conventions of court drama.

Rather than attempting to exhaust the subject, my intent has been to present sufficient evidence to demonstrate that Calderón's court spectacles are indeed "plays of power," in every way *except* the way they have traditionally been viewed—mere toys for the entertainment of the powerful. To comprehend their power requires a full "composición de lugares" by the modern reader, a triple contextualization of Calderón's dramatic texts.

The first stage of contextualization consists of restoring to the printed word Calderón's masterly exploitation of the full polyphony of the dramatic idiom. While court spectacles all over Europe included poetry, music, dance, perspective scenery, and stage machinery, these components often functioned as discrete or competing elements. Calderón, however, integrated them effectively to heighten the power of his dramatic text. Thus, dissonant chords and awkward rhythms contribute to the infernal scene in *Fortunas de Andrómeda y Perseo*, and in that same play, Discordia alternately sings or recites to indicate that she operates in both the divine and the human spheres. Calderón uses rapid changes of scenery and drop-in sets not just to dazzle the audience but to unify his plots as he presents Perseo's birth as a flashback and shows Leonido a vision of the threat mounting against him in another kingdom in *Hado y divisa de Leonido y Marfisa*. Stage machinery also underlines symbolic movements within the play, as, for example, in *La estatua de Prometeo,* Minerba carries the rational Prometeo upward toward the sun while Palas draws the emotional Epimeteo back and down into a dark grotto. Nor does Calderón neglect the value of poetry itself: witness his use of contrasting meters to personify Minerba and Palas, or Andrómeda's monologue as she is attached to the sacrificial rock. By effectively integrating all these elements, Calderón created plays of power in the sense of the full utilization of all elements of theatrical representation to maximize dramatic impact.

As those other codes heighten the theatrical power of Calderón's central story, so do the "minor" pieces that surround it increase the complexity of its discourse. Calderón employs the loa for a dual purpose, one of which is a dramatic exposition of his poetics of the court spectacle. In the loa for *Las fortunas de Andrómeda y Perseo*, he shows how music, art, and poetry joined by stage machinery present the king's play; in the loa for *Hado y divisa de Leonido y Marfisa*, he dramatizes how the power of representation presents the very king himself. At the same time, Calderón uses the loa to set the connections between the onstage gods and the royal spectators necessary to both the text of royal power for all court spectacles and the political text of the particular play. The other minor pieces reinforce that connection and sometimes play parodically on the conventions of the court play, as in the *Triunfo de Juan Rana.*

To recover the text of royal power and the political text of these events depends on the second and third stages of contextualization, that is, the appreciation of the performance within the physical space of its representation and within the political context of its day. Publication of the text of royal power depended on the splendor of the theatre and the prominence of the royal family as both primary spectator and first pole of the spectacle for the rest of the audience. This image was augmented by the hierarchical arrangement of other guests, the solemn ceremonies of royal entry and exit, and the dramatic encomium of the loa, which elevated the royalty to the realm of mythic deities. Having established this flattering connection between the king and the gods, Calderón could then avail himself of the imperfections of those mythic figures to consider, through the tactful medium of dramatic illusion, political issues troubling the court.

At the same time, in his most successful plays, he organized the plot so that it would also offer a particular text, not anchored to the political figures and issues of the day but sufficiently subjunctivized or universalized so that each viewer-reader might read meaning into it through his particular world of experience. Calderón could create this polyvalent text and expect his spectators to accept it because the hermeneutics applied to classical mythology, as to biblical stories, traditionally yielded multiple readings of the same tale. These are not "layers of meaning" arranged hierarchically from the superficial to the profound, but simultaneously present in a interrelationship of productive tension.

The result in these plays is a discourse of power more complex than that which generally prevailed on other European stages. What were the factors that made its creation and acceptance possible? An important element is of course Calderón's combination of dramatic genius and intellectual rigor, the same combination of talents that enabled him to produce annually autos sacramentales that were at once brilliant pieces of theatre that captured the attention of the broad public in the streets of Madrid and doctrinally accurate dramatizations of Catholic dogma. With these gifts, he earned a secure stature in the court that gave him a degree of control over all elements of the court spectacle that few dramatists in other courts could enjoy.

A second factor was the strength of the professional dramatic tradition in Spain, which made the spectacle play performed by professional companies the court spectacle of choice. This generic preference facilitated the presentation of an oppositional discourse within the plot that was not possible in the allegorical forms predominating in other courts. There the opponent was represented as an evil already defeated, or at most staged in the simple black-and-white confrontation of an antimasque over which the masque triumphed.

The third factor was certainly the political situation in the Spanish court and the philosophical concept of the nature of royal authority. With all the difficulties they faced, the Hapsburg kings were not threatened by any viable *internal* opposition. There was not, therefore, the same incentive for them to employ the court spectacle primarily as a dramatic defense of their moral right to absolute power.[2] Furthermore, one of the limits placed on absolute power by Spanish political philosophers from Quevedo to Mariana was the obligation to permit and to heed legitimate criticism.

A fourth and admittedly speculative factor that may have enabled a discourse of power in Spain that did not occur in other European courts involves the personalities of the kings to whom the spectacles were addressed. Since we can easily imagine the possibility of such a discourse in the power vacuum that followed the death of Felipe IV, the question centers on its feasibility during his lifetime. As his letters to Sor María de Agreda and Sor Luisa demonstrate, Felipe IV combined a love of the theatre with a sense of personal guilt for the disasters that beset his country. If this sense of responsibility kept him from silencing preachers who poured out to him litanies of the problems of his realm from the pulpit, he was no more likely to silence a play-writing priest who wrapped his critical analysis in the tactful and entertaining form of dramatic spectacle.

If we can perform this triple contextualization to place Calderón's court spectacles in the dramatic, physical, and political environment in which they were performed, we can come to a new appreciation of his genius as a dramatist and a richer understanding of the complexity of his world view. His court spectacles are plays that display in full force his mastery of the theatrical idiom, works in which he serves the powerful while examining the bases of that power and the fissures that threaten it. They are "plays of power" in every positive sense of the word.

NOTES

CHAPTER ONE. INTRODUCTION

1. See Buck 23–24, 248–249; Durán 18.

2. Calderón was also charged with frivolity in the "carelessness" or "ignorance" with which he treated the classical myths. The few critics who commented on the plays in the early twentieth century tended to focus on this "misunderstanding" of the stories. See, for example, Martin and Paris.

3. The reevaluation of the myth plays began with Valbuena Prat, in a chapter devoted to them in his book *Calderón*. Among the most important contributors are Chapman; Parker, "Metáfora y símbolo" and "Segismundo's Tower"; Neumeister, *Mythos*; ter-Horst; Sullivan; Wardropper; De Armas, *Astrea*; and Stein on music; editions of several of the plays by Aubrun, Wilson, and others; and many articles on various plays and aspects of their production, particularly those of Varey. For a general review of the reception of the mythological plays, see the introduction to Calderón, *La estatua de Prometeo* 97–104.

4. As Gadamer points out, we can never become conscious of all our prejudices, nor can we hope, from our own historically conditioned moment, to reconstruct fully the grounds of understanding of a past epoch, yet it is only in the attempt at fusing those two horizons that we can increase our understanding of both ourselves and the past.

5. Lope's relative financial independence did not necessarily provide full artistic freedom; whether in jest or in seriousness, in his "Arte nuevo," he defended his neglect of classical precepts by claiming that he had placed himself under the alternative dictatorship of the tastes of the "vulgo" who bought his wares.

6. E.g., Barrionuevo 1:237, 247, and 2:199–200; Maura, *Carlos II* 2:503.

7. Foucault also explores this problem in his essay "What Is an Author." Since the seventeenth or eighteenth century, he says, literary (as opposed to scientific) works have been accepted only in relation to an "author function," distinct from the writing subject, essentially bounded by the criteria for authentication of texts inherited from Christian exegis. As propounded by St. Jerome, this means excluding from the body of works attributed to an author anything substantially different in style or doctrine from his norm. "The author is also the principle of a certain unity of writing—all differences having to be resolved, at least in part, by the principle of evolution, maturation, or influence. The author also serves to neutralize the contradictions that may emerge in a series of texts: there must be—at a certain level of his thought or desire, of his consciousness or unconscious—a point where contradictions are resolved, where incompatible elements are at last tied together or organized around a fundamental or originating contradiction" (111). This mode of critical operation has worked first to exclude Calderón's court plays from consideration on the basis of their stylistic difference/"inferiority" and subsequently has biased critics toward reading them through the lens of his allegorical religious drama, long accepted as quintessentially "Calderón." One of the notable exceptions is Wardropper, who points out how the image of Calderón as the conservative defender of traditional institutions has impeded appreciation of his later works (41).

8. This work differs from the norm, however, in that it is totally sung, a true opera.

9. This date is disputed; see Chapter 6.

10. In addition, Calderón wrote an early version of the Narcissus story, probably for Carnival of 1639, for which he was paid 1,500 *reales*. This text has been lost. He may have written *La fábula de Dafne*, also lost, performed on 28 July 1636. See Shergold, *History* 287, 292. The Dafne play is elsewhere attributed to Lope de Vega, however.

11. We have no performance records assuring spectacular court production of this two-act work, but the stage directions it includes indicate several changes of perspective scenery, and its music also seems to have been more sophisticated than the norm of its time (see Stein 191–205). Confusion often arises because Calderón used the same story and title for an auto sacramental, and there is also a very different three-act play with the same title written by Calderón (Act III) in collaboration with Rojas and Coello.

12. See his letter (in Cotarelo y Mori, *Calderón* 287–288) to his superior, the Patriarch of the Indies, Alonso Pérez de Guzmán, who had withdrawn the chaplaincy of the Reyes Nuevos de Toledo previously bestowed on Calderón because he thought it not fitting for a man who wrote plays and then ordered him to write the autos sacramentales for that year. Calderón forced his hand by asking that he either be allowed to write for all suitable occasions or excused from all dramatic writing on the grounds that it was unsuitable for a priest.

13. See Gordon 168–169 and Strong, *Art* 98–125, 153–170. The role of image making in political consolidation is of course not exclusive to absolutist systems. In the case of the Republic of Venice, Muir demonstrates convincingly the importance of elaborate civic ritual in promoting the myth of Venice as an ideal example of beauty, religiosity, liberty, peacefulness, and republicanism, thereby preserving the reality of oligarchic control by a less-than-ideal aristocracy.

14. See Timothy Murray's excellent article on Richelieu's use of the theatre to underscore his ruling position.

15. Jonson was less sanguine about their universal comprehensibility; he added a footnote explaining certain figures to his printing of *Hymenaei*: "And for the Allegorie, though here it be very cleare, and such as might well escape a candle, yet because there are some, must complaine of darknesse, that haue but thick eyes, I am contented to hold them this Light" (qtd in Gordon 161–162). Even the primary regal spectator could sometimes have "thick eyes," Ewbank implies, for during the performance of Jonson's *Pleasure Reconciled to Virtue*, a masque subsequent critics have praised for "its union of ritual structure with visual and verbal symbolism," the king grew impatient. "James I interrupted the performance . . . by shouting out: 'Why don't they dance? What did you make me come here for? Devil take you all, dance' " (qtd in Ewbank 307).

16. Lawrenson (9) points out, however, that only in Italy were there attempts at authentic reconstruction of ancient theatres, whereas the French took from the Vitruvian tradition only what suited their purposes, which in many cases was limited to superficial decoration. The same proviso applies to developments in Spain, where only the disposition of the temporary theatre constructed in Aranjuez for the 1622 performance of Villamediana's *La gloria de Niquea* could be considered a remote link with reconstruction attempts through its kinship with the Olympic Theatre of Vicenza. Amadei de Pulice (23–26) describes this theatre in considerable detail.

17. Since Renaissance poets and musicians had no actual music from Greek drama, this development was based on their interpretation of ancient writings about music. See Grout 11–14, 34–39; Donington 81.

18. See Seznec for a full explanation of the passage of classical myth to the Renaissance.

19. Pyle suggests that they would better be referred to as "favole mitologiche" because it is their mythological subject matter that binds them together. Scholars of early music and drama differ substantially about the appropriate designation and classification of these pieces and subsequent forms. Pirrotta (37) calls Correggio's and Taccone's works "*drammi mescidati*, hybrid dramas," because they attempted to combine the regularities of classical theatre with the greater freedom with regard to time, action, plot, and meter characteristic of popular religious theatre. For a detailed account of the evolution of music and theatre to Monteverdi, see Pirrotta and Povoledo's study.

20. Pirrotta and Povoledo discuss in detail the music and staging of the intermedi, and the dramatic function of the different types within the total spectacle.

21. Other forms were not excluded, however. Intermedi coexisted with opera in seventeenth-century Italy (see Grout 27–28; Pirrotta and Povoledo 236, 271); in France, there were *pièces à machines*, such as *L'Andromède* of Corneille or Moliere's *Psyche*; and *máscaras* were often part of court festivities in Spain, although some of these seem to have consisted of masqued balls with no important theatrical elements.

22. For details of the development of theatre construction, scenery, and machinery, see Lawrenson, Strong, *Splendour* and *Art*, Amadei de Pulice, and Wickham.

23. The article by Rodríguez G. de Ceballos contains interesting information on Italian developments in scenography and stage technique, and their application in Spain; that of Pérez Sánchez provides valuable data on painters of perspective scenery in the Madrid court. Both of these articles, in the Egido volume on baroque scenography, came to my attention too late for incorporation here. I am grateful to Sebastian Neumeister for sending me this volume.

24. A contemporary chronicler suggests humorously that his sudden death might have been a summons to work in a higher court: "Bacho el tramoyista, lunes, viniendo desde el Retiro a Madrid, se cayó muerto en el Prado. Debe de ir a hacer a la otra vida alguna comedia para San Juan, pues va tan de prisa" (Barrionuevo 1:286).

25. Hurtado de Mendoza (9) made similar observations on the relative importance of verse and spectacle in Villamediana's court "invention," *La gloria de Niquea*.

26. He had written one act of *Polifemo y Circe* the previous year; Mira de Amescua and Pérez de Montalbán wrote the other two acts.

27. See her articles "Manuscrito Novena," "Música existente para comedias de Calderón," and "La plática de los dioses." A revised and expanded version of her dissertation, "Music in the Seventeenth-Century Spanish Secular Theater, 1598–1690," will be published by Oxford University Press in 1992.

28. A musical and poetic form structured around an *estribillo* (refrain), akin to the French *virelai* and the Provençal *dansa*, dedicated either to rustic and popular themes or to religious subjects, particularly the Nativity.

29. Stein, "Music" 10. For the information in the following section on the use of music in Spanish court spectaculars, I have drawn heavily on her dissertation.

30. *Comedia* is a generic term applied to three-act plays in Spain, whether comic or tragic.

31. See in particular Brown's excellent article, "Music—How Opera Began"; also Donington 40–42, 68–100; Grout 34–77; and Pirrotta 22, 36, 197–280.

32. Throughout the century, the royal family and household were regularly entertained by *particulares*, private command performances by professional troupes of plays from the public theatres.

33. This was a prescient bit of casting, given his subsequent amorous inclinations.

34. This was a shortened version of a play previously written for the public stage. Even in its abbreviated form, it seems to have reached a climax different from that intended when the scenery caught fire, giving occasion for a bit of real-life heroism, for the king was reported to have carried the queen and the infanta to safety in his arms. Several later reports by foreign travelers confuse the plays, saying that the blaze began during the performance of *La gloria de Niquea*. All sorts of rumors grew up around the incident, some saying that the fire was deliberately set by Villamediana so that he could rescue the queen, of whom he was reported to be enamored. Villamediana was murdered a few months later, adding new fuel to the blaze of gossip. Another interpretation had it that the king and the count were rivals for the affections of a court lady, the Portuguese beauty Francisca de Tabora. After his death, Villamediana was indicted for sodomy, but this action may have been an attempt to quash widespread gossip about his courtship of the queen. See Shergold, *History* 273–274; Gómez de Liaño and Infantes 487–489.

35. Stein, "Music" 138–139. The verse was of course no innovation, for Italianate verse had been widely used by Spanish poets for a full century since Garcilaso's masterpieces demonstrated its flexible beauty. Dramatists regularly employed it in their plays, but in limited passages to achieve special effects.

36. Some of this scenery may have been reused in the subsequent production of *Querer por sólo querer*.

37. With her research in the State Archives in Florence, Whitaker has settled longstanding disputes about this work—its date, whether it was truly an opera, and whether the music was composed by a Florentine or Spaniard.

38. Gonçalez de Salas would have conceded no priority to the neighboring French in the field of dance, for he says that after the Greeks and Romans, "ninguna otra Provincia ha usurpado tanto su elegancia como la Nuestra, en donde con perficción summa hoi pertenece, i con singular semejança de los Antiguos" (f.119).

39. Tuccaro, a famous acrobat who settled in France in 1571, provided an almost painfully detailed development of this idea: "Toutes lesquelles choses [les retrogradations et diversités des conjonctions des planettes] si on vouloit considérer parfaictement, on pourroit paravanture congoistre qu'elles sont iustement imitées et representées au bal; d'autant que la diversité des mouvements faicts a l'opposite l'un de l'autre par ceus qui dancent, n'est qu'une générale imitation de divers mouvements des cieux, et le retour qu'on faict en arrière au bal et à la danse n'est autre chose que vouloir imiter honnestement la retrogradation des planettes. Il y a plus, que les passages qui sont representéz tenants un de leurs pieds arrestéz et remuants de l'autre: c'est comme une similitude des estoiles errantes, quand elles sont, suyvant les Astrologues en leur degré. Et les voltes dont on use en ballant, ne sont autrechose que les espris qu'on tient estre és cieux, les conionctions alternatives qu'on faict après une separation proportionnée du bal et de la danse: et

puis ces belles et diverses retraictes, droictes et obliques, qu'on exerce avec tant de grace, sont les mesmes conionctions et oppositions triangulaires et quadrangulaires voire sexangulaires qui interviennent quasi tous les jours entre les planettes en leurs spheres celestes" (qtd in McGowan 20–21).

40. This seems to represent a confusion between the names Jubal and Tubal. Genesis 4:21–22: "His [Jabal] brother's name was Jubal; he was the father of all those who play the lyre and pipe. Zillah bore Tubal-cain; he was the forger of all instruments of bronze and iron." The *General estoria* of Alfonso el Sabio (bk. 1, chaps. 16–19) develops extensively the story of the invention of musical instruments by Jubal; Tubal is described as the first metalsmith, an "omne lidiador" who taught men how to fight and invented arms to that end. His only contribution to the development of music was accidental: Jubal invented music on the inspiration of the "notes" he heard struck by Tubal's hammers in his forge.

41. Felipe's skill as a dancer was also praised by Cesare Negri, who dedicated to him his book *Nuove Inventioni de Balli* (Milan, 1604), and by the Venetian ambassador Simon Contarini (Stein, "Music" 105 n.15).

42. Stein, "Music" 119–120; *Diccionario de Autoridades*; Brooks 159–160. Brooks, a dancer herself, includes a useful glossary with more technical descriptions of a number of steps and dances, from which the following are quoted: "*pavana*— . . . pavan, the stately court dance to music of a binary rhythm, which was usually performed with the *gallarda*. It was built from arrangements of simple and double steps, moving forward and backward. Depending on the version performed, the dance might be embellished with low jumps and runs, and small stamps"; "*gallarda*—one of the most frequently performed courtly dances of the Renaissance, it was the gay and lively partner dance to the stately *pavana*. The *gallarda* was performed to a sprightly six-beat musical accompaniment, and its simplest version consisted of four steps, a spring into the air on the fifth beat, and a landing on the sixth count with the feet in fourth position. Many variations of the step were invented"; "*turdión*—the predecessor to the six-count galliard, and featured the same sorts of steps, but generally with less virtuosity expected in the jumps and *batterie*" (388–394).

43. Brook says the pie de gibao was a stately dance related to the pavana, while the alemana was "a sedate dance in duple meter considered to be of German origin, consisting of a slow walking section, a musical interlude, and a repetition of the dance section at a faster tempo and with some light jumps" (388, 392).

44. Brooks: "*españoleta*—lively Renaissance dance in a triple meter, often performed by groups of three, with light jumps and hops, and complex leg work"; "*jácara*—a southern Spanish dance used widely in the theater and in court balls in the seventeenth century, but originating in the underworld of the Andalusian Moors" (388, 392).

45. See Act I, l. 386, and Act III, l. 68, of my edition and Introduction, p. 12.

46. Stage direction following Act I, l. 680, in the Varey and Shergold edition.

47. Stage directions describe the geometric arrangement with which this "movement" of the loa begins: ". . . los doce Meses, significados . . . en doce airosos Jóvenes, que al pie cada uno de su Signo, formaban entre todos en dos bandas cuatro diagonales líneas tiradas al centro con tan regular medida en su declinación las estaturas, que desmentidas unas de otras, dejaban verse todas" (Calderón, *Fieras* 64–65).

48. See Shergold and Varey, *Representaciones* 24, 70–71, 76.

49. At the same time, it provided a happy release from the dark ambiguity of the preceding play. See Chapter 6.

CHAPTER TWO. CALDERÓN, MASTER OF POLYPHONY

1. Calderón had written several court-spectacle plays before this date. His first, *El mayor encanto, amor,* will be considered in detail in the following chapter. His next mythological play, *Los tres mayores prodigios,* reminiscent of the intermedi in its loose thematic construction and of the auto sacramental in its performance on three staging carts, consisted of three stories: Jason, Medea and the Golden Fleece; Theseus and the Minotaur; and Hercules and Deianira. There was a hiatus in such production in the 1640s due to a series of political catastrophes and the deaths of Cosimo Lotti, the queen and the crown prince. When Felipe IV married Mariana de Austria in 1649, public and court theatres came to life again. Calderón's 1652 spectacle play, *La fiera, el rayo y la piedra,* also contains three stories, but they are effectively melded into one unified play. The texts of two other early Calderonian court plays, one on the story of Daphne (1636) and another about Narcissus (about 1639), have not survived. See Shergold 287, 292. Neumeister includes a useful chronological list of Calderón's mythological court plays but limits it to plays in which mythological deities make at least a fleeting appearance and excludes plays such as *Hado y divisa de Leonido y Marfisa* and *El jardín de Falerina* that introduce no classical divinities. He also mistakenly dates *Apolo y Climene* and *El hijo del sol, Faetón* in 1661 rather than 1662.

2. In his introduction to Corneille's *Andromède,* Delmas lists a number of other versions of the story. However, he incorrectly dates the Lope de Vega play as 1618–1620 rather than ca. 1613 and Monteverdi's melodramma in 1608 instead of 1618–1620.

3. A bust Romano made of Beatrice is now in the Louvre.

4. Each of the previous two acts of this five-act drama also ended with the music of hidden instruments.

5. The second-act exchange between Mercurio and Siro, and the closing scene sung by Apollo.

6. See Strong, *Art and Power* 36 and Plates 23 and 24, which show on facing pages Leonardo's sketches for *Danae* and a reconstruction of a Brunelleschi *apparato* in which the angel of the Annunciation descended from heaven. Strong describes Leonardo's drawing as "a celestial appearance of a deity in the clouds," but his own clear reproduction of the sketch refutes this. Steinitz describes the drawings more accurately and completely.

7. A mandorla is an almond-shape aureola of light that from about the sixth to the fifteenth century traditionally surrounded Christ in paintings of the Transfiguration and the Ascension. Part of the Brunelleschi device mentioned above consisted of a mandorla that transported the angel of the Annunciation.

8. The date of its first performance is uncertain. McGowan lists it for the year 1606, but I have been unable to find a confirmation of that date. The Philidore ms. dates it in 1608, while the manuscript copy of the text (Bibliothèque Nationale Ms. fr. 24352, f.308) says it was danced "avant Louis XIII vers 1609 ou 1610" and also has "Henri IV" written in the upper right-hand corner. Bibliothèque Nationale Ms. fr. 24357 (p. 479) lists it as one of five ballets danced for Louis XIII in 1611.

9. In André Philidor, "Ballets Dansez sous le Regne de Henry IV," Bibliothèque Nationale Ms. Res.F. 496. The Andromeda ballet is on f.82.

10. His arrival apparently constituted the climactic scene in the 1611 performance for the young Louis XIII; the manuscript source says that only four stanzas were danced—stanzas one, two, six, and nine—and the Bataille music reflects that shorter version. It consists of only music for only one stanza, with the other three printed on a facing page for performance to the same music.

11. Or possibly Henri Clarnère, one of the most famous fireworks engineers of the time.

12. The Bibliothèque Nationale possesses a fascinating engraving of this spectacle, reproduced by Christout, which shows the Tower of Nesles, Andromeda chained to the rock as the monster and Perseus approach, and the dancers on the float, all spouting flames, with other towers and chateaux of Paris in the background and spectators watching in boats downriver.

13. A notable exception is the article of Bianconi and Walker, "Production, Consumption," which analyzes the relationship between political structures and the production and reception of opera in various European cities in the seventeenth century.

14. The first unit concludes Book 4 of the *Metamorphoses*, and the second opens Book 5.

15. Cassiopeia is sometimes said to have boasted that she herself was fairer than the Nereids, Neptune's daughters. In other versions, she boasts that it is her daughter who outshines them. Campeggi has her lament her vanity without making precise its exact nature.

16. This introduction of Nereus, or Neptune in other versions of the story, is a departure from the Ovidian tale, probably drawn from *Orlando furioso,* in which Ariosto recounts Orlando's rescue of Olympia from Orca, a sea monster who swallows maidens of the island of Ebuda offered up in an attempt to appease Proteus (often confused with Nereus) for the king's slaying of his beautiful daughter, who was carrying Proteus's child (bks. 8 and 11). Calderón also makes Nereo one of the offended gods in his play.

17. "L'architetto della prospettiva e delle macchine fu Cosimo Lotti, il quale con l'esempio delle cose passate, si è portato di maniera che, dato la parità del sito, non è stata punto inferiore alle passate, nè di vaghezza, nè di ricchezza, nè d'invenzione" (qtd in Solerti 127).

18. A Jesuit, Giovan Domenico Ottonelli, in his treatise on the theatre, *Della christiana moderatione del theatro* published in 1652, classified "sung plays" into three types according to the patrons supporting them: (1) princely, "given in the mansions of the great princes and other lords, be they laymen or of the church"; (2) academic, given by "a group of gentlemen or virtuous citizens, or erudite members of academies put on according to the occurrence of some good reason . . . [and] composed by capable musicians after they have been written by celebrated professors of the poetic art" (qtd in Bianconi and Walker, "Febiarmonici" 54–55); and (3) those performed by "mercenary" musicians formed in traveling companies that performed for a diverse public. Bianconi and Walker point out that the boundaries between these types were not really clear-cut, and early Venetion opera, such as that of Ferrari and Manelli, falls "somewhere between the 'princely' and the 'academic' " ("Febiarmonici" 64).

19. The libretto was published by Francesco Suzzi in Ferrara in 1639. There is a copy

in Ferrara, Biblioteca Comunale Ariostea, MF218, 1. I am grateful to Thomas Walker for calling my attention to this piece and securing a copy of the libretto for me.

20. Pio di Savoia creates a Fineo so distasteful that he borders on the comic—perhaps deliberately so, since the description published with the libretto praises the event for its great variety of pleasures, including "vaghissima scherzi" (3). Fineo is clearly in love with the power to be gained by marriage to Andromeda rather than the maiden herself, and curses everyone from Cefeo to the gods when they oppose him: "Non conosco altro Giove, & altro giusto, / Chè ne miei Cavalieri, e nel mio gusto" (95). When the queen suggests that he might have risked his life to save Andromeda from the monster, Fineo tells her in effect that women should "shut up and tend to their knitting": "Chiudi l'ardita boca / Donna superba, e sciocca / . . . / Chè Donna haver non deve altro per uso, / Chè maneggiare la conocchia, e'l fuso" (92).

21. The king's men are appropriately attired entirely in the whitest of whites, "in segno forse dalla sincera causa, che difendevano" (98). The published account describes in great detail all the brilliantly colored costumes used in the event.

22. While the text leaves nameless the musicians who sang the work, the names of the twenty-eight nobles who performed as Cavalieri and their Padrini are printed in bold letters, with the two squadrons of cavalieri tactfully arranged in alphabetical order.

23. Although there are no specific performance records, the conjunction of textual references and external evidence compiled by McGaha argues very convincingly for its performance in that year (McGaha introduction to Vega Carpio, Perseo 3–9).

24. Profeti questions the idea of mutual influence between them, however. See her article "Jacopo Cicognini e Lope de Vega."

25. Anachronistic because Amphitryon was the grandson of Perseus.

26. A number of other Lopean changes also derive from Bustamente and Pérez de Moya, including the location of Polidetes' kingdom in Acaya and Andromeda's home in Tyre rather than Ethiopia; the alteration from burnished bronze to "cristalino espejo" of the shield that averts Medusa's fatal gaze; and the idea that Polidetes sent Perseus off on the presumably fatal mission of slaying Medusa because he feared the young man would usurp his power. From Pérez de Moya's allegorical interpretations Lope drew the idea of Atlas as an astrologer and his depiction of Perseus as virtue and Medusa as vice.

27. De Armas ("Lope de Vega and Titian") documents Lope's familiarity with Titian. There was also an important series of frescos painted by Gaspar Becerra between 1563 and 1568 in the southwest tower of the palace of El Pardo. Perseus's story decorated the ceiling, with episodes drawn from Book 4 of the Metamorphoses of Ovid. The story of the liberation of Andromeda was painted on the walls, but unfortunately nothing remains of the latter series. Another series of frescoes was painted in the palace of the Marqués de Santa Cruz in Viso about 1580, and paintings of individual scenes were popular, particularly that of Andromeda on the rock. In the sixteenth century, according to López Torrijos, the theme was popular with the king and great lords because of its possibilities for heroic exaltation and political and religious allegory, and because esthetically pleasing nude scenes of Andromeda and Danae could be justified by their classical descent against Spanish moralistic critics who disapproved of nudity in painting. See López Torrijos 231–242.

28. Menéndez y Pelayo noted its epic structure long ago. He praised Lope for trans-

porting "épicamente" to the stage "la primitiva unidad orgánica del mito" (qtd in Vega Carpio, *Perseo* 18).

29. Lisardo is a somewhat awkward suitor, however. On learning from Apolo that only gold can penetrate the tower in which Acrisius has locked Danae, Lisardo shoots an arrow into her prison with a note asking her whether he should give the gold to her or use it to bribe her guards.

30. See vv. 671–781, 973–974; McGaha, Introduction 5–7.

31. Its importance is ironic on two counts. In *El peregrino en su patria* (427–429), Lope scorns the introduction of fabulous elements in poetry and specifically names the use of winged horses, saying: "Pues a ninguno parezca nuestro Peregrino fabuloso, pues en esta pintura no ay cauallo con alas, chimera de Bellerophonte, dragones de Medea, mançanas de oro, ni palacios encantados"; furthermore, he condemns reliance on scenic effect.

32. This and the preceding three verses allude to the double Bourbon-Hapsburg engagement.

33. He poses a comic counterfoil to Perseo's spectacular aerial appearance on Pegaso when he says from below and on foot that he is also on horseback and on his way to liberate Andrómeda, but with a disadvantage in his steed: "Pero vengo por el suelo; / que de comer zanahorias / está pesado de cuerpo" (2810–2812).

34. Although these figures ultimately descend from chivalric material, I suspect also a link with Campeggi's *Andromeda*, in which Envy and Jealousy arise from the underworld at Nereus's bidding to incite Phineus to revenge against Perseus.

35. "Ya . . . estamos de partida para Ventosilla. El miercoles se hará en aquel jardín, si quiere el agua, la comedia destos caballeros del Duque. . . . Muy metidos andamos en haçer dragones y serpientes para este teatro; . . . No sé cómo ha de salir, que ha entrado el agua y en este tiempo no cessa fácilmente, y en jardín no es a propósito" (La Barrera 145).

36. See Allen 37–40, 69.

37. In the "Prólogo dialoguístico" to the *Parte XVI* of his *Comedias*, the very volume in which the *Perseo* was published, Lope has the theatre itself complain that "Yo he llegado a gran desdicha, y presumo que tiene origen de una de tres causas: o por no haber buenos representantes, o por ser malos los poetas, o por falta de entendimiento de los oyentes; pues los autores se valen de las máquinas; los poetas de los carpinteros, y los oyentes de los ojos." Lope's Teatro then asks the figure Poeta: "¿Tenéis algunas comedias nuevas?" to which the poet answers, "Después que se usan las apariencias, que se llaman tramoyas, no me atrevo a publicarlas" (qtd in Amadei Pulice 12–13).

38. McGaha believes that both the dazzling display of literary virtuosity and the use of allegory in this play were designed to demonstrate Lope's qualifications for the office of court chronicler. The didactic element, says McGaha, was Lope's attempt to prove his moral seriousness despite his scandalous life (Vega Carpio, *Perseo* 29).

39. He was demonstrably less successful in serving his own interests, for when the post of court chronicler next became available in 1620, it did not go to Lope.

40. Delmas believes that a considerable number of versions of the story were probably available to Corneille in the large library Mazarin had collected (Corneille lxii–lxiii).

41. Significantly, in defending his mixture of lyric strophes with the proselike Alexandrine line, Corneille cited the example of Spanish drama (Corneille 154).

42. Delmas also finds echoes, in both the structure and verse of his play, of the creations of Pio di Savoia and of Boissin de Gallardon, *La délivrance d'Andromède et les malheurs de Phinée, La Perséenne,* published in *Tragédies et Histoires saintes* (Lyon, 1618).

43. The description appears in a special issue of the *Gazette de France,* 18 February 1650, included in the Delmas edition, pp. 156–169.

44. The addition was perhaps inspired by Ferrari's less well integrated use of Venus, who appears from the sea and tells Astrea that she will intercede on Andromeda's behalf with Neptune while Astrea goes to speak to Jupiter. Venus was also associated with the Perseus-Andromeda story in a series of frescoes in the palace of the Marqués de Santa Cruz in Viso, which may indicate a considerable circulation of the idea. See López Torrijos 237.

45. Color was an important element in the overall effect, as Corneille's description of the last set demonstrates, emphasizing the brilliant light reflected from the gleaming bronze surfaces of the temple.

46. More than purely aesthetic concerns may have motivated Corneille's declaration, however, during the years of the Fronde. Opposition to Mazarin included opposition to Italian opera productions he promoted at court. Those who considered the prime minister a "meddling Italian" charged that he used these and other spectacles to divert and control the young king; on musical grounds, French listeners objected that the text was obscured by musical decoration in the Italian mode (Isherwood 119–126). "When the Fronde commenced in June 1648, there was a veritable castrato hunt in the streets of Paris: Torelli was incarcerated; Rossi and Melani fled the country. Introduced for political reasons, Italian opera fell for political reasons" (Isherwood 125).

47. For an interesting analysis of the role of this technique in the representation of reality in the Golden Age, see Pring-Mill.

48. Rupp points out the same contrast between Jonson's prose explanations of his masques and Calderón's deliberate omission of marginal glosses to his autos, because, as he says in his preface, "para el docto no hacen falta y para el no docto hicieran sobra" (Calderón, *Autos* 42). Says Rupp: "Jonson would exchange his audience for a public of learned readers; Calderón asks that his readers transform themselves into spectators" (21–22).

49. Baccio had studied with Giulio Parigi, taught perspective drawing in Florence, and constructed fortifications for the Medici at Livorno and other Tuscan sites. Massar has found in Florentine collections drawings of a costume design and of two great birds that are probably Baccio contributions to Florentine theatrical productions (365–367).

50. The existence of a number of low-quality paintings of the Perseus theme shows that the story achieved considerable popularity at a relatively popular level, which López Torrijos attributes to the influence of the theatre (241–242).

51. Ms Typ 258. Published editions of the play, which probably derive from shortened productions in the public theatres or a simplified repeat court production, omit the preface, the final spectacular temple scene, and other significant passages. John Varey and Jack Sage are preparing a critical edition based on the Harvard manuscript, and Alicia Pulice will publish a facsimile edition. Varey describes these drawings and the political implications of court plays in " 'Andromeda y Perseo', Comedia y Loa de Calderón."

52. In a letter of 8 April 1653, the year of this play, Felipe wrote to Sor Luisa, who had been a lady-in-waiting to the former Queen Isabel and governess of María Teresa before

taking the veil in 1648: "De gran aflicción me sacó Su Divina Merced dando salud a la reina, porque os aseguro que llegó a estar de mucho peligro y con gran cantidad de viruelas. Hartas muchas le han quedado, y creo que no se librará de algunas señales, pero vuelvo a repetir aquí lo que dije delante de la Rubia [María Teresa] . . . que como yo la viese buena no se me daría nada que quedase con más costurones que Mortara." In a letter of 3 June he repeats his joke about the smallpox scars and mentions a play, which may well have been *Andrómeda y Perseo*: "Muy buena a sido la comedia, y vuestro amigo Juan Rana [the famous gracioso Cosme Pérez, now retired from the public theaters but still performing at royal request] a cumplido famosamente con sus obligaciones; bien creo que si le hubiérades visto, se atreviera la risa a inquietar la función. La gente moza se ha entretenido harto, y, a Dios gracias, estamos todos buenos, y yo, tan bien hallado con mi compañerita, que vuelvo a ratificarme en el chiste de los costurones" (Pérez Villanueva 197, 200).

53. "La Poesía trayá vn libro dorado en que escribía. Y la Pintura, vna lámina; en que al parecer pintaua" (f. 5).

54. Poetry speaks of her numbers because according to Pythagorean tradition, the rhythmic order of poetic meter imitates the mathematical perfection of the movement of the heavenly spheres and, together with the connections made through metaphor and the well-wrought design of the poem, helps to raise the soul to contemplation of cosmic harmony.

55. In fact, a quartet: since "stage machinery" could in no way be worked into the decorum of such a scheme, it had to offer its services as an appropriately silent but powerful ally.

56. I thank Louise Stein for calling my attention to this connection. She discusses Rospigliossi's role in introducing Italian opera in Spain in "La plática" 32–33.

57. Folio 4v of the manuscript reproduced in facsimile in Brown, vol. 8.

58. The use of a prologue for such purposes is of course not unique to Rospigliosi and Calderón. As Hanning points out (2–4), in Renaissance dramatic literature the prologue frequently served to express the author's views on the art of drama as well as to set the mood, introduce the plot, gain audience sympathy, and praise patrons, and the author frequently used comments on local circumstances both to win sympathy and provide a transiton from the real to the fictional world. Another prologue similar to those of Rospigliosi and Calderón also opened a 1652 opera in Naples, *Veremonda L'Amazzone d'Aragona* (by Luigi Zorzisto, music by Francesco Cavalli, stage machinery and dance by Giovanni Battista Balbi) with a dispute between poetry, music, and architecture. "The victor is Archittetura, pregnant with the changes of scene, the machines and the dances which would be seen in the opera" (Bianconi and Walker, "Febiarmonici" 8–9). The opera was performed as part of the festivities to celebrate the retaking of Barcelona from the Catalan rebels in October 1652, and Bianconi and Walker ("Febiarmonici" 7, 23–30) point out that it was intended to impress a restless Neapolitan populace with a visible display of Spanish power.

59. The loa also reinforces dramatically a philosophical reading of the play as a reassuring vision of the integration of the microcosm that is man in the harmoniously ordered macrocosm of Pythagorean-Platonic tradition. For an elegant and convincing reading of the play as a Neoplatonic allegory of the defeat of discord and evil by reason and order, see Merrick.

60. "Algo se me oluidó al cuento / pues aun pega todavía."

61. As a bridge can be crossed in two directions, so this comic skeptic can lead the incredulous to connect through his humor with the fantastic world of the play and also serve as a distancing mechanism for the overly credulous.

62. For the significance of this passage in a political reading of the play, see Chapter 4.

63. See note 1.

64. The portrait now hangs in the Real Academia Española de la Lengua.

65. A noble man of arms, not a mere "letrado."

66. For another example of Calderón's use of Corneille and the history of the controversy over whether he knew French, see the Cruickshank introduction to *En la vida todo es verdad y todo mentira*, lxxvi–xcv.

67. For the thematic importance of this alteration to the story, see Chapter 4.

68. Calderón does disregard D'Aubignac's stipulation that sets be in place at the beginning of an action. The Spanish dramatist changes them freely within acts as the situation demands, but he (and/or the director of his play) does anticipate the potentially disruptive audience reaction of which the French critic speaks. When the maritime scene for Perseo's rescue of Andrómeda was revealed, complete with moving waves, fish, boats, and the rocky coastline, the audience burst into applause, and as the description reports, the company waited until the applause had passed before the musicians led Andrómeda on stage in mourning attire (f.87v–88).

69. The description of this appearance demonstrates an awareness of the problem of human scale in perspective scenery. They appeared, it says, "en el primer claro de los dos vastidores, (desde cuya mayor altura, aun no hauía empeçado a declinar la línea de la perspectiua;)" (f.36v).

70. The fear amidst the audience was not groundless, for actors sometimes were hurt from falling off the tramoyas, and at least one was killed. See Shergold 314, n.1. Actors were sometimes paid the seventeenth-century equivalent of a stuntman's fee for going up on the machines.

71. See Stein's discussion of this first example of recitative in Spain: "Music" 229–236.

72. My summary is drawn from her dissertation, "Music" 229–245, which will be published shortly in revised form.

73. Varey, "Scenes" 57. Varey discusses the varied psychological and philosophical implications of the staging of this and other cave and grotto scenes in "Cavemen in Calderón." Here it places Perseo in a shadowy world of nonbeing and at the same time represents the beginning of a process of education.

74. "En el primer termino de su habitación se vio Danae, biçarramente compuesta de galas cortesanas, sentada en el estrado; y con ella algunas damas, meninas, y dueñas: vnas con labores, y otras con instrumentos, en la forma que dirá la siguiente estampa" (f.41).

75. Stein, "Music" 240–241. Calderón uses the same song in *La desdicha de la voz*. A somewhat different setting attributed to Juan Blas had earlier appeared in the Cancionero de Sablonara, and it was included in the many printings of the Segura *Primavera* collection between 1629 and 1659 (Stein, "Plática" 43–47, which includes samples of the settings by Blas and the composer of *Fortunas*).

76. This popular demand performs the same function as did the winds in Corneille, freeing Cefeo from the cruelty of sacrificing his daughter. Calderón has in fact arranged the story in such a way that no negative king figure appears on stage. Acrisio is only

mentioned; Politides is Perseo's champion, not his would-be assassin; and the shadowy Cefeo plays only a passive, lamenting role.

77. Because Lully's *Persée* (1682) comes much later and his work cannot have served as a model for Calderón, I have not included it in my survey, although he clearly accomplished an artistically effective synthesis in his *tragédie lyrique*.

CHAPTER THREE. POWER AT PLAY

1. The descriptive text of *Andrómeda y Perseo* repeatedly underlines the importance of this operation, calling attention to the accompanying drawings of the stage sets to help the reader visualize the scene and lamenting that the sketches cannot supply the "soul" of the machine effects, which is their movement, nor can the score transmit the effect of the voices that performed it (f.73). This emphasis inclines me to think that the description may have been written by Calderón himself.

2. What we would today call the Spanish Empire was called by contemporaries the monarquía. See Brown and Elliott 9. For a good summary of that sense of decline, see Elliott, "Self-Perception."

3. Brown and Elliott (18) desribe the Articles as "a strange medley . . . ranging from the prohibition on the import of foreign manufactures to the closing of brothels."

4. "War, while making long-delayed reforms indispensable, created conditions which made their fulfillment impossible" (Elliott, "The Spanish Peninsula" 460).

5. As such, he provided a striking contrast to Louis XIII and his disordered household. "Thwarted in his desire to make Louis XIII the focal point of a splendid and cultivated court, Richelieu created his own court at the Palais Cardinal. By contrast, Olivares, living an austere personal life, devoted his great gifts for stage-management to projecting the image of his monarch as the epitome of royal patronage and splendor, the *rey planeta*, Europe's first Sun King." Elliott, *Richelieu and Olivares* 47–48.

6. For a description of the rather haphazard progress of its design and construction, see Brown and Elliott, chaps. 3 and 4.

7. Although contemporary testimony is contradictory, opening night was apparently postponed and took place somewhere between 25 June and 4 July, and a second series of performances was given between 29 July and 3 August. No plays were performed in the two public theatres between 25 June and 3 August because the theatre companies (one that of Roque de Figueroa) were occupied with rehearsals and performances of *El mayor encanto, amor*. See Shergold, "First Performance." Based on a letter from Bernardo Monanni, the secretary of the embassy of the grand duke of Tuscany (ASF Mediceo, filza 4960), Brown and Elliott (276 n.20) date the first performance on 29 July.

8. Entry for 24 April 1658. See also entries for 28 February and 7 and 21 March 1657.

9. To condemn "murmuración" was a standard topic, as we see in the Cervantine *novela ejemplar* "El coloquio de los perros," but Saavedra explains its corrective value in Empresa 14: "Lo que no alcanza a contener o reformar la ley, se alcanza con el temor de la murmuración, la cual es acicate de virtud y rienda que la obliga a no torcer del camino justo. . . . No tiene el vicio mayor enemigo que la censura. . . . Y así, aunque la murmuración es en sí mala, es buena para la república, porque no hay otra fuerza mayor sobre el magistrado o sobre el príncipe. ¿Qué no acometiera el poder, si no tuviera delante a la murmuración? . . . La murmuración es argumento de la libertad de la república, porque

en la tiranizada no se permite. Feliz aquélla donde se puede sentir lo que se quiere y decir lo que se siente. Injusta pretensión fuera del que manda querer con candados los labios de los súbditos, y que no se quejen y murmuren debajo del yugo de la servidumbre. . . . Ni es posible poder reprimir la licencia y libertad del pueblo. Viven engañados los príncipes que piensan extinguir con la potencia presente la memoria futura, o que su grandeza se extiende a poder dorar las acciones malas. . . ." (177–179). Interestingly, he says that in ancient republics, satirical pieces in the theatre served the same function (183).

10. This condemnation of flattery was a standard topic in all treatises on the education of the prince and related studies. Mariana dedicates an entire chapter (bk. 2, chap. 11) to the topic.

11. That Júpiter is his father is of course a pleasant rather than unpleasant truth for Perseo but one that risks bringing Juno's wrath down on him if Perseo or anyone else declares it openly. Calderón put on stage the problem of how to speak unpleasant truths to the powerful from the beginning of his career, in *Amor, honor y poder,* a comedia performed in the palace in June 1623 for the king and perhaps also for Charles, Prince of Wales, who was then in Madrid negotiating his possible marriage to the Spanish infanta. Enrico, a young nobleman whose sister Estela's honor is threatened by the king's passion for her, kneels before the king, who is hiding in the garden after attempting to seduce Estela. Pretending to believe that he is before a very realistic statue of the king, Enrico reminds the monarch that he is bound by law and by his obligation to the community that defends his realm:

> Este es del Rey tan natural retrato,
> que siempre que su imagen considero,
> llego a verle quitándome el sombrero,
> con la rodilla en tierra: [así le acato].
> Y si el rey me ofendiera
> de suerte que en la honra me tocara,
> viniera a este retrato y me quejara,
> y entonces le dijera
> que tan cristianos reyes
> no han de romper el límite a las leyes;
> que miráse que tiene sus Estados
> quizá por mis mayores conservados,
> con su sangre adquiridos,
> tan bien ganados como defendidos (79).

The ruse does not work; the king jails Enrico, and only his sister's bravery saves him from death. As De Armas (*Astrea* 65–66) points out, this play could well be read as a critique of the willful and lustful nature of the young Felipe IV.

12. One notable exception is *The Triumph of Peace,* written by James Shirley in consultation with the barristers of the Inns of Court and staged by Inigo Jones, which upheld the power of law against Charles's assertion of a conception of divine right that made his will law. Charles was pleased by the splendor and adulation of the masque and overlooked the political point it sought to make. See Orgel, *Illusion* 78–83. Gentle criticism of monarchical policies seems also to have been tolerated in court entertainments of the Hapsburg court in Vienna during the reign of Leopold I. The Venetian ambassador to Vienna

reported that court audiences at operatic performances there took as much pleasure in satirical allusions to personalities at court as in the music (Bianconi and Walker 261–262). One opera libretto went so far as to chide Leopold, portrayed as Alexander the Great, for excessive leniency in curbing vices harmful to the community (Dietrich 205).

13. Andrés Sánchez de Espejo, "Relación aiustada en lo possible, a la verdad, y repartida en dos discursos. El primero, de la entrada en estos Reynos de Madama María de Borbón, Princesa de Cariñan. El segundo, de las fiestas, que se celebraron en el Real Palacio del Buen Retiro, a la elección del Rey de Romanos" (Madrid, 1637, f.9v–10r; cited in Varey, "L'Auditoire" 80).

14. The undated drawing is in AP Legajo 667, with documents from the end of the seventeenth and the first decade of the eighteenth century.

15. A document sent to the marqués de Santa Cruz on 4 December 1633 stipulated that the entry to an entertainment in the plaza of the Buen Retiro should be as follows: "El Cauallero mayor de la Reyna a de entrar por la escalera del patio de los oficios que sale a la saleta de mi quarto y lo mismo sus mayordomos y primer caualleriço y sus mugeres por la escalera de la leonina puerta del prado y los caualleriços de la Reyna por la escalera de madera que sube del patio de los oficios a la galería de Madrid y sus mugeres por la escalera principal de los conssejos que mira a Madrid y el contralor grefier y despenssero mayor y thessorero tanbién an de entrar por la otra escalera de madera que sube del patio de los oficios a la galería de Madrid y sus mugeres destos oficiales por la portería de las damas como se os auissó particularmente por la primera relación que os envié con orden mía y de todas auéis de enbiar relación al Alcayde de en la forma que tenéis entendido y el os auissará de quien ubiere de cuidar de la comodidad de estas perssonas." AP Caja 11.744, Expte. 11.

16. In a Biblioteca Nacional manuscript that has been published by D. Casiano Pellicer, *Tratado histórico sobre el origen y progresos de la comedia y del histrionismo en España* (Madrid, 1804), Part 2, 146–166; also included as a preliminary to the Hartzenbusch BAE edition, vol. 7, 587–590. After the event, someone added a title in the preterit: "Fiesta que se representó en el estanque grande del Retiro, invención de Cosme Lotti, a petición de la Excelentísima Señora condesa de Olivares, Duquesa de San Lucar La Mayor, la noche de San Juan." The text, however, is in the future tense and is clearly a proposal, not a description of an accomplished fact.

17. The memorandum specifies: "Formaráse en medio del estanque una isla fija, levantada de la superficie del agua siete pies. . . ." This is confirmed by a Jesuit newsletter of 31 July, which reports: "Hicieron en medio del estanque un tablado grande, y en él un bosque muy espeso con grandes montañas y árboles, fuentes, volcanes de fuego" (qtd in Shergold, "First Performance" 25).

18. It is also possible that the loa was presented quite differently because the final effect in Calderón's text is the arrival of Galatea in a chariot pulled by two large dolphins. Either he moved the effect to the end for a spectacular conclusion or used the same idea twice.

19. This and other significant details of his Circe story Calderón probably drew from Tasso's tale of Aminta and Rinaldo. See *Gerusalem liberata,* Cantos 15 and 16.

20. Lotti's plot summary had included a good deal of burlesque humor, mostly centering around men turned into pigs; Calderón's is considerably more subtle and better incorporated into the plot line, and some of it is extremely telling in the political reading.

21. For an excellent comparison of the two works, see LeVan.

22. Susana Hernández-Araico found similar data and came to much the same conclusion as De Armas; she has not yet published her findings.

23. Calderón had explicity linked the Retiro gardens and palace to a very different dramatic world the previous year in his auto *El nuevo palacio del Retiro*. See my article "Bodies of Power." His public was therefore prepared for political allegories centered on the new palace.

24. It was axiomatic in treatises such as those of Mariana, Quevedo, and Solorzano that the king's physical presence before his troops was their greatest incentive to heroic action. See Mariana 295; Quevedo 2:ch. 23; and Solorzano, Emblem 92.

25. Although Lotti has Júpiter send the moly by Mercury, as the myth was usually told, Calderón changed the donor to Juno and the messenger to Iris. The choice of Juno is consistent with her support of the Greeks in the *Aeneid*; it could also be argued that by this change, Calderón provided a supportive mythic figure for Queen Isabel, who, like Juno, had ample reason for jealousy over her husband's escapades. At the end of the play, as Ulises flees Circe's realm, he begs Juno's forgiveness:

> Hermosa Juno, no culpes
> El mayor encanto, amor,
> Pues, aunque tus flores tuve
> Pude vencer mil encantos,
> Y aqueste solo no pude (409).

26. Citing Gregorio Marañon, *El Conde-Duque de Olivares*, 5th ed. (Madrid: Espasa-Calpe, 1965), 196.

27. Brown and Elliott make the mistake of equating Lotti's memorandum with a description of the actual performance. The auto sacramental *El nuevo palacio del Retiro* depicted the Buen Retiro in the favorable light Olivares preferred, but the court play did not.

28. Brown and Elliott (62) also suggest that the vast expansion of the Buen Retiro might have been motivated in part by a desire to outbuild the Lermas, who had a large estate right across the street.

29. It is possible, however, that this term originated not with Calderón but with his friend and editor Vera Tassis. The three earliest editions, published during Calderón's lifetime but from imperfect texts with little or no editorial intervention on his part, give the line as "pues lo monado basta," which is one syllable short. One of these editions, designated "Q" by Cruickshank (4–6, 21), was missing part of the first scene, an encounter by Ulises and his men with Lísidas and Flérida, converted to speaking trees by Circe. Since that passage is also missing in the Vera Tassis edition, from which all modern editions descend, he presumably based his edition on the Q text. The same line in the Vera Tassis edition reads, "pues ya lo enmonado basta"; Vera Tassis did in some instances have alternative manuscripts on which he based his corrections, but he also frequently "corrected" without such authority. On average, when compared to other witnesses not available to Vera Tassis, slightly less than 50 percent of his corrections prove to be accurate, and the rest arbitrary (see Hesse 50; Greer 191). The verbal play "enmonado-enamorado" may, then, (1) have originated with Calderón, been garbled by a printer and restored by Vera Tassis, either on the basis of another manuscript or on his own consider-

able familiarity with the author's style or (2) have been an "improvement" invented by Vera Tassis, suggested by the clear Ulises–Clarín parallel that Calderón had drawn.

30. This was a recondite solution, which Calderón explained at considerable length in the text. Galatea is Ulises' champion because he took revenge against Polifemo for his murder of her "husband," Acis. At least some members of the audience did not follow the explanation, for a Jesuit newsletter said that it was Circe who arrived in the chariot: "luego vino en carro triunfal Circe por el agua, tirado de dos delfines, a deshacer los encantos, cosa de peregrina invención" (qtd in Shergold, "First Performance" 25). This was both a logical and physical impossibility since she was already on the scene.

31. "Rematóse la fiesta con danzas en tierra y en el agua; la riqueza de los vestidos fué increíble, y la variedad de las cosas prodigiosa; duró seis horas, y se acabó a la una de la noche. La costa se deja al juicio, que por ser bueno el del piadoso lector, verá cuánta puede ser" (Jesuit newsletter, qtd in Shergold, "First Performance" 25).

32. McGowan points out the irony of the fact that "Henri III's reputation for justice and virtue, and his control over political events, were never more precarious than at the precise times when artists exerted themselves to present a picture of the king's merits and omnipotence" (Beaujoyeulx 36).

33. Furthermore, as we shall see in Chapter 5, in the discussion of what I have tagged the "particular text," the palatability for the royal spectator of the political text in this and other Calderonian court spectacles was increased by the fact that it was not the only available coherent interpretation. Spectators could also read this play as the Ulysses–Circe story has more traditionally been interpreted, a "quest romance" (Fischer 111) or the journey of life, "the human conflict between duty and passion, between reason and lust" (Sloman 129–130). Calderón did not preach to the king bluntly, like Padre Bautista, but with discretion, enmeshing the political text within a more "universal" way of appropriating the text and applying its message.

Chapter Four. The Problem of Don Juan José

1. At least seven or eight of his illegitimate children survived him at his death, although Davies (85) says that some authors put the number as high as thirty, while only three of his thirteen legitimate children were alive in 1665: María Teresa, married to Louis XIV; Margarita María, who would marry Leopold I of Austria; and Carlos II.

2. See a facsimile of the baptismal certificate in Maura, Corte 1:169.

3. The two plays, El hijo del Aguila and El águila del agua y batalla naval de Lepanto, were written by Luis Vélez de Guevara. The second was licensed for performance on 29 July 1642; since it is a second part of El hijo del Aguila, the first part was presumably written shortly before that date.

4. For readings of the play that focus on its enduring truth to human nature, see Merrick's intelligent exposition of Perseo as the triumph of love and order, and Hivnor's conception of the play as a universal "romance quest theme" centered on "the ritual of initiation and self definition" (246).

5. Or Tavara, or Tabara as she is listed in the cast list of Villamediana's Gloria de Niquea.

6. See Rosales; Gómez de Liaño and Infantes.

7. Bances did not always follow his own rules of discretion; Wilson and Moir suggest that the audaciousness of *La piedra filosofal* led to Bances Candamo's retirement from his court post and return to the provinces in 1693 (142).

8. In the ceremonious Hapsburg court questions of precedence and forms of address were considered of utmost importance. On recognizing Don Juan José as his son, Felipe IV issued a lengthy royal cédula, specifying in great detail forms of address and precedence. A particularly sensitive matter was whether, in what form, and at what point the parties involved should remove and replace their hats, since the highest level of nobility was signaled by the right to remain "covered" in the presence of royalty. To the grandes (highest nobility), the archbishop of Toledo and most important ambassadors, for example, he was to remove his hat and bring it down to his waist. In receiving lesser titled figures, first sons of grandes, bishops, viceroys, etc., "se apartaría dos pasos de la mesa donde hubiera dejado su sombrero, para que, mandándoles cubrir y no haciéndolo él, como le haría á presencia de Grandes y asimilados, tampoco ellos se cubrieran." Felipe specified in the same cédula that Prince Baltasar Carlos and Princess María Teresa should call him "mi hermano" and Queen Isabel should address him as "mi hijo"; Isabel acceded, at least to the extent of allowing envelopes to him to be so addressed, but Mariana later refused to accord him this title. (Maura, *Corte* 1:173–175, 178).

9. Qtd in Maura, *Corte* 1:190. See also Barrionuevo 2:283–291, from whom Maura draws most of his material.

10. Nearly every galán enamored of a lady of higher status compares himself in some way to Faetón. For a survey of poetic treatments, see Gallego Morell. Covarrubias seconds Pérez de Moya's interpretation in his *Tesoro de la lengua castellana o española* of 1611.

11. A "mal fin" was very nearly the fate of the entire 1662 premiere of *El hijo del sol, Faetón,* as the rivalry between Faetón and Epafo found its real-life parallel and nearly brought the production to an end in real flames. On the morning of 14 February, the day the play was to be produced, a workman found what appeared to be a trail of dust on stage; the "dust" proved to be gunpowder, three packets of which had been hidden in the scenery, along with a fuse that had failed to ignite. Investigators found that the gunpowder had been planted by a slave of the marquis of Heliche, former governor of the Buen Retiro, who had been replaced by the duke of Medina de las Torres in December and did not want the duke to get credit for his work on the production. Before his own arrest, the marquis tried to bribe the governor of the prison in which his slave was being held to poison him or fake a suicide by hanging, so that the slave could not reveal the truth under torture. Heliche also made two attempts to escape from prison; on the second, he got out dressed as a woman but was discovered when the unusual haste of some workers loading a box on board ship made the dock police suspicious and they opened the box to find the marquis in it (Shergold, *History* 325–326).

12. The date of both plays is often given as 1661. However, we know from evidence presented at the trial of the Marquis that *Faetón* was performed in 1662. We have no such documents attesting to the date of *Apolo y Climene,* but since the play ends with a reference to a forthcoming second part that will tell the story of Faetón, the usual assumption is that both plays were written for performance during Carnival of 1662. For the alternative of Hernández-Araico, see p. 117.

13. Paris says that this name was Calderón's invention, but it appears in the historical explanation Pérez de Moya gives of the myth: "Phaeton fue vn verdadero hombre, y

aunque no fue hijo del planeta Sol, fue hijo de vn poderoso Rey de los Argiuos llamado Merope, o Apis, que fue habido por Dios, por la fama de sus hazañas, y llamaronle Sol, o Phebo. Este Merope enamorose de Climene hija de Oceano, en quien vuo vn hijo llamado Astarcho, o Eridano, que despues se nombro Phaeton" (f.85). The older Erídano is Climene's father in *Faetón* and therefore grandfather to Faetón and a priest of Diana.

14. Such human fieras are a standard feature in Calderonian drama. Their exclusion from society is either a result of a violent seduction or rape to which they have been subjected or to political intrigues from which they are being sheltered. They are thus victims of human passions for the flesh and for power, often difficult to separate. See Maurin for a discussion of related symbolism in *La vida es sueño*.

15. The blending of sacred and profane images was fairly common in religious paintings of the era, as still appears in the Monasterio de las Descalzas Reales in Madrid. This convent of Franciscanas Clarisas was the home of many daughters of royal blood, both legitimate and illegitimate. On the walls of the Salón de Reyes hangs a portrait of Don Juan José portrayed as San Hermenegildo. A painting attributed to Claudio Coello in the Casita de Sor Margarita depicts Santa Clara, the founder of the order, making her profession before San Francisco; she is portrayed with the features of the "second Sor Margarita de la Cruz," illegitimate daughter borne to Don Juan José by the daughter of the painter José Ribera. She entered the convent at six years of age, and there are two other portraits of her as a nun in the Salón de Reyes. The convent also contains a painting of a beautiful and richly dressed young woman combing her hair with one hand while the other holds what could be a white headdress; she is supposed to be Don Juan José's mother, "La Calderona," although no concrete proof of this attribution is available. The support of the royal family for this convent was literally painted on its walls; a fresco over the grand staircase depicts the spiritual "presence" of Felipe IV, Mariana, Margarita María, and Felipe Próspero, represented as if on a balcony overlooking the scene. When Don Juan José came to power, he donated the Capilla del Milagro to the convent, and repeated this depiction of his presence "al fresco," as if in a royal tribunal overlooking the chapel. He is accompanied in the fresco by another figure, who may be Carlos II (see Tormo Monzo and Ruíz Alcón).

16. Calderón often included self-conscious references to the theatrical setting in his mythological plays. Earlier in this play, Batillo explains the disappearance of Amaltea and Galatea by saying, "Que algún tramoyero dios / Se andaba haciendo apariencias" (187).

17. Were this Tirso de Molina, who wrote knowingly of the weaknesses of some hermits and nuns in plays such as *El condenado por desconfiado* and *La Santa Juana*, I could believe that this was an intentional irony; deliberate irony in relation to religious institutions seems less likely in Calderón, perhaps because of the weight of his "ideal biography" and the "author function" described by Foucault (see Chapter 1). He did treat religious topics humorously in burlesque pieces such as the *Mojiganga de las visiones de la muerte*.

18. "Nada habrá que tú me pidas / Que otorgarte no procure, / En desagravio del tiempo / Que hizo el temor que te oculte" (195).

19. Underlining the parallels between Don Juan José and Faetón in terms of illegitimate birth, sensitivity, pride, and ambition has perhaps distorted the picture of both the fictional character and his real-life referent. Don Juan José was, despite his faults, both an appealing and a generally popular figure, as we will see in Chapter 5. While Calderón shows the flaws in Faetón's character that will lead to his downfall, he makes clear the

psychological grounds for those failings and leads the reader to share in the young man's frustration over his position in an unjust world.

20. The birth of Felipe Próspero in 1657 did indeed bring joyous celebration in Spain, to which Calderón contributed the court play *El laurel de Apolo*; their reaction to the birth of Carlos was considerably more subdued because it followed by only a few days the death of Felipe Próspero and because the sickly Carlos seemed likely to follow Baltasar Carlos and Felipe Próspero to an early grave.

21. This loa is not printed with any standard edition of the play, but it does appear in Cotarelo y Mori, *Colección de Entremeses* 1:33 (BAE 17) and in another version edited from BN Ms. 16.539, in Neumeister, *Mythos* 315–331. All references herein refer to the Neumeister edition.

22. "Un sacro laurel, / rey del monte, cuya altiva / copa el sol ciñe de oro / . . . / de los embates de un cierzo, / sentía tocadas sus hojas" (321).

23. Due to Felipe's having been "metido en un hoyo hasta los pechos, esperando un lobo que no quiso ir a besarle la mano," aggravated by a difficult return trip in which his carriage was stuck for more than two hours (Maura, *Corte* 1:106).

24. Calderón offers this pleasure fairly frequently: for example, he cites the sunless days of December in the loa for *Fieras afemina Amor* and the winter cold in which Felipe Próspero was born in that for *El laurel de Apolo*.

25. In August 1661, the French ambassador to Madrid, who had been sounding out Spanish opinions on the subject, reported that Don Luis de Haro, Felipe's prime minister at the time, did not consider the renunciation valid; furthermore, Spain's failure to pay the dowry specified in the treaty gave the French a good pretext for declaring it void (Kamen, *Spain* 383–384).

26. For other instances of the equivocal use of "austro" to refer to the house of Austria, see Rosales 63, 68.

27. A satirical poem of the period poked fun at the situation:

> El Príncipe, al parecer,
> por lo endeble y patiblando,
> es hijo de contrabando,
> pues no se puede tener.
>   La Infanta no llega a ver
> a su recíproco amor;
> y aunque está el Emperador
> quejoso, y tieso que tieso;
> ¿Qué se le da al Rey de eso? (qtd in Maura, *Corte* 1:87 n. 1)

28. The themes of the loa are carried over into the play in suggestive ways. In the first scene, the chorus sings about a sublime laurel who functions as a sort of lighthouse, crowning with hope the pilot who sees him (176). In an insult-trading contest between Galatea, who favors Faetón, and Amaltea, who supports Epafo-Peleo primarily to spite Faetón, Galatea calls her a "Caduca deidad de flores, / sujeta a embates del cierzo" (183), reinforcing the link between Peleo and the frail new prince. And when Faetón questions why Amaltea has turned against him, Batillo says, "Será que como los pobres / todos son flores, sospecha / que le has de gastar las suyas" (187). This sibylline response seems to have no logical explanation within the strict confines of the plot and can perhaps best be

explained as a reference to the humble flowers described in the loa and their disenchant-ment with Don Juan José's losses in the Portuguese campaign.

29. The song also appears in other plays by Calderón and other poets. See Stein, "Music" 529; Wilson and Sage 124–125.

30. See Stein's discussion of the limited use of music in this play: "Music" 268–270.

31. One possible argument for a significant chronological separation of the plays might be that surviving documents for palace performances in the last quarter of the century indicate that each play was performed separately at least twice, including one gala performance apiece in the Coliseo. No surviving record indicates a performance of both in the same year. After their first performance, then, each play was seen as having a separate existence. But later Madrid audiences already knew both plays; we cannot pre-sume that Calderón or his patrons gave them a similar independence at first appearance.

32. Of course, history proved it extremely ironic, for Carlos II not only did not sire an Aquiles to defend Spain, but his incapacity to father any children brought the end of Hapsburg rule in Spain.

33. See Parker, "Metáfora" and "Father-Son Conflict."

34. "¿Quién pudo hacer resistencia / a dos tentaciones? una / (que es la que me hizo más fuerza) / chismar el secreto; y otra, / que a quien se le chisme sea / Céfiro, en quien la codicia / pactó con la conveniencia" (152).

35. Virtually all the critical arguments about Basilio's role and the fulfillment of prophecies that have been devoted to *La vida es sueño* are equally applicable to this play. His actions are not based on a proud overevaluation of his own reason, as in Basilio's case, but an equally damnable reliance on Fitón, who employs illegitimate "sciences" and represents himself as serving Admeto, Climene, and the state, while in fact he is interested only in demonstrating his own power. To my knowledge, no privado after Olivares was accused of such witchcraft, but virtually all were charged for a similarly self-serving duplicity.

36. Don Juan José's predilection for painting was well known, and he is traditionally considered to have painted *La Huida a Egipto* in the Capilla del Milagro, which he do-nated to the Descalzas Reales (Ruíz Alcón 66).

37. Margarita was of course too young to be married in fact, but she could be dis-patched to Vienna to continue her maturation there, a fairly common practice in the case of early royal marriages. Numerous councilors of the king were also encouraging him to give Don Juan an ecclesiastical habit, which he consistently refused. The primary reason given was that it was safer to have him on the council of state as a cleric than in command of military forces, the truth of which would later be proved.

CHAPTER FIVE. AN OPTIMISTIC ANSWER

1. For a related view of the social production of meaning, see Holquist. Arguing against the personalist view of meaning grounded in the unique individual and the de-constructionist negation of its possibility, Holquist postulates the generation of meaning in a dialogue between *parole* and *langue*, between the individual psyche and the system of culture in which it operates.

2. In his use of the term *subjunctivized*, Bruner draws on Wolfgang Iser's definition of the narrative speech act as one characterized by an indeterminacy which allows a spec-

trum of actualizations. It is "a text whose intention is to initiate and guide a search for meanings among a spectrum of possible meanings" (25).

3. Despite having started their investigations independently and from different perspectives, two other students of Calderón's court drama have come to related conclusions with regard to its polysemous nature. Stephen Rupp, in the dissertation cited above, focuses on the auto, which he compares with the Jonsonian masque, and makes the important connection with the tradition of fourfold exegesis. Dipuccio takes the interpretive clue from Barthes' observation that " 'one can conceive of very ancient myths, but there are no eternal ones; for it is human history which converts reality into speech, and it alone rules the life and death of mythical language. . . . Mythical speech is made of a material for communication . . .' " (Barthes, *Mythologies* 10). Focusing on the communicative process in the mythological comedias, says Dipuccio, "releases these plays from the boxes with which critics previously confined these works. Categorizing these works as spectacular extravaganzas and/or religious allegories becomes ludicrous. . . . The totality of the dramas does not fit neatly into either category, nor any other classification. On the contrary, the communicative patterns in these plays prove the impossibility of discovering the 'core' and 'truth' defined by the ancient and modern mythographers. Any point chosen as the core, whether it is the title, a prophecy, a central theme, or a character's psychological development, is elusive and defies insistent categorization. Instead, it unfolds multiple interpretations. This expansion underscores the openness of myth, which demands constant reinterpretation, reworking and redefinition" (24–25).

4. In the loa to the auto *El laberinto del mundo*, Calderón has Faith herself pronounce this defense of the use of pagan myth:

> . . . Entre los Gentiles
> asienta, que convirtieron
> en fábulas las Verdades;
> porque como ellos tuvieron
> sólo lejanas noticias
> de la Luz del Evangelio,
> viciaron sin ella nuestra
> Escritura, atribuyendo
> a falsos dioses sus raras
> maravillas, y queriendo
> que el Pueblo sepa, que no
> hay fábula sin misterio,
> si alegórica a la Luz
> desto se mira, un ingenio,
> bien que humilde, ha pretendido
> dar esta noticia al Pueblo (1558).

5. For a survey of the history of the Prometheus myth and Calderón's sources, see the introduction of my edition of the play, pp. 105–132. While he could have read Aeschylus's drama in the 1655 Latin translation, the Greek tragedian's works were not influential in Spain until the romantic era, and the fundamentally different plot structure argues against his direct knowledge of that work. He did, however, draw Minerba's defense of Prometeo from Lucian's parodic version of the myth.

6. For a history of the Prometheus story throughout Europe, see Trousson.

7. For further details of this tradition, see Panofsky 24, 156–160, and my introduction, 125–126.

8. Although we cannot be sure of the exact date of the first performance of *La estatua de Prometeo*, the most probable one is December 1670. It could not be earlier than 1669, for the theatres were closed after Felipe IV's death in 1665, and court performances were not resumed until 1669. Nor could it be later than 1674 because the play was presented on a reduced scale in August 1675, which would not have occured unless it had already had a gala opening. The 1671 performance for the Queen Mother's birthday was Calderón's *Fieras afemina Amor*, that for 1672 was *Los celos hacen estrellas* of Juan Vélez de Guevara, and for 1673, *Los juegos bacanales* of Agustín Salazar y Torres. Possible dates for the first performance of *La estatua de Prometeo*, then, are 1669, 1670, and 1674. For further informaton, see Varey and Shergold's introduction to their edition of Vélez de Guevara's *Celos*, xlv–liv; my introduction to the *Prometeo*, 93–94; emendations regarding the date of *Fieras afemina Amor* given in Chapter 6.

9. See Varey and Shergold introduction to *Celos*, cv–cviii.

10. For further details, see my edition, 94–95, 127–128. There is a copy of the libretto in Vienna in the Oesterreichische Nationalbibliothek as well as a manuscript (M 148/82) containing the music for the first two acts.

11. We have established by verse structure and marginal notations on a manuscript version that the surviving text of the play has been cut by at least one quarter and perhaps as much as a third, and therefore presents the reader with a text that is more condensed, and probably more difficult, than Calderón's full original (208–216).

12. Most readers also draw on their own conception of the seventeenth century, which in turn reflects a conjunction between the written and plastic testimony of a prior age and the shaping force of the reader's cultural milieu.

13. In his "Five Questions Concerning the Mind," in Cassirer 207–208.

14. In Calderón, *Entremeses* 371–384.

15. Prometeo and Epimeteo are not titans but men—"dos nobles caudillos del pueblo"—in Calderón's presentation.

16. Palas, the envious opponent of reason, is a partial exception to this rule. Epimeteo suggests that a goddess who is envious might be ignorant too (II, 133–135), and Palas does later display at least a partial ignorance of Epimeteo's true motives (II, 539–42).

17. The inclusion of the Chaldeans is one of the details Calderón drew from Pérez de Moya. They were considered the first "modern" astronomers in the sense of being the first who observed the heavens for the purpose of learning rather than as astrologers, to make predictions (Ley 8–9).

18. Cipriano, in *El mágico prodigioso*, broaches the same problem in a different framework as he reasons toward a concept of the existence of a single supreme God. The ultimate question of cause and effect for Christian theology is that of the cause of evil; if God is First Cause, and God is wholly good, then why and how does evil exist in the world he created? Prometeo does not pose the question in these terms, but it is implicit in the search for the origin of dualism, considered a defect in comparison with the philosophical perfection of unity, and is explicitly suggested in the refrain "¡Ai de quien el bien que hiço / en mal combertido vio!" (III, 1013–14, 1099–1104).

19. In Ficino's cosmology, this astrological influence on character takes place as the nascent pure soul descends from God to its earthly body, taking on a "veil" of corporeality as it passes through the heavens; the original seven gifts from God are differently

reinforced according to the particular astrological conjunction that prevails when the soul makes its descent (Couliano 42–43).

20. In this element, Calderón follows in the line of Plato (*Protagoras* 131), who used the Prometheus myth to explain how human beings came to live in a political society, and Boccaccio (bk. 4, chap. 44, 268–269), who concludes that humanity is a double creation, shaped by God as a natural being but then debased by original sin until Prometheus intervened to give humanity its second, social, or civilized being.

21. Ficino describes a similar process of purification for the soul that seeks to ascend toward higher degress of truth and ultimately the vision of God. See, for example, his *Platonic Theology*, Book 9, Chapters 2 and 3.

22. See also Curtius, "Calderón und die Malerei" and "Calderón's Theory of Art."

23. The political utility of religion was generally recognized in the seventeenth century, which saw it as the first foundation of community. See Maravall, *Teoría del estado* 105–106 and Saavedra Fajardo, Emblem 24.

24. In *Las visiones de la muerte*, Calderón pokes fun at lying as an innate frailty of the human body. Cuerpo and the Carretero trade insults:

CARRETERO: Mientes como cuerpo humano.
CUERPO: Tú como humano pellejo. (382)

25. Calderón parodies the idea of the soul's ascent toward heaven in *Las visiones de la muerte*. It is not the liquor of knowledge that transports Alma but that of the grape: Caminante comments as he watches Alma consume the contents of his wineskin, "bota": "Como el alma es tan devota, / se eleva mirando al Cielo" (381).

26. Nor was such a figure present in the accounts available to Calderón. Aeschylus's drama was not commonly known, and the rebellious aspect of the myth was not emphasized again (except by Giordano Bruno) before Shelley and Goethe. The absence of defiance in Calderón's Prometeo therefore should not be attributed to some inherent conservatism on Calderón's part that caused him to soften the story as he knew it, to downplay rebellion against the established order. He took the incoherent, contradictory, and generally medieval account as he found it in the mythographers of his time and made of it a drama of the human dilemma unequalled in its profundity since the days of Aeschylus.

27. In the *auto El lirio y la azucena*, it is Discordia instead who summons her cohort Guerra:

Tú, cuya furia al mundo introducida,
en civil y campal vio dividida,
no sólo entre el vasallo y enemigo
cualquier mortal; pero entre sí y consigo,
según de Job se indicia,
pues el hombre doméstica milicia
se llama, siendo en su confuso abismo
(dentro de sí) batalla de sí mismo;
oye mi voz. (916)

28. The dramatic transition that brings about the "happy ending" is as abrupt as the above sentence. The "felicity" of this ending seems an inorganic appendage to an essen-

tially tragic tale. The drama contains all the philosophic elements to justify—intellectu-ally—such an ending, but the emotional effect on a reader is nevertheless rather violently unsatisfying. While the immediate explanation may be the desirability of a positive end-ing for the court play and the lesson it delivers, its abruptness may also stem from a similar dichotomy within the playwright, between a fundamentally tragic sense of life and an intellectual—and inorganic—optimism.

29. If the goddess of reason herself resorts to violence, does this means that reason itself is a disguised form of violence, as Bandera points out in the case of Basilio? Is Bandera right in saying that Calderón signals the onmipresence of violence as the central fact of human society? Bandera says: "La violencia, nos dice Calderón, no es nada externo, nada trascendente, nada sagrado. La violencia se origina siempre en el interior de la ciudad y en ella participan todos" (199). This is surely an accurate observation, yet the basic issue dramatized in *La estatua de Prometeo* is not the universality of violence but the universal dualism that calls this violence into being.

30. It is possible to see Epimeteo as the recently fallen Nithard or the rising Valen-zuela, or a blend of both. His enthusiastic championship of new religious rites might link him with the Jesuit valido, while his espousal of building a magnificent temple could recall the image of Valenzuela as a builder. Along with the provision of spectacular entertainment, Valenzuela used an ambitious program of building and public works to impress the public (Kamen, *Spain* 154, 337). On the other hand, Epimeteo's passionate ignorance might be seen as linking him with the feeble-minded Carlos.

31. In the political theology developed throughout Europe in the Middle Ages and early modern period, the King as embodiment of the political authority of the monarchy was held to be imperishable and separable from the mortal body of the king as individual. See Kantorowicz and Marin.

32. Wardropper, without focusing specifically on *La estatua de Prometeo*, also maintains that Calderón's late dramas contradict the received idea that he was a rigid traditionalist, a "blue-blooded conservative." Citing Calderón's innovations—"the subtle symbolic expression through spectacle" and "the reconstruction of ancient myths"—he says that these later works "point, with a perceptive surreptitiousness, to possible ways of entering an unpredictable, but certainly different, future, without discarding a glorious past" (41).

33. "It is in the precognitive aspects of the theological code, and the requirement for its contents to be expressed in essentially narrative categories, that the ultimate structural limits and distortions of the political consciouness of a religious and precapitalist period are to be sought. When we turn to the artistic and cultural expressions of such religious impulses, however, we confront the figural mode again, as it were to the second power. Is it possible that this second-degree process of figural articulation—the process of cul-tural production generally—may do more than simply replicate the first; indeed, that it may in some central way serve to foreground and to bring out the contradictions and structural limits of its primary theological raw material?" (45–46).

CHAPTER SIX. A PESSIMISTIC VIEW

1. These include an earth-goddess, Cibele, and the leader of the Muses, Calíope. Calderón introduces a vision of Mt. Parnassus that is only marginally more functional in the play than that of Lope in his *Perseo*, and he employs the Pegaso mechanism for Hér-

cules' battle with the dragon that guards the golden tree in the garden of the Hespérides, for reasons probably more akin to entertaining the eleven-year-old Carlos II than for purposes of the plot.

2. With the exception of his last, nonmythological play, *Hado y divisa de Leonido y Marfisa*.

3. The text in an excellent edition left unfinished by Edward M. Wilson at his death and completed by Don W. Cruickshank and Cecilia Bainton; the accounts in AP Legajo 667. Subirats and Varey, "Mayordomía" have both utilized this document. Varey and I will publish a transcript of it in a forthcoming volume in the Tamesis *Fuentes para la historia del teatro en España* series.

4. The cover sheet of the accounts remarks on the cost, saying, "Ymportó esta parte del dicho gasto 277,861 reales de vellón líquidos—de que se puede hazer a que llegarían todos los demás gastos, de theatro, alumbramientos, ayudas de costa en dinero, refrescos y otros."

5. Lengths of blue and green taffeta; silver and white and pink [*encarnado*—"pink" or "flesh-colored"] gauze; *nuán*, a light cotton fabric; *holandilla*, a lining material; red and white silk thread (for embroidery, apparently); gold braid; gold and silver lace; white thread (six pounds) for sewing [*bastezer*]; *angulema,* another kind of lining material; tinsel to cover the shields of the signs of the zodiac; and colored ribbon.

6. By extrapolating from the accounts for *Hado y divisa de Leonido y Marfisa* (1680), however, we can get an idea of the complex organization required to operate them. A total of sixty-nine men were paid to operate the machinery for the stage effects for ten to fourteen days (for three performances and the rehearsals) and another thirty-six men to quick-change the perspective scenery (Varey and Shergold, *Representaciones palaciegas* 123–126).

7. The description included with the text calls him "Dios del ingenio" and says he is a "jeroglífico de el que, osadamente vano, intenta sofrenar al vulgo" (58). I do not see the connection between these interpretations and the theme of the play; while Calderón may well have written the descriptions that accompanied *Las fortunas de Andrómeda y Perseo* and *Hado y divisa de Leonido y Marfisa,* it seems doubtful that he was responsible for this one.

8. The description and the costume accounts seem somewhat contradictory with regard to the nymphs' costume, for the description say that the nymphs, along with the signs of the zodiac and the months, were attired in blue and silver with curling blue and white plumes, while the costume accounts speak only of white and silver gauze for the nymphs and blue taffeta for the signs and months.

9. "Era su prespectiva de color de cielo, hermoseado de nubes y celajes; y desde su primer bastidor hasta su foro, cuajada de caladas estrellas, que al movimiento de artificiales luces, obscureciendo unas y brillando otras en luciente travesura, campeaban alternadas" (64).

10. The extensive use of blue may have been an indication of opulence, for blue dyes were the most expensive (Reade 14). The description in the text says that the musicians were also dressed in blue. According to the accounts, three extra costumes for men like those of the months were made, which must have been for the musicians. No extra blue dresses for women were made. Certainly more than three musicians were required, so it seems likely that only the guitar players of whom Baccio de Bianco had complained were on stage, and the rest of the instrumental group was hidden.

11. Although the focus throughout is steadily on Mariana, Calderón also inserts flattering references to her daughter and grandaughter, Margarita and María Antonia, and to her son Carlos.

12. Varey ("Audience" 404) has also observed the deliberate blurring of the line between the "circumambient reality and the spectacle proper" in Juan Vélez de Guevara's *Los celos hacen estrellas*.

13. Judging from the accounts, the Hespérides were played by Manuela de Bustamente, Mariana Romero, and Micaela Fernández. Hesperia and Verusa have more important roles in the play, so it is probable that they were played by Manuela and Mariana, both of whom played "primera dama" roles, Manuela in the company of Félix Pascual from 1665 to 1671, and Mariana Romero with that of Manuel Vallejo from 1670 to 1674. Their dresses were apparently alike except in color. Each required twenty varas of a lightweight brocaded fabric from Seville "de Seuilla de Uelázquez" and twenty varas of taffeta for lining (probably including a visible underskirt). Manuela de Bustamente's dress was in green and gold with red lining; that of Micaela was blue and silver with blue lining; and Mariana Romero's was honey-colored (*caña*) and silver with blue lining. Each was trimmed with four-inch silver lace from Venice, but either Micaela was much slenderer or her role less important, for only fifty-four varas of lace were provided for her while sixty varas each were ordered for Mariana and Manuela. Information on actors and actresses taken from Rennert, Shergold, and Varey, *Autos*; Pérez Pastor; and the *Genealogía, origen y noticias de los comediantes de España* as well as from the accounts and Wilson edition of the play.

14. In the traditional version of the Iole story, Eurytus, king of a city in Boetia, had initially promised to marry his daughter Iole to Hercules but then changed his mind. Hercules killed him, destroyed his city, and carried off Iole. Deianira's resulting jealousy over his relationship with Iole eventually led to Hercules' death. It was Omphale, queen of Lydia, to whom Hercules had been enslaved in punishment for killing Iphitus, who dressed him in women's clothes and set him to women's work. For more details, see Calderón, *Fieras*, note to line 1073.

15. See Tate's article for the use of the Hercules myth by early Spanish historians.

16. Orso finds the presence of this painting disturbing, and a detraction from the heroic theme of the hall. In his recent book *Philip IV and the Decoration of the Alcázar of Madrid* (55, 60–63), he hypothesizes that Felipe IV commissioned Rubens's *Hercules and Antaeus*, a more appropriately heroic vision of Hercules, to replace it. This painting, of approximately the same size as the *Hercules and Omphale*, was finished by Jacob Jordaens after Rubens's death, and it was listed in the 1686 inventory of the Hall of Mirrors, while the Gentileschi painting was not, and its subsequent fate is unknown. The episodes in both paintings are dramatized in Calderón's play, but if the heroic Rubens Hercules replaced the Gentileschi painting in the Hall of Mirrors, Omphale had her dramatic revenge in *Fieras afemina Amor*.

17. Hércules was played by Alonso de Olmedo, the leading man in Escamilla's or other companies from 1660 to 1681.

18. The captives were not presented as abject or mean figures, however; according to the accounts, they were attired equally in costumes of powder-blue taffeta.

19. She was a celebrated actress who regularly played "primera dama" roles for Antonio de Escamilla (including the years 1670–1672) and other companies, and the accounts show for her a silver and honey-colored dress apparently similar in design to those of

Egle, Verusa, and Hesperia. She was dressed like a princess rather than a tramoya-borne goddess.

20. She might have had such a portrayal in the opening performance. María de Quiñones was called a "zélebre representanta en la parte de damas" (475) by the *Genealogía, origen y noticias de los comediantes de España*. She was no young woman at the time of *Fieras afemina Amor*, already acting in 1640, she had been playing lead roles at least since 1659, and she continued acting until well over seventy years of age. She seems to have been in demand offstage as well, for according to Barrionuevo (370), a *regidor* of Madrid, Gaspar de Valdés, arranged to have Francisco Paz, a knight of the Order of Santiago killed on her account on 24 March 1661. But Alonso de Olmedo, who definitely played Hércules, was if anything even more celebrated as a leading man. According to the *Genealogía*, Olmedo "hizo galanes en las compañías de Madrid muchos años con grandísimo aplauso y tanto que compitió con Seuastián de Prado, y diuididos en la Corte los parezeres y sentires se reduxo el aplauso de entramuos opiniones" (161). The son of a successful theatre company owner, he was much better educated than the majority of actors, for he had studied at the University of Salamanca before opting for a stage career and was praised as "hombre de mui buen juizio y buena comuersazión y de mui buenos prozedimientos, cortesano y atento." He also wrote a number of theatrical bailes and entremeses and "mui buenas coplas así para Palazio como para la Villa" (*Genealogía* 161). Like María de Quiñones, he had been acting since at least 1640 and playing leads by 1659. He was something of a galán offstage as well as on, and had children with more than one actresss. Yet he was also the victim of the violence done to women, for his wife was kidnapped by a nobleman shortly after their marriage according to the *Genealogía*. Would his enormous popularity with the public, combined with the general acceptance of Hercules as the hero who represented Spain itself, have combined to condition the audience toward the sort of sympathy with Hércules that Wilson felt, or did he transform himself into full-fledged antihero? Lope, in his *Arte nuevo*, said that actors who played the part of a traitor might find shopkeepers no longer willing to sell to them, while those who played loyally heroic roles would find themselves feted, even by princes. In the context of a court performance presided over by Mariana, we must include in our speculations the possibility that the reaction of the audience might have depended on their leanings toward the poles of the offstage axis of male-female competition, that between Mariana and Don Juan José de Austria.

21. In contrast, the similar use of a vision of Andrómeda in drawing Perseus into the cave of Morpheus was employed to enlighten and protect him.

22. That this was his intent seems to have been general knowledge; Leopold wrote to von Pötting with regard to the event, "Der Astillano hat meo judicio eine feine Narretei gethan, 120.000 escudos sic dicendo zum Fenster hinauszuwerfen; allhier würde nit leicht einem ein solche Tentation ankommen" (*Fontes* 57:21).

23. If Astillano was involved in the subject for the play as well as the costumes, we might even see in these comments a hint of another possible scenario for its choice: conceivably, the príncipe suggested a play about Hércules, thinking of him as the sort of inspiring Alcides described above, and Calderón, disgusted with the prevailing climate of political machinations, saw the ambiguous possibilities in the Hércules-Yole-Omphale story.

24. I believe a fascinating parallel could be drawn between the sort of three-dimensional, theatricalized perspectivism of the Calderonian court play made explicit in this

entremés and the complex perspective of Velázquez's *Las hilanderas* and *Las meninas*. Both bind together regal or divine and "normal" spectators, observing the same event from different psychological, if not physical, points of view. Neumeister (277–287) has done this, but I disagree with his conclusion that it amounted to little more than an exaggerated instance of royal solipsism.

25. Profeti uses the terms *condensation* and *displacement*, the mechanisms which Freud believed allowed the subject to escape the barriers of self-censorship in dreams; the same mechanisms, she maintains, allow the transgression of community-censored conduct in the entremés. A comment of Mariana, ever a harsh critic of the theatre, supports this view, for he says that censors should pass judgment on any play to be produced, "including also the pieces for between the acts, by which the greater harm is accustomed to creep in" (360).

26. The use of such a parodic episode in the entremés clearly illustrates the distance between the French model of adulatory court spectacle and the complex discourse of power present in Calderonian court fiestas. Isherwood notes that Italian troupes in France delighted audiences at the Hôtel de Bourgogne with parodies of the spectacles that Lully presented to Louis XIV, poking fun at Quinault's plots, Lully's recitatives, machine-borne gods; "even the regal pomposity of the sacrosanct prologues was burlesqued" (Isherwood 242). Whereas Lully studiously ignored such satire, this Calderonian fiesta made a "domesticated" parody part of the court spectacle itself.

27. A note in the Wilson edition explains "Cribas" as equivalent to "Cristo"; "a euphemistic oath comparable to English 'Crikey': '¡Voto a Cribas!'" (236).

28. Bergman (67) says 1672; Rennert (555), 1673.

29. See Pérez Villanueva 61, 76, 81, 102, 121, 153, 200, 221, 303.

30. The entremés refers to this pension, referring to the temple of Fame, "donde tienen / comida y casa pagada / todos los hombres insignes" (117).

31. See Bertaut description, chap. 3, p. 137.

32. Almost certainly Felipe Próspero. Rodríguez and Tordera (216) believe this entremés to have been written in 1658. It was published in 1660.

33. These uses in turn gesture toward the fiesta in which they are contained, as the reference to the temple of fame and the muses on Mt. Parnasus point back to the plot of the play, while its adoption for the king's garden refers to the physical setting and the royal presence.

34. Here, however, a distinction should be made between the artistic representation as a corporeal entity and the meaning its viewers construct from its structure, between the "statue" that is the subject of this entremés and the entremés as a structure of meaning. As a physical object, the artistic representation could be appropriated by those with the most political and economic power; *Las meninas* would decorate the king's walls, and court plays would exist with their full value as an original only in the presence of the royal spectator, although copies of Velázquez's paintings might circulate outside the palace walls and Calderón's plays might be staged in the absence of the king or even, in simplified form, in the corrales. However, as a structure of meaning, the entremés is constituted in the "possible world" constructed by each viewer, from the overlap between the on-stage action and his own world of experience (see Chapter 4), and in this form, it is outside the physical control of the "soldiers of the king." It was, obviously, subject to another kind of power, that exercized by a common cultural and literary tradition that delimited the general boundaries of probable interpretation.

35. Rodríguez and Tordera (120) state that palos and the baile are interchangeable as methods of closure, an observation that merits further consideration.

36. Judging by the costume accounts, in this case the "soul" wore brighter plumage than the "body." Juan Rana himself was dressed in a silver-gray felt, from beret to cape and breeches, with matching linings and stockings, and silver trim and buttons. Manuela's costume "de bobo" brocaded red taffeta for *sayo* with *mangas asidradas* and breeches. She also wore a hat "de color chanbergo" decorated with colored ribbons. One wonders whether the choice of color for the hat was a purely aesthetic decision or whether it was meant as a subtle reminder of the problems posed by the presence of the regiment of that name.

37. This "Sol" is of course Mariana.

38. There was no parody in this *sainete*, unless it was in the mind of an author who wrote it tongue in cheek or an audience that received it as such, for Mariana was neither beautiful, intelligent, nor much loved in Spain where she was known as "la alemana."

CHAPTER SEVEN. THE END OF THE LINE

1. In the latter works, however, some sort of suprahuman being generally intervenes at least briefly, as does the magician Megera in *Hado y divisa*.

2. For a convenient summary of the official and unofficial mechanisms of government, see Kamen, *Spain,* Chapter 2.

3. It was performed twenty-one times, first in the Coliseo of the Buen Retiro on 3, 4, and 5 March for the court and foreign dignitaries and thereafter for the general public, the latter performances apparently taking place in the corrales. See Pérez Pastor, *Documentos* 364–365; Varey, *Teatros y comedias 1666–1687* 124, 180; and Varey, *Representaciones* 106–107.

4. They are on ff.88–184 of BN Ms. 9.373, a curious collection of printed works and manuscript copies of historical, administrative, and legal documents primarily from the seventeenth century, bound together in a parchment cover bearing the title "Difere⟨n⟩tes Materias historicas y de Nobleza." As Hartzenbusch observes in a footnote (355–356) to his edition, which is based on this manuscript, the description names Calderón with his titles "caballero de la órden de Santiago, y capellan de honor de su Majestad" but without any of the glorifying adjectives with which it prefaces the names of the stage engineer and others responsible for the events. On this evidence, Hartzenbusch makes the plausible suggestion that the dramatist himself wrote the description.

5. Printed in Varey, *Representaciones* 106–140.

6. "Sobre estas columnas cargaba el arquitrabe, friso y cornisa; y dando la vuelta ella de un extremo en otro en proporción de círculo, guarnecía un medallón que servía de clave. En él se miraba de relieve el augustísimo blasón de España: un león coronado descansando sobre un orbe, al cual asistía una cruz, cetro y espada, jeroglíficos de la religión y el poder. Pendía de su cuello el toisón, insignia de nuestros monarcas: todo esto de brillantísimo oro, uniéndose amigablemente la ferocidad con el resplandor" (356).

7. The verb employed is *tremolar*, regularly used to apply to military banners.

8. Interestingly, the describer does not call them "little Cupids" as he does those of the stage curtain. It would seem, then, that these were a suggestion of the progeny he hoped would soon be forthcoming.

9. Since the account specifically says that the Latin motto was above the lion's head, this placard was surely below the medallion, although he does not specify its location.

10. Cf. Pye's commentary on Hobbes's analysis of monarchical authority. Discussing the specular interdependence of the king's dazzling gaze and the empowering regard of his subjects, Pye says: "the vulnerability and the terrifying power of the king's visible presence are, in fact inseparable . . . the subject's desire to reduce the sovereign presence to the fully exposed object of his sight lends the regal eye its penetrating, and impenetrable, power" (281).

11. By the Thomistic conception of the human mind that Calderón followed, the external senses, reacting to stimuli, transmit the information to the internal, *sensus communis,* which organizes the information from the different senses into complete images, or phantasms. The imagination can thereafter present to the mind things that have previously been perceived by the senses but are no longer present, while the faculty of memory engraves these images in our "gray matter" and makes it possible for us to recall past images, knowing that they are past. The phantasm is the starting point for the working of all intellectual processes; the "fantasía" could either recall phantasms previously engraved or recombine them to generate new phantasms, new images. See Brennan.

12. Wardropper accepts Neumeister's analysis of the setting, despite the fact that he recognizes that "Calderón delicately cajoled and instructed the king through symbolism" (40). In a recent article, "Escenografía," Neumeister recognizes the didactic value of this arrangement for the king: "Los antepasados amonestan al heredero a hacerse digno de ellos. Se requiere la prudencia, calidad imprescindible del príncipe: reúne el pasado, el presente y el futuro" (155). Neumeister continues to emphasize, however, the essentially solipsistic nature of the event. In an essay lacking the intellectual rigor of Neumeister's and Wardropper's approach, Valbuena Briones makes a related judgment when he calls *Hado y divisa* "un entretenimiento intelectual escapista" (172).

13. As the years went by and repeated rumors that Marie-Louise was pregnant proved false, the Spanish populace turned against her, and a well-known *pasquín* made a witty play on the verb *parir,* "to give birth," to suggest her fate:

> Parid, bella flor de lis,
> que, en aflicción tan extraña,
> sí parís, parís a España,
> si no parís, a París. (qtd in Maura, *Corte* 1:394)

14. See Jago; Kamen, Chapter 9; and in a more general sense, Rabb, for consideration of the position of the aristocracy in Spain and elsewhere in this period. Cohen (384–390) links both *La vida es sueño* and *Hado y divisa* to Shakespearean works such as *The Winter's Tale* and *The Tempest,* which for him are "pastoral tragicomic romances" that reflect the failure of the aristocracy to adapt to the move toward capitalism.

15. Lundelius also finds ironic notes in Calderón's treatment of chivalric motifs in *El castillo de Lindabridis.*

16. Carlos II reportedly became enamored of Marie-Louise through her portrait and laudatory reports of her beauty (Davies 147).

17. There is an ironic note, however, in the use of the cowardly gracioso to present his chivalric pedigree and the humorous tone in which it is recounted.

18. Calderón also uses the vision to unite dramatically the action in two separate realms and to indicate their simultaneity, as he had in *Fortunas de Andrómeda y Perseo*.

19. The flying serpent and hydra may not have been Calderón's idea. As well as the complete manuscript which contains the detailed description of this play, there is another manuscript copy of the text alone in the Biblioteca Nacional, Ms. 16.743. Except for minor copyist's errors, the text is the same, but the stage directions are much simpler and similar in length and placement to those in Calderón's autograph manuscripts of later plays such as that of *El gran príncipe de Fez*. They are also written in the future or present tense, specifying the effects that are to be staged, rather than a past-tense description of a past performance. Generally, the stage directions in this manuscript specify the same staging as in the long description, albeit in briefer terms. However, they make no reference to her steeds, and at the end of the first act, she does not even seem to have been airborne.

20. This lovely play is one of the most accessible to a modern audience because of its relevance to the perennial problems of sexual identity and parent-child relationships in the turbulent period of adolescence. The "political text" of this play was, I believe, a warning of the danger of achieving a strong and stable personality in the atmosphere of the court. Isolated from reality and surrounded by adulation, princes and princesses could easily drown in the self-absorption of a Narcissus or, becoming dependent on flattery, be reduced to an echo of others' opinion of her, as was the poor nymph.

21. These are the first two strophes of the "Romance de Luis Vélez," which Calderón had used in three previous plays and had been reworked both seriously and satirically by many other poets. Vélez himself offered another version: "Escollo armado de hiedra, / yo te conocí servicio; / ejemplo de lo que vale / la m . . . de los validos." See Wilson and Sage 60–62.

22. *Transversal* in this context means indirect line of descent; the *Diccionario de Autoridades* quotes Castillo Solórzano to illustrate: "Habiendo naturales / En vuestro Reino, vengan trasversales / Principes a posseerle."

23. This scenic link may not have been part of Calderón's original plan for the drama, however. Like Megera's flying serpents, it is not mentioned in the stage directions of the other manuscript copy. Whether it was an idea that occurred to the dramatist after he wrote the text as the scribe copied it or it originated with a stage architect, however, Calderón adopted it enthusiastically, as the description attests.

24. Although a fall from a horse in Calderón is generally interpreted as a sign of runaway passions, I suspect that the more practical reason for such an opening in this play was that of capturing the attention of a monarch whose favorite entertainment thus far had been bullfights.

25. See Daniel L. Heiple, "The Tradition Behind the Punishment of the Rebel Soldier in *La vida es sueño*," *BHS* 50 (1973): 1–17, and Donald McGrady, "Calderón's Rebel Soldier and Poetic Justice Reconsidered," *BHS* 62 (1985): 181–184.

26. In general terms, the Marxist explanation of the origin and decline of public theatre in the two countries in Cohen's thoughtful work would seem to be true; however, he contradicts his own careful periodization by lumping together *La vida es sueño* and *Hado y divisa*, separated by over forty-five years and differences as important as the plot similarities Cohen finds, and by overlooking the fact that Calderón was writing romantic come-

dies such as *La dama duende, Casa con dos puertas mala es de guardar, De una causa dos efectos,* and *El galán fantasma* during the same period that he wrote *La vida es sueño.*

27. The importance of loyalty, courage, and fidelity in love are not questioned, but the military function that was still the theoretical justification for the ascendency of a knightly class (although it had long since ceased to fulfill this role in fact) is undercut in a variety of ways in this fiesta. In contrast to the image of battle as the hero's natural duty in *El mayor encanto, amor,* warfare here can be presented negatively or comically. Casimiro calls war a "Monstruo que de humana sangre / Hidrópico se alimenta" (381); Merlin talks about a civil war between a frog and a mosquito over whether it is better to die in wine or live in water (387); and the "Baile de las flores" by Alonso de Olmedo that was danced between the second and third acts consisted of a civil war between flowers in which sovereignty was disputed between the rose and the lily, with the tulip serving as a foreign spy and double agent.

Also intriguing is the musical interlude with which Calderón opened Act II. Neither Stein nor Wilson and Sage found any other occurrences of this ballad, and we may therefore presume that Calderón wrote it specifically for this play. The scene opens with Marfisa, previously seen in a cave dressed in skins, now elegantly attired and seated in a "gabinete real" (370). Ostensibly singing of the fluctuations of the sea, two choruses pose questions with an obvious social application:

CORO 1:	*Si yo gobernara el mar . . .*
CORO 2:	*Si yo tuviera el poder . . .*
CORO 1:	*Yo le quitara el crecer . . .*
CORO 2:	*Yo le quitara el menguar.*
VOZ 1:	*Si cuando más en la suma*
	Inconstancia de su esfera
	Ser monte de nieve espera,
	Vuelve a ser golfo de espuma,
	Porque ser nadie presuma
	Más de lo que nace a ser . . .
CORO 1:	*Yo le quitara el crecer.*
VOZ 2:	*Poco a su espiritu debe*
	Quien de su parte no hace
	Por ser más de lo que nace;
	Y yo que a monte se atreve
	Naciendo golfo de nieve,
	Porque lo llegue a lograr . . .
CORO. 2:	*Yo le quitara el menguar.*

Marfisa answers ambiguously that she neither approves nor reproves the law of the seas, "Y así, dejado en su ser . . . / (*Canta*) *Ni le quitara el crecer / Ni le quitara el menguar*" All the musicians then repeat, "*Si yo gobernara el mar, / Si yo tuviera el poder, / Ni le quitara el crecer / Ni le quitara el menguar*" (370). The outcome of the play as a whole also sidesteps the question of social mobility in the way characteristic throughout Golden Age literature; the protagonists that apparently go from poverty to glory prove to be of noble or royal blood. The social hierarchy is also brought into question, albeit ambiguously, by the

Entremés de la tía between the first and second acts, in which three *hidalgos* who live a parasitical existence on the margins of court life are ridiculed, and the concluding entremés, *El labrador gentil-hombre,* an abbreviated Spanish version of *Le Bourgeois gentil-homme* in which Molière's urban merchant is transformed into a "simple rico de aldea" who comes to court to see the queen and marry a princess.

28. Ironically, the *Hado y divisa* manuscript is followed in Ms. 9.373 by an undated printed *romance* accompanied by a "philosophical commentary" meant to serve the same purpose of molding and encouraging a young king. It describes itself as "Romance, y prossa, en que se prueba con Real Philosophia, que para ser vn Rey grande, y perfecto, tal vez son providencias, algunos contratiempos, y guerras en su Reynado, y principalmente siendo joben: porque vno, y otro descubre las Prendas naturales del Príncipe, para ser buen Rey, y en la experiencia acrisoladas, y perfectas, escusa el defecto, que sin ella tener pudo; mas ya practicado, y experto en la Regia pensión, y pesadumbre de la Corona, y Ceptro, con sabia Magestad, y aciertos, vence sus dificultades. Haziéndose temido, se haze amado, en guerra, y paz siempre victorioso. . . ." The irony is that the advice it offers is not directed toward Carlos II but toward either Felipe V or Luis I, his first Bourbon successors. (The "philosophical commentary" is credited to Joseph de Grimaldo, Felipe V's powerful secretary. Since the caption of the romance begins "Es enigma el rey del rey," I suspect that it was intended for Luis I, who was briefly "rey del rey" when his father abdicated in his favor. Luis soon succumbed to smallpox, and Felipe V resumed the throne.)

CHAPTER EIGHT. CONCLUSION

1. Some years ago, Hesse applied a Freudian approach to this play with interesting results, and Larson has recently studied its complex treatment of time.

2. Jonathan Brown has observed that Felipe IV, although an even more extensive art collector than Charles I of England, did not commission works of art for the sort of royalist political statement characteristic of the English king. (Lecture on Charles I of England and Felipe IV, Princeton University, 11 November 1987.)

BIBLIOGRAPHY

LIST OF ABBREVIATIONS

BAE	Biblioteca de Autores Españoles
BHS	*Bulletin of Hispanic Studies*
HR	*Hispanic Review*
MLR	*Modern Language Review*
NBAE	Nueva Biblioteca de Autores Españoles
PMLA	*Publications of the Modern Language Association of America*
RF	*Romanische Forshungen*

Allen, John J. *The Reconstruction of a Spanish Golden Age Playhouse: El Corral del Príncipe, 1583–1744.* Gainesville: University of Florida Press, 1983.

Amadei de Pulice, María Alicia. "Hacia Calderón: Las bases teórico-artísticas del teatro barroco español." Diss. University of California, Los Angeles, 1981.

Archivo del Palacio, Madrid. Legajo 667, Caja 11.744.

Ariosto, Ludovico. *Orlando furioso.* Trans. Guido Waldman. Oxford: Oxford University Press, 1983.

Arnold, Denis. *Monteverdi.* London: J. M. Dent and Sons, Ltd., 1975.

Asensio, Eugenio. *Itinerario del entremés.* Madrid: Gredos, 1971.

Aubrun, Charles. Introduction. *La estatua de Prometeo.* By Pedro Calderón de la Barca. Paris: Centre de Recherches de l'Institut d'Etudes Hispaniques, 1965. v–xxxiii.

Bances Candamo, Francisco. *Theatro de los theatros de los passados y presentes siglos.* Ed. Duncan W. Moir. London: Tamesis Books, 1970.

Bandera, Cesáreo. *Mímesis conflictiva.* Madrid: Gredos, 1975.

Barrionuevo, Jerónimo de. *Avisos. (1654–1658).* Ed. A. Paz y Meliá. 2 vols. Biblioteca de Autores Españoles 221–222. Madrid: Ediciones Atlas, 1968.

Barthes, Roland. *Essais critiques.* Paris: Editions du Seuil, 1964.

Bataille, Gabriele. *Airs de differents autheurs, mis en tablature de luth.* Ed. Pierre Ballard. Paris: 1611. Vol. 3 of facs. ed. Geneva: Minkoff Reprints, 1980. 6 vols.

Beaujoyeulx, Baltazar de. *Le Balet comique de Royne.* Ed. facs. and Intro., Margaret M. McGowan. Binghamton, N.Y.: Center for Medieval and Early Renaissance Studies, 1982.

Bergman, Hannah. "Juan Rana se retrata." *Homenaje al Prof. Rodríguez-Moñino.* 2 vols. Madrid: Castalia, 1966. 1:65–73.

Bianconi, Lorenzo, and Thomas Walker. "Tales of the Febiarmonici: On the Spread of the Opera in Seventeenth-Century Italy." Forthcoming in the *Drammaturgia Musicale Veneta* series. Revised version of "Dalla *Finta pazza* alla *Veremonda*: storie di Febiarmonici." *Revista italiana di musicologia* 10 (1975): 379–454.

―――. "Production, Consumption and Political Function of Seventeenth-Century Opera." *Early Music History* 4 (1984): 209–298.

Bibliothèque Nationale Ms. fr. 24352, f. 308 and Ms. fr. 24357, ff. 178–179; Ms. Res. F. 496.

Blue, William R. *The Development of Imagery in Calderón's Comedias*. York, S.C.: Spanish Literature Publications, 1983.

Boccaccio, Giovanni. *Genealogía de los dioses paganos*. Eds. María Consuelo Alvarez and Rosa María Iglesias. Madrid: Editora Nacional, 1983.

Booth, Wayne. *A Rhetoric of Irony*. Chicago: University of Chicago Press, 1974.

Brennan, Robert Edward. *General Psychology: An Interpretation of the Science of the Mind Based on Thomas Aquinas*. New York: MacMillan Co., 1937.

Brooks, Lynn Matluck. *The Dances of the Processions of Seville in Spain's Golden Age*. Kassel, Germany: Edition Reichenberger, 1988.

Brown, Howard Mayer. "Music—How Opera Began: An Introduction to Jacopo Peri's *Euridice* (1600)." *The Late Italian Renaissance*. Ed. Eric Cochrane. London: Macmillan, 1970. 401–443.

Brown, Jonathan, and J. H. Elliott. *A Palace for a King: The Buen Retiro and the Court of Philip IV*. New Haven: Yale University Press, 1980.

Bruner, Jerome. *Actual Minds, Possible Worlds*. Cambridge, Mass.: Harvard University Press, 1980.

Buck, Donald C. "Theatrical Productions in Madrid's Cruz and Príncipe Theaters during the Reign of Felipe V." Diss. University of Texas at Austin, 1980.

Calderón de la Barca, Pedro. *Amor, honor y poder*. Ed. Angel Valbuena Briones. Madrid: Aguilar, 1960. Vol. 2 of *Obras completas*. 53–88.

———. *Apolo y Climene*. Ed. Juan Eugenio Hartzenbusch. BAE 14:151–174.

———. *Autos sacramentales*. Ed. Angel Valbuena Prat. Madrid: Aguilar, 1952. Vol. 3 of *Obras completas*. 3 vols. 1952–1960.

———. *Eco y Narciso*. Ed. Angel Valbuena Briones. Madrid: Aguilar, 1959. Vol. 1 of *Obras completas*. 1952–1990.

———. *Entremeses, jácaras y mojigangas*. Eds. Evangelina Rodríguez and Antonio Tordera. Madrid: Clásicos Castalia, 1982.

———. *La estatua de Prometeo*. Ed. Margaret Rich Greer. Kassel, Germany: Edition Reichenberger, 1986.

———. *Fieras afemina Amor*. Ed. Edward M. Wilson. Kassel, Germany: Edition Reichenberger, 1984.

———. *Las fortunas de Andrómeda y Perseo*. MS Typ. 258. Houghton Library, Harvard.

———. *El gran príncipe de Fez*. Ed. Angel Valbuena Briones. Madrid: Aguilar, 1952. Vol. 1 of *Obras completas*. 1407–1454.

———. *Hado y divisa de Leonido y Marfisa*. Ed. Juan Eugenio Hartzenbusch. BAE 14:355–394.

———. *El hijo del sol, Faetón*. Ed. Juan Eugenio Hartzenbusch. BAE 14:175–198.

———. *El laurel de Apolo*. Ed. Angel Valbuena Briones. Madrid: Aguilar, 1952. Vol. 1 of *Obras completas*. 2171–2195.

———. *El laberinto del mundo*. Ed. Angel Valbuena Prat. Madrid: Aguilar, 1952. Vol. 3 of *Obras completas*. 3 vols. 1952–1960. 1553–1580.

———. *El lirio y la azucena*. Ed. Angel Valbuena Prat. Madrid: Aguilar, 1952. Vol. 3 of *Obras completas*. 3 vols. 1952–1960. 916–939.

———. *El mayor encanto amor*. Ed. Juan Eugenio Hartzenbusch. BAE 14:385–410.

Campeggi, Ridolfo. *Poesie. Parte seconda*. Venetia: Vberto Fabri, 1620.

Capdet, Françoise, and Jean-Louis Flecniakoska. "Le Batard Don Juan d'Autriche, personnage de théatre." *Dramaturgie et Société: Rapports entre l'œuvre théâtrale, son inter-*

prétation et son public aux XVIe et XVIIe siècles. Ed. Jean Jacquot. Paris: Editions du Centre National de la Recherche Scientifique, 1968. 125–132.

Carballo, Luis Alfonso de. *Cisne de Apolo*. 2 vols. Ed. Alberto Porqueras Mayo. Madrid: Consejo Superior de Investigaciones Científicas, 1958.

Cascardi, Anthony. *The Limits of Illusion: A Critical Study of Calderón*. Cambridge: Cambridge University Press, 1984.

Cassirer, Ernst., Paul Oskar Kristeller and John Herman Randall, Jr., eds. *The Renaissance Philosophy of Man*. Chicago: University of Chicago Press, 1948.

Chapman, W. C. "La comedias mitológicas de Calderón." *Revista de Literatura* 5 (1984): 35–67.

Christout, Marie-Françoise. *Le Ballet de cour de Louis XIV, 1643–1672*. Paris: Editions A. et J. Picard and Cie., 1967.

――――. "Les Feus d'artifices en France de 1606 à 1628. Esquisse historique et esthétique." *Fêtes de la Renaissance*. Ed. Jean Jacquot. Vol. 1. Paris: Editions du Centre Nationale de la Recherche Scientifique, 1956. 247–264.

Cicognini, Jacopo. *L'Andromeda, favola marittima. Scorso di penna in un corsi di sole. Poesia drammatica del Sig. Giacomo Cicognini, con la quale si descrive la favola d'Andromeda. Rappresentata . . . l'anno 1617 in Firenze*. Biblioteca Riccardiana n. 2792, cc. 130–167.

Cohen, Walter. *Drama of a Nation: Public Theater in Renaissance England and Spain*. Ithaca, N.Y.: Cornell University Press, 1985.

――――. "Shakespeare and Calderón in an Age of Transition." *Genre* 15 (1982): 127–137.

Corneille, Pierre. *L'Andromède*. Ed. Christian Delmas. Paris: Librairie Marcel Didier, 1974.

Cotarelo y Mori, Emilio. *Colección de Entremeses, Loas, Bailes, Jácaras y Mojigangas desde fines del siglo XVI a mediados del XVIII*. NBAE 17. Madrid: Casa Editorial Bailly-Baillière, 1911.

Cotarelo y Mori, Emilio. *Ensayo sobre la vida y obras de D. Pedro Calderón de la Barca*. Madrid: Tipografía de la Revista de Archivos, Bibliotecas y Museos, 1924.

Couliano, Ioan P. *Eros and Magic in the Renaissance*. Trans. Margaret Cook. Chicago: University of Chicago Press, 1987.

Covarrubias, Sebastián. *Tesoro de la lengua castellana o española*. Madrid: Ediciones Turner, 1979.

Criuickshank, Don. Introduction. *En la vida todo es verdad y todo mentira*. By Pedro Calderón de la Barca. London: Tamesis Books Ltd., 1971

Cruickshank, Don, and Seán Page. Introduction. *Love is no laughing matter*. By Pedro Calderón de la Barca. Warminster, Eng.: Aris and Phillips, 1986.

Curtius, Ernst Robert. "Calderón und die Malerei." *RF* 50 (1936): 90–97.

――――. "Calderón's Theory of Art and the *Artes Liberales*." *European Literature and the Latin Middle Ages*. Princeton: Princeton University Press, 1973. 559–572.

Davies, R. Trevor. *La Decadencia Española, 1621–1700*. Barcelona: Editorial Labor, 1972.

De Armas, Frederick A. "Lope de Vega and Titian." *Comparative Literature* 30 (1978): 338–352.

――――. *The Return of Astraea: An Astral-Imperial Myth in Calderón*. Lexington: University Press of Kentucky, 1986.

Deleito y Piñuela, José. *El rey se divierte*. Madrid: Espasa Calpe, 1935.

Dietrich, Margret. "Le Livret d'opéra et ses aspects sociaux a la cour de Léopold Ier." *Dramaturgie et Société: Rapports entre l'œuvre théâtrale, son interprétation et son public aux XVIe et XVIIe siècles*. Ed. Jean Jacquot. Paris: Editions du Centre National de la Recherche Scientifique, 1968. 203–210.

Dipuccio, Denise. "Communicative Structures in Calderón de la Barca's Mythological 'Comedias.'" Diss. University of Kansas, 1982.

Donington, Robert. *The Rise of Opera*. New York: Charles Scribner's Sons, 1981.

Donogue, Denis. *Thieves of Fire*. New York: Oxford University Press, 1974.

Draghi [?], Antonio. *Benche vinto, vince amore. O Il Prometeo*. [Vienna]: Mateo Cosmerovio, Stampatore di Corte, [1669?].

Durán, Manuel, and Roberto González Echevarría. "Calderón y la crítica." *Calderón y la crítica: Historia y antología*. Vol. 1. Madrid: Editorial Gredos: 1976. 2 vols.

Eco, Umberto. "Possible Worlds and Text Pragmatics: 'Un drame bien parisien.'" *VS* 19/20 (1978): 5–76.

——. "Semiotics of Theatrical Performance." *The Drama Review* 21 (1977): 107–112.

Elam, Keir. *The Semiotics of Theatre and Drama*. New York: Methuen, 1980.

Elliott, J. H. *The Count-Duke of Olivares: The Statesman in an Age of Decline*. New Haven: Yale University Press, 1986.

——. *Richelieu and Olivares*. Cambridge: Cambridge University Press, 1984.

——. "Self-Perception and Decline in Early Seventeenth-Century Spain." *Past and Present* 74 (1977): 41–61.

——. "The Spanish Peninsula, 1598–1648." *The Decline of Spain and the Thirty Years War, 1609–48/59*. Ed. J. P. Cooper. The New Cambridge Modern History. Vol. 4. Cambridge: Cambridge University Press, 1970. 435–473.

Esquivel Navarro, Juan de. *Discurso sobre el arte del dançado*. Sevilla: Iuan Gómez de Blas, 1642.

Ewbank, Inga-Stina. "'The Eloquence of Masques': A Retrospective View of Masque Criticism." *Essays Principally on Masques and Entertainments*. Ed. S. Schoenbaum. Renaissance Drama, New Series. Vol. 1. Evanston, Ill.: Northwestern University Press, 1968. 307–327.

Fenlon, Iain. "Mantua, Monteverdi and the History of *Andromeda*." *Claudio Monteverdi. Reinhold Hammerstein zum 70. Geburtstag*. Laaber: Laaber-Verlag, 1986. 163–173.

Fernández de Heredia, Juan Francisco. *Trabajos y afanes de Hércules. Floresta de sentencias, y exemplos, Dirigada al Rey nuestro señor Don Carlos II*. Madrid: Francisco Sanz, 1682.

Ferrari, Benedetto. *Andromeda*. Venice, 1637.

Foucault, Michel. "What is an Author?" *The Foucault Reader*. Ed. Paul Rabinow. New York: Pantheon Books, 1984. 101–120.

Gadamer, Hans-Georg. *Truth and Method*. New York: Crossroad, 1988.

Gallego Morell, Antonio. *El mito de Faetón en la literatura española*. Madrid: Consejo Superior de Investigaciones Científicas, 1961.

Genealogía, origen y noticias de los comediantes de España. Eds. N. D. Shergold and J. E. Varey. London: Tamesis Books Ltd., 1985.

Gómez de Liaño, Ignacio, and Víctor Infantes. "Fábula de una muerte anunciada." *El Crotalón* 1 (1984): 485–497.

Gonçalez de Salas, Jusepe Antonio. *Nueva idea de la tragedia antigua, o Ilustracion última al libro singular de Poética de Aristoteles Stagirita*. Madrid: Franc. Martinez, 1633.

Goodman, Nelson, and Catherina Z. Elgin. "Interpretation and Identity: Can the Work Survive the World?" *Critical Inquiry* 12 (1986): 564–575.

Gordon, D. J. *The Renaissance Imagination*. Ed. Stephen Orgel. Berkeley: University of California Press, 1980.

Gracian, Baltasar. *El Criticón*. Ed. Santos Alonso. Madrid: Ediciones Cátedra, S.A., 1980.

Grass, Günther. *On Writing and Politics*. Trans. Ralph Manheim. London: Secker and Warburg, 1985.

Greenblatt, Stephen. *Renaissance Self-Fashioning*. Chicago: University of Chicago Press, 1980.

Greer, Margaret R. "Bodies of Power in Calderón: *El nuevo palacio del Retiro* and *El mayor encanto, amor.*" *Conflicts of Discourse, Spanish Literature of the Golden Age*. Ed. Peter Evans. Manchester: Manchester University Press, 1990.

Grout, Donald Jay. *A Short History of Opera*. 2d ed. New York: Columbia University Press, 1965.

Hanning, Barbara Russano. *Of Poetry and Music's Power: Humanism and the Creation of Opera*. Ann Arbor, Michigan.: UMI Research Press, 1980.

Heiple, Daniel L. "The Tradition behind the Punishment of the Rebel Soldier in *La vida es sueño.*" *BHS* 50 (1973): 1–17.

Heninger, S. K., Jr. *Touches of Sweet Harmony. Pythagorean Cosmology and Renaissance Poetics*. San Marino, Calif.: The Huntington Library, 1974.

Hernández-Araico, Susana. "Mitos, simbolismo y estructura en *Apolo y Climene* y *El hijo del sol, Faetón.*" *BHS* 64 (1987): 77–85.

Hesse, Everett W. "Calderón's *Eco y Narciso* and the Split Personality." *Theology, Sex and the Comedia*. Madrid: José Porrúa Taranzas, S.A., 1982. 53–61.

———. "The 'Terrible Mother' Image in Calderón's *Eco y Narciso.*" *Romance Notes* 1 (1960): 133–136.

Hivnor, Mary E. "The Perseus Myth as Defined by Calderón and Corneille." *Bulletin of the Comediantes* 40 (1988): 237–247.

Hollander, Robert. *Allegory in Dante's Commedia*. Princeton: Princeton University Press, 1969.

Holquist, Michael. "The Politics of Representation." *Allegory and Representation*. Ed. Stephen J. Greenblatt. Baltimore, Md.: The Johns Hopkins University Press, 1981.

Hurtado de Mendoza, Antonio. *Fiesta que se hizo en Aranjuez a los años del Rey Nuestro Señor D. Felipe IIII*. Madrid, 1623.

———. *Obras poéticas*. Ed. Rafael Benítez Claros. Vol. 1. Madrid: Gráficas ultra, 1947.

Isherwood, Robert M. *Music in the Service of the King. France in the Seventeenth Century*. Ithaca: Cornell University Press, 1973.

Ivanova, Ana. *The Dancing Spaniards*. London: John Baker, 1970.

Jago, Charles. "The 'Crisis of the Aristocracy' in Seventeenth-Century Castile." *Past and Present* 84 (1979): 60–90.

Jameson, Frederic. "Religion and Ideology: A Political Reading of *Paradise Lost.*" *Literature, Politics and Theory*. Ed. Francis Barker, et al. London: Methuen, 1986.

Kamen, Henry. *Spain in the Later Seventeenth Century, 1665–1700*. New York: Longman, 1980.

———. *Una sociedad conflictiva: España, 1469–1714*. Madrid: Alianza, 1984.

Kantorowicz, Ernst H. *The King's Two Bodies: A Study in Mediaeval Political Theology*. Princeton: Princeton University Press, 1957.

La Barrera, Cayetano Alberto de. *Nueva biografía de Lope de Vega*. BAE 262. Madrid: Ediciones Atlas, 1973.

Larson, Catherine. "Playing for Time, Playing with Time in Calderón's *Eco y Narciso*." *Bulletin of the Comediantes* 39 (1987): 115–126.

Lawrenson, T. E. *The French Stage and Playhouse in the XVIIth Century: A Study in the Advent of the Italian Order*. 2d ed. New York: AMS Press, 1986.

Lesure, F. "Le record de ballets de Michel Henry." *Fêtes de la Renaissance*. Ed. Jean Jacquot. Vol 1. Paris: Editions du Centre Nationale de la Recherche Scientifique, 1956. 205–219.

Ley, Willy. *Watchers of the Skies: An Informal History of Astronomy from Babylon to the Space Age*. New York: Viking Press, 1966.

Livermore, Ann. *A Short History of Spanish Music*. London: Duckworth, 1972.

López Piñero, José María. *La introducción de la ciencia en España*. Barcelona: Ediciones Ariel, 1969.

López Torrijos, Rosa. *La mitología en la pintura española del Siglo de Oro*. Madrid: Catedra, 1985.

Loyola, St. Ignatius. *The Spiritual Exercises of St. Ignatius Loyola*. Ed. Joseph Rickaby, S.J. London: Burns and Oates, Ltd., 1915.

Lundelius, Ruth. "Vélez de Guevara's *El Caballero del Sol* and Calderón de la Barca's *El castillo de Lindabridis* (A Response to Professor Valbuena Briones)." *Antigüedad y actualidad de Luis Vélez de Guevara: Estudios críticos*. Ed. C. George Peale. Purdue University Monographs in Romance Languages 10. Philadelphia: John Benjamins Publishing Co., 1983. 52–57.

Maraniss, James E. *On Calderón*. Columbia: University of Missouri Press, 1978.

Maravall, José Antonio. *La cultura del barroco: Análisis de una estructura histórica*. 2d ed. Barcelona: Editorial Ariel, 1980.

———. *La teoría española del estado en el siglo XVII*. Madrid: Instituto de Estudios Políticos, 1944.

Mariana, Juan de. *The King and the Education of the King (De Rege et Regis Institutione)*. Trans. George Albert Moore. Washington, D.C.: The Country Dollar Press, 1948.

Marin, Louis. *Le Portrait du roi*. Paris: Minuit, 1981.

Mariscal, George. "Caldéron and Shakespeare: The Subject of Henry VIII." *Bulletin of the Comediantes* 39 (1987): 189–213.

Martin, Henry M. "The Perseus Myth in Lope de Vega and Calderón with Some Reference to Their Sources." *PMLA* 46 (1931): 450–460.

Massar, Phyllis Dearborn. "Scenes for a Calderón Play by Baccio del Bianco." *Master Drawings* 15 (1977): 365–375.

Maura Gamazo, Gabriel. *Carlos II y su corte. Ensayo de reconstrucción biográfica*. 2 vols. Madrid: F. Beltran, 1911.

———. *Vida y reinado de Carlos II*. 2 vols. Madrid: Espasa Calpe, 1954.

Maurin, Margaret. "The Monster, the Sepulchre and the Dark: Related Patterns of Imagery in *La vida es sueño*." *HR* 35 (1967): 161–178.

McGowan, Margaret M. *L'Art du ballet de cour en France, 1581–1643*. Paris: Editions du Centre National de la Recherche Scientifique, 1963.

McGrady, Donald M. "Calderón's Rebel Soldier and Poetic Justice Reconsidered." *BHS* 62 (1985): 181-184.

Menéndez y Pelayo, Marcelino. *Calderón y su teatro*. 3d ed. Madrid: Imprenta de A. Pérez Dubrull, 1884.

———. Introduction. *Teatro selecto* by Pedro Calderón de la Barca. Madrid: Librería de Perlado, 1918.

Merrick, C. A. "Neoplatonic Allegory in Calderón's 'Las fortunas de Andrómeda y Perseo.'" *MLR* 67 (1972): 319–327.

Monteverdi, Claudio. *The Letters of —*. Trans. and Ed. Denis Stevens. Cambridge: Cambridge University Press, 1980.

Mooney, Paul Arthur. "A Reevaluation of Past and Current Critical Opinion on the *comedias mitológicas* of Pedro Calderón de la Barca." Diss. Pennsylvania State University, 1973.

Muir, Edward. *Civic Ritual in Renaissance Venice*. Princeton: Princeton University Press, 1981.

Mujica, Barbara. *Calderón's Characters: An Existential Point of View*. Barcelona: Puvill, 1980.

Murata, Margaret. *Operas for the Papal Court, 1631–1668*. Ann Arbor: UMI Research Press, 1981.

Murray, Timothy. "Theatrical Legitimation: Forms of French Patronage and Portraiture." *PMLA* 98 (1983): 170–182.

Neumeister, Sebastian. "Los retratos de los Reyes en la última comedia de Calderón (*Hado y divisa de Leonido y Marfisa*, loa)." *Hacia Calderón: IV Coloquio Anglogermano. Wolfenbüttel, 1975*. Ed. Hans Flasche. Berlin: Walter de Gruyter, 1979. 83–91.

———. *Mythos und Repräsentation*. Munich: Wilhelm Fink Verlag, 1978.

———. "Escenografía cortesana y orden estético-político del mundo." *La escenografía del teatro barroco*. Ed. Aurora Egido. Salamanca: Ediciones Universidad de Salamanca y Universidad Internacional Menéndez Pelayo, 1989. 141–159.

O'Connor, Thomas A. "Calderón and Reason's Impasse: The Case of *La estatua de Prometeo*." *La Chispa '81: Selected Proceedings of the Second Louisiana Conference on Hispanic Languages and Literatures*. Ed. Gilbert Paolini. New Orleans: Tulane University, 1981.

———. "Hércules y el mito masculino: La posición 'feminista' de *Fieras afemina Amor*." *Estudios sobre el Siglo de Oro: En homenaje a Raymond R. MacCurdy*. Eds. Angel González, Tamara Holzapfel, and Alfred Rodríguez. Madrid: Cátedra, 1983. 171–180.

Orgel, Stephen. *The Illusion of Power: Political Theater in the English Renaissance*. Berkeley: University of California Press, 1975.

———. "The Royal Theatre and the Role of the King." *Patronage in the Renaissance*. Eds. Guy Fitch Lytle and Stephen Orgel. Princeton: Princeton University Press, 1981. 262–273.

Panofsky, Dora y Erwin. *La caja de Pandora: Aspectos cambiantes de un símbolo mítico*. 2d rev. ed. Barcelona: Barral Editores, 1975.

Paris, Pierre. "La Mythologie de Calderón: Apolo y Climene—El hijo del sol, Faetón." *Homenaje ofrecido a Menéndez Pidal*. 3 vols. Madrid: Librería y Casa Editorial Hernando, S.A.: 1925. 1:557–570.

Parker, A. A. "Metáfora y símbolo en la interpretación de Calderón." *Actas del Primer Congreso Internacional de Hispanistas*. Oxford: Dolphin Book Co., 1959. 141–160.

Parker, A. A. "Segismundo's Tower: A Calderonian Myth." *BHS* 59 (1982): 247–256.

———. *The Allegorical Drama of Calderón: An Introduction to the autos sacramentales.* Oxford: Dolphin Book Co., 1943.

———. "The Father-Son Conflict in the Drama of Calderón." *Forum for Modern Language Studies* 2 (1966): 99–113.

Pasero, Anne M. "Male vs. Female: Binary Opposition and Structural Synthesis in Calderón's *Estatua de Prometeo.*" *Bulletin of the Comediantes* 32 (1981): 109–115.

Pérez de Moya, Juan. *Philosofía secreta.* Madrid: Francisco Sánchez, 1585.

Pérez Pastor, Cristóbal. *Documentos para la biografía de D. Pedro Calderón de la Barca.* Madrid: Fortanet, 1905.

Pérez Sánchez, Alfonso E. "Los pintores escenógrafos en el Madrid del siglo XVII." *La escenografía del teatro barroco.* Ed. Aurora Egido. Salamanca: Ediciones Universidad de Salamanca y Universidad Internacional Menéndez Pelayo, 1989. 61–90.

Pérez Villanueva, Joaquín. *Felipe IV y Luisa Enríquez Manrique de Lara, Condesa de Paredes de Nava. Un epistolario inédito.* Salamanca: Caja de Ahorros y Monte de Piedad de Salamanca, 1986.

Pio di Savoia, Ascanio. *L'Andromeda.* Ferrara: Francesco Suzzi, 1639.

Pirrotta, Nino, and Elena Povoledo. *Music and Theatre from Poliziano to Monteverdi.* Trans. Karen Eales. Cambridge: Cambridge University Press, 1982.

Pitou, Spire. *The Paris Opéra. An Encyclopedia of Operas, Ballets, Composers, and Performers.* Vol. 1. *Genesis and Glory, 1671–1715.* Westport, Conn.: Greenwood Press, 1983.

Porter, William V. "Cicognini, Jacopo." *The New Grove Dictionary of Music and Musicians.* Ed. Stanley Sadie. 1980.

Pribam, Alfred Francis, and Moriz Landwehr von Pragenau, eds. *Privatbriefe Kaiser Leopold I an den Grafen F. E. Pötting, 1662–1673.* Vols. 56 and 57 of *Fontes Rerum Austriacarum.* Vienna: Carl Gerold's Sohn, 1903.

Pring-Mill, Robert D. F. "Some Techniques of Representation in the *Sueños* and the *Criticón.*" *BHS* 45 (1968): 270–284.

Profeti, Maria Grazia. "Condensación y desplazamiento: La comicidad y los géneros menores en el teatro del Siglo de Oro." *Los géneros menores en el teatro español del Siglo de Oro.* Ed. Luciano García Lorenzo. Madrid: Ministerio de Cultura, 1988. 33–46.

———. "Jacopo Cicognini e Lope de Vega: 'Attinenze strettissime?'" *Quaderni di Lingue e Letterature* 11 (1986): 221–229.

Pye, Christopher. "The Sovereign, the Theater, and the Kingdome of Darknesse: Hobbes and the Spectacle of Power." *Representing the Renaissance.* Ed. Stephen Greenblatt. Berkeley: University of California Press, 1988. 279–301.

Pyle, Cynthia Munro. "Politian's Orfeo and the favole mitologiche in the Context of Late Quattrocento Northern Italy." Diss. Columbia University, 1976.

Quevedo Villegas, Francisco de. *Política de Dios, Govierno de Christo.* Ed. James O. Crosby. Madrid: Castalia, 1966.

Quintero, María Cristina. "Political Intentionality and Dramatic Convention in the *Teatro Palaciego* of Francisco Bances Candamo." *Revista de Estudios Hispánicos* 20 (1986): 37–53.

Rabb, Theodore K. *The Struggle for Stability in Early Modern Europe.* New York: Oxford University Press, 1975.

Reade, Brian. *The Dominance of Spain, 1550–1660*. Costumes of the Western World Series. London: George G. Harrap and Co., Ltd., 1951.

Rennert, Hugo Albert. *The Spanish Stage in the Time of Lope de Vega*. New York: Hispanic Society of America, 1909.

Rodríguez, Evangelina, and Antonio Tordera. *Calderón y la obra corta dramática del siglo XVII*. London: Tamesis Books Ltd., 1983.

Rodríguez G. de Ceballos, Alfonso. "Escenografía y tramoya en el teatro español del siglo XVII." *La escenografía del teatro barroco*. Ed. Aurora Egido. Salamanca: Ediciones Universidad de Salamanca y Universidad Internacional Menéndez Pelayo, 1989. 33–60.

Rosales, Luis. *Pasión y muerte del Conde de Villamediana*. Madrid: Gredos, 1969.

Rosenthal, Albi. "Monteverdi's 'Andromeda,' A Lost Libretto Found." *Music and Letters* 46 (1985): 1–8.

Rouanet, L. "Un autographe inédit de Calderón." *Revue Hispanique* 6 (1899): 196–200.

Rousset, Jean. "L'Eau et les Tritons dans les fêtes et ballets de cour (1580–1640)." *Fêtes de la Renaissance*. Ed. Jean Jacquot. Vol 1. Paris: Editions du Centre Nationale de la Recherche Scientifique, 1956. 235–245.

Rozas, Juan Manuel. Introduction to Villamediana, *Obras*. Madrid: Clásicos Castalia, 1980.

Ruiz Alcón, María Teresa. *Monasterio de las Descalzas Reales*. Madrid: Editorial Patrimonio Nacional, 1987.

Rupp, Stephen James. "Articulate Illusions: Art and Authority in Jonson's Masques and some *Autos sacramentales* of Calderón de la Barca." Diss. Princeton University, 1984.

Saavedra Fajardo, Diego. *Empresas políticas. Idea de un príncipe político-cristiano*. Ed. Quintín Aldea Vaquero. 2 vols. Madrid: Editora Nacional, 1976.

Said, Edward. *The World, the Text, and the Critic*. Cambridge, Mass.: Harvard University Press, 1983.

Segura Ortega, Manuel. *La filosofía jurídica y política en las "Empresas" de Saavedra Fajardo*. Madrid: Academia Alfonso X el Sabio, 1984.

Seznec, Jean. *The Survival of the Pagan Gods: The Mythological Tradition and Its Place in Renaissance Humanism and Art*. Rev. ed. Trans. Barbara F. Sessions. New York: Pantheon Books, 1953.

Shakespeare, William. *Cymbeline*. Ed. Robert B. Heilman. In William Shakespeare, *The Complete Works*. Gen. ed. Alfred Harbage. New York: The Viking Press, 1969. 1290–1333.

Shergold, N. D. *A History of the Spanish Stage from Medieval Times until the End of the Seventeenth Century*. Oxford: Oxford University Press, 1967.

———. "The First Performance of Calderón's *El mayor encanto amor*." *BHS* 35 (1958): 24–27.

Shergold, N. D., and J. E. Varey. *Los autos sacramentales en Madrid en la época de Calderón, 1637–1681. Estudio y documentos*. Madrid: Artes Gráficas Clavileño, 1961.

———. *Representaciones palaciegas: 1603–1699. Estudio y documentos*. London: Tamesis Books Ltd., 1983.

Shklar, Judith N. "Subversive Genealogies." *Daedalus* 101 (1972): 129–154.

Smith, Peter. "Giaccobi, Ghirolamo." *The New Grove Dictionary of Music and Musicians*. Ed. Stanley Sadie. 1980.

Solerti, Angelo. *Musica, ballo de drammatica alla Corte Medicea dal 1600 al 1637*. New York: Benjamin Blom, 1968.

Solórzano Pererya, Juan de. *Emblemas regio-políticos*. Valencia: Bernardo Noguès, 1658.

Stein, Louise. "El 'Manuscrito Novena': sus textos, su contexto histórico-musical y el músico Joseph Peyró." *La Revista de Musicología* 3 (1980): 197–234.

———. "Música existente para comedias de Calderón de la Barca." *Actas del Congreso Internacional sobre Calderón y el Teatro Español del Siglo de Oro*. 3 vols. Madrid: Consejo Superior de Investigaciones Científicas, 1983. 2:1161–1172.

———. "Music in the Seventeenth-Century Spanish Secular Theater, 1598–1690." 2 vols. Diss. University of Chicago, 1987.

———. "La plática de los dioses: Music and the Calderonian Court Play, with a Transcription of the Songs from *La estatua de Prometeo*." Chap. 2 of Introduction of *La estatua de Prometeo* by Pedro Calderón de la Barca. Ed. Margaret Rich Greer. Kassel, Germany: Edition Reichenberger, 1986.

Steinitz, Kate M. "Le Dessin de Léonard de Vinci pour la représentation de *La Danae* de Baldassare Taccone." *Le Lieu Théâtral à la Renaissance*. Ed. Jean Jacquot. Paris: CRNS, 1964. 35–40.

Stradling, R. A. *Europe and the Decline of Spain: A Study of the Spanish System, 1580–1720*. London: George Allen and Unwin, 1981.

Strainchamps, Edmond. "Belli, Domenico." *The New Grove Dictionary of Music and Musicians*. Ed. Stanley Sadie. 1980.

Strong, Roy. *Art and Power: Renaissance Festivals, 1450–1650*. Berkeley: University of California Press, 1984.

———. *Splendour at Court: Renaissance Spectacle and Illusion*. Boston: Houghton Mifflin Co., 1973.

Subirats, Rosita. "Contribution à l'Etablissement du Répertoire Théâtral à la cour de Philippe IV et de Charles II." *Bulletin Hispanique* 79 (1977): 401–479.

Sullivan, Henry. "Calderón and the Semi-Operatic Stage in Spain after 1651." *Calderón and the Baroque Tradition*. Eds. Kurt Levy et al. Waterloo, Canada: Wilfrid Laurier University Press, 1985. 69–80.

Taccone, Baldassare. *La Danae. Commedia, 1496*. Ed. A. G. Spinelli. Bologna: Società Tipografica Assoguidi, 1888

Tate, R. B. "Mythology in Spanish Historiography of the Middle Ages and the Renaissance." *HR* (1954): 1–18.

Teresa de Jesús, Santa. *Libro de mi vida*. Mexico: Porrúa, 1972.

terHorst, Robert. *Calderón: The Secular Plays*. Lexington, Ky.: University Press of Kentucky, 1982.

Tomashevskii, Boris. "Literature and Biography." *Readings in Russian Poetics*. Eds. Ladislav Matejka and Krystyna Pomorska. Cambridge, Mass.: Massachusetts Institute of Technology Press, 1971.

Tormo y Monzo, Elías. *En las Descalzas Reales: Estudios Históricos, Iconográficos y Artísticos*. Madrid: Junta de Iconografía Nacional, 1917.

Traugott, John. "Creating a Rational Rinaldo: A Study in the Mixture of the Genres of

Comedy and Romance in *Much Ado about Nothing.* " *Power of Forms in the English Renaissance.* Ed. Stephen Greenblatt. Norman, Okla.: Pilgrim Books, ca. 1982. 157–181.

Trousson, Raymond. *Le Thème de Prométhé dans la littérature européenne.* 2 vols. Geneva: Librairie Droz, 1964.

Valbuena Briones, Angel. "Calderón y las fiestas de Carnaval." *Bulletin of the Comediantes* 39 (1987): 165–174.

Valbuena Prat, Angel. *Calderón: Su personalidad, su arte dramático, su estilo y sus obras.* Barcelona: Editorial Juventud, 1941.

Varey, John E. "'Andrómeda y Perseo', Comedia y loa de Calderón: Afirmaciones artisticoliterarias y políticas." *Revista de Musicología* 10 (1987): 529–545.

————. "The Audience and the Play at Court Spectacles: The Role of the King." *BHS* 61 (1984): 399–406.

————. "L'Auditoire du *Salón Dorado* de l'*Alcázar* de Madrid au XVIIe Siècle." *Dramaturgie et Société: Rapports entre l'œuvre théâtrale, son interprétation et son public aux XVIe et XVIIe siècles.* Ed. Jean Jacquot. Paris: Editions du Centre National de la Recherche Scientifique, 1968. 77–91.

————. "*Casa con dos puertas*: Towards a Definition of Calderón's View of Comedy." *MLR* 67 (1972): 83–94.

————. "Cavemen in Calderón (and Some Cavewomen)." *Approaches to the Theater of Calderón.* Ed. Michael D. McGaha. Washington, D.C.: University Press of America, 1982. 231–247.

————. "La mayordomía y los festejos palaciegos del siglo XVII." *Anales del Instituto de Estudios Madrileños* 4 (1969): 145–168.

————. "Scenes, Machines and the Theatrical Experience in Seventeenth-Century Spain." *La Scenografia barocca.* Ed. Antonio Schnapper. Bologna: Editrice C.L.U. E.B., 1982. 51–63.

Vega Carpio, Lope de. "Andrómeda." *Colección escogida de obras no dramáticas de Frey Lope Félix de Vega Carpio.* Ed. Cayetano Rosell. BAE, vol. 38. 492–497.

————. *Colección de las obras sueltas.* Vol. l. Madrid: Don Antonio de Sancha, 1776.

————. *La fábula de Perseo, o la bella Andrómeda.* Ed. Michael D. McGaha. Kassel: Edition Reichenberger, 1985.

————. *El peregrino en su patria.* Ed. Myran A. Peyton. University of North Carolina Studies in the Romance Languages and Literatures, No. 97. Chapel Hill: University of North Carolina Press, 1971.

————. *La selva sin amor. Egloga pastoral que se canto á su majestad, que Dios guarde, en fiestas de su salud.* In *Colección escogida de obras no dramáticas de Frey Lope Félix de Vega Carpio.* Ed. Cayetano Rosell. BAE, vol. 38. 300–312.

Vélez de Guevara, Juan. *Los celos hacen estrellas.* Eds. J. E. Varey and N. D. Shergold. Music ed. Jack Sage. London: Tamesis Books Ltd., 1970.

Villamediana, Juan de Vera Tassis, Conde de. *Obras.* Zaragoza: Juan de Lanaja y Quartanet, 1629.

Walker, Thomas. "Echi Estense negli spettacoli musicali a Ferrara nel primo seicento." Forthcoming in Lene Waage Petersen and Daniela Quarta, eds. [Title?] Modena: Panini, n.d.

Wardropper, Bruce. "Calderón de la Barca and Late Seventeenth-Century Theater." *Record of the Art Museum, Princeton University* 41 (1982): 35–41.

Whitaker, Shirley. "Florentine Opera Comes to Spain: Lope de Vega's *La selva sin amor.*" *Journal of Hispanic Philology* 9 (1984): 43–61.

Wickham, Glynne. *A History of the Theatre.* Cambridge: Cambridge University Press, 1985.

Williams, Raymond. *Marxism and Literature.* Oxford: Oxford University Press, 1977.

Wilson, Edward M., and Duncan Moir. *Golden Age Drama, 1492–1700.* New York: Barnes and Noble, Inc., 1971.

Wilson, Edward M., and Jack Sage. *Poesías líricas en las obras dramáticas de Calderón.* London: Tamesis Books Ltd., 1964.

Yates, Frances A. *Astrea. The Imperial Theme in the Sixteenth Century.* Boston: Ark Paperbacks, 1985.

INDEX

absolutism: and court spectacle, 3, 7
Accademia degli intrepide, 42
Accademia del disegno, 12
Aeschylus, 155, 224n.5, 226n.26
Alberti, Leon Battista: *Della pittura*, 10
Alcázar Palace, 21, 106, 119, 121–122; Hall of
  Mirrors, 125–129, 162, 229n.16; Salón
  Dorado, 21, 82
Alciati, André, 8
Aleotti, Giovanni Battista, 11
Alfonso X, el Sabio, 187, 207n.40
Amadei de Pulice, Alicia, 204n.16, 212n.51
Ana of Austria (queen of France), 45
Andromeda (Ferrari/Manelli), 41–42, 209n.18,
  212n.44
Andromeda (Marigliani/Monteverdi), 40–41,
  208n.2
Andromeda, L' (Pio di Savoia/Rossi), 42–43,
  210nn.20–22
Andromeda, favola marittima, L' (Cicognini/
  Belli), 39–40
Andromeda. Tragedia. Da recitarsi in Musica
  (Campeggi/Giacobbi), 36–39, 211n.34
Andromède, L' (Corneille), 41, 49–54, 57, 59,
  66–67, 205n.21, 208n.2, 212nn. 45 and 46,
  214n.76
Angeletii, Francesco, 42
Aranda, Francisco de, 79
Aranjuez Palace, 91
Ariosto, Ludovico, 39, 50, 194, 209n.16
Asensio, Eugenio, 64
Astillano, prince of, 157–158, 171, 173,
  230nn. 22 and 23
Aubignac, François Hédélin, abbé d', 52–53,
  214n.68
Aubrun, Charles, 5, 151

Bainton, Cecilia, 173, 228n.3
Balbi, Giovanni Battista, 42, 213n.58
Balet Comique de la Royne, Le (Beaujoyeulx),
  24–25, 28, 94
Ballet d'Andromède dansé l'an 1608, 35
Ballet d'Andromède exposée au monstre marin, 35,
  208n.8

ballet de cour, 10, 24–25; libretto of, 15, 21, 35
Baltasar Carlos (prince), 78, 100, 193, 208n.1,
  220n.8, 222n.20
Bances Candamo, Francisco: *Cómo se curan los
  celos y Orlando furioso*, 104; *El esclavo en grillos
  de oro*, 104; *La piedra filosofal*, 104, 220n.7;
  Por su rey y por su dama, 104; *Theatro de los
  Theatros de los passados y presentes siglos*, 104
Bandera, Cesáreo, 227n.29
Barrionuevo, Jerónimo de, 79, 81, 112, 121,
  230n.20
Barthes, Roland, 31, 224n.3
Bautista, Nicolas (friar), 81, 219n.33
Beaujoyeulx, Baltazar de. See *Balet Comique de
  la Royne, Le*
Becerra, Gaspar, 210n.27
Belli, Domenico, 39
Benche vinto, vince amore. ò il Prometeo (Draghi?),
  129
Bernarda, Manuela, 158
Bertaut, François, 85
Bianco, Baccio del, 58, 205n.24, 228n.10; his
  arrival in Spain, 13, 54; and Calderón, 15;
  and *Fortunas de Andrómeda y Perseo*, 54–55,
  59, 64; in Italy, 212n.49
Bianconi, Lorenzo, 209nn. 13 and 18, 213n.58
Bisucci, Giovanni Battista, 42
Blas, Juan, 214n.75
Bloemaert, Cornelius, 126
Boccaccio, Giovanni, 124, 128; *Genealogiae
  deorum gentilium libri*, 32, 50, 226n.20
Boiardo, Matteo María, 194
Bologna, 36
Borja, Fernando de, 79
Borja, Mariana, 158
Brooks, Lynn Matluck, 28–29, 207nn.42–44
Brown, Jonathan, 12, 78, 91, 145, 215nn. 3
  and 6, 218nn. 27 and 28, 236n.2
Brunelleschi, Filippo, 10–11, 34, 208nn. 6 and
  7
Bruner, Jerome, 223n.1
Bruno, Giordano, 226n.26
Buen Retiro Palace: Coliseo theatre, 11, 13,
  82, 84–85, 223n.31, 232n.3; gardens, 87,

249